Please remember that this is a library book,
and that it belongs only temporarily to each
person who uses it. Be considerate. Do
not write in this, or any, library book.

WITHDRAWN

MERCHANTS, FARMERS,
& RAILROADS

MERCHANTS, FARMERS, & RAILROADS

Railroad Regulation and New York Politics
1850–1887

LEE BENSON

NEW YORK / RUSSELL & RUSSELL

Studies in Economic History
Published in Coöperation with
The Committee on Research in Economic History

FOR MY MOTHER AND FATHER

Preface

In 1850 the state of New York enacted a free railroad law which represents perhaps the most sweeping legislative endorsement of *laissez faire* in American history. With remarkable speed, state after state paid the ultimate flattery to New York doctrines of political economy; that commonwealth's expression of faith in the wonder-working qualities of the "natural laws of trade" soon was copied throughout the length and breadth of the land. Despite the tribute of such rapid acceptance, however, by 1887 the passage of the Interstate Commerce Act formally signaled the end of *laissez faire* in transportation and presaged its eventual decline in all other important segments of the national economy.

Ironically, perhaps, it was the continued development of the economic instrument for the encouragement of which the New York law of 1850 was adopted — the railroad — which led to the most sustained attack against *laissez-faire* doctrines that the country had yet seen. Not theory nor intellectual debate but pragmatic events made it obvious that railroads, above all the trunk lines dominating transportation to and from the Atlantic seaboard, had matured to the point where competition alone no longer functioned in this area — if it ever had anywhere — as a guarantee of order in the economic world. Trunk lines were not really akin to grocery stores or even textile factories, and the time was soon past when the differences could be ignored. Not surprisingly, several of the more perceptive railroad leaders came to recognize that the positive use of state power was an indispensable supplement to private, self-policing agreements. Trunk-line pools and government regulation were twin aspects of the same economic fact; unaided, the free workings of the natural laws of trade could no longer be expected to harness an aggressive private-enterprise system.

But if not the natural laws of trade, what, or who, was going to do it? And how? The questions, at least in form, were unprecedented, the pressure great, the pace of economic change dynamic. As a result, the answers given by all leading participants from time to time were so opportunistic and so narrowly viewed in terms of self-interest that it is impossible to discern any comprehensive, logically consistent ideological approach to the railroad problem in the period. That opportunism, not logic, was indeed the striking characteristic of the discussion may be seen in the spectacle of the presidents of the New York Central and Erie Railroads and the substantial merchants of the New York Chamber of Commerce angrily accusing each other in 1879 of preparing the way for "Communism." Both sides had vested interests to defend or advance, and it appears safe to say that their respective attitudes toward railroad regulation were shaped less by abstract theories concerning the proper role of government in human affairs than by devotion to those interests.

Viewed as conflicts between different sets of entrepreneurs adjusting to the new economic environment created by development of a vast, intricate railroad network, the leading controversies of the period lend themselves more readily to accurate analysis, and are deflated to less sensational proportions, than the contemporary designations of "crusade," "revolt," or "uprising" would have us believe. Looked at in this way, moreover, the central issue of the era emerges as the important, but hardly revolutionary, question of how the profits of the private-enterprise system were to be divided among various groups of entrepreneurs and how the system itself was to be best preserved. Merchants, railroaders, financiers, and farmers had considerably different ideas as to the proper allocation of economic rewards and they expressed these ideas pungently, forcefully, and frequently; yet the area of agreement among contending parties was impressively large, for at no point was the enterprise system itself a focus of attack. Herein, indeed, lies the paradox which is the central theme of this study: far from attacking property rights and the private enterprise system, the late nineteenth-century assault on *laissez faire* was designed to protect both more effectively. Free competition fell but private enterprise remained; and as America entered the twentieth century, the trinity upon which its institutions were based — the sanctity of private property, the philosophy of economic individualism, and presumptively a harmony of self-interest and social welfare — remained substantially unaltered.

In the making of this book, a number of intellectual debts have been incurred which it is a pleasure to acknowledge. Paul W. Gates of Cornell University directed the doctoral dissertation from which the book derives. But I am indebted to him for much more than skilled training in historiography, fruitful suggestions, perceptive criticism, and generous sharing of accumulated historical knowledge. His devotion to independent research and his uncompromising integrity have served me as a genuine source of inspiration, and I would be proud to think that he regards this book as a worthwhile product of his seminar. John G. B. Hutchins and Herrell De Graff of Cornell University also labored to improve my understanding of economic history and agricultural economics, and I trust that their scholarship and advice have been drawn upon in ways not displeasing to them.

Arthur H. Cole, Chester M. Destler, and James C. Malin were kind enough to read the original manuscript, and their criticisms and suggestions have contributed much to the final version. On behalf of the Committee on Research in Economic History, Edward C. Kirkland went far beyond the call of duty; he read the original manuscript not once but thrice, and I have profited heavily from his painstaking and acute analysis. The chairman of the committee, Dr. Cole, has been consistently generous and thoughtful in helping to smooth the transition from raw manuscript to finished book and, moreover, has initiated me into some of the more recondite mysteries of academic publication. From the beginning of this study some seven years ago, David M. Ellis has given me the benefit of his expert knowledge concerning New York and transportation history, and made available for my use unpublished research notes of considerable value. It is probably superfluous to add that I alone should be the target of critical slings and arrows.

I have also to acknowledge debts of a fiscal character. The Committee on Research in Economic History was good enough to award me a grant which materially aided the completion of the present book; and I have been the beneficiary of a postdoctoral fellowship from the Social Science Research Council, which enabled me to improve my understanding of economic theory. Walter Isard, then of Harvard University, supervised my explorations in that field, and helped to bridge the gap for me between economic history and economic theory.

In my search for basic materials, a number of individuals were generous to me. Mr. Francis B. Thurber of New York City made available to me important manuscript collections relating activities of his father, Francis B. Thurber, which materially contributed to my understanding of the regulation movement, and gave his permission for the publication of excerpts; Alice Gardner of Brooklyn, New York, was kind enough to place at my disposal manuscript materials originally in the possession of her father, Frank S. Gardner, of the New York Board of Trade and Transportation; Robert Garrett of Baltimore granted me permission to use the Garrett Family Papers in the Library of Congress and to publish excerpts, as did Thomas Boylston Adams of Boston in connection with the manuscript diaries of Charles Francis Adams, Jr., in the Massachusetts Historical Society; while both M. D. Griffith of the New York Board of Trade and Harold M. Stanley of the New York State Grange facilitated my research into their organizations' past. The present editor of *The American Grocer,* Sidney Kocin of New York City, let me disrupt his normal operations in order that I might examine the paper's files for the late nineteenth century.

I have had occasion to use the resources of a number of libraries and manuscript depositories and have benefited from the expert knowledge and cheerful assistance of various staff members of the Cornell University Library, Columbia University Library, Harvard University Library, New York Public Library, the Massachusetts Historical Society, the New York Historical Society, the National Archives, the Library of Congress, and the Collection of Regional History at Cornell University. Edith Fox of the latter institution was most helpful in aiding my search for source materials, and I am also especially thankful to Josephine Tharpe of the Cornell Library, Stephen Riley of the Massachusetts Historical Society, and Dorothy C. Barck of the New York Historical Society for helping me to make more intelligent use of the resources of their respective institutions.

Finally, I should like to acknowledge my debt to the many scholars whose researches in one fashion or another have contributed to my better understanding of historical development. Though to the best of my knowledge all concepts and data directly derived from secondary works have been cited in the footnotes, the process of unconscious absorption is a subtle one. No doubt I am unaware of the extent to which this book has been shaped by the writings of others. Any reader who feels that his work has been drawn upon but not cited explicitly is probably right, and my apologies are offered in advance for the omission.

Bureau of Applied Social Research   LEE BENSON
Columbia University

Contents

Illustrations

MERCHANTS, FARMERS,
& RAILROADS

CHAPTER I

Early Movements for Railroad Regulation and Cheap Transportation

> As the supply and value of nearly every article of necessity and luxury are affected by the means and cost of transportation, and as the productions of some sections, like the farming products of the great West, are largely excluded from the Atlantic markets, while various articles of the seaboard are similarly debarred from profitable distribution through the interior states, the interests of every section of society and of the country are directly connected with and essentially affected by this branch of our inquiries.
>
> Hiram Walbridge in *Proceedings of the National Commercial Convention, Held in Boston, February, 1868*, p. 58.

Detailed account of New York activities on the transportation front will begin with the year 1873 but something more than the customary excursion backwards in time is necessary. Several basic features of the postwar railroad problem were operative during the 1850's and the significance of developments after 1873 is best appreciated by comparison with their historical antecedents. Such comparison reveals underlying continuities but it is even more revealing of the manner in which the Communication Revolution forced new and surprising departures in the Empire State.[1] As seen here, what emerges is a conflict pattern pressing towards logical climax in the late seventies and early eighties. Lacking the benefit of hindsight New York trunk-line officials responded to transportation innovations by adopting policies offensive to a growing number of entrepreneurial groups. In turn, resistance to those policies led once antagonistic entrepreneurs to band together against the unchecked exercise of railroad economic and political power. Because the participants' actions were influenced by events outside state boundaries, a summary, highly selective analysis is given below of national railroad developments as they affected New Yorkers.

FREE RAILROAD LAWS

Railroad regulation in the United States dates from the very beginning of railroad operation. Each charter had to be procured individually and with the charter went the power of eminent domain. Derived from the earlier canal and turnpike acts in England and transmitted from one state to another, American railway charters had major features in common. With few if any exceptions, they avowed the public purpose for which the franchise and privileges were given. Although variations existed from state to state, and from company to company, they usually contained some sort of regulatory provision.[2] The states, therefore, through the chartering process, exercised at least rudimentary safeguards against abuse of the public powers granted to private enterprisers.

As a rule, charters were believed to be self-enforcing. But dependence upon voluntary fulfillment of obligation was not the only form of early regulation. Particularly in New England, boards of commissioners were established to deal with a wide set of problems, and general statutes affecting railroads existed in several states. Almost everywhere a variety of public officials had a degree of legal control over transportation companies. In addition, outraged citizens could petition the legislature, resort to the courts for redress, or bring complaints to the attention of officials charged with responsibility.

The practical effect of all these regulatory devices was another matter. Apart from the economic and political pressures that the roads could exert, the regulations themselves and the provisions for enforcement were rather less than perfect.[3] Contrary to contemporary belief, the railroad was not just another common carrier, and turnpike and canal companies hardly furnished adequate precedents. Yet, despite obvious weaknesses, the early attempts at regulation were of fundamental importance in the history of the railroad problem. They amounted to clear recognition and acceptance of the concept that railroads were public corporations created to satisfy a public need and therefore subject to state control. Proponents of regulation later were to point to these legal precedents with telling effect.

By the early 1840's, displeasure with the unrestrained functioning of railroads was evident in New York. Strikingly similar to those voiced after the Civil War, the general grievances included high rates, poor service, rate discriminations, financial corruption, monopolistic tendencies, watered stock, and free passes.[4] A convenient example of local complaints and proposed remedies may be taken from an area in which hostility to railroad management persisted throughout much of the nineteenth century. In 1843, a pamphlet was circulated denouncing the "selfish and blind policy" of the railroads between Albany and Buffalo, and the "careless inattention of the Legislature to a subject so deeply interesting to their constituents." The roads were deficient, passenger rates were exorbitant, service was bad, and a reduction of fare to two cents a mile was demanded by legislative action; preferably, the state should purchase the existing roads or build a new one. Such action was preferred because railroads were certain to supersede canals, and if New York interests were to secure the western trade, "the connecting railway between the great Valley of the Lakes and the Mississippi on the one hand, and the New England States and the City of New York on the other, should be owned, not by mammoth monopolies, but by your State government." [5]

The author was a keen analyst, good prophet, and skillful agitator, but the times were not suited to such analysis, prophecy, and agitation. A decade was to pass before the legislature imposed the two cents per mile limit upon New York Central passenger rates, and two more before the merchants of the metropolis undertook a vigorous campaign in behalf of a government-built (not operated) road to hold the western trade for New York. In 1843, the trend was distinctly in the opposite direction. Disillusionment with the policy of state-owned internal improvements and state aid to private enterprise had been developing, and the New York Constitutional Convention of 1846 reflected the prevalent mood by unanimously approving a prohibition against aid of this character.[6]

Another important subject treated by the convention was the relation of "incorporated companies" to the state. In the words of A. B. Johnson, a bank president, corporate promoter, and political economist of the period: "the course of events having disproved the narrow arguments against corporations, the convention that formed the constitution of 1846, became, therefore, intent on removing from corporate agency its monopoly character, which was so generally odious as to excite, at one time, an ill-directed zeal for the disallowment of any corporate grants . . ." [7] Moreover, the charges of corruption accompanying procurement of charters from the legislature had also contributed to the movement for free enterprise. Potential "undertakers" were reluctant to run the legislative gauntlet or outbid established entrepreneurs for the right to serve the public weal.[8]

Published in 1850, Johnson's article on the history of corporate legislation in New York illustrates both the contemporary trend and the prewar meaning of antimonopoly. Subtitled, "On the Progress of Liberal Sentiments," the article hailed the work of 1846:

> It retained corporate agency as an allowable and valuable facility of social progress, but removed its monopoly features, by permitting under general laws, every person to obtain a corporate organization who desired the facility; and by interdicting only special grants of corporate powers. And thus was consummated the greatest triumph that our American experiment of equal rights has ever achieved in practical results.[9]

In effect, the Constitution of 1846 proclaimed the end of that "paternal character of government" once typical of the state.[10] Its framers drew up a body of fundamental law dominated by the assumptions of nineteenth-century liberalism. Far from encouraging state ownership or strict regulation of transportation, the Constitution paved the way for the General Railroad Law of 1850 which carried laissez-faire precepts to unprecedented lengths in New York and the country at large. But the constitutional section lending itself to a "free railroad law" also contained a statutory provision guarding against corporate invocation of the Dartmouth College doctrine to protect charter privileges.[11] Thus, the Constitution simultaneously facilitated the triumph of *laissez faire* and made possible its eventual overthrow.

Although the Constitution of 1846 was designed to bring about that happy day when all citizens could enjoy equal legal facilities in enterprise, the section on corporations cited above left the legislature with important discretionary powers. Special privileges were forbidden but an exception was made in favor of cases "where, in the judgment of the Legislature, the objects of the incorporation cannot be obtained under general laws." [12] One of these exceptional cases was the railroad, and several years were to pass before "adventurers" in that field of enterprise were able to disport themselves uninhibited by legislative declarations of approval or disapproval.

Yielding to the demand that railroads be removed from the category requiring special acts of incorporation, a Senate committee in 1847 reported out a general bill providing for the creation of railroad companies. Buttressed by references to Magna Charta, the noble "Barrons at Runne-Mede," and the far-sighted framers of the Federal Constitution, the committee deliberately emasculated the bill in advance by reserving the "sacred and important trust" of eminent domain to the legislature. Interestingly, the committee anticipated by some forty years the painfully acquired conviction of trunk-line officials that not everyone who so desired should be allowed to organize a railroad. Its report contended that if a general law were passed authorizing an indefinite number of associations to take private property without legislative assent in each case, a general scramble would ensue for the first choice in the location of railroads. "By such a law, the sacred right of eminent domain would be virtually parcelled out to an indefinite number of self-created, and perhaps irresponsible corporations, and the right of private property would soon come to be less respected here, than under any despotic government in the Christian world." [13]

To meet this line of argument the advocates of a general law had proposed the appointment of a tribunal whose certification would be necessary before any projected work was declared a "public utility" and granted the right of eminent domain. However, the Senate committee deemed the right too precious to be delegated away by the people's representatives.[14] The general law enacted in 1848, therefore, still required each corporation to secure legislative confirmation of its public utility status before it was given the power of eminent domain.[15] As the committee had foreseen, this kind of procedure left things about where they were and a leading periodical observed that "by far the most exciting questions of the [1849 legislative] session related to railroads." [16]

In 1850 legislative resistance to free competition in transportation was overcome, and the general law of that year went so far as to dispense with the tribunal proposed three years earlier to certify each work as a public utility.[17] According to its provisions, the mere filing of articles of incorporation by any twenty-five or more persons made them a railroad corporation possessed of the power of eminent domain, free to run lines wherever and however they saw fit, subject only to certain limitations in cities. Several potentially important restrictions were imposed but, unlike the Free Banking Law of 1838, railroads were not placed under the theoretically watchful eyes of state overseers or administrators. The later sarcastic comment of Simon Sterne, the New York lawyer and student of the railroad problem who conducted the Hepburn investigation, is worth noting to indicate the significance of the Act. As Sterne saw it, with minor exceptions the 1850 Act marked a complete surrender of the state's right to regulate railroads, and "introduced the era of what was supposed to be competition." [18]

Sterne must have been somewhat carried away with himself when he made this observation because several provisions of which he was well aware were overlooked. Apart from a number of regulations concerning the method of organizing companies, constructing roads, handling passengers, etc., passenger rates were fixed at three cents a mile, comprehensive annual reports had to be filed annually with the state engineer and surveyor, and the roads were restricted to 10 per cent dividends upon *capital actually expended in construction*. The legislature reserved the right to alter the rate of freight, fare, or other charges when higher dividends were paid.[19] Though the reports as filed were almost meaningless, and the 10 per cent restriction wholly ignored, in later years these provisions assumed considerable importance. Together with the passenger fare maximum, they also demonstrate that the victory of free enterprise in transportation was not complete, and that the power of eminent domain was not granted to private corporations without restriction. Even at the high point of the "let alone" policy in New York, railroads were held to have a public character and a distinction was made between them and the usual run of corporations.

Despite such strictures, the phrase, "the era of what was supposed to be competition," catches the essential quality of the 1850 Act. As long as free railway laws did not exist and each charter granted a legal monopoly to a certain extent, the right of the state to protect the public against abuses logically followed. But the victory of *laissez faire* overthrew charter limitations and abolished law-created monopolies. Necessarily, the corollary of full freedom to engage in enterprise was to make dependence upon the laws of competition primary instead of the laws of government. Unrestricted competition was now viewed as the most efficient instrument which could be devised to protect the public from any form of monopoly or sustained abuse.[20]

Another aspect of Sterne's comment deserves attention here. The significance of transportation developments in New York outran the state borders. The Free Railroad Law of 1850 rapidly became the model for legislation all over the country, and Henry V. Poor, unlike Sterne, paid tribute to the "wise policy" pioneered by New York. Poor was a leading authority on railroads and in his version the most marvellous results followed from making "railroad construction everywhere . . . as free to the people of the United States as the air they breathed," and seeing to it that "the only *role* of government has been that of a *police officer*." [21] Such contrasting evaluations only underscore the point that the New York legislation basically shaped the legal character of the American railroad system for several decades after 1850, and markedly influenced contemporary attitudes towards the proper relation between railroads and government.

But important qualifications are necessary to correct the impression given by Sterne and Poor that the victory of laissez-faire concepts in transportation was overwhelming. The legislative history of railroads in New York during the 1850's appears to prove two propositions: nearly absolute freedom of railroad action was not due to theory but to neglect and lack of implementation of the law; the relation of railroads to the state at any given moment depended more upon the state of relations between railroads and their antagonists, and the balance of political power, than upon dogma.

THE FIRST NEW YORK RAILROAD COMMISSION

As noted above, the law of 1850 contained some important provisions which limited railroad freedom of action. Except for the maximum passenger rate provision, however, the limitations were more theoretical than real since no administrative machinery was established to enforce them.[22] The fallacy of regulation by statute was recognized from the start,[23] and by 1855 it led to the establishment of a Board of Railroad Commissioners with considerable power.[24]

Studied in the light of the board's subsequent actions, its first report is most revealing of the reasons for its creation and the group instrumental in its enactment. Not only the public in general but stockholders in particular were disturbed by the conduct of railroad officials and the deep veil of secrecy thrown around the mysteries of railroading. The commissioners spoke harshly of the "prominent cases of fraud which have, of late years, so startled the community," and resulted in the misapplication of funds and interests entrusted to railroad officers. They were even more unsparing in castigating what later was known as "stock-jobbing," i.e., speculation in stocks by railroad officials able to juggle values for their own profit.[25]

Conflicts between stockholders and railroad officials, and the failure of the latter to regard themselves as trustees of the property entrusted to them, were important aspects of the railroad problem in the nineteenth century. According to the commissioners, the 1855 law was calculated to furnish relief to injured stockholders. It was also designed to provide the public with fuller and more reliable information, and the legislature with data enabling it to modify the law as the necessity arose.[26] The statute creating the railroad commission reflected the motives for its passage. The board consisted of three members, the state engineer and surveyor, an appointee of the governor, and one man selected by the stock and bond holders of all rail corporations in the state. No provision was made for rate regulation but the commissioners were given sweeping powers to investigate the books, documents, and other records of the companies, question under oath all officials and employees, and require them to provide any information they deemed necessary. Moreover, no railroad or portion thereof could be opened without inspection and certification by the board that its condition was satisfactory. A major limitation, however, was that the commissioners were not empowered to enforce the law but could only report violations to the Attorney General and make recommendations to the legislature.

Upon establishment the board set to work with vigor and determination. It drew up a revised form for the railroad companies' annual reports and pressed for accuracy and completeness in the returns. After its first year of operation a Senate committee hailed the board's activities as having produced "a greater amount of information in regard to every road in the State than any railroad reports which have ever before been made in the United States." [27] Displaying such zeal, the commissioners were hardly inclined to ignore their power to recommend legislation. Their first annual report stated that changes should be made in the law but deemed it advisable to wait until further experience had clarified the commissioners' views.[28] Since the tenor of the report was extremely critical of railroad management, the subsequent clarification of views took a strange direction.

No sooner had the report been published than a bill was introduced to abolish the railroad commission and restore the law of 1850 to its self-enforcing condition. The Senate committee appointed in 1856 to consider the bill strongly opposed it. Instead, they turned in a report affirming the "imperative duty of the Legislature" to define the railroads' powers and duties and "to retain such a supervision and control over them, as may be necessary to maintain the just rights both of those who contribute to the construction of the road, and the traveling public who contribute to its maintenance." [29]

Reintroduced in the next legislature, the bill to abolish the railroad commission received a more sympathetic hearing. And reflection apparently had caused a majority of the board to reconsider their views. In reply to a resolution of the Senate inquiring into the delay in publishing the commission's report for 1857 they recommended their own dissolution.[30] This time no senatorial statement of the necessity for a railroad commission was forthcoming. In fact, the bill to repeal was introduced by the same senator who a year before had signed the report affirming the imperative need for a supervisory body.[31] Within a week, the legislature overwhelmingly passed the bill, the governor signed it, and the first railroad commission in the state of New York passed into history.[32]

The uses and abuses of history are legion and the peculiar circumstances surrounding the abolition of the board might forever have remained a mystery if the attorney for the New York Central some two decades later had not decided to bolster his case by appealing to "history." Arguing against the New York merchants' demand for a railroad commission, he emphasized that the "scheme" was not new and claimed that the earlier experiment had been abandoned because of the commissioners' scandalous conduct and utter uselessness.[33] Appeals to history always carry weight and it became necessary for the proponents of a railroad commission to set the record straight. Fortunately, they were in an excellent position to do so for in their ranks they now boasted General Alexander S. Diven.

Divens had been the attorney of the Erie Railroad during the 1850's, and he gave the Hepburn Committee the inside story of the roads' reaction when they found the existence of a board of commissioners "embarrassing." Somewhat hazy on the details — he couldn't remember at first whether the sum involved was $125,000 or $25,000 but finally decided upon the latter figure — he did recall that Dean Richmond of the New York Central had handled the arrangements. Richmond, an almost legendary figure in the annals of New York political lobbying, "arranged" matters so that the commission recommended repeal of the law and the legislature happily complied with their request.[34] Thus the brand of persuasion was revealed which led railroad commissioners and senators in 1857 to reconsider their firmly held convictions of 1856.

The significance of the first New York railroad commission's dissolution is not confined to the light it throws on prewar railroad legislative methods. Apparently for some years to come the commission form of regulation was viewed with suspicion in the state. Despite intense public discussion and strong support for a variety of measures during the late fifties, a careful reading of the pertinent material has failed to uncover any sentiment for establishing a regulatory commission to solve the railroad problem. After the peculiar developments of 1857, it would appear, boards of commissioners were not deemed the answer to transportation difficulties in New York until the passage of time blurred memories.

RAILROAD TOLLS, PRO RATA, CANAL IMPROVEMENT

The New York canal system was so integral a part of the state's economy in the middle of the nineteenth century that the coming of the railroad was bound to have an unsettling effect upon important vested interests. During the 1850's when the major trunk lines emerged, competition between land and water routes reached the point where resort "to the people" became mandatory for the injured parties. In its immediate origins the conflict dates from 1851 when the railroads paralleling the Erie Canal secured the abolition of tolls upon freight carried by them. From then on they paid nothing to the state canal funds. At the same time, in order to cheapen transportation upon the canals, tolls were reduced and substantial appropriations voted to complete the enlargement first approved in 1835. Rather than bringing peace to the transportation front, both decisions only prepared the way for more intense conflict.[35]

No longer subject to tolls the railroads were now better able to compete directly with the canals, and organizational and technological improvements during the decade tipped the scales heavily in favor of the land routes for certain kinds of traffic. Moreover, rivalry between the newly consolidated and extended trunk lines in New York, Pennsylvania, and Maryland, that is, the four railroads reaching from the seaboard to the Great Lakes or the Ohio River,[36] also injured the water carriers. Canal revenues declined sharply and the difficulties of paying for improvements and meeting the charges upon the waterways' funded debt mounted. Especially in areas remote from the canals, resistance to direct taxes for their construction and upkeep had been strong for decades. One solution to the problem was to reimpose railroad tolls, and in 1855 the governor recommended its adoption. His recommendation was immediately responded to with enthusiasm[37] and what turned out to be the first full scale "war" against railroads in the United States was on.

Since transportation affected a number of diverse economic groups in New York, hostility to railroad management found expression in other forms than the restoration of tolls.[38] For some time before 1858 upstate commission merchants and millers had felt the effects of western competition, but in that year trunk-line progress and rivalry brought on the novel state of affairs whereby rates from the West to New York City were little higher than from Buffalo;[39] in 1859 the rates from the West were actually lower.[40] Other places along the canal suffered even greater discrimination, and shippers at local points in the interior of the state failed to appreciate the situation which forced them to pay high rates so that railroads might provide cheap transportation for their western competitors.

As severe depression intensified resentment, Assemblyman Parsons of Rochester introduced a bill in 1858 to make railroad tariffs directly proportionate to distance.[41] His stated objective was to improve the competitive position of Rochester's "mills and manufactories," and he therefore was cool to the restoration of tolls upon the New York Central.[42] Assemblyman Parsons reflected the views of those commercial and industrial groups lined up behind pro rata but commercial interests had still another solution. Primarily they wanted to cheapen rather than raise the cost of transportation, and they viewed the completion of the Erie Canal enlargement as indispensable to that end.

Notwithstanding the fact that the tolling, pro rata, and canal improvement movements represented different approaches to the transportation problem, their supporters were realistic enough to merge forces in order to overcome the railroad lobby's political power. Perhaps it helps to clarify the complexities of the prewar transportation agitation in New York if its three main phases are presented in oversimplified fashion.

Canal forwarders and contractors directly tied to the prosperity of the water route campaigned for railroad tolls to restore the competitive position of the canals. They also approved of canal enlargement and pro rata — anything which would better the water route's competitive position. These two groups constituted the driving force behind the tolling movement from 1855 on.[43]

Upstate merchants and millers, from Buffalo to Albany, supported canal improvements but tended to oppose tolls as burdensome to commerce and beneficial to other sections of the state at the expense of their own. Moreover, they knew that New York City mercantile interests frowned on projects to raise transportation costs and feared that railroad tolls plus pro rata would drive the metropolis into fatal opposition. Passage of the pro rata bill to end place discrimination, and retention of their location advantages relative to western competitors were their basic objectives.[44]

At the ocean end of the canal, mercantile interests generally favored all plans to cheapen transport costs to New York and deplored all plans tending towards other results. Owners of large scale transportation companies, canal forwarders, warehousemen, grain merchants, or men convinced that an efficiently administered and improved canal system must be superior to railroads and thus guarantee New York's supremacy, were especially interested in preserving and improving the waterways. Aware that the dominant sentiment in the metropolis favored all-out competition between improved canals and railroads, the canal champions in the city found it necessary to oppose the tolling movement. Instead, they proposed direct taxes to pay for canal improvement rather than railroad tolls which would raise transportation costs. However, to insure the aid of upstate merchants and millers for canal enlargement, and to preserve for the canal traffic necessary to its permanent existence, they endorsed the pro rata demand.[45]

Other considerations aside, the metropolitan interests pressing for canal enlargement had to weigh the fact that the most logical allies of the pro rata militants were the farmers. Upstate merchants, millers, and farmers were primarily concerned with place discrimination favoring western competitors, not the absolute level of rates, nor the conflict between railroad and canal. Farmers, those remote from the canals above all, were susceptible to appeals to sell the waterways to private interests and thus avoid taxes on internal improvements benefiting the West. Faced with the possibility that an upstate coalition might be formed placing major emphasis upon place discrimination rather than canal improvement, the metropolitan transportation militants went along with pro rata despite the opposition of the Chamber of Commerce which expressed the dominant sentiment in New York.

As was only to be expected, strenuous efforts were made to win farmers over to all three positions, i.e., railroad tolls, pro rata, canal improvement. In the process the boundaries of logic and truth were stretched beyond permissible limits. Men working hard at projects to cheapen the cost of transportation from the West via canal passionately addressed farmers on the iniquities of corporations which had cheapened the cost of transportation from the West via railroad. Handicapped by isolation, and lacking any organization capable of exerting continuous political pressure, farmers played only a subordinate role in the tolling and pro rata movements. Their support was essential if legislative success was to be achieved, but the more compact, better organized, and more mobile groups clearly regarded them as innocents to be led down the garden path.[46]

Although they worked hard at giving the appearance of representing all citizens (except railroad managers) in all parts of the state, the groups championing the three different positions were not nearly as catholic in their interests or appeal. Located directly along the line of the canal from Buffalo and Oswego to New York, their agitation was essentially localistic in nature and marked by conflict within the ranks. Yet in 1858, before the agitation had crystallized and attained political power, internal splits did not come to the fore. To win any of the objectives it was necessary to stir up "the people," overcome the power of the railroad lobby, and bring about a measure of cohesive action by interests sharing at least one thing in common, antagonism to railroad policy as it developed in the late fifties. Thus, in December 1858 a large convention was held in Syracuse to win popular support and persuade the legislature to take positive action on transportation problems.[47]

The omnibus character of the convention may be judged from the resolutions adopted. Among others, they called for a referendum authorizing a loan to pay the Floating Canal Debt, and legislative enactment of a direct tax to complete enlargement of the canal system, passage of a pro rata freight bill, reimposition of tolls on railroads, and prohibition of free railroad passes to government officials.[48] To achieve these ends, a committee was appointed to prepare an address setting forth the sentiments and opinions of the "Convention of the Friends of the Canal System." [49]

Henry O'Reilly of New York City was a member of the committee but the *Address* did not trouble itself with the problems of the metropolis. On the contrary, it asserted that at a time of commercial distress the Empire State could not afford to let the western trade pass through unrestricted.[50] Such views obviously found little favor in New York, now deeply concerned with the diversion of trade accompanying the railroad rate wars. Only a few months earlier a convention of trunk-line officials had established a differential railroad rate system assigning lower tariffs to Baltimore and Philadelphia on the basis of their relative proximity to the West. With New York's supremacy facing its first real challenge since the construction of the Erie Canal, restriction upon the western trade was not precisely an attractive slogan in the metropolis.[51]

One feature of the Syracuse *Address* is of particular significance as an indication of the extent to which laissez-faire views had come to prevail by 1858, and the counter-arguments designed to meet it. Pro rata was justified on the legalistic ground that in surrendering the right of eminent domain the people of New York made an implied contract with the roads to receive equal treatment "with other communities who have made no similar sacrifices. This contract has been constantly and oppressively violated." Returning to a defense of regulation some pages later, the *Address* maintained: "Although it may seem to conflict with the laws of free trade and unrestricted competition for the State to pre-scribe rules and dictate terms of freighting to railroads, yet when a corporation already powerful has won from the State . . . vast addi-tional power . . . under the pretense and pledge of greatly promoting the interest of the State . . . [statement of abuses] we say, in view of such abuse of power, all the great interests of the State, her agriculture, her commerce, and her manufactures — the great interests which both canals and railroads promise to subserve — invoke the protection of the State under the right reserved to the Legislature 'to alter, modify, and repeal charters.' " [52] Thus the Syracuse *Address* constitutes an early invocation of the public utility doctrine to combat the arguments of laissez-faire advocates.

Designed to arouse the people to demand their rights, the Syracuse Convention was at least partially successful. Petitions poured in upon the legislature "praying the passage of a law to regulate the tariffs of railroads," and a select committee was appointed to study the matter. The committee majority turned in a strongly worded report demonstrat-ing the degree of discrimination against localities and groups within the state. Like the authors of the Syracuse *Address,* they stressed the legalis-tic aspect of the public utility doctrine; regulation was called for because discrimination was an abuse of chartered privileges. Though the report attempted to meet the objection that a pro rata law would divert traffic from New York City, its signers obviously were animated by the desire to protect interior and canal interests. They therefore favorably reported a bill to regulate the freight tariffs of railroads on the pro rata prin-ciple.[53]

A contradictory report was turned in by the committee minority. Both signers were from New York City, and one, George Opdyke, a member of its Chamber of Commerce.[54] After demonstrating to *their* satisfaction that pro rata violated the spirit and letter of the Constitu-tion of 1846, and the General Railroad Act of 1850, they proceeded to take up other matters than "the law and morality of this question." [55] Among these other matters was the claim that the economics of trans-portation justified higher proportionate charges for local traffic if ter-minal and operating costs were considered, something pro rata advocates chose to ignore.[56] But the following sentence from the minority report best expresses the dominant New York view and succinctly states the chief argument of the metropolis and its railroads against regulation before the Civil War:

The competition with rival lines of roads and rival cities on the seaboard for the western trade has but just commenced, and it would be suicidal for our legislature to interfere at this time and put such restrictions on the roads of this State, as would drive the business they now enjoy from them and from the State.[57]

Faced with determined opposition from the railroads and from the metropolis, the pro rata and tolling advocates were not yet well enough organized to get either bill passed in the Assembly or the Senate during the 1859 session. To remedy that situation, another convention "of the Friends of the Canal System" was scheduled for Rochester in advance of the state elections so that "we shall make our mark where it can be read by all." [58] Shortly before the convention met on September 1, 1859, the friends of the railroad system unintentionally contributed towards making it a greater success than its sponsors had anticipated.

The August issue of the leading commercial journal in the United States contained an article which deplored pro rata and tolling bills, and maintained that the superiority of railroads over canals was no longer in question. The highly embarrassed condition of the state's finances, its author argued, made it necessary to stop spending money on the canals: "It certainly appears to us high time that the State paused in its career of borrowing and expenditure." [59] In previous years, *Hunt's Merchants' Magazine* had published stronger articles explicitly calling for the sale of the canal system to private interests without provoking comparable reaction.[60] But trunk-line rate wars now lent substance to the charge that the article was part of a "Railroad Conspiracy" to discredit the canals "for the sake of diminishing their revenues, with a view at last of bringing them under the hammer." [61]

Harshly worded editorials to this effect in the New York *Times,* *Herald,* and *Tribune* reflected the alarm felt by metropolitan interests. On behalf of the New York delegates to the canal convention, Henry O'Reilly drew up and circulated an address urging the need for popular action to ward off "the apparently organized efforts to revolutionize our canal system by its conversion from a public highway into a private monopoly." But O'Reilly's address is noteworthy in two respects: heavy emphasis was placed upon the Chamber of Commerce as the "great conservator of the business interests of the City of New York"; no mention was made of pro rata or tolling, and action was called for only in regard to canal preservation and improvement.[62]

As a result of the intense excitement created by "discovery" of a railroad "conspiracy" to destroy the canals, the Rochester convention unexpectedly became a center of public attention. Despite all the conspiracy ballyhoo, the convention hardly confined itself to a program defending the canals against their "mortal enemies." It reaffirmed the omnibus resolutions of the first convention at Syracuse, set up a "State

Central Committee of Ten" (nine upstaters and Henry O'Reilly), and made railroad tolls and pro rata bills key platform planks. Though the division of opinion upon tolls came into the open, it did not become a source of heated controversy until the Utica convention four weeks later. Led by O'Reilly as spokesman for the New York City delegation, and featured by charges of bad faith on both sides, the opposition to tolls was forceful but unsuccessful.[63]

Strong reaffirmation of the tolling resolution at Utica notwithstanding, Carlos Cobb and Henry O'Reilly, the two leading figures carrying on the antirailroad agitation, continued to play it down.[64] Cobb was a Buffalo flour and grain commission merchant and chairman of the State Executive Committee;[65] O'Reilly was also a member of the Executive Committee but his main function was to serve as chairman of the Clinton League, the title adopted in 1859 by the New York friends of the canals. Though the two men worked closely together, the League really was a separate organization "for Promoting the completion of the Canal System," and its ties to the state body were tenuous.[66]

Shrewdly exploiting the "Railroad Conspiracy" to destroy the canals, Cobb and O'Reilly were remarkably successful in stirring up agitation on the transportation question in the fall of 1859. As chairman of the State Executive Committee, Cobb could not ignore railroad tolls; the "interrogatories" he addressed to candidates for public office asked them to state their position on that issue, as well as others. The Clinton League's questionnaires only dealt with canal enlargement, opposition to sale of the canals, and pro rata.[67] Private exchanges between Cobb and O'Reilly testify to the gratifying response to their activities,[68] but more public acknowledgment was also forthcoming. All major party candidates for state office in the November election answered in the affirmative to the questions addressed them by the Clinton League.[69] Local candidates were also eager to get on the bandwagon and their letters were published as soon as received. By November 1 the League alone had issued 77 documents.[70]

With no presidential contest to complicate the issues, the questions posed by the Clinton League and the State Executive Committee were a main feature of the 1859 elections.[71] When the legislature convened, the Assembly lost little time in passing pro rata and tolling bills. The Senate, however, refused to go along with pro rata[72] and passed a tolling bill unacceptable to the Assembly.[73] Apart from the pressures exerted by the roads, and the diversity of interests dissipating the strength of the antirailroad groups, the opposition of the New York Chamber of Commerce was an important factor in the defeat of both bills.

The New York trunk lines had abandoned the differential agreement favoring other cities and the Chamber, unlike the Clinton League, looked to railroads rather than canals to preserve the city's supremacy. It therefore demanded that no restrictions be placed upon the roads and that they be left "perfectly free to exercise their full capacity" for the greater glory of New York commerce. Considering its postwar attitude towards railroad regulation, the Chamber's statement of its point of view in 1860 is interesting. Warning against "arbitrary interference with the natural laws of trade," the Chamber attempted to combine liberal theory with an appeal to hard reality: "what right has the State to legislate in favor of one interest [canallers], at the cost of others? Why unjustly interfere with the chartered rights of railroad companies, and diminish their profits, when they are already seriously depressed?" [74]

Defeated in 1860, the pro rata and tolling bills faded from sight with the coming of the Civil War. Railroad tolls were never again an important issue in the Empire State but the pro rata movement was far from dead. As will be noted below, it revived after the war and in the form of a long-haul short-haul restriction upon railroads again was agitated in New York. In this form it also became a key section of the Interstate Commerce Act of 1887.

The main purpose of this extended discussion of pro rata and tolls has been to indicate the different responses of New York City and up-state economic groups to the emergence of trunk-line railroads during the 1850's. Two decades later, further development of the railroad system and other features of the Communication Revolution caused New York merchants to reverse their positions sharply. In the 1870's, they took the lead in the campaign to "interfere with the chartered rights of railroad companies," worked hard at rallying upstate interests to that program, and emphasized the need for a free canal (free of tolls) to prevent railroad diversion of trade from the metropolis.

ANTIMONOPOLY MOVES WEST AND THEN BACK EAST AGAIN

Until this point the railroad rate wars of the late 1850's have been discussed solely in terms of New York developments. But the impact of trunk-line competition and progress was widely felt east of the Alleghenies. Stimulated by depression after 1857, merchants and farmers in the other seaboard states also pressed for legislative protection against place discrimination favoring the West. Having its center in New York, the pro rata campaign of 1858–1861 extended as far south as Virginia and constituted the first *sectional* movement against railroads in the United States.[75]

But, as in New York, the eastern protests against railroad discrimination were soon submerged under the wartime wave of prosperity. Now the center of agitation over railroad rates shifted westward to the region

New York Canals and Railroads, 1855

beyond Lake Michigan. The closing of the Mississippi, and the large agricultural production increase in the region to meet wartime demands, strained its railroads' carrying capacities. With water competition diminished, freight outrunning facilities, and increased operating costs stemming from inflation after 1862, transport rates soared. Merchants and farmers dependent upon railroads resented the rapid increase in charges and found it difficult to believe that the roads were not taking undue advantage of the war to profiteer. This conviction was strengthened by the organization in 1863 of an extraordinary combination between the Mississippi steamboats plying the upper river and the railroads operating in the region. In effect, a transportation monopoly was created, with all the attendant abuses.[76]

Against this background, and with eastern agitation still fresh in mind, it is understandable that the 1863–1866 period was marked by popular feeling against the roads.[77] Conventions and meetings denounced transportation abuses, demanded state regulation, and set up machinery which aroused considerable interest and sympathy for the movement in Chicago and Milwaukee. Eastern commercial interests were also concerned since the seaport towns had profited from the increasing volume of western produce. Receiving its major impetus from the sharp drop in commodity prices just after the end of the war, the agitation reached its climax in the so-called "antimonopoly revolt" of 1865–1866.[78] Yet it is instructive to note that the movement disintegrated with the return of prosperity early in 1866, and the granting of a few concessions by the transportation companies.[79] The movement's sudden collapse makes it clear that the "antimonopoly revolt" was not a broad-gauge demand for reform. Hostility to the railroads in various sections of the West during the nineteenth century, particularly agrarian hostility, was keyed to business cycle fluctuations and was acutely responsive to lowered or raised freight charges relative to commodity prices.

But interest in transportation problems had not been confined to the region west of Lake Michigan during the Civil War; the strain upon carrying facilities was generally felt in the Middle West and, indirectly, in the East. It was soon obvious that existing lines of communication would be increasingly inadequate and virtually every group concerned with the problem joined in the demand for better and cheaper transportation. Not too surprisingly, each city and region had a pet solution all its own.[80]

As the nation's largest interior market Chicago acutely felt the shortage of facilities and, among other projects, it urged the rapid improvement of the Erie Canal. New York was agreeable — provided that Congress paid for such improvements. Unfortunately, Congress did not subscribe to the proposition. To bring New York to terms Chicago thereupon proceeded to rally the West behind a plan to improve the Canadian waterways as an alternate route. Within six months the country was aroused to the problem and in the spring of 1863 a large canal convention met in the Windy City.[81] Many localities were represented but the Chicago and New York delegates prevailed. In good log-rolling tradition the resolution finally agreed upon called for the national government to improve both the Illinois and New York canals.

The Chicago meeting in 1863 marked the peak of the wartime agitation nationally. Generally speaking, the railroads and water routes had successfully adjusted to the new demands upon them by this time and commodity price rises produced a more favorable freight cost ratio. With the close of the war, however, falling prices and increased volume of produce seeking a market again brought the demand for cheap transportation to the fore. Detroit now was made the site of a large commercial convention and various groups supported a plan for a ship canal around Niagara Falls on the American side. But another and more fruitful idea arose from the convention. First advanced at Detroit, the successful proposal for a national Chamber of Commerce to deal with transportation and related matters is indicative of the strong mercantile interest in the problem.[82]

Before discussing the organization of the National Board of Trade in 1868 as an outgrowth of the Detroit convention, reference is necessary to Henry O'Reilly's postwar activities and to his part in keeping the transportation issue alive after the Western antimonopoly movement collapsed. Upon the outbreak of the Civil War, O'Reilly lent his organizing and pamphleteering talents to the cause of the Union, and to the Democratic League formed to uphold it. Among his co-workers was an erstwhile resident of Madison County, New York, one Lorenzo Sherwood. Both men had been active in New York during the 1840's on the canal issue then agitating the state, and they were brought together again by the Democratic League.[83] After hostilities ended they combined energies and talents to "solve" the transportation questions; the result, the "National Anti-Monopoly Cheap Freight Railway League, for Promoting Reform in Railroad Management, by Securing Equal Rights and Cheap Transportation, with Consequent Increased Development of Our Industrial Energies and National Resources." [84] Early response to their agitational efforts in 1867 can only be described as phenomenal.

The title of the organization indicates a good deal about its antecedents, immediate origins, and objects. As in the case of the "Clinton League" and the "Democratic League," O'Reilly worked out of an office in the Wall Street district of New York City and was in charge of arranging and distributing "documents." [85] Comparison of the Clinton League and National Anti-Monopoly Cheap Freight Railway League publications reveals identical techniques employed: reprints of letters, editorials, proceedings of meetings, testimonials of prominent men, etc. Even the same miserable small type! The old slogan, "Equal Rights," reflects O'Reilly's and Sherwood's political education in the Barnburner wing of the New York Democracy during the forties when it made "monopoly" a swear word in the state.[86] And emphasis upon "anti-monopoly" was only logical since Sherwood had conceived the plan underlying the League's activities in 1866, a year in which the western "antimonopoly movement" for cheap transportation reached its peak.[87] Finally, the reference to "National Resources" stems from Sherwood's conviction that: "As a developing agency in a country like the United States, the railway will stand preeminent . . . A new plan is about to be inaugurated for the rapid and cheap handling of ponderous material. The want of this is now the greatest defect in our means for development." [88]

Sherwood's "new plan" derived from his indoctrination in that "grand school of political economy" claiming De Witt Clinton as its foremost exponent.[89] Designed to establish a series of double track freight trunk lines under Congressional legislation, it called for financial aid from the national and state governments. No proposal was made that the nation or states exclusively own or control the main trunk lines, but they would be permitted to subscribe up to 75 per cent of the stock in companies chartered by Congress to build them, and to donate land to aid in their construction. Congress also would be empowered to fix freight rates and appoint an officer charged with the responsibility of protecting the public from impositions on behalf of private stockholders. The roads were to be open "to free competition in transportation, as much so as the Erie Canal." Any company or individual would be allowed to put on inspected rolling stock and engage in business by conforming to the prescribed rules and requirements. A moderate and uniform rate of speed was to be adopted for all trains, which, with other economies, would result in reducing freights to one-third of current charges.[90]

Sherwood presented a memorial to Congress in January 1867, explaining in detail the plan inspiring Senator Henderson of Missouri to introduce a bill to connect the Gulf States with the Pacific Railroad. Before the session was out two more western senators had introduced similar bills, and four others were in preparation making the benefits available to all sections of the land. No Congressional enactments having followed, however, the National Anti-Monopoly Cheap Freight Railway League was organized to remedy that deficiency.[91]

Henry O'Reilly cast his letters, pamphlets, circulars, etc., upon the waters and the responses flowing back to 24 Pine Street, New York, were highly gratifying. The citizens of New York City whose interests were, as O'Reilly reminded them, "so largely connected with the question of Cheap Railway and Telegraphic Inter-communication with all parts of the United States," [92] particularly appreciated the merits of the plan. A special session of the New York Association for Advancement of Science and Art, Cooper Institute, was called to consider holding a public meeting to present its virtues for national consideration. Among those signing the call advocating the meeting were the editors of the *Evening Post, Railroad Journal, Daily Times, Brooklyn Eagle,* and numerous leading journalists, merchants, bankers, and others.[93]

With much fanfare, arrangements were made for the public meeting and O'Reilly was soon able to write of the "New York Anti-Monopoly Cheap Freight Movement. The Progress of the Age is signally illustrated in the movement now made by men and journals of all parties in New York, for promoting the Anti-Monopoly Cheap-Freight Railway Policy . . . All shades of all parties, all varieties of interests, are represented among the signers of the Call for the proposed assemblage at the Cooper Institute, on the 17th October, instant." [94] O'Reilly's description need not be taken literally but on the appointed evening, with assembled dignitaries on the platform, and lesser ones in the audience, Lorenzo Sherwood addressed "the largest meeting I ever saw assembled on an occasion like this." [95]

Launched on a flood of well-publicized oratory at the Cooper Union meeting, the League rapidly secured impressive support. Tributes poured in from the country at large,[96] and even from across the Atlantic, praising the wisdom of the "Cheap-Freight Policy" and the marvelous results certain to flow from it.[97] Auxiliary leagues were formed in various places and the high point of the campaign is probably to be noted in a published letter by the "President of the National Cheap Freight Railway League and others, to Citizens of Texas." Dated November 21, 1867, it congratulated them on their efforts to organize support for the cheap-freight policy. What makes the document so significant are the "others" associated as "Co-Operators" with Sherwood. Comprising most of the prominent politicians in the country, they included Senators Wade, Chandler, Sumner, Conkling, and Representatives Sam Randall, Julian, Holman, Butler. In all, as a separate printed slip signed by B. F. Wade boasted, there were "28 other Senators, 19 Governors and Ex-Governors, and 146 Members and Ex-Members of Congress, besides hosts of other sensible men." [98]

With such distinguished, or at least politically powerful supporters, it would be reasonable to have anticipated speedy enactment of legislation carrying out the policy of the Cheap Freight League. Why then did the League decline to the point where Lorenzo Sherwood was reduced to speaking on street corners in Chicago on the eve of the Republican Convention, May 20, 1868? The answer could not have been a sudden awareness of the plan's impracticability. As late as 1876 an organization of New York merchants still urged its adoption and Congressional bills and reports followed its principles for a number of years. In the rather pathetic but unyielding speech Sherwood delivered at the corner of Randolph and Dearborn — or more accurately, in the Court House Yard where the Chicago police finally allowed him to talk undisturbed — he gave his answer. As soon as wide Congressional support had been secured, the "monopolists," in and out of Congress, "joined forces to put back the scheme of the Cheap-Freight Railway League. The antimonopolists in Congress tamely submitted to the arrangement lest the harmony of party might be disturbed." [99]

Sherwood's explanation is consistent with what we know of Gilded Age politicos but another factor was also significant. Soaring commodity prices did not reach their peak until late in 1868 and in the sunshine of bright, if short-lived, prosperity, his cheap transportation movement rapidly dried up. [100] Before the year was out even the semblance of organization had disappeared. No longer was application for pamphlets to be made to Henry O'Reilly: "Such as desire the documents of the Cheap-Freight Railway League, please drop a note to Mrs. L. Sherwood, Ebbitt House, Washington, and she will send them free and post paid." [101] All was lost save determination — except, apparently, something with which to mail literature to interested parties.

THE NATIONAL BOARD OF TRADE

Still other phases of the postwar agitation against railroad management might be mentioned to put the organization of the National Board of Trade in perspective. For one thing, the commanding personality of Commodore Vanderbilt served to bring railroad developments to public attention in 1867 and to keep them there. As a case in point, Vanderbilt's efforts to win control of the New York Central led to the celebrated affair whereby passengers arrived at Albany one wintry day only to find that the customary connection with his Hudson River Railroad no longer existed. Men, women, and children bound for places along the east bank of the river were forced to emulate Eliza crossing the ice, and cries of indignation went up from the press. Indignation was soon translated into legislative bills to protect travelers and the Assembly Railroad Committee conducted a widely reported investigation of the incident. [102]

Given the fact that railroad policy had already revived demands for pro rata in New York, the arbitrary disruption of traffic at Albany and Vanderbilt's successful battle to control the Central resulted in the well worn specter of "monopoly" again haunting the Empire State.

Then came the "Erie War" which threatened to make the specter an expensive near-reality and negate the basic concept underlying the Free Railroad Law of 1850.

The key theoretical argument against regulation had been that competition between railroads guaranteed the public interest. Necessarily, attempts to lessen or eliminate competition were viewed with disfavor. (Even the original consolidation of the New York Central in 1853 had been criticized on the ground that independent companies were destroyed to create a monopoly.) In 1867, Vanderbilt's achievement in combining the roads from New York City to Buffalo further appeared to vitiate the free competition assumption. Thus, the long drawn-out conflict between Vanderbilt and the Drew-Fisk-Gould group in 1868 for mastery of the Erie Railroad tended to reinforce fears among the metropolitan merchants of a "restrictive monopoly."[103]

It deserves emphasis that the New York Chamber of Commerce opposed Vanderbilt's attempt to add Erie to his railroad portfolio and that it held a special meeting on March 12 to deal with the subject.[104] Scandalous conduct by judges, legislators, and railroad officials during the Erie War was the immediate cause of the meeting but more lasting grievances existed. The preamble and resolutions adopted on March 12, and a subsequent memorial to the legislature, both expressed sharp dissatisfaction with the roads' basic policies.[105] Summarily stated, the Chamber complained that continuous lines of railroads could now compete successfully with water lines for freight, the metropolis could no longer rely upon the river and canals to maintain its supremacy, and the New York roads were lagging behind competitors in pushing rail connections and lowering freight charges. Rates to and from the West were cheaper at Boston, Baltimore, and Philadelphia, and trade was being diverted from the metropolis. To add to these troubles a new danger threatened:

it may almost be claimed that the prosperity and progress of this City and the material interests of this State are under the control of two corporations, and if a consolidation of these be effected, will lie in the hands of a great moneyed monopoly.[106]

In time, Vanderbilt's failure to gain control of the Erie dissipated the alarm but the latent hostility to railroads at the metropolis had been given impetus. Significantly, the merchants' demands were not yet for regulation but for preservation of competition, extension of the New York roads' connections to the West, and institution of a low rate, high volume traffic policy.

New York complaints that other cities enjoyed better connections and cheaper rates point up the fact that railroad innovation made trunk-line competition even sharper than before the war. Development of "compromise cars" to overcome the difficulties of different gauges, and the mushrooming of "fast freight lines" to insure continuous shipment over separate roads, represented progress. Protests by places and persons that they were discriminated against, stockholder charges of profits siphoned off into freight companies owned by railroad managers, represented the growing pains of progress. In Pennsylvania and Ohio they resulted in legislative investigations and reports during 1867–68 which enlightened the public in general and merchants in particular about rate making practices and railroad policy. But indignation failed to find statutory expression in an era when legislatures were commonly regarded as another form of railroad property. Despite the introduction of a comprehensive regulatory bill in Ohio, the net result was only a railroad commissioner who functioned as a statistician.[107]

With railroads so prominently brought to the attention of the commercial interests of the country, the Boston Board of Trade gave first place to transportation problems in its call for the convention which led to the formation of the National Board of Trade. Every important city sent delegates and the resulting organization was the most representative commercial body existing in the United States.[108] For some years after June 1868 no other segment of the economy was nearly as well mobilized to advance its interests.

A study of the Board's *Annual Proceedings* discloses its sustained preoccupation with transportation and suggests this conclusion: until the "Granger Movement" erupted briefly in the Upper Mississippi Valley, commercial groups throughout the country, particularly those representing major coastal and interior cities, dominated the campaigns centering on transportation issues.[109]

The National Board of Trade focused attention upon the subject at its meetings, conventions were held on a sectional basis in the South and West, and individual Chambers of Commerce, Boards of Trade, etc., also were active.[110] Moreover, in addition to the material presented above, a brief summary of developments during the late sixties and early seventies appears to document the generalization that the so-called "Granger Movement" climaxed the first major phase of postwar railroad agitation rather than initiated it.

THE GRANGER MOVEMENT

The Erie War was scarcely over when consolidation and improvement of main lines by Commodore Vanderbilt and Jay Gould again alarmed railroad patrons in New York (and elsewhere). Correctly anticipating that they would be called upon to pay the costs accompanying baptism by stock-watering can, shippers soon generated enough resentment to bring on further legislative investigations.[111] Moreover, sporadic railroad wars strengthened demands for pro rata in certain localities, and canal conventions denounced the resulting diversion of trade from the metropolis and the losses visited upon "the friends of the canals." [112]

Though not usually thought of in this connection, the collapse of the "Tweed Ring" in 1871 added to the antirailroad uproar. Tweed and associates were closely tied to the "Erie Ring" and had also proved their freedom from prejudice by good deeds on behalf of the New York Central. One direct result of Tweed's downfall was the famous coup deposing Jay Gould from the presidency of Erie.[113] Together with the Credit Mobilér exposures, Gould's ouster in 1872 gave the public throughout the land additional insights into the mores of railroad officers and owners.

At the very time that Gould literally was being thrown out of office, the "Oil War" began in the Pennsylvania fields as a result of rebates to Standard Oil. Railroad operations thereupon became a matter of concern to influential groups in Pennsylvania, Ohio, and New York.[114] In addition, the organization of the Massachusetts Board of Railroad Commissioners in 1869 had given Charles F. Adams, Jr., an opportunity to write annual reports which attracted so much attention that he rapidly acquired a national reputation.[115] Finally, the two volumes containing the report and testimony of the Windom Committee, appointed late in 1872, make it abundantly clear that the cry for low freight charges and transportation regulation was nation-wide. Angry outbursts in the Old Northwest against railroad policies simply sounded one variation on a general theme. Yet two points deserve stress: nowhere did agitation attain greater intensity during the early seventies than in the Upper Mississippi Valley; intense agitation there undoubtedly had a catalytic effect upon developments elsewhere.

Spectacular they were, but unfortunately the short-lived series of events in the West have fostered the impression that interest in transportation problems was sectional instead of national. Moreover, the success of its opponents in pinning the epithet, "Granger," upon the movement for regulation has served to confuse the issue further and make the agitation appear agrarian in direction and tendency. A number of recent studies have helped to revise that concept and a somewhat different thesis may be offered in its place:

Farmers, particularly *dirt farmers,* were only one of several groups engaged in diverse movements to secure regulation in the Old Northwest, and the Grange itself played only a supporting role in securing the misnamed "Granger Legislation." Dirt farmers, Grangers proper, and members of agricultural clubs undoubtedly came to join in the procession and supply the mass agitation and political potential necessary to enact regulatory statutes. But midwestern mercantile groups appear to have set the movements rolling and generally directed their course. And the postwar eagerness of Democratic politicians to find new issues to distract from the recent past can not be overlooked in the revival of western antimonopoly movements.[116]

Evidence that midwestern commercial interests continued to be concerned with the transportation problem after the "antimonopoly revolt" of 1863–1866 collapsed is abundant in the *Annual Proceedings* of the National Board of Trade cited above. It is further borne out by the Windom Committee testimony, and the *Proceedings* of the American Cheap Transportation Association from 1873 to 1875, treated below. Large-scale landowners (who may well have had other business interests) were also prominent in the agitation but they appear to have worked closely with the commercial organizations. After all, merchants paid the freight bills, not farmers, and as Albert Fink once pointed out to the Cullom Committee, mercantile profits and operations were more directly affected by transportation charges and their fluctuations than agrarian interests.[117] Moreover, the early operations of the Interstate Commerce Commission after 1887 demonstrate that mercantile complaints of place and personal discrimination, originating in the North, South, East, and West, led all the rest.[118] On the basis of impressions gathered in the course of the present study, the speculative thesis might be advanced that wherever agitation against railroad rate policy achieved any intensity after 1865, merchants (jobbers and wholesalers above all) were actively at work.

Two examples perhaps illustrate the part played by merchants and large-scale landowners in directing what seems destined to go down in history as the "Granger Movement" — as federalists are imperishably entitled Anti-Federalists, and nationalists known as Federalists. (The Granger Movement discussed here is strictly confined to transportation.) In almost the same manner that upstate New York merchants sought to arouse farmers before the war, Chicago merchants campaigned to convince Illinois farmers that the abuses of warehouse owners and railroads could only be curbed by state regulation. Established in 1871 after several years of agitation, the Illinois Board of Railroad and Warehouse Commissioners was not so much the product of spontaneous indignation on the prairies as a monument to the strategic talents of the Chicago Board of Trade.[119] That the leaders of the agrarian agitation were hardly dirt farmers is illustrated in the person of W. C. Flagg. President of both the National Agricultural Congress and the Illinois State Farmers Association, Flagg was not only a relatively large-scale landowner and agricultural editor but a Yale graduate of the class of 1854 "with high honors." [120]

A perceptive contemporary analysis (1876) of the factors making for regulatory legislation in Iowa emphasized the resentment against railroads expressed by local merchants and manufacturers.

> The railroads were accused of practicing . . . [personal discrimination] to such extent as practically to drive small shippers out of the business, and to make the business along their line a monopoly in the hands of a few large operators . . . Perhaps the strongest argument, and the one producing the greatest effect, was the practice of the roads in discriminating against the local business of the State, or charging as much and in many cases more to and from the interior points in the State to the Mississippi River as from the same points to Chicago, and in making a different classification for all kinds of grain on their local traffic from the one enforced on their joint tariffs.
>
> Another ground of complaint was the charging of a less rate for long distances than for short distances, the former applying to competitive business, and the latter to noncompetitive business. This was practiced by all the roads.[121]

Despite the importance of place and personal discrimination, irritation at railroad arrogance, sectional antagonism, opportunistic Democratic politicians, etc., as factors influencing the Granger Movement, historical perspective seems to establish cheap transportation as the chief reason for the re-emergence of widespread hostility in the Old Northwest. Over and above local considerations, world-wide developments depressing commodity prices, and their repercussions upon all segments of the then basically agrarian American economy, explain the movement's rapid rise and even more spectacular fall in the seventies. Although most of the factors mentioned above were present before and after 1871–1874, only in those years did the economic situation permit them to find significant expression.

With one exception, a clear-cut resemblance exists between the "Granger" agitation of 1871–1874, and the "antimonopoly movement" of 1863–1866.[122] The exception, however, was crucial, for commercial interests at leading interior and seaboard cities no longer were merely sympathetic to the complaints of local merchants and farmers; they now were vitally concerned.[123] For a short time in 1866–67 the prevalence of high level commodity prices induced a relative lull in antirailroad activity. But when widespread agitation resumed it followed almost the identical pattern as before. High prices and rapid land settlement stimulated a large increase in agricultural production, and eastbound freight began to outrun carrying capacity; hence the enthusiastic reception at first accorded the National Anti-Monopoly Cheap Freight Railway League late in 1867. Freight rates went up but so did commodity prices until the world markets cracked in 1868–69.[124] This time a much longer period ensued in which freight charges remained high (except for sporadic and short-lived rate wars) while foodstuffs dropped sharply in value. The greater the disparity between the two, the greater the anger among western merchants and farmers and eastern merchants eager to trade with the interior. Something had to give and the explosion occurred in the panic year of 1873. Railroad regulation was again the watchword and the Windom Committee hearings demonstrate that interest in cheap transportation was felt everywhere, except in the ranks of eastern farmers.

But despite continuing depression, tension in the West was now relieved by the drastic rate reductions accompanying railroad wars of the mid-seventies. The Baltimore & Ohio placarded the area with proclamations that help was on the way and when the road entered Chicago in November 1874 it was hailed as the "Grangers' Friend." [125] By December, Illinois spokesmen were applauding the beneficial effects.[126] For reasons discussed in detail below, both the rail and ocean rates structure collapsed shortly thereafter. Commodity prices also declined but western movements for railroad regulation tended to disintegrate in the mid-seventies. Local rates probably remained high yet they did not appear to have resulted in high total costs of shipments to the seaboard.[127] As evidence that local rates could not have been too important an issue, when legislative solutions to end the continuing depression were again sought late in the decade, the West now turned almost exclusively to monetary panaceas. Greenbacks were the new war cry and "money kings" replaced "robber barons" in western popular disfavor.

In the West railroad rate wars pricked the volatile bubble of agitation; in New York City and State they had the opposite effect. While railroad innovations and abuses continued to affect groups and localities adversely the country over, neither in magnitude nor duration were the difficulties comparable to those experienced by the concentration of interests tied to the port of New York. For a variety of reasons, some economically justifiable, others more dubious, trunk-line officials found it necessary, or desirable, to rearrange rate and traffic patterns at the expense of an ever widening circle of economic groups in and out of the metropolis. Other features of the Communication Revolution operated to the state's disadvantage, and other factors aroused mercantile and nonmercantile discontent, but the trunk lines' threat to its locational supremacy best appears to explain why after 1873 railroad agitation centered in New York for the third time.

Convinced that railroad magnates endangered their prosperity, the mercantile interests most directly affected were too powerful and aggressive to remain passive while New York's lead was whittled away. With the organization of the American Cheap Transportation Association in 1873, they formally embarked on a sustained campaign to preserve their unique locational advantages. In its political phases their campaign

CHAPTER II

New York City and the Pattern
of Transportation Change

A speaker at the meeting the other night compared New York to an old and well established mercantile house, which had grown rich in the course of years, and slackened its efforts to control trade, resting securely in its prestige, and the confidence that no one could compete with it. But while the old house was resting upon its laurels, younger and more vigorous houses were working hard, and almost before the old house was aware of it they had become very serious competitors, affording better facilities for doing business and naturally taking the trade.

B. B. Sherman in *Minutes* of the first meeting of the Board of Managers of the New York Cheap Transportation Association, September 17, 1873.

The meeting referred to above had been held in the large hall of Cooper Union on September 10, 1873, and marked open recognition by the New York mercantile community that its near-monopoly of the import trade was at last seriously threatened. Such recognition had been growing for several years past, but it is significant that it found organized expression in 1873. In that year the demand for cheap transportation re-echoed through the country and attained a new pitch of intensity. Among the eminent men seated on the platform at the meeting which created the New York Cheap Transportation Association were the senators of the Committee on Transportation Routes to the Seaboard, more popularly known as the Windom Committee. Their presence testified not only to the importance of the meeting's sponsors, but to the fact that the country was aroused on the question.[1]

New York's wealth and prestige had contributed to its lagging behind other places in considering organized action upon the railroad problem after the Cheap-Freight Railway League collapsed in 1868. An abortive effort was made in 1870 but the metropolis did not join the general movement on a large scale until three years later. Participation in the movement involved more than an abstract concern for the hard-pressed farmers at the West. New York was beginning to appreciate the fact that its trade was slipping and decided to end this unusual state of affairs. As the *Times* candidly admitted in its editorial approving the Cooper Union meeting, "just now we are not so much seeking to relieve the farmers as to save ourselves." [2]

In 1873 the situation was obviously different than it had been for a few years after the Civil War. Economic activity had largely expanded as a result of the war, and New York had expropriated the major share of the increased foreign commerce, as well as a handsome portion of the internal trade. Apart from its status as the focal point for foreign trade, the city served as a key domestic distributing, financial, and manufacturing center. Not only did her own citizens pay tribute to New York's supremacy; that perfect Bostonian, Charles Francis Adams, Jr., hailed it in 1868 as a model of commercial enterprise and intelligence. According to Adams, the latter place exemplified the blessings of a cosmopolitan economy, whereas the Hub, in all conscience, could only be described as "provincial" [3] — no doubt his cruelest epithet.

COMMUNICATION REVOLUTION VERSUS NATURE

If there was one subject upon which unanimity existed in contemporary commercial circles it was that the Erie Canal had been responsible for New York State's preëminent economic position.[4] Yet good grounds exist for questioning the view that De Witt Clinton and his co-workers made New York the Empire State in fact as well as name. In place of Clinton the credit might go to Mother Nature, and in place of the Erie Canal, the natural advantages of New York deserve emphasis. Actually, the state and its metropolis were in the front rank before a foot of "Clinton's Ditch" had been dug, or, for that matter, before the entrepreneurs of New York City and the decisions of British traders after the War of 1812 had lent Nature a hand.

Taken together, the natural advantages of New York far surpassed those of any other port. It had a superb harbor, excellent coastwise and trans-ocean position, the agriculturally valuable Hudson, Mohawk, and Genesee valleys in its hinterland,[5] and the unique benefit of a topographical trough across the Allegheny Mountains to the Great Lakes. No other equivalent depression existed for a thousand miles to the south, and only New Orleans was better equipped naturally to secure the western trade. The latter city, however, was not as favorably endowed in other respects, and if geography had been the sole determinant, New York would have had an even greater lead than it did. But geography had not been the sole determinant affecting the development of the port and its hinterland.

In broad terms, even more than the French and Indian power blocking access to the West and inhibiting settlement in the Upper Hudson-Mohawk region, the notoriously illiberal land system in the Province of New York caused its development to lag before 1776. After the Revolution the Indian barrier was gone, the land system became less repressive, and settlement was encouraged.[6] New York State ranked fifth in population at the 1790 Federal Census and first in 1820; New York City attained the lead in its class by 1810. Neither state nor city was ever surpassed.[7] Significantly, the rate of population growth was distinctly higher in the state than in the city until the 1820–1830 decade. With the most rapidly growing hinterland in the United States at its disposal, it would have been surprising had New York City not shot to the fore. In large measure, the colossus at the mouth of the Hudson did not make the Empire State but was made by it.[8]

What the canal did was to capitalize upon the natural advantages of the port and help to increase its population lead. By 1797 New York had already surpassed Philadelphia's volume of foreign trade and, thereafter, topped the nation in that category. But not until the completion of the Erie Canal further accelerated its hinterland's development was New York's lead firm, and not until canal enlargement was well underway after 1835 did the port's primacy become overwhelming.[9] Bringing an ever increasing volume of commodities down to New York harbor, the canal also transported merchandise inland cheaply, functions for which rival Atlantic ports had no comparable instrumentality until three decades later. As a result, New York was able to dominate the foreign trade, as well as the coastwise and internal commerce which by the early fifties had become much greater.[10] After New Yorkers improved upon Nature no other city was so well equipped to handle these three interdependent categories.

From the completion of Clinton's Ditch to the beginning of serious railroad competition, New York was without peer as the commercial entrepôt of the North. A series of canals such as the Champlain, Oswego, Black River, and numerous lateral branches fed the system, enabling New York to tap a great portion of the northern states and, through the lake connections at Buffalo, pull into its sphere a considerable portion of the commerce of the Old Northwest. Moreover, canals in that section only added to the effectiveness of the New York system.[11]

Little need exists to labor the point. Phenomenal growth of New York City and the cities springing up along the canal and river routes pushed the development of a good portion of the state directly, and an even greater area indirectly. Stimulus was given to enterprise much beyond the state borders and expansion generated throughout the entire area which could reach the New York market most economically. In turn the development of its hinterland fed the commerce of the city still further, and so the process went — a mutual kind of interaction within the over-all metropolitan economy. Furnishing the largest outgoing and incoming cargoes, shipping necessarily concentrated at the port, warehouses grew in size and number, branch houses from other cities in short order became the main offices, and the apparatus of trade and finance generally flourished.[12] In time these cumulative advantages came to be fully appreciated, for transportation innovations then permitted New York's rivals to offer more effective competition.

COMMUNICATION REVOLUTION VERSUS NATURE

As long as artificial waterways using horsepower constituted the most economical form of transportation along the Atlantic Slope, New York's rivals were overwhelmed by her natural advantages. As steam power applied to land carriage increased in efficiency, the mountain barriers were cut down proportionately and the advantages of New York's water route diminished. The greater the technical progress, the less decisive the advantages of topography.[13] During the late 1850's, the emergence of trunk-line railroads brought on rate wars and differentials which advanced the process still further. Though they still favored New York, the actual costs of transportation began to lose importance as the determining factor fixing rates to the West. By 1860, its Chamber of Commerce's remonstrance against pro rata bills and railroad tolls emphasized the fact that the transportation advantages once enjoyed by the metropolis were now endangered.[14]

What might have happened had the Civil War not come along must be left to the imagination; what did happen was that wartime circumstances resulted in New York's appropriating a larger share of the total foreign trade than she had ever enjoyed. In 1858 — the first year in which the city was measurably affected by trunk-line competition — she had roughly 47 per cent of the total foreign trade of the eleven principal ports and 42 per cent of the entire country's. In 1865 the comparable figures were 77 per cent and 64 per cent,[15] and New York's ability to beat off competitors correspondingly improved.

Precisely because of her enviable position, New York was bound to be the prime target at which every potential and existing trade center trained its fire, at least in part. Rivalry with other established Atlantic seaports was only the most obvious aspect of the situation. Boston, Philadelphia, and Baltimore had long felt the crushing superiority of New York and their efforts to break it were predictable. But as a result of the closing of the Mississippi during the war, New York had largely gained at New Orleans' expense, and that hitherto important Gulf port was determined to regain what it regarded as its own. To the north, the

Canadian government was vigorously pushing the St. Lawrence and Welland canals, and the improved water route terminating at Montreal threatened the once unchallenged Great Lakes-Erie Canal-Hudson River line.[16] Numerous smaller Atlantic and Gulf ports were either engaged in improving their facilities, or on the verge of such activities. And keen students of the problem could recognize that the Pacific Coast ports at some future date would provide considerable trouble for New York, both west and east of the Rocky Mountains.

In many respects, interior cities posed almost as serious a threat to the domestic and foreign trade of the metropolis. Chicago, St. Louis, Cincinnati, and others had long been clamoring for a change in the customs regulations to permit importation without appraisement at the exterior port where foreign goods were first landed. The Act of July 14, 1870, marked attainment of their objective. As a result, interior wholesalers and jobbers were better equipped to compete with seaboard rivals and direct exportation was stimulated. Commercial arrangements between business houses in the interior and the United Kingdom and Continent facilitated a two-way traffic, and the opportunity was readily grasped.[17] In addition, for a long time after the coming of the railroad New York had been the main market and commercial entrepôt of large sections of the northeastern states, and those western and northwestern (Old Northwest) states readily accessible to the Great Lakes. In fact, many New England interior and coastal points, even Boston itself, had secured western grain via New York and such transshipments were soon uneconomic.[18] Within the boundaries of the Empire State competition was intensified, for wholesalers in Syracuse, Rochester, Utica, and other growing cities were determined to oust New York jobbers and wholesalers from their home markets.[19]

Adequate statistics do not exist to measure fully the impact of the varied assaults upon the metropolis' commerce. Though the domestic trade was approximately seven times the foreign by the early eighties,[20] no data were collected which permit detailed comparisons between rival cities. And the postwar development of through trade meant that even the foreign trade statistics cannot be taken at face value. Seaports were increasingly serving as way stations between the interior and Europe,[21] and figures for given ports include transactions which actually represent a diversion of trade from the merchants of those ports. It is possible, however, to suggest the postwar trends by comparing the changes in the volume of foreign trade at the eleven principal Atlantic and Gulf ports, and in the total receipts of all grain at the five principal Atlantic ports from 1865 to 1880 (including Montreal).

New York's share of the imports and exports was 77 per cent in 1865, dropped to 63 per cent in 1867, and oscillated around that figure until 1897 when it dropped to 58 per cent.[22] Grain receipts at New York were 58 per cent in 1865, and declined erratically to 50 per cent in 1880.[23] Another set of statistics measuring grain receipts at six American Atlantic ports provides a supplemental series. Its figures give New York 61 per cent in 1873, drop to 52 per cent in 1880, oscillate around there until 1892, and in that year fall to 47 per cent. Thereafter, the decline is steady to 38 per cent in 1898.[24]

Comparable statistics for the internal trade do not exist and it is necessary to rely on impressionistic evidence. Reading the angry statements of New Yorkers concerned with that branch of commerce, it is clear that they genuinely believed a substantial diversion away from their city took place in the 1870's; they would also appear to have been in a good position to know. Treated at greater length below, the subject is mentioned here to supplement the statistics on foreign trade, and to emphasize that misleading conclusions are bound to be drawn if the far more voluminous internal commerce is not taken into account.[25]

The statistics given above are all in relative figures; in absolute terms there was a decided increase. But the great overriding fear of the New York merchants was that a relative decline in her position would spur rivals on to even greater efforts and strengthen them to the point of effecting an absolute decline. From their own experience the merchants knew how easy it was for a process of pyramiding to set in and how rapidly quantitative advances transformed themselves into more formidable qualitative gains. In fact, can a better example be found than the rise of New York to illustrate the pyramiding process possible once transportation innovations produced significant relocalizations of economic activity? [26]

Four developments might be singled out as especially contributing to making New York more vulnerable to the competition of rival cities after 1865.[27]

First, as a happy by-product of her position as the leading shipping center, commercial intelligence (information) concerning markets throughout the world had been better at New York than elsewhere in the United States. This important advantage soon was considerably diminished when, after the completion of the Atlantic Cable in 1866, the transmission of information became only a matter of minutes instead of days or weeks.

Second, Canadian enterprise in pushing the St. Lawrence and Welland canals caused serious concern. Those mercantile circles convinced that water routes would always be cheaper than rail, at least in the grain trade, envisioned Montreal as cutting deeply into New York's supremacy. In the same category were the various projects for improving the Mississippi River route and improving New Orleans as a river and ocean port.

Third, in regard to ocean shipping, in the later seventies New York lost a considerable number of the advantages she had once enjoyed. American imports as compared to exports were falling, and cut-throat competition between sailing and steam ships as a result of over-tonnage meant that a large number of sailing ships came to the Atlantic Coast in ballast, totally dependent upon outbound freight. Instead of discharging high value imports at New York, and therefore willing to take out cargoes cheaply, they were now available at about the same low rates at any point above Norfolk. Sharply slashed rates also meant that if ocean differentials still favored New York they had to be small in size. And the Atlantic Cable reduced the advantages of regular lines of steamers and clipper ships between specified points, advantages previously favoring New York. Now outbound ships could proceed to Cork, Ireland, for orders, and from there be sent with grain to any European port, depending upon market conditions. Philadelphia and Baltimore had been handicapped by deficient shipping facilities and the changes sketched here improved their position.

Finally, despite these changes, if New York could continue to transport goods to and from the interior more cheaply or quickly than other cities, or at least as cheaply and quickly, her dominant position would have tended to maintain itself. Trade channels are difficult to redirect, at least in the short run, and the city's supremacy as a money market, her established commercial relations, strong commodity exchanges, etc., gave her immense advantages. But improvements in rail transportation enabled rival cities to enlarge the economic hinterland in which they could provide cheaper or quicker facilities than New York and thereby tip the balance sufficiently in their favor to attract trade. Moreover, the conditions under which trunk-line competition developed forced railroad officials to nullify many natural and cumulative advantages possessed by the metropolis. Rail transportation thus became the leading problem confronting the New York mercantile community for it permitted rivals to take advantage of all the new opportunities presented by the Communication Revolution.

When the railroad system was made up of short, disconnected, high-cost freight lines, serving essentially as feeders to major water routes, in important respects they added to rather than subtracted from New York's sphere of influence. Interior points were freed from their dependence upon the city for various commodities and other Atlantic ports could enlarge their hinterland, but the net effect was an increased geographic area most effectively serviced by the Lakes-Erie-Hudson route.

Furthermore, the same topographical advantage enabled the New

York Central to construct a route much superior to that of its northern and southern rivals when railroad technology was crude. The roads along the lake and canal route also profited from their location in well-developed regions providing a relatively large passenger traffic, a considerable amount of high value or perishable freight better handled by rail than by water, and an appreciable amount of local freight.

During the 1850's, therefore, though the trunk lines cut sharply into the passenger and high-value freight of the water route, New York possessed unrivaled facilities to handle eastbound and westbound traffic of all kinds.[28] Before 1860, railroad innovations were not matched by those in ocean shipping and communication, and New York's superior position in the latter respects still made it the most desirable port for some regions easily accessible by rail to other cities. Once the roads ceased feeding passengers and merchandise to water routes and became effective competitors for low-value, long-distance freight as well, and once New York's shipping superiority receded measurably, a different situation obtained. Both developments came together in the seventies (rail preceding ocean), and their direct and indirect results underlay the growing hostility to railroad management in the metropolis. It was not so much that New York lagged behind in pushing her rail net, but that her supremacy was now more susceptible to aggressive competition. Topography no longer gave her unique position.[29]

The implications of this last point may be clearer if attention is drawn to one of the period's organizational innovations which particularly hurt New York. Probably the leading economic development of the ten or fifteen years after the Civil War was the wave of consolidations characterizing their railroad history. By 1875 five great systems extended continuously from the Atlantic seaboard to Chicago and the West — the New York Central, the Pennsylvania, the Erie, the Baltimore & Ohio, and the Grand Trunk. All five lines had connected scattered units and established complete through routes.[30] William H. Vanderbilt's comment tersely sums up the result of the organizational and technical advances after 1865: "five great railroads to New York, with only business enough for two." [31]

In an industry characterized by high fixed costs, large excess capacity, and a somewhat inelastic demand relative to price (at least in the short run), five trunk lines and business enough for two spelled out only one thing: cut-throat competition. Total demand for transportation of grain to the seaboard in the short run was relatively inelastic, but rate competition also meant route competition. Competition of routes among the improved railroads of the 1870's adversely affected New York City because the Erie Canal faced the loss of its most valuable traffic, eastbound grain.

RAILROAD RATE WARS AND THE ERIE CANAL

Rate wars, differentials, and informal pools were already evident by the 1850's.[32] A comprehensive study of these developments is still lacking but it is possible to indicate some general characteristics which distinguish the pre-1874 varieties from their successors. Fundamentally, little difference existed. In the late fifties, and again in the late sixties, a falling off in business sporadically gave new urgency to the problem of excess capacity. Rate wars were the natural by-products. As the price of peace, trunk lines not having access to New York demanded differential rates favoring rival cities in order to secure a "fair share" of traffic. Conventions were held, agreements signed, differentials established, promptly disregarded, and soon the process began again.[33] But the early rate wars centered more on passenger traffic and westbound high-value goods than did those of the mid-seventies which centered around eastbound freight.[34] The conditions governing the over-all traffic pattern explain the shift in direction.

Until the Atlantic Cable was completed and created a full-fledged international commodity market in which transactions were carried out almost instantaneously, the railroads' time-saving advantage was not too important in the export grain trade. And export grain constituted the key eastbound traffic for which rival cities and roads fought, since domestic requirements were actually "local" traffic, not subject to serious competition by "foreign" roads after trunk-line connections were well developed.[35] (Competition did exist between the canal and the various roads into New York, and no road exclusively handled all the domestic grain of any city.)

Soon after its completion in 1866, the Atlantic Cable brought about drastic changes in business practices. Transactions could be made with rapidity and they increased in volume. Capital was turned over rapidly and profit margins tended to be reduced to the bare minimum by sharp competition. Following the Panic of 1873, the closest kind of figuring was necessary to secure business. One or two cents a hundred now constituted the margin between profit and loss, and savings in interest upon grain in transit, or the opportunity to take rapid advantage of a slight change in prices, necessarily took on more importance.[36]

Significantly, the roads only really began to challenge the water route's predominance as a grain carrier in the period 1866–1868.[37] But two factors tended to delay serious competition by the trunk lines for the export grain. The rail rates were too high to take much traffic away, particularly during the open season of navigation, and the expansion of agricultural production in the West provided an amount of traffic which actually taxed the capacity of all carriers to the seaboard. Inadequate facilities resulted in high rates for both rail and water carriers. Under these profitable circumstances little disposition existed to engage in sustained rate competition.

As might be expected, the enlarged demand stimulated an enthusiastic expansion of facilities. Such a state of affairs lasted long enough to balance supply and demand. Now the demand curve lagged behind for the rapid rate of traffic growth suddenly halted in 1873.[38] Add to this the severe panic and the long depression which followed, and the explosive potentialities of the situation are obvious. Economically (and politically) the resultant shock was felt almost immediately in the United States, not long after abroad, and indirectly it soon came to affect most aspects of life in the western world.

Confronted by these developments, the trunk lines and the cities identified with them were hard pressed to enlarge or protect their share of the export grain traffic. The result was to slash rates to levels as low as 10 cents a hundredweight from Chicago to the seaboard. Unprecedented low rates such as this meant that the days of unchallenged water superiority were over.[39] The Erie Canal continued to carry significant quantities of grain right down to 1890, particularly wheat during the peak seasons of movement, and during the uneasy rail truces that broke out from time to time. But its proportionate share of the tonnage dropped rapidly. Water rates also dropped to all time lows, but even the most drastic cuts could only enable the canal to hold its own for a number of years and then to fall rapidly behind.

Though railroad competition with the Erie Canal for freight was evident as early as the 1850's, the rivalry at first had been in limited categories, that is, merchandise, provisions, and live animals.[40] Now the grain traffic was added to the growing list of commodities best served by the roads. Analysis of the decline in exports from New York demonstrates the decreased effectiveness of the water route. That the decline in the export trade was almost entirely due to the canal's relative decline is shown by comparing New York's share of the seaboard receipts with her share of the seaboard exports, and noting the percentage figures of the receipts by rail and canal.[41]

Clearly, the Erie Canal was the principal victim of the sharp competition of routes which developed in the mid-seventies. But the increased tonnage carried by the railroads was not particularly remunerative to them for "war" between the trunk lines and the canals also required a war between the individual trunk lines. While there had been sharp clashes from time to time for the eastbound traffic, they were only skirmishes compared to the ones which followed the entrance of the Baltimore & Ohio into Chicago in November 1874.

Year	Rail	Canal and coast-wise	N.Y. receipts	N.Y. exports
1873	28.8	32.6	61.4	77.9
1874	33.0	29.5	62.5	74.8
1875	33.1	24.9	58.0	67.6
1876	28.8	18.2	47.0	49.4
1877	25.0	26.5	51.5	54.8
1878	29.9	23.7	53.6	54.1
1879	31.8	19.3	51.1	53.0
1880	28.1	24.1	52.2	56.3
1891	41.5	13.0	54.5	52.9
1895	41.2	5.2	46.4	47.6
1896	30.3	6.3	36.6	33.7

RATE WARS AND DIFFERENTIALS

Just as rate wars were of a different kind and magnitude after 1874, differentials and pools took on new form and content. By this time the American railroad system had developed to the point where competition revealed basic problems demanding sustained attempts at solution.[42] Given the economic situation in the mid-seventies it would have taken a miracle to avoid severe rate wars. But John Garrett's plans ruled out the possibility of any such divine intervention. Garrett, president of the Baltimore & Ohio, enthusiastically conducted forays into the Pennsylvania Railroad's territory and he was also determined to acquire a secure New York outlet for his road.[43] Even before the Baltimore & Ohio actually entered Chicago on November 15, 1874, Garrett cut the westbound rates from New York to the West. Since his road got into New York over the Pennsylvania's connections, the latter road was urged by the other lines to deny access to Garrett.[44]

The key factor in the railroad war was the progress of the Baltimore & Ohio's line to Chicago. Garrett was convinced "that upon the completion of his lines, like another Samson, he could pull down the temple of rates around the heads of these other trunk lines . . ."[45] A Chicago terminus was the source of his confidence. He intended to apply the leverage gained by entering that city to achieve all his major objectives, including unconditional entrance to New York over the Pennsylvania lines at a pro rata of the tariff.[46] As the line pounded westward in 1874 a series of sharp clashes occurred and efforts were made to stave off a full scale rate war. The Saratoga Compact signed in August of that year was not the first meeting of like character to be held but became the most famous. A generous schedule of rates was adopted, each signatory line pledged to uphold them, and a Board of Arbitration was appointed to enforce the covenant. But the refusal of the Baltimore & Ohio and the Grand Trunk to enter into the agreement made it something less than a firm contract.[47]

Notwithstanding the sharp skirmishes of 1874, rate levels did not really get out of control until early in 1875. From the middle of February through September "ruinously low rates" prevailed. The fact that the war began during the closed season of water navigation makes clear both its serious nature and the differences which set it apart from predecessors. Previously, rate conflicts were more likely to be carried on during the navigation season when the roads did not have much to lose. But for some years to come more basic issues overrode these prudent considerations.

Though the contest in 1875 at first was limited to the Pennsylvania and the Baltimore & Ohio, the American railroad system had now reached that stage where other roads could not stay out for long. Shipping was more easily attracted to Philadelphia and Baltimore than during previous rate wars, and traffic, therefore, could also be more easily diverted to those ports. Nevertheless, not wanting to extend the area of conflict and thus bring the entire rate structure tumbling down, the New York roads tried to keep out of the fight. Since the Pennsylvania did not want rates to be cut on its traffic to New York, it attempted to coöperate with them.[48]

The dilemma of the managers of the New York roads is easily appreciated. At a time when the volume of traffic to match enlarged capacity was considerably below expectations, more than ever their problem was to weigh the revenue losses due to traffic diverted to the warring roads against the amount of revenue lost if rates were cut on the traffic they still had. Yet they could not afford to ignore the long range effect of traffic diversion, that is, the increased strength of the Pennsylvania and Baltimore & Ohio relative to themselves. Another complication gave them trouble. The water-carriers would hardly be idle while their grain traffic was snatched away. When navigation opened they would be certain to cut rates and then the New York roads would really be hit. Finally, the Grand Trunk, which together with the Baltimore & Ohio had refused to sign the Saratoga Compact, was bringing grain into Boston at two-thirds of the rate to New York.[49]

Whatever the precipitating factor was, by the middle of March 1875 efforts to maintain the Saratoga agreement were abandoned, and the war was on. Rates plunged to new lows and on eastbound business no regular tariffs existed for most freight. In its weakened condition the Erie rapidly succumbed and went into bankruptcy. At A. J. Drexel's intervention, a temporary truce was effected in June between the Baltimore & Ohio and the Pennsylvania. (Drexel's intervention stemmed from his banking firm's connection with both roads.) But the northern trunk lines were not consulted and the *Railroad Gazette* commented in late August, "notwithstanding the long-past treaty of peace between the chief contending powers, the present condition of things is unlike peace." As the *Gazette* had pointed out the month before, a major disturbing factor was the New York roads' fear that the rates to Philadelphia and Baltimore would be made much lower than to New York.[50]

No longer could the New York roads tolerate substantial differentials on eastbound traffic, or the New York merchants permit them to do so unchallenged. In reality, the differentials had never been put to the test. The near-chaotic state of railroad rate-making had precluded the possibility that schedule tariffs be taken seriously for any length of time. Apart from that, even had the nominal differentials previously been enforced, the result would have been much less inimical to New York than if they were put into effect in 1875. By the mid-seventies the innovations grouped together here under the term Communication Revolution had largely contributed to the drastic decline of staple commodity prices. They had also appreciably diminished the transportation advantages of New York. With fractional advantages now determining the course of trade, differentials assumed unprecedented importance. A contemporary put it this way: "the difference of six or even sixteen cents a hundred might have been but very little felt by New York in the period from 1855 to 1870, whereas a cent or two cents a hundred changed the current of trade between 1875 and 1880 from New York to Baltimore." [51]

Aware of these considerations, New York trunk-line managers hesitated to end the war in 1875 until they were convinced that the Baltimore & Ohio and the Pennsylvania had not concluded a peace disastrous to their roads. Actually, the war did not end. An uneasy kind of truce prevailed for some months after the nominal settlement in June, but eastbound rates were not raised. During the conflict large shippers had taken out time contracts which still had some months to run, and not much additional revenue would be secured in any case. The warlike peace, or peaceful war, dragged on for several months; it finally resulted in the differential agreement of March 1876 which, unlike the Saratoga Compact, included all four trunk lines.[52]

Before turning to the developments of 1876 it is necessary to consider the westbound differentials. In theory, differentials on freight to the interior had been established in the 1850's as a basic trunk-line principle; in practice, they were almost non-existent. As George Blanchard testified before the Hepburn Committee, his method in fixing rates on the Baltimore & Ohio prior to 1875 was to pay "no attention whatever to these differences, but on many classes of dry goods made the difference fifty cents a hundred under New York, or whatever we could get; we had no schedule of differences, and we had no rule of differences established, but when we got the tariff of the New York roads we simply sat down and made our rates what we pleased; because there was no agreement and no condition to the contrary." [53]

The operational phrase is "whatever we could get." These four words fairly well sum up the situation before the formal establishment of a westbound pool in 1877. No matter what agreement had been reached by the roads the basic consideration always was to maximize revenue. Rate wars broke out, not because differentials were ignored but because sufficient traffic was diverted from one road to another to make the situation appear intolerable. Whether the diversion of traffic was due to rate cutting, improved facilities, new connections, etc., was immaterial. None of the roads would passively permit traffic "belonging" to them to be handled by rivals, particularly at times when the total amount of traffic failed to meet expectations and needs.[54]

On the westbound traffic the roads out of Boston were the chief problem for the Central and the Erie. The Hub of the New England manufacturing complex, Boston had excellent financial resources, good shipping connections, a substantial import and jobbing trade, and the necessary apparatus to handle even greater amounts, as Philadelphia and Baltimore did not. Thus, the Grand Trunk and Vermont Central combination (the latter's connections gave it entry to Boston) had some basis for their expectations of an increased share of the total westbound traffic. To compete with the more efficient Boston and Albany-New York Central alliance, they demanded, and got, a differential out of Boston consistently under that maintained by the better route.[55] The Grand Trunk-Vermont Central combination, therefore, carried westbound freight under the New York rates — always a source of irritation to the latter city.

In key respects New York was more likely to be hurt by rate wars on the westbound traffic than on the eastbound. Of the four trunk lines (the Grand Trunk was not then awarded the accolade) only the New York Central, through its connection with the Boston & Albany, carried much traffic to and from the Hub. And the proportion of its westbound business was small compared to New York; the *Railroad Gazette* in 1875 estimated the ratio as 1 to 10.[56] Thus, whenever the Central or the Boston & Albany felt compelled to meet the Grand Trunk rates, a powerful inducement existed to hold rates firm at New York. If the rate-cutting extended to that city all the major roads would become involved, with enormous revenue losses. Understandably, the New York managers were under great pressure to attempt to limit the war to Boston.

Perhaps the extent of the squeeze against New York is best appreciated by noting that at times goods from New York to Chicago went there via Boston. That was only the beginning. At certain times, when the Boston rates really ran wild, goods would be shipped by water from New York to Boston, then back to New York over the Erie Railroad's connections, and then on to Chicago at a total cost much below that directly from the metropolis. This state of affairs reflected the pressures operating to hold the New York rates firm and the economic absurdities to which the roads were reduced in their efforts to prevent a general war.[57]

Vanderbilt's method of dealing with the protests from New York in early 1875 on the westbound traffic was characteristic — cut rates were granted to leading shippers to pacify them.[58] Either the Boston rates were not slashed deeply enough in the winter of 1874–75 to cause much trouble, or the cuts did not last long. In any event the clamor soon died down. It was a different matter in the winter of 1875–76 when the same squeeze play was on. Protests from the New York merchants attained new heights and apparently had some effect upon the trunk lines. Whether the protests really were the cause or merely the occasion, the result was the same. The roads out of New York met the Boston rates and after a sharp but brief struggle with the Grand Trunk a temporary truce was worked out.[59]

Railroad competition had reached the point, however, where truces were for increasingly shorter duration. Baltimore and Philadelphia were desirous of competing with New York as export centers for western produce, and, because of substantial improvements in their railroad lines and excellent terminal facilities, they actually were getting a growing percentage of the trade.[60] Moreover, one result of the 1875 railroad war had been to drive rates down to the point where the trunk lines could appropriate traffic from the canals. Since the possibility now existed that lower rates could be more than balanced by gains in tonnage, long drawn out conflicts appeared less unattractive to ambitious railroad managers.

AFTER THE RATE WARS CAME THE POOL

With the lowering of freight rates and the perfecting of the various railroad systems, the interrelationships between the five major eastern groupings became increasingly intimate and sensitive. Activities and policies of one road quickly impinged upon the others and it was almost impossible to localize the areas of conflicts. If one road changed its rates on one kind of traffic, the impact was felt on virtually all traffic and all roads. Under these circumstances the agreement of December 1875 soon proved ineffectual. The Grand Trunk was bought off by giving it a share of the traffic but trouble began elsewhere.

Early in February 1876 the Erie and the New York Central renewed rate cutting on all eastbound through-traffic and the cycle started again.

After a few weeks another meeting was held and a new plan drawn up to settle the difficulties. The agreement of March 2, 1876, therefore, was an attempt to deal with the problems arising out of both eastbound and westbound freight wars. In place of the nominal *fixed* differentials below New York, new nominal *percentage* differentials were substituted based on mileage. Boston still had equal rates but the Baltimore and Philadelphia charges from Chicago were 13 and 10 per cent less, respectively. Without any better enforcement provision than the pledged word of the railroad presidents, it failed. Less than six weeks later the battle was on again, openly. In fact, the rate cutting never seems to have stopped; that brief truces were sometimes indulged in would be a more accurate description. The Central may have been naïve enough to maintain the contract rates while its rivals stole traffic but such *pro forma* protests need not be taken seriously.[61]

Far from being a victim of unscrupulous rivals, the New York Central apparently was now eager to show its strength. During the winter of 1875–76 it had become obvious that a considerable diversion of grain from New York was taking place. The other lines banded together to ask Commodore Vanderbilt to grant the Grand Trunk a differential on eastbound freight so that it might be persuaded to enter the trunk-line agreement. (It already had a westbound differential.) Seemingly this proved to be the proverbial straw. The Pennsylvania and the Baltimore & Ohio had gotten differentials because of their shorter lines. Now Vanderbilt was being asked to give a differential to the Grand Trunk because of its longer line.[62] The Commodore's answer was to deny the justice of the differentials altogether, and to take a no-compromise position. "Now, in order that we may live on proper charges, we cannot make concessions which shall offset our natural advantages. Is it just that we should? I say it is not." [63]

A good deal is still unknown about the real motivations of the various participants in the rate wars. As indicated below, after the pooling agreement of 1877, the suspicion — not a new one by any means — began to permeate the New York business community that the rate wars were essentially "stock-jobbing tricks." But during 1876 the conviction grew widespread that the Commodore had made his stand and was now prepared to fight for the principle that New York be given equal rates on competitive traffic. Obviously, he had the full support of the metropolis in such an undertaking. For various reasons New York was securing a smaller percentage of trade than before and the differentials were assigned a good deal of the blame.[64]

Signatures on agreements to the contrary, the differentials still had not been observed. Instead the New York roads, particularly the Central, had allowed some traffic to slip away because of an understandable desire to ward off rate wars.[65] In this sense differential rates to and from other cities did exist. Viewed as symbols the differentials explain the constant charge that the New York roads did not have the interest of "their city" at heart, as the Baltimore & Ohio and the Pennsylvania were supposed to have had. Differentials had come to symbolize *all* developments which tended to give rival cities lower rates than New York.

The course of the railroad war in 1876, however, was taken as proof that Vanderbilt had finally realized that trade was slipping away to a dangerous extent, and that the Central as well as New York was suffering from the diversion. In 1876 his road went over to the offensive. Rates such as 8 and 10 cents a hundred on grain from Chicago to the various ports seemed to make it abundantly clear that no sham battle was being waged. To New Yorkers, the railroad agreement of December 16, 1876, signalized the complete abolition of the differentials. The *Commercial and Financial Chronicle* exultantly expressed the general opinion: "New York has secured the vital principle of one uniform rate to all the three cities on grain, provisions, and etc., for export." [66]

Rejoicing was premature and had New Yorkers been given access to the correspondence of several leading figures in the drama they would have known that no happy ending was in store for them. Far from the New York Central's having won, the Pennsylvania and the Baltimore & Ohio officers were convinced that victory was theirs. Again A. J. Drexel of Drexel, Morgan and Company was active in the cause of peace — on the side of the Philadelphia and Baltimore roads. Early in December he had written to John W. Garrett that "Col. Scott [of the Pennsylvania] intends acting very forcefully with Vanderbilt . . ." A week later: "Let me congratulate you [Garrett] on the settlement of the Railway disputes, which . . . [Scott] informs me is now an accomplished fact — I hope that it will be a permanent one, and that the experience of the past will not be lost on Mr. Vanderbilt." [67]

But Drexel apparently did not believe that Vanderbilt was really prepared to learn the lessons of history and thought Tom Scott oversanguine in expecting the agreement to be honored. "I hope he is correct in his opinion but I confess I have very little faith in either of the New York parties. Col. Scott took occasion to express his great satisfaction at the harmonious working of the Balt. & Ohio & Pa Central roads & feels satisfied that together you can accomplish a great deal." [68] Drexel's letter to Garrett points up a significant aspect of trunk-line competition in 1876. During the rate wars from 1873 to 1875 the Baltimore and Philadephia roads were the major contestants; now they jointly fought against the New York roads to secure differentials favoring their termini. And they obviously did not regard the agreement of December 16, 1876, as a defeat.

Whether deliberately or not, the agreement was loosely drawn and soon went the way of many railroad compacts of that day. Under its terms Baltimore and Philadelphia retained differentials on goods for *local* consumption, and shippers readily took advantage of this loophole. In addition, a dispute broke out over what the agreement really meant. Did equal export rates mean equal from the West to the seaboard or all the way to Europe? The Baltimore and Philadelphia roads backed the latter interpretation and gave their shippers rebates to cover the alleged differences in ocean shipping. New York disputed this reasoning since it would merely mean differentials in new dress.[69]

It seems difficult to believe that the railroad presidents were unaware of the agreement's ambiguities. As Charles Francis Adams, Jr., observed at the time, it "settles nothing" and admits of "infinite wrangling." [70] Whether they wanted to achieve a breathing spell or indulge in some "stock-jobbing" is not clear, but the battle was soon on again. It lasted (publicly) until July, though a formal agreement ending the war was signed on April 5, 1877. This time the agreement brought few cheers in New York. Rather than guaranteeing the metropolis equality of rates, it was designed to insure permanent inequality, and, in a short time, provided the machinery to enforce it.[71]

Representing an overthrow of the 1876 percentage principle based on mileage, the new differentials reverted to the early system of fixed amounts and were much smaller than before. Their ostensible purpose is well stated in the agreement:

> To avoid all future misunderstandings in respect to the geographical advantages or disadvantages of the Cities of Baltimore, Philadelphia and New York, as affected by rail-and-ocean transportation, and with the view of effecting an equalization of the aggregate cost of rail and ocean transportation between all competitive points in the West, Northwest, and Southwest, and all domestic or foreign ports reached through the above cities . . .[72]

In this respect the agreement does not differ fundamentally from its numerous predecessors and merely expressed the eternal affirmation in favor of peace. Notwithstanding, the war continued unabated and the April memorandum probably would have followed its predecessors into discard if something new had not been added in June. The feature which converted the agreement into a new departure was the establishment of enforcement machinery. A trunk-line pool was formed and Albert Fink was appointed commissioner and given a permanent staff to supervise the agreement. (Like legislators, railroad managers had to learn the hard way that paper rules and regulations were not self-enforcing.) Fink had won his reputation as a result of the successful operation of the Southern Railway and Steamship Association and the trunk-line pool was based on a similar plan.[73]

The four trunk lines agreed to divide the westbound traffic out of New York on the basis of tonnage allotment. Daily returns of all shipments from New York to the West were made to Commissioner Fink's office and each week the totals were compared. If a road carried more than its allotment, it would then be required to turn over to the road or roads which had suffered a deficit the amount of tonnage necessary to balance accounts. Unmistakably, division of tonnage was the core of the pooling system and the agreements of 1877. Once the roads were able to agree on the proper percentage of tonnage alloted to each road the rate structure would fall into line. After all, the main purpose of rate wars was to attract traffic from each other, and only secondarily from the water route. Under the pooling system tonnage was fixed and, in theory at least, no incentive existed to cut rates on traffic covered by the agreement.[74]

Several features of the pooling plan are of particular interest. As first put into practice it only applied to westbound freight out of New York. New York freight made up much the largest share of the total, and the plan was to institute the pool there and gradually extend it to include all the ports. Since the trunk lines made the rates on the westbound traffic, it was easier for them to come to terms than to achieve agreement on eastbound freight. In the latter case a larger number of roads were involved and considerably increased the difficulties. Allotments were on the basis of 33 per cent each to the Erie and New York Central, 25 per cent to the Pennsylvania, and 9 per cent to the Baltimore & Ohio.[75]

In theory the plan appeared to be fool-proof; in practice it was something else. Two minimum conditions had to be satisfied before stability could be achieved. First, sufficient total traffic had to exist for all the roads to keep reasonably busy. Secondly, the actual flow of traffic had to conform closely with the agreed percentages. If one road was consistently over its allotment it became restive and wanted the percentages rearranged to accord with that factual proof of its superiority. Contrariwise, roads consistently under their assigned share were under heavy pressure to attempt to gain traffic in order to resist demands for change. In this connection, the continuing efforts made by each road to perfect its system were serious disruptive factors. New facilities and new connections meant that the percentages were always subject to re-division; at best a precarious equilibrium existed.

Other important problems existed to complicate the situation but these can be left for later consideration. Here the concern has been to delineate the basic structure of the pool and to stress that the pooling arrangement rather than the differential rates was expected to solve the problem. Ceremonial rites of compact-signing had been staged frequently during two decades of trunk-line competition, and the disastrous rate wars of the mid-seventies had demonstrated their farcical nature. Men such as Albert Fink, George R. Blanchard (vice-president of the Erie), and Charles Francis Adams, Jr., were firmly convinced that the successful establishment of the pooling system was indispensable to the continued healthy functioning of American railroads.[76]

Rate wars had not only proved the need for pools, they had done something more important. The railroad managers were now in the mood to accept them. No one seemed to have any affection left for unrestricted competition, and all seemed to realize that nature and its well-advertised laws simply could not be left to take the natural course. "Never, at any time, has the spirit of yielding and harmony among themselves been so manifest in railroad men as during this year . . . ," and 1877 therefore went down in railroad history as the "pooling year." [77] As far as the managers of the trunk lines were concerned, until 1881 the system seemed to be working so well that they gradually extended it to include all westbound traffic and energetically tackled the eastbound to boot. Surface harmony to the contrary, however, the trunk-line pool rested on a shaky structure and contained elements of obvious weakness.

IRRESISTIBLE FORCES AND IMMOVABLE OBJECTS

In many respects the formation of the trunk-line pool marked a distinctly new era of railroad history. As late as November 1874 Albert Fink employed this line of argument in defending railroads against government regulation:

> Discriminations are the necessary result of competition, and competition is the best protection against extortionate charges — much more efficient than any artificial legislative device. To take away the right from railroad proprietors to establish their tariffs upon the recognized principles that guide all other commercial transactions, and substitute fixed tariffs or arbitrary rules on which they must be based would destroy the great usefulness of railroads.[78]

Less than a year later, Southern railroad demoralization had progressed so far that Fink left his post as general manager of the Louisville & Nashville to organize the Southern Railway and Steamship Association, an Association firmly dedicated to the proposition that unrestricted competition was the death of the railroad business.[79] Success in that post had led to a call to head the far more important Trunk Line Pool in 1877. If Fink had been given to such practices, its organization might be said to have constituted public confession that railroad tariffs could *not* be established "upon the recognized principles that guide all other commercial transactions."

What now might be described as the conditions of large-scale oligopoly (few sellers) had developed; and railroad oligopoly had some characteristics of its own which created peculiarly difficult problems. For one thing, probably more than in any other form of enterprise, driving a rival into bankruptcy was a consummation devoutly *not* to be desired. Once in receivership the road was relieved of the necessity of paying the interest and dividends which normally took such large portions of railroad revenues. Under these circumstances, the bankrupt road tended "to run wild" and threaten its solvent rivals with the same fate unless concessions were granted.[80] Apart from the dangers of bankrupt roads with little to lose, serious trouble stemmed from the fact that in the mid-seventies few things were easier to start than a railroad war, and once begun, few were harder to stop.

Irrespective of the motives and desires of the originators, the pressures generated by rate wars almost invariably meant that they got out of hand. John W. Garrett's vision of himself as another Samson was more prophetic than he could have realized; unfortunately for him, when the pillars of the railroad rate structure were pulled down the Baltimore & Ohio did not escape the falling debris. Under the stimulus of conflict, freight charges dropped to levels which railroad managers had really believed impossible and produced a qualitative change in the entire transportation system. The changes were of such magnitude that they had serious effects not only upon railroads and inland water lines, but upon merchants, farmers, manufacturers, etc. And still another group was vitally affected by the consequences of the rate wars: European investors in American railroads and the banking houses handling their transactions. To a considerable extent, increasing European skepticism regarding the value of American railroad investments was a factor leading to the Trunk Line Pool of 1877. Particularly after the Panic of 1873, European investment bankers constituted the court of last resort for hard-pressed American entrepreneurs and their views carried increasing weight.

After a falling out between John W. Garrett of the Baltimore & Ohio and the firm of Baring Brothers, the former turned to J. S. Morgan and Company, then the leading American banking firm in Europe.[81] In 1876 negotiations were under way for Morgan to place a bond issue of the Baltimore & Ohio in the English financial market. One factor tending to complicate the transaction, Morgan informed Garrett, was that "the public [in England] are becoming alarmed at the rumours which reach them as to the result of the terrible war of traffic which seems to be going on between the railways on your side — I dare say that these fears are exaggerated, but they exist to a very considerable extent." [82] Several months later these fears had crystallized to the point where, in Morgan's judgment, "the wise course will be to hold our hand, for a while, at least . . ." [83] By December 1876 the collapse in the Philadelphia & Reading and New Jersey Central roads had alarmed investors concerning the prospects of *"all* American Railroad securities, even the very best." Morgan, however, took the occasion to compliment Garrett on his sound financial policy in contrast "with what some other companies have done in dividing to their shareholders, *all* their earnings and loading themselves with debt, either floating or mortgage, or both." [84]

The London banker was due for a rude shock some months later but apparently he then had unquestioned faith in the Baltimore & Ohio's financial condition.[85] Nonetheless, as more details of the sad plight of American railroads were made public, and as European investors came to appreciate the ingenious vagaries of American financial reports, suspicions deepened and receptivity to new issues declined even more precipitously.[86] Thus, it is not surprising that early in March 1877 Garrett attempted to reassure Morgan concerning the future prospects of the Baltimore & Ohio by describing his activities on behalf of trunk-line peace and higher rates:

> I have recently spent a week in New York engaged in what will prove, I hope, the most important conferences ever held between the Trunk Lines. Mr. Wm. H. Vanderbilt, Mr. Jewett, Mr. Scott and myself held frequent, full, and free conversations upon all the subjects that pertain to the demoralization which has so long existed in rates of transportation . . . The great principle upon which we all joined to act upon was, to earn more and to spend less — to fix a system under which reasonable and equitable rates between all points can be established and maintained . . . Mr. Vanderbilt for the first time in my knowledge at such a meeting — fully representing his entire lines — showed an appreciation of the dangers to which railway interests have been exposed, and a sincere desire to meet and adopt, in a cooperative spirit, all measures necessary to protect and advance the general railway interests.[87]

Among other interesting information contained in Garrett's letter were references to the continuance of "friendly and cooperative relations" between the Pennsylvania and the Baltimore & Ohio, and the expectation that Morgan's influence would be used with the English directors of the Grand Trunk to bring the Canadian road into line. Garrett's efforts must have impressed the House of Morgan, for a short time later they were being praised in the most extravagant terms by one of its partners, and he was nominated for "a place among the greatest benefactors of this country." [88]

By May preparations for the Baltimore & Ohio's bond issue were well advanced and Garrett again wrote to Morgan describing his continuing efforts to attain railroad peace. He assured him that even Vanderbilt — the chief troublemaker according to Garrett — was now amenable, and "I believe, that, with the simple and plain agreements finally made, we may look for permanently good results." [89] Rates were to be restored to near 1873 levels and freight classifications also would be changed to increase revenues. As usual, Garrett boasted of the excellent condition of the Baltimore & Ohio; no hint was given of the financial pressures inspiring him to work so ardently for peace in contrast to his former aggressiveness.

A stern letter from J. S. Morgan to Garrett at the end of June helps to explain why the trunk-line pool was entered into at that time. His carefree air of early May to the contrary, Garrett had been forced to apply for a cash loan. In the process J. Pierpont Morgan obtained some revealing "facts and figures" from him. Upon receipt of these facts and figures by cable the elder Morgan adopted a far less ingratiating tone than had once been his practice: "I am somewhat staggered by the amount of your floating debt which he [Pierpont] puts at upwards of $8,000,000. I see enough ahead to show me that the position is a very grave one and one which considering this exceptional state of affairs, and the sensitive and suspicious state of the public mind in respect to all such properties, will require great care and be handled with great good judgment if we would bring the ship safely around upon its course again." And Morgan warned Garrett of the difficulties that would ensue unless a conservative policy was adopted and railroad affairs set in order.[90]

Before long, Garrett was in receipt of a stiff note from Pierpont stating the need for "copper-fastening agreements" to avoid anxiety "should any emergency arise"; it also requested immediate and humiliating assurances that he had neither sold nor hypothecated his Baltimore & Ohio stock.[91] To add injury to insult, the Morgan official who had four months earlier denominated Garrett the savior of America soon pressed for speedy repayment of the cash loan.[92] If the Baltimore & Ohio had such difficulties, there is little reason to doubt that the other trunk lines were also feeling the strain. And the violent railroad strikes during July and August only increased the pressures upon railroad managers. It thus seems small wonder that 1877 was the "Pooling year" par excellence.

With the wisdom granted by hindsight we can appreciate the point that once railroad competition was openly abandoned as a viable principle — local traffic had rarely, if ever, experienced its benefits — some new economic and political relationships had to be worked out. Abandonment of competition was an admission that fundamental changes in economic activity had taken place in the decade after the Civil War. In turn, railroad attempts to adjust to these changes helped to set off a chain of reactions which found formal expression a decade later in the Interstate Commerce Act of 1887. The railroad system had reached the point where the free play of economic forces could no longer be permitted, and the trunk-line managers viewed the pool as the device best suited to the new situation. But as far as New York City was concerned the roads she regarded as peculiarly her own, that is, the New York Central and the Erie, had callously sacrificed her interests to satisfy their own requirements.

Many were the grievances which the merchants of the metropolis could lay at the door of the railroads; yet the Trunk Line Pool overshadows all others. Quite definitely an exaggeration, some of the underlying realities are best grasped if the Interstate Commerce Act of 1887 is regarded as New York's answer to the Trunk Line Pool of 1877. No implication is intended that the ICC was in any sense the exclusive creation of the metropolis. But the statement appears warranted that its merchants played the leading role in the campaign to achieve national regulation of railroads.

Specific grievances against the roads will be taken up more fully in the next chapter and it is only pertinent here to indicate the basic issue involved. Clearly, railroad development must have in time destroyed some of the advantages New York once possessed as a distributing center for categories of freight involving simple transshipment functions. To losses of this nature the merchants were resigned, and if not resigned, at least had no rational basis for complaint. Nonetheless, even among New Yorkers who granted that the Erie Canal was increasingly ineffective compared to the railroads, no disposition existed to concede that the city had to lose any portion of its valuable import or export traffic. Nor was there any disposition to accept displacement as a jobber or wholesaler of domestic products, except for those obvious categories of freight indicated above.

Some solid foundations existed for the New York merchants' conviction that they could hold their own. Important advantages accrued to the metropolis as a result of its long headstart and they were counted on to beat off the challenge of assorted rivals of interior and coast. Given these advantages, the argument ran, no reason existed for the railroads' inability to serve New York as the water route had once done. As a matter of fact the roads could do more. Not only did the New York Central have the same topographical blessing as the Erie Canal, but because of the nature of railroad transportation, substantial economies of scale went to lines possessing a large volume of traffic. Both the Erie and New York Central roads obtained the benefits of the volume of freight furnished by the Empire State and its seaport, a volume and quality of traffic much superior to that given to their rivals by Maryland or Pennsylvania. Therefore, if they were managed honestly, operated efficiently, and worked in the interest of "their state and city," they could easily surpass the lines leading to other ports, tap a larger geographic hinterland than the water route was capable of, and bring to New York an even greater share of the nation's commerce than before.[93]

If the railroads did their duty, as the merchants conceived that duty to be, the destiny Providence had mapped out for Manhattan Isle would be gloriously realized. The real desire of many merchants was to bring about all-out competition between rival termini, with the roads "belonging" to each city firmly allied to the separate mercantile communities. It was widely, if erroneously, held at the time that such a condition of affairs expressed the true relationships between city and railroad.[94]

But the managers of the New York roads had a different concept of their function than that subscribed to by New York merchants. These clashing concepts formed the chief grievance of the metropolis. The Erie Canal, exploiting New York's unique geographical trough across the Alleghenies, had been operated completely in the commercial interests of the Empire State, more especially its seaport and assorted satellites. In the 1870's the trunk lines tapping the interior definitely surpassed the canal as a transportation instrument but they refused to assume its function as the strong commercial arm of New York. The New York Central and the Erie, subject to the general pressures of a global economy, and the particular requirements of trunk-line competition, necessarily refused to conduct operations exclusively in the interests of their "home city." Only in this sense did the New York merchants regard the increasing effectiveness of railroads as a threat to their continued supremacy. The roads were denounced, not for having overtaken the Erie Canal, but for having refused to take over its function.

Under any conditions the merchants would have been angry at the displacement of the canal if accompanied by the refusal of the railroads to take its place as New York's transportation instrument. Coming at a time when commercial depression was severe, the loss was more keenly felt by New York merchants still painfully subject to the "natural laws of trade" and resentful of the railroad's attempt to seek exemption from their workings via "pools." Several years of experience had already impressed upon New York the unenviable distinction of being the port where rates tended to be most firm. Now the trunk-line agreement seemed destined to saddle that load upon it permanently while rivals suffered no such handicap.[95]

As the implications of the pool became apparent, it was taken as proof that the roads were willing to sacrifice the interests of their terminus whenever present difficulties and "past corruption" required it. Some specious attempts to stake out an ideological position aside, the New York merchants' opposition was not due to a stand against pooling in principle. On the contrary, they were well aware that in many respects the pool was more to be desired than the fluctuating rates and capricious discriminations preceding its formation. Not an unshakeable passion for economic liberalism but realization that the pool's basic purpose was to subordinate the interests of New York to the larger requirements of railroad harmony explains their antagonism to it.[96]

Because of the heterogeneous nature of the New York mercantile community, the roads might well have committed almost every crime in the railway decalogue and gotten away with it for a long time. As a matter of fact, they already had,[97] and without provoking effective opposition. But to commit their roads openly, at a time of great depression, to a position permanently destroying New York's "natural advantages," indeed actually favoring her rivals, was too much for mercantile endurance. As the merchants pictured it in their more heated moments, the once immutable laws of trade had been abrogated by a handful of men presuming to set themselves up as arbiters over the economic life of the country. Threatened by such usurpation, it was mandatory that the state control their activities lest they demoralize and depress the interests of non-railroad entrepreneurs whenever they chose. In the name of the entire community, therefore, the merchants set themselves to cry halt and to denounce the roads for taking advantage of their superior economic power to jeopardize other groups operating in a competitive economy.

That the railroad managers had any inkling of the resistance forces they activated when their peace treaty was signed in the summer of 1877, is highly doubtful. Skillful lobbying by Chauncey Depew had "managed" the New York legislature in the past, and no reason existed to suppose that Gilded Age politicos would suddenly cease to be amenable to his persuasive talents and resources. Barely six months were to pass, however, before it became obvious that railroad calculations had failed to take into account the possibility of alliance between metropolis and hinterland on transportation issues. Past experience might perhaps have seemed proof enough that such alliance was too unnatural to be conceived, or to be viable. But if the merchants could not persuade the railroads to function exclusively in the interest of New York, they had the option to attempt to *force* such conviction. Much of the history of railroad regulation in the next decade is summed up in the observation that the New York merchants exercised their option.

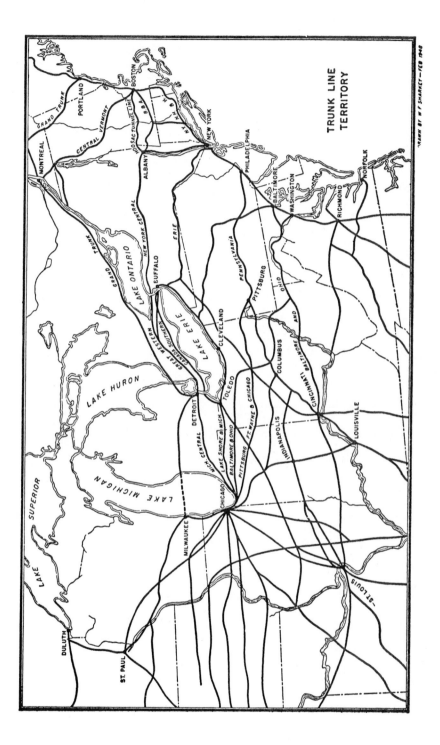

TRUNK LINE
TERRITORY

DRAWN BY W.F. SHARKEY—FEB 1946

CHAPTER III

New York Fights Back

Now, Mr. President and gentlemen, if the time has not fairly come for the merchants of New York to arouse themselves to some determined and united action in connection with this whole question of freights, and the interests dependent upon it, we must either be dreaming, or we are satisfied to quietly allow the business which has made our city the great market and commercial centre of the Western Continent to slip away from us, and pass into the control of others, whose interests and sympathies have but little in common with our city or ourselves.

C. C. Dodge at the Chamber of Commerce, January 30, 1878, in *Twentieth Annual Report,* Part 1:106.

The broad scope of the previous discussion has resulted in a considerable amount of oversimplification. For the most part New York merchants have been treated as a collective entity; perhaps the impression has been given that they more or less shared similar interests and opinions, and were prepared to move together with some degree of unanimity. Such an impression needs modification. To a certain extent all the merchants, indeed all property and enterprise in the city, had a vested interest in its prosperity. And since New York owed so much of her wealth to trade and commerce, a general feeling did prevail that her supremacy had to be maintained. Beyond these obvious generalizations it is unsafe to venture without making some distinctions.

The very size of the city (Brooklyn included), its dispersed locational patterns, the large number of individual firms and companies, and the variety of business and property interests involved are enough to suggest the difficulties. Primary focus here will be given to the heterogeneous mass comprising the New York merchants (retailers are excluded). Increasingly, historians are becoming aware that the *casual* use of generic terms, such as farmers, merchants, workers, etc., is an occupational disease to be avoided. Possibly no better example than the New York merchants could be found to point up the dangers. But the nature of this study precludes detailed description and some broad classifications have to be adopted. They are essentially empirical in that they are based upon the direction of traffic flow; that is, one group of merchants primarily concerned with eastbound freight, the other group made up of merchants whose shipments went west (southwest, northwest, etc.).

For our purposes the first category is composed mainly of grain and produce merchants and the men directly tied to their operations, such as warehouse owners, canal forwarders, etc. The second category is more complex but essentially includes wholesalers or jobbers handling foreign and domestic merchandise, manufactures, groceries, and high value raw materials. Titles such as "Dry Goods," "Importers and General Merchants," "Grocers," would be likely to adorn their business cards. Within each category a further distinction is necessary between those houses, usually large firms, enjoying close relations with railroads and blessed with special rates, and those houses not so favorably treated, including some of considerable size. Intimately tied up with the welfare of both categories were the shipping and harbor interests. More generally concerned with the position of the Port of New York than with any particular direction of inland flow, these interests were likely to support any action favorable to either the export or import trades.

For some time after the Civil War a substantial degree of overlapping existed in the two major categories delineated above. Some houses shipped freight in both directions and dealt in exports and imports. No attempt is being made to set up rigid patterns of demarcation but the separate categories contain firms clustered around a core characteristic important to this study. Thus, the grain and produce houses were more concerned with inland water transportation than were wholesale grocers who invariably shipped by rail. The former possessed a good deal of freedom of action and had the option of either water or rail, while the latter were firmly tied to the land route. Moreover, fewer places competed with New York for the eastbound export trade than the number handling westbound domestic and imported goods. Finally, the eastbound trade almost exclusively comprised through-traffic from major interior centers to the coast, and then abroad; westbound shipments involved local interior points taking high rates, as well as shipments to major termini. As a result, westbound shippers had much more complex relations with the railroads than did fellow New Yorkers dealing in grain and produce.

The differences between the two categories found expression organizationally and programmatically. All the commodity merchants, large and small, functioned through various exchanges, the Produce Exchange being the largest and strongest. Commodity merchants were in close daily contact, were fairly homogeneous, and tended to band together more easily to achieve common purposes, usually directly involving their business operations. The other category included a wide diversity of interests. Its members did not do business through exchanges, were difficult to unite around any particular program, and were only sparsely organized. Its major organizational focus, the Chamber of Commerce, though heterogeneous in composition and smaller in number, had far more prestige and power than did the Produce Exchange. The Chamber also dealt with some problems directly affecting its members' daily operations, but its deliberations usually touched upon major problems of commerce affecting New York, and national as well as international interests.

On issues which really aroused and united its membership the Chamber exercised a potent force because the organization included the leading figures in the various branches of commerce and finance, and because the officers of the Chamber generally owned or controlled the wealthiest and most renowned firms in the metropolis. Some of the wealthier Produce Exchange members also belonged to the Chamber. Overlapping in membership was accompanied by an overlapping in program; yet essential differences existed and grew more marked as time went on. Their positions might be stated roughly in this fashion: both organizations were interested in New York's securing all possible advantages of transportation, but the Produce Exchange concentrated more on maximizing the city's advantages by water while the Chamber was primarily concerned with its advantages or disadvantages by land.

Although these two organizations were not necessarily at cross purposes in their respective programs, definite disadvantages existed because they failed to work together. And a number of smaller mercantile associations further reflected the diverse character of the New York business community. To remedy this lack of liaison, and to achieve optimum effectiveness, an organization of merchants was set up in 1873 to deal solely with transportation problems. At first known as the New York Cheap Transportation Association, it thereafter took on the name of the Board of Trade and Transportation, and is today the powerful New York Board of Trade. From the early seventies to the passage of the Interstate Commerce Act in 1887, the Cheap Transportation Association (in its various forms) was the most important organization to deal with the problems of railroads and regulation in New York and, it is maintained here, the nation at large.

THE AMERICAN CHEAP TRANSPORTATION ASSOCIATION

Reference has been made in a preceding chapter to various developments that sporadically revived hostility to railroad management in New York after the demise of the National Anti-Monopoly Cheap Railway

League. The "Erie War" in 1868, consolidation of the New York Central and Hudson River railroads in 1869, passage in the same year of the Erie Classification Act designed to prevent Jay Gould's overthrow by his Board of Directors, renewed pressures for pro rata legislation, the downfall of the Tweed Ring in 1871 followed by the overthrow of Jay Gould in 1872, the "Oil War" over rebates to the Standard Oil Company, complaints over discrimination against New York city, exposure of the Credit Mobiliér, all this tended to focus interest upon railroads.

Whether from a keen scent for which way the wind was blowing, or perhaps as he claimed, from genuine repentance, a self-confessed, erstwhile member of the Albany Lobby came forth in the autumn of 1872 to do battle for the "plundered people" against the "unjust and oppressive management of railroads." George O. Jones was not to be a voice crying out in the wilderness for he sounded slogans and demands in tune with the times, so much so that they were largely appropriated by the New York Cheap Transportation Association upon its organization in 1873. Railroad corruption and discrimination of a flamboyant kind had seen to it that a receptive audience existed for the pamphlet published by him with this title: "To the Merchants and Property Owners of New York City. The Causes Which Are Driving Commerce from Your Doors, Forcing Trade into Other Cities, Destroying the Value of Your Property, and Impoverishing the Country." [1]

As Jones saw it the causes were simple. The New York roads, particularly the Central, were unjust and oppressive carriers. Railroad managers had pocketed tens of millions of dollars by financial manipulations which caused the stocks and bonds of the Erie and the Central to total several times the amount of money actually expended upon them.[2] Jones claimed that the stock and bonds of the New York Central and Hudson River Railroad, amounting to $105,000,000 in all, represented no more than $25,000,000 of real investment. More to the point, in his pamphlet, and in subsequent testimony before the Windom Committee, he proved the charge from the annual reports submitted to the state surveyor and engineer by the line and its component parts.[3]

Jones also maintained that excessive rates, personal and place discrimination, and the corruption of the processes of government to secure and protect ill-gotten gains taxed the commerce of the state, injured its farmers, and threatened the very foundations of free institutions.[4] His main remedies may be summarized in this fashion: scale the roads' obligations down to capital actually expended in construction; limit dividends to eight per cent; set up long-haul short-haul regulations; make free passes illegal; force railroads to give full publicity to their various transactions; finally, create a Board of Railroad Commissioners with power to fix rates, abolish discrimination, and regulate the roads' operations.[5] According to Jones, appropriate legislation had been blocked because Vanderbilt owned the legislature and Tweed was his agent. In the past year "to my knowledge, over eighty-five of its members left Albany with his money in their pockets." [6] But the reformed lobbyist maintained that if the New York merchants held one of their traditional public meetings, the state and the nation could be aroused to appropriate action.[7]

Approximately a year was to elapse between publication of the pamphlet and the Cooper Union meeting founding the New York Cheap Transportation Association which may be regarded as its logical sequel. For Jones in his call to action had made the point later stressed by the founders of the New York Cheap Transportation Association; that is, given the aroused state of public opinion, the metropolis had the opportunity to jump on board the bandwagon and guide it deftly to continued commercial glory.[8]

During the interim between publication of the pamphlet and the Cooper Union meeting, angry demands were made throughout the nation for cheap transportation, and they found quick response in the metropolis.[9] Early in 1872 the Union Farmers' Club of Avon, Illinois, had publicly suggested the need for a convention on transportation. After some correspondence, S. M. Smith, of the Wethersford Farmers' Club, issued a call for a meeting to be held at Kewanee, Illinois, in October. At that meeting a committee was set up, went to work, and in January 1873 the Illinois State Farmers Association was born. Formation of local units was rapid in Illinois, and similar developments took place throughout the West and South.[10] Apparently inspired by the western agitation and probably in touch with its leaders, R. H. Ferguson, a grain dealer of Troy, New York, in April 1873 sent out a circular on transportation to state governors and prominent public figures. His intention was to crystallize the country-wide sentiment through a meeting at New York City which would be attended by delegates from various interested organizations. As a result, the American Cheap Transportation came into existence at the old Astor House of New York City, May 6 and 7, 1873,[11] and the metropolis soon was again the center of railroad agitation.

Light is thrown on the number and type of "farmers" leading the "Granger Movement" by the roster of delegates in attendance at the first and later conventions of the association. The May 1873 meeting was headlined "Farmers Opposing Monopolies" (the "sturdy farmer" has always had disproportionate political appeal in America since at least the days of Jefferson), and prominent farm leaders *were* key figures in its deliberations. But the bulk of the delegates at its convention were from commercial organizations or represented large scale planters and landowners. The largest single delegation at the first meeting was from the Dubuque (Iowa) Board of Trade, and representatives of New York City, Buffalo, Chicago, St. Louis, Milwaukee, etc., were all prominent thereafter. The national character of the organization was evident in its list of vice-presidents and indicates that no basis exists for confining interest in transportation reform to one section.[12]

Debates at the conventions have a pronounced non-agricultural flavor, despite the presence of men who led the best-known national and state farm groups. In regard to the western representatives at the first meeting, little reason exists to doubt the basic accuracy of a New York *Times* correspondent's later assessment that they "were all either politicians or fancy farmers; they were not the farming yeomen." [13] A more appropriate and less jaundiced description of the delegates to the association's conventions was probably this one: "men of a high order of intelligence and business capacity, most of whom are known throughout the country." [14] Of more importance is the fact that the association, largely made up of representatives of western and southern commercial and agricultural interests, quickly came under the direction of eastern merchants and railroad reformers opposed to the "robber barons."

Josiah Quincy, Jr., who at least as early as 1867 was publishing pamphlets advocating cheap transportation in line with the tenets of the Cheap Freight Railway League,[15] was elected president and retained that position until he resigned two years later because of ill health. R. H. Ferguson of the Troy, N. Y., Grain Dealers' Association, the man who had called the organization into being, was its secretary. But the most influential member of the organization and its real driving force was the treasurer, Francis B. Thurber, a partner in one of the largest New York wholesale grocery houses. Thurber was also the chairman of its Committee on Railroad Transportation and practically dictated the organization's stand on the subject.[16] Together with Josiah Quincy, Jr., he seems to have provided the largest share of the funds necessary to get the organization in motion.[17]

A letter from Quincy to Thurber points up contemporary recognition of eastern leadership in the association and the sectional problems involved in the movement for railroad regulation:

> The gentlemen who were placed with me on the Committee to prepare the address [to the people] have promised me their views on the subject, and as soon as I receive them, I shall endeavor to put them in shape. I wish to have the Western members satisfied, if possible, with it, as I find that the enemies of the movement, wish to persuade the people there that as the officers are from the East their interests will be neglected . . . Hoping we may be able to do something to abate the will of monopoly . . .[18]

Other letters to Thurber from western leaders indicate his influential role, as well as his awareness of the necessity for close liaison if the movement was not to become sectional.[19] But the published proceedings and newspaper accounts of the four meetings of the American Cheap Transportation Association demonstrate that this was only wishful thinking. They testify both to an intense desire for improved and cheaper transportation cutting across sectional lines, and to the difficulties inherent in getting representatives of different geographic areas to work together on a common program. Western merchants and landowners wanted higher net returns and wider markets. Southern landowners wanted cheap food from the West for their laborers and southern merchants wanted to improve their competitive positions. Eastern merchants wanted low freight rates to stimulate commerce generally, enable them to achieve the economies of large-volume turnover of capital, allow American grain to compete more readily in the world market, and facilitate shipments of merchandise to a prosperous West. And commercial centers everywhere were eager to secure cheaper transportation, provided, of course, that they were the beneficiaries thereof.

Despite the high-flown principles voiced, basic considerations governing the positions of the various delegations were sectional advantages or disadvantages. With sectionalism and localism rampant, the platform of the organization tended to be the result of compromise and log-rolling, and no real national strength could be developed for any particular policy or principle. In this respect the conventions of the American Cheap Transportation Association were almost carbon copies of their counterparts held by the National Board of Trade.

Editorializing upon the Richmond Convention of the association, the *Railroad Gazette* observed that a fundamental difficulty in the movement was the sharp competition between cities for local advantages.[20] Major splits at conventions took the form of a conflict between improved waterways or improved railroads but local or sectional considerations usually determined the line-up on these issues, and on other subsidiary questions involved.[21]

Like so many other organizations springing up after the Civil War, the American Cheap Transportation Association split up on the twin rocks of localism and sectionalism. Its conventions reveal that no broad-gauge program appealing to discontented groups throughout the country at large was possible, and the rate wars of the middle seventies finished the association. The last convention was in December 1875, but brevity of existence should not be interpreted as proof of insignificance. The primary objective of cheap transportation had been achieved, even if the means were none of its doing. Nonetheless, together with the National Board of Trade, the association had been a potent force in the campaign for improved transportation facilities and railroad regulation, and had served to educate the country on these issues.[22] The famous

Windom Committee Report of 1874 specifically reflects the association's influence and was shaped in part by its recommendations.[23] Probably the chief significance of the association lies in the fact that it was the first body to effect a national union of commercial and agricultural interests on the transportation problem. Thereby, it set the stage for later, more significant developments.

NEW YORK CHEAP TRANSPORTATION ASSOCIATION

Among other things, the Astor House convention of May 1873 called for the formation of subsidiary organizations to achieve "the true solution of the problem of cheap transportation." Action to achieve a "true solution" was already under way, for the Importers' and Grocers' Board of Trade in New York had begun agitation on the general subject of transportation in December 1872. Members of the board quickly seized the opportunity to advance their program presented by the convention. Not only had the convention been well publicized but for some months prior to it the New York papers had been carrying accounts of the proceedings of the Select Legislative Committee investigating the Erie Railroad. A day by day unfolding of the fraud and corruption involved in the Erie's management had prepared New Yorkers for the hard-hitting final report of the committee, released on May 16, 1873.[24] It was during the course of this investigation that Jay Gould enunciated his now classic statement of a railroad manager's political duties:

we had to look after four States, New York, New Jersey, Pennsylvania, Ohio, and have helped men in all of them; it was the custom when men received nominations to come to me for contributions and I made them and considered them good paying investments for the company; in a republican district I was a strong republican, in a democratic district I was democratic, and in doubtful districts I was doubtful; in politics I was an Erie railroad man every time.[25]

Gould's candor and arrogance, as expressed above, and in numerous other instances, together with the actual details of railroad policy revealed in the investigation, shocked even blasé New Yorkers able to swallow the Credit Mobiliér scandal on top of the Tweed Ring revelations of 1871.[26] The impact of the investigation is summed up in the committee's report:

It is not reasonable to suppose that the Erie railway has been alone in the corrupt use of money . . . but the sudden revolution in the direction of this Company has laid bare a chapter in the secret history of railroad management, such as has not been permitted before.[27]

Here was strong support for men bearing grievances against railroad management, and the Erie Investigation, together with western agitation for cheap freight rates, served to arouse New York merchants to action.

The shape of forthcoming events had already been sketched in the *American Grocer,* a trade journal published in the metropolis and controlled by the Thurber family. Prior to the Astor House convention it published a series of articles upon the abuses of the existing freight system, and called for a "National trunk road built and owned by the Government, just as the Erie Canal was built and is owned by the State of New York." (Obviously, the memory of the Cheap Freight League lived on in the metropolis.) As in Belgium and other European countries, government ownership of such a road would influence the entire transportation system and result in a more desirable state of affairs. Possessing this orientation, the *Grocer* hailed the forthcoming meeting of the "Grangers of the West" and urged local merchants and shippers to give them "such a welcome as the importance of the visit deserves." Faced by a combined, organized movement of farmers and merchants the railroad companies would be forced to give way. But the *Grocer* predicted that the fight would not be easy and advocated "thorough organization" as the first step.[28]

To achieve the requisite "thorough organization," two anonymous pamphlets were issued shortly after the Astor House convention. Entitled *The Commercial Interests of New York as Related to Our System of Transportation,* they were almost certainly written by Francis B. Thurber.[29] The pamphlets proposed the formation of a local auxiliary to the American Cheap Transportation Association and argued that unless such action was taken trade would continue to be diverted to other cities.[30] On the other hand, certain that public opinion throughout the country would soon force government regulation of railroads and improved transportation facilities between East and West — "probably at the next session of Congress" — Thurber warned the metropolis that it must quickly take control of the movement.

An association such as the merchants of New York propose to form can, in connection with a constituency throughout the country, have much to say in regard to what projects shall be undertaken and so guide the movement, that unwise and unprofitable schemes will not be undertaken by Government, and the commercial interests of New York may be looked after and fostered.[31]

On Friday, June 13, 1873, at the rooms of the Importers' and Grocers' Board of Trade, a few merchants took the initial steps in the organization of the New York Cheap Transportation Association. Among the firms represented at the meeting were H. B. Claflin & Company, Dry Goods, Charles Pratt, Petroleum, H. K. Thurber & Company, Grocers, and several others of prominence.[32] A second conference was held on June 18 to which a few additional branches of trade sent spokesmen. Encouraged by the response, the founders decided to hold a public meeting at Cooper Institute to form a permanent organization. In traditional

New York fashion a committee was appointed to circulate a call among the merchants and to raise funds. As was to be the case with several later organizations, Thurber served as secretary and got things rolling. Other outstanding merchants serving on the committee were H. B. Claflin, head of the largest dry-goods house in the United States, Franklin Edson, president of the Corn Exchange, John F. Henry, a wholesale drug merchant, and B. B. Sherman, soon to assume the presidency of the Mechanics' National Bank.[33]

The call was circulated together with copies of the pamphlets cited above — pamphlets well calculated to interest merchants sensing the approach of hard times. In forceful language the nation's financial stringency was attributed to inadequate and too costly transportation facilities,[34] and the argument was employed that railroad combinations and consolidations formed to perpetuate these abuses must be met by similar organizations on the part of the people. "Unless merchants, manufacturers and consumers at the East, organize and co-operate with the producers of the West, our commerce will be permanently injured." [35] Eastern farmers, it might be noted, obviously were not expected to greet the movement for cheap transportation with enthusiasm.

As early as August 1, the response was such that a newspaper article headlined, "Revolt of the Merchants," noted that although "there is no class in the community so reluctant as to unite for the correction of fancied wrongs as the mercantile," the progress of the movement already foreshadowed "a MOST MOMENTOUS UPRISING against the steadily increasing oppression of the railway monopolists." [36] Whatever the reasons for the favorable response, it was claimed that the call met with great success and had been signed by more than "Five Hundred of the First Mercantile Houses in New York." Confirmation of the claim is found in a *Tribune* editorial urging heavy attendance at the meeting and stating that "Several hundred of the best commercial names in the city are appended to the call which appears in our columns this morning." [37] The *Times'* editorial declared the subject important enough to warrant one of the largest and most earnest meetings ever held in the metropolis.[38]

The presence of the Windom Committee upon the platform of the Cooper Union that evening was no accident. Senator Windom had seen an account in a western paper of the call issued by "certain gentlemen connected with the importers and grocers Board of Trade," and wrote to them on August 6 for further information. Specifically, he was interested in securing their coöperation in the work of his committee and wanted data on stock watering and fast freight lines.[39] During the correspondence that ensued it was arranged to have the committee visit New York.

The Cooper Union meeting was especially set for September 10 so that "the committee would be able to avail themselves of the benefit of the mature thought of these gentlemen who will present the subject of transportation on behalf of the commercial interests of N.Y. City." Thurber had originally made the proposal and it was enthusiastically seconded by Joseph Nimmo, Jr., then serving as secretary to the Windom Committee.[40] (One important by-product of the correspondence was the friendship which developed between Thurber and Nimmo. Nimmo soon became chief of the Bureau of Statistics and in that position issued valuable reports concerning the railroad system of the United States. Moreover, the strategic position occupied by Nimmo enabled him to aid his friend's projects in various ways and at various times.)[41]

Although fairly well attended, the Cooper Union meeting was not nearly as successful as had been anticipated from the response to the call. "It was evident that most of the principal members of the mercantile community, while aroused to enough interest in the movement to give their names to a summons for a gathering in its favor are not yet sufficiently enthusiastic to encourage the effort by their presence and energy of action." [42] But vigorous speeches were made denouncing railroad abuses and affirming New York's claim as the "natural outlet" of a great part of the continent; officers were elected, resolutions passed, and the association officially launched. Cheap transportation was declared to be one of the great material wants of the nation, discrimination against the city was denounced, and the maintenance of New York's commercial supremacy was proclaimed the duty of her merchants and citizens. Next morning both the *Times* and *Tribune* hailed the organization as positive evidence that merchants were at last aware of the metropolis' dangers and would now take appropriate measures.[43]

Despite the fact that George O. Jones (author of the pamphlet asserting that one such meeting would have instantaneous effect) graced the platform, a long, hard fight had yet to be waged before his predictions of legislative success were realized. Notwithstanding its professed aim to mobilize all metropolitan interests around a common transportation program, the organization was not really representative of the mercantile community, either in composition or in program. In theory it was designed to concentrate the efforts of all existing trade bodies on problems conceived in broad national terms and solved by methods beneficial to all metropolitan interests; in practice, because the major impetus came from wholesale grocers, jobbers, and importers, interested primarily in westbound freight, it was not representative. Apart from irritation at lower westbound rates to other seaports, they were particularly disturbed by the roads' increasing tendency to grant special rates to interior jobbers and wholesalers.[44] And special rates were not yet a problem for eastbound shippers.

Since retailers paid the freight on goods consigned them, they found it more advantageous to buy from wholesalers enjoying special rates in their home areas than to make the expensive and time-consuming journey to New York. (After the Panic of September 1873, things were too difficult for retailers to welcome, or afford, the "inconvenience" of a sojourn in the metropolis.) Differential rates granted interior wholesalers against retailers explain to a considerable extent why the New York *Herald* could observe in June 1874: "the depression in dry goods is vastly greater and infinitely more marked in New York than anywhere else." [45] Contrariwise, Chicago and Cincinnati papers were able to gloat over New York admissions that the "jobbing trade was leaving that city," and declare that: "The gradual transfer of the trade of Western dry goods merchants from New York and other Eastern cities to home markets is one of the most remarkable features in the present aspect of the Western trade." [46]

A circular from a well-known New York house conceding that western jobbers undersold them in certain classes of goods was pounced upon as proof of interior superiority. The New York firm — members of the Cheap Transportation Association — claimed that this was true only on domestic goods. It therefore recommended that retailers buy "domestics" at home but "all their foreign and fancy goods from New York." The reasoning concerning New York's advantages in the latter category was clearly specious and the Cincinnati *Gazette* took delight in pointing that out. The *Gazette* wound up on a note of commercial triumph: "The West stands to-day the successful competitor of the East, and neither drummers nor circulars can arrest the progress of the Western dry goods jobbing trade." [47]

Under the combined assault of both seaboard and interior rivals, New York wholesalers became alarmingly aware that railroad rates were a key factor in the noticeable diversion of trade. For example, Francis Thurber claimed that his interest had first been drawn to the subject of transportation when he found his house losing trade because freight charges from New York were higher than from rival cities. [48] Personal interest in the westbound trade aside, their recognition that the canal would be surpassed by the railroads caused them to hammer away at the proposition that New York's supremacy had to be maintained by way of the land route. [49]

In its conviction that railroads had superseded canals the association now constituted an avant-garde group. Only after several years was its program modified to include emphasis on waterways, and thereby made more attractive to the grain merchants. [50] Interestingly enough, in the interim, the latter group had changed their own views concerning the relative merits of land and water transportation after trunk-line rate wars proved a potent educational force. As long as the rate wars were on, however, little reason existed for merchants interested in eastbound freight to become terribly vexed with railroad managers.

Rate wars attained the primary object of cheap transportation, and when trunk-line competition was unrestrained New York was far more likely to benefit from place discrimination than to suffer from it. True, temporary agreements favoring other cities during lulls in competition, lack of adequate railroad terminal facilities, and personal discrimination gave cause for complaint. These tended to be relatively unimportant, however, when sharp competition prevailed and almost anyone could get special rates at unprecedentedly low levels. It is significant that the Produce Exchange did not really join in the agitation against railroads until after Albert Fink was established as Trunk Line Pool Commissioner and serious efforts were made to enforce the *eastbound* differentials.[51]

Apart from inertia and devotion to *laissez faire,* other reasons existed in addition to those noted above for the Cheap Transportation Association's failure to mobilize the major mercantile organizations on behalf of railroad regulation. At first hailed with enthusiasm in almost all circles (exceptions were those frequented by railroad managers), the "Granger Movement" rapidly fell into disfavor after the Panic of 1873.[52] Though the logic was faulty and the facts in error, the charge came to stick in the East that railroad regulation in the West had caused the Panic.[53]

Diversity of business interests probably accounted for the marked susceptibility of many New York merchants to the argument. For example, as the legislative representative of the New York Cheap Transportation Association, Simon Sterne continually pressed in its behalf for laws protecting stockholders' interests against unscrupulous boards of directors, and the association continually emphasized that many of its members owned railway shares.[54] To the extent, therefore, that merchants believed railroad regulation and agitation had depreciated their stocks and caused the Panic, the campaign to eontrol railroads was set back.

The Cheap Transportation Association had been launched at a time when New Yorkers could be asked to jump aboard an agitational bandwagon rolling in high gear to secure their commercial glory; as leading business spokesmen now depicted it, the road map chosen led in a different direction. And there can be little doubt that the Panic-caused-by-agitation version was widely accepted. As indicated below, the same Cheap Transportation Association which out-Grangered the "Grangers" in December 1873 was scornful of Illinois extremism and appreciative of Massachusetts conservative wisdom in March 1874.[55] Perhaps the retreat was dictated only by tactical considerations, but it does point up the duality of mercantile interests which seriously handicapped men hoping to unite the metropolis against railroad discrimination.

The interesting case of Charles Pratt illustrates another difficulty both in achieving a solid antirailroad front and in holding on to soldiers already in the ranks. One of the largest New York oil refiners, Pratt at first saw little merit in the rate discrimination enjoyed by the Standard Oil Company through railroad favoritism. During the "Oil War" of 1872 his firm led the fight to abolish personal discrimination in the trade. Since Standard Oil continued to enjoy secret rebates, railroad promises to the contrary, Pratt's status as a charter member of the Cheap Transportation Association and one of its directors is understandable. But upon becoming convinced that Standard Oil was not going to be beaten Pratt followed the old American maxim. He joined them in October 1874. In a short time his name no longer honored the directory of the Cheap Transportation Association, and, presumably, he no longer saw anything wrong in personal discrimination practiced by common carriers.[56]

Pratt was not the only one successfully tempted to desert the ranks when discrimination was held out as a blessing rather than a burden. Thurber later commented scornfully upon the many members who had fallen by the wayside because they had been offered, and had accepted, special rates.[57] But by that time the leaders of the Cheap Transportation Association had learned that the path to regulation was much steeper and rockier than it had appeared in the summer and fall of 1873 when almost everybody damned the railroads and praised the "Grangers."

CHEAP TRANSPORTATION ASSOCIATION AS EDUCATOR

Following the organizational structure of the Chamber of Commerce, the association's activities were mainly performed by committees. Monthly meetings of the Board of Directors were held at which the various committees reported, made proposals, and argued out plans. Meetings at first were attended only by directors but copies of the minutes were printed and mailed to every member. While this procedure enabled the small group of men who really dominated the association to function with maximum flexibility, it also assured close contact with the membership.

In a certain sense the Cheap Transportation Association and its successors may be said to have been the work of three men, Francis B. Thurber, John Henry, and Simon Sterne. The first two were merchants who were keenly aware of the need for thorough organization and political action to achieve desired results. In fact, Thurber served as the pamphleteer of the trio and contributed numerous anonymous pamphlets to the cause. Interestingly, at least as late as October 1872 he was a staunch Grant Republican and opposed the Liberal-Republican party.[58] Henry had been an adherent of the antislavery wing of the Republican Party, later was that party's candidate for mayor of Brooklyn, and may be said to have represented the "Jeffersonian liberal" element within it.[59] Sterne was a lawyer, prominent free trader, and leading Democrat, who had made study of the railroad problem a particular field of investigation. As Secretary of the Committee of Seventy to overthrow the Tweed ring he was intimately aware of the nature of politics and legislation in the Gilded Age.[60] Together, the three made an effective team, and they maintained a long range perspective which enabled them to overcome temporary discouragements.

Because its manuscript records are no longer in existence, it is difficult to calculate the total strength of the Cheap Transportation Association from year to year. Its composition is even harder to analyze. At the start a number of the most prominent houses in the city were represented but the bulk of the membership was probably drawn from medium size firms. Dues were relatively low, $10 a year, and membership was actively solicited, not granted as a privilege. Unlike the more restrained Chamber of Commerce, in November 1873 the association appointed a general agent whose primary function was to secure new members.[61] Apart from aggressive attempts to recruit members, several other features characterized the work of the organization. Conceived of as an instrument to effect liaison between the various existing commercial organizations, it tried to swing the full weight of the mercantile community behind specific solutions to the transportation problem. But the association also was to serve as the political arm of the existing commercial organizations for they tended to stay aloof from electioneering.[62]

To carry out its political functions, a questionnaire, similar to the "interrogatories" of the prewar Clinton League, was distributed by the association in October 1873 to several thousand businessmen dealing with various aspects of the transportation question. These questionnaires were to be submitted to candidates for the legislature and to put them on record as favoring the association's proposals. Sent out too late in the campaign to have much effect, the questionnaires are indicative of the basic political approach dominating the association's work. They also reveal historical continuity for one of the directors of the association was Carlos Cobb, formerly of Buffalo, and leader of the pro rata movement before the war. Though he does not appear to have been too active in the association, in all likelihood he gave its leading spirits the benefit of advice drawn from experience.[63]

Probably the most important activity carried on during the early years was educational work via pamphlets and circulars. The first major publication of the association was a report by Thurber on railroad transportation and it indicates the broad approach employed from the start, as well as the advanced position taken by New York merchants in 1873.[64] Designed for national circulation the report naturally placed its emphasis upon the general welfare of the country. The particular interests of New York City were played down and diversion of freight and rate differentials were not touched upon. Cheap transportation was highlighted, and appropriate legislation and other measures were urged to achieve the desired objectives. Apparently the metropolitan merchants were confident of their ability to protect New York's interests once national sentiment had crystallized into organizational form.

According to the pamphlet, exorbitant charges stemmed from the fact that the people had neglected to shut the door against the evils accompanying the application of steam to transportation. By combination and consolidation, powerful monopolies had arisen which now prevented or crushed competition. Thus, railroads, which in this age were the people's highways, had become instruments of oppression, and corporations theatened the prosperity and institutions of the very country which gave them life.[65] The pamphlet got down to cases and outlined a legislative program, as "radical" as can be desired for those times, to remedy railroad abuses:[66]

1. A Board of Railroad Commissioners clothed with power to establish and regulate rates in New York, and to prescribe a uniform system of railway accounts.
2. Proportional or minority representation of the stockholders on railroad boards of directors.
3. Railroad companies to be prohibited from paying dividends or interest beyond a fair return on actual cost of their property.
4. Prohibition of discriminatory rates against non-competitive points.
5. Prohibition of railroads delegating their business to separate corporations known as fast freight lines.
6. Prohibition of leasing, consolidation, or combination of parallel lines to destroy competition.
7. Prohibition of railroad corporations holding more real estate than necessary for the operation of their roads, engaging in mining, or in any business other than transportation.
8. Prohibition of free passes to public officials or any persons other than regular railroad employees.

All provisions were intended for national enactment but were applicable to the separate states as well. Several touched upon the question of competition but *"The Great Good to be Realized from This Latter Power Must Come From —* A National Double or Quadruple Track Railroad Exclusively for Freight, to be Built and Operated in the Interest of the

Whole People." [67] In this relatively early stage of the railroad problem competition was still assumed to be the real solution. What New York really wanted was a freight road to the West to be run in its interest, just as the Baltimore & Ohio and the Pennsylvania were supposed to favor Baltimore and Philadelphia, respectively. Despite the fact that the 1873 pamphlet, designed for national circulation, was not explicit on this point its proposed location for a national freight road was a giveaway. The proposed road would run from New York directly west to a point in Ohio and then branch off to Chicago and to St. Louis — a plan which obviously would bring little joy to other seaboard cities. [68] (No inhibitions existed when the association printed material tailored for local consumption; then the proposed road was explicitly described in terms of New York's needs.) [69]

Strongly advocated for several years, the rate wars of the seventies and the growing severity of the depression caused the freight railroad project to be shelved. [70] Increasingly, legislation was emphasized as the means by which New York could overcome its difficulties in the matter of transportation, and the focus shifted from national to state action. Aside from the pertinent consideration that a national constituency no longer existed for transportation agitators, the most specific complaint of the New York merchants was susceptible to local action.

After the Vanderbilts took over the New York Central the practice became widespread of granting certain upstate wholesalers special contracts substantially below the standard tariffs available to retailers. A variety of reasons appear to have dictated the policy of awarding special contracts. Possibly the most important one stemmed from the disparity between the eastbound and westbound tonnage. The large number of empty freight cars heading west constituted a serious barrier to efficient railroad operation. Traffic managers apparently were convinced that considerable advantages accrued to the road if it dealt with a relatively limited number of wholesalers shipping regularly on a large scale, rather than with numerous retailers shipping in a more limited and less regular manner. Here it must also be remembered that such discriminations were standard mercantile practice and that transportation was still more or less governed by mercantile principles. Another reason for the discrimination, as William H. Vanderbilt publicly stated, was to reduce the pressure in the interior for pro rata legislation. [71] The favored merchants usually wielded considerable influence in their localities and could be counted on to support the railroads in regard to pro rata bills and other legislation. And differential rates of this type lost no traffic to the Central — the diversion was merely from one merchant to another.

Less flattering motives were also attributed to railroad managers granting special rates. They were charged with profiting personally from these rates to firms in which they had a personal interest, or profiting through favors to friends and sycophants. But according to Simon Sterne, the best explanation of special rates stemmed from the extraordinarily high freight tariffs of 1865. Rather than reduce these rates as wartime inflation receded, the roads attempted to maintain the rate structure as a whole, giving way only as individual pressure was exerted upon them for lower charges.[72]

Whatever the reason, there can be no denying the facts testified to by men who were in the best possible position to know, namely William Vanderbilt, James H. Rutter, and Samuel Goodman (all of the New York Central). Like their counterparts at the West, retail merchants in upstate New York found it cheaper to buy from local wholesalers in Utica, Syracuse, Rochester, etc., than to buy from metropolitan merchants and pay high rates on freight, F.O.B. New York City. Here was a prime source of the long bitter conflict between the railroads and the seaboard merchants which eventually came to the attention of the Interstate Commerce Commission.[73] Here too was a major reason for New York merchants to concentrate upon state legislation to prevent discriminatory rates; even had a "national constituency" remained for railroad agitation in the seventies it was not then believed that *intrastate* freight could be regulated by a federal agency.[74]

In March 1874 a special committee of the New York Cheap Transportation Association initiated what became an annual pilgrimage to Albany to urge passage of a bill establishing a Board of Railroad Commissioners. The bold demands of December seemed to have been winter-killed by the frigid reception now accorded "Grangerism" in the East. In marked contrast to the proposals outlined in the 1873 pamphlet, the bill was explicitly patterned after the Massachusetts precedent and relied on publicity rather than enforcement power.[75] Its rapid retreat accomplished little, for the association soon had to acknowledge that railroad control of the legislature was firm enough to bury even the mild bill. This obvious display of railroad power at least had one valuable result for the merchants: it convinced them that it was necessary to marshal strong public sentiment behind their proposals rather than to go before the legislature armed only with earnestness and moderation. For some time thereafter the association, taking the lesson to heart, concentrated on educational rather than legislative work.[76]

By January 1875 the executive committee of the association was able to report encouraging results. At first many businessmen displayed either indifference or ignorance concerning the influence of the transportation system upon commerce but "this difficulty has been in great measure overcome." Many reports and documents of an educational character had been distributed and "a gratifying interest in the subject is now manifested by our business men generally." Expenditures for publications had been large and were to continue so. Distribution of pamphlets had not been confined to New York; copies had been sent to public officials, prominent men, and trade bodies throughout the country. As a result, the association had received a "great number" of communications from all over the nation and "a great deal of valuable contact" came about. Two full-time employees had been engaged to carry out the work on a sustained basis. The executive committee report claimed that all this activity had brought about unprecedented growth for a commercial organization; as proof, the 300 members of January 1874 had been increased to 1,045 by January 1875.[77]

On another front the association also had made considerable progress. After failing to achieve satisfactory coördination with other commercial organizations despite numerous attempts, it solved the problem by a simple expedient. Beginning with the October 1874 meeting of the Chamber of Commerce, a high proportion of the association's leaders joined the Chamber and proceeded to work for their program in both organizations.[78]

No time was lost by the Cheap Transportation Association men in making their influence felt. For example, a special committee of the Chamber was created to secure the adoption of certain state constitutional amendments concerning the canal system. John F. Henry and Francis B. Thurber were appointed to it. Almost immediately, a broad committee was formed representing various commercial bodies in the city, and documents and ballots were sent to each of the 218,000 registered voters in Manhattan and Brooklyn with very satisfactory results.[79]

Such an auspicious beginning paved the way for more far-reaching developments in 1875. In that year, as indicated in the previous chapter, westbound rates favored Boston more than usual. By December the discrimination against New York amounted to approximately 100 per cent and could no longer be tolerated. To prove that it wouldn't be tolerated, a general meeting of merchants (non-members included) was held at the Chamber of Commerce to consider appropriate action. Significantly, B. G. Arnold, a prominent figure in the Cheap Transportation Association, chaired the meeting, and C. C. Dodge and A. A. Low of the Chamber played leading roles in the deliberations. Railroad discrimination against New York was denounced strongly and a committee set up to meet with the officers of the New York Central. A conference finally took place late in December, but not until the force of public opinion and the pressure of the other trunk lines had reduced the New York rates below the Hub's. Among the prominent merchants meeting with W. H. Vanderbilt were William E. Dodge, Jackson S. Schultz, and

B. G. Arnold. The merchants thanked Vanderbilt for reducing the rates, and he assured them that henceforth New York City would be put on an equal basis with its rivals. Next morning the *Times* hailed the conference as recognition by both parties that they shared common interests, and it expressed the hope that the meeting would lead to amity and coöperation.[80]

Against this background, mercantile reactions to the rate wars which resumed in the spring of 1876 can better be appreciated. Stirring proclamations by the Vanderbilts against differentials delighted the merchants and the minutes of the Cheap Transportation Association reveal a sharp break in the customary criticism of railroads. In May, Francis Thurber formally reported on the position taken by the New York roads in favor of equal eastbound rates and extended the thanks of the association to their managers. To indicate, however, that full peace and harmony still did not prevail, Thurber insisted that the metropolis really deserved lower rates than other cities. Moreover, he complained, special contracts to interior wholesalers continued unabated and New York jobbers still were affected adversely on westbound freight. But he "respectfully hoped" that since the roads had come to see the error of their ways regarding eastbound freight, they would now reconsider the entire transportation situation as it affected the city.[81]

The shrewd businessmen leading the association did not confine themselves to "respectfully" hoping that the railroad magnates would see the light. Caution had been induced by the bad beating given the railroad commission bill in 1874, but it was reintroduced in March 1876 and fought for during the remainder of the legislative session.[82] Simon Sterne's argument before the New York Senate Railroad Committee testified to the conservative thinking of the association, as well as to the real nature of the New York movement for railroad regulation. He claimed to represent thirteen hundred business firms supplying at least two-thirds of the shipping and forwarding interests of the state, all of whom "cannot for a moment be charged with opposition to the railways." [83] What they were opposed to was railroad *mismanagement* and disregard of the public interest. They proposed "this mild measure of reform" so that "a solution may be found for the difficult problem of reconciling both public and private interests in the management of these corporations." Warning against the dangers of permitting "an ignorant multitude [to] frame party platforms about this matter," Sterne argued that the bill was actually beneficial to railroad interests since it would stave off demands for confiscation of railway franchises.[84]

Sterne was a fairly good prophet (demands were later made for railroad nationalization); yet some years were to elapse before railroad presidents generally came around to his way of thinking. However, the educational work of the association had progressed to the point where the Chamber of Commerce went on record in 1876 as favoring a Board of Railway Commissioners for New York similar to that of Massachusetts. The preamble and resolutions were offered by Francis B. Thurber and he was requested to prepare a memorial embodying these views to be sent to the governor and appropriate legislators.[85] Things were looking up for the small group of New York merchants who had banded together in 1873 to tackle the railroad problem.

RAILROAD CONTRIBUTIONS TO MERCANTILE ORGANIZATION

Without underestimating the importance of the Chamber's resolution, the position taken by the Vanderbilts in the railroad wars was probably of more lasting significance in the struggle for regulation. Prior to their declarations of equality, the Central had been denounced as a New York road in name only, carrying more freight to New England than to the metropolis.[86] The bitter railroad war of 1876, conducted according to the Vanderbilts to put all the seaboard ports on an equal basis, seemed to destroy the basis for such denunciation.[87] At long last it appeared that New York was going to have a strong railroad devoted to advancing her commerce. Therefore, despite the gloom induced by the increasingly severe depression, the prospect of a better competitive position now appeared to bring cheer to the metropolis.

Rosy optimism induced by the railroad war of 1876 made doubly severe the disillusionment suffered soon after the resumption of hostilities in 1877. Unequivocal pledges and manifestos notwithstanding, William H. Vanderbilt and Hugh Jewett, the president of the Erie, signed the April and July agreements which in one form or another have operated against New York until this day. And shortly thereafter the trunk lines, except for the Grand Trunk, entered into the westbound pool. For the first time elaborate machinery existed to enforce the differentials, or more meaningfully, to arbitrarily divide the traffic.

Mercantile charges to the contrary, something more than railroad duplicity accounts for the reversal between the December 1876 and the April and July 1877 agreements. The fact is that the roads whose main termini were Philadelphia and Baltimore simply could not permit New York to have equal rates with those cities on competitive traffic. Unless the New York roads were willing to accept tonnage allotments and differential rates, the Pennsylvania and the Baltimore & Ohio threatened a permanent war of rates, even though the pressures upon them might not have allowed them to carry out the threat. Faced with this unappetizing prospect the Central and the Erie preferred to yield, and the westbound pool of 1877 and the eastbound pool of 1879 were the results.[88]

The caution must be noted, however, that even after 1877 the allotments and differentials were never strictly observed. Whenever too much traffic was diverted rate concessions were made to hold the proportion of tonnage properly "belonging" to New York.[89] Within certain limits the near-monopoly once held by the metropolis was definitely ended by the trunk-line pool of 1877, but neither the New York railroads nor the merchants intended to surrender the city's commercial supremacy. The antagonism existing between them stemmed from the exigencies of railroad competition which forced the roads to go further in the direction of making concessions than the merchants held to be permissible; to the latter group, *any* concession was intolerable.[90]

As might be expected, the merchants were out of sympathy with the idea that trunk-line competition forced the New York roads to sign the differential agreement. For one thing the railroad managers took the weakest possible ground and attempted to justify the differentials on the basis of the shorter distances to Baltimore and Philadelphia — an argument which the Vanderbilts themselves had denounced in 1876.[91] For another, the conviction grew that the railroad war had been nothing but a "Stock-Jobbing Trick." The extremely conservative *Commercial and Financial Chronicle* attacked the abandonment of the "vital principle" of New York equality and accused the railroad managers of manipulating their roads for personal profit on the stock exchange:

A railroad war of the trunk lines is about as certain in recurrence as the small-pox or the change of seasons. Periodically, and with many formalities, agreements are made between the rival parties, and periodically but without any formality, the agreements thus made are disregarded and broken. So unfailingly a part of each year's history has this little by-play become, that it might safely be advertised in advance as one of the regular sensations of the Stock Exchange . . . We claim that a memorandum of this kind, to which no one is really bound, and which is therefore subject to repudiation at any moment on any impulse, is a mere deception. As a temporary expedient it will enhance the value of stocks, perhaps save the protest of notes coming due; but the bad use it can be put to is seen in the course of our Stock Exchange the past week. Any one of the contracting parties has it in his power, whenever it is his interest to do so, to precipitate a semi-panic in securities.[92]

One month later the *Chronicle* was able to cite as evidence a sensational report of "The Stock Exchange on Corporate Management." This report charged that it was impossible for stockholders to get truthful accounts of the real position of corporations (particularly railroad corporations), that the interests of the stockholders were ruthlessly disregarded by the officers, and it urged every member of the exchange to exert his individual efforts to secure necessary reforms in corporate management. The *Chronicle* strongly agreed, and the *Times* said the report traced public distrust of corporation stocks to the "systematic evasiveness" of railroad managers. According to the latter paper, the report justified all the distrust of railroad managers which then prevailed.[93]

Searching criticism was directed against New York railroad managers on grounds other than current adventures on the stock exchange. From the start of agitation in 1873 the charge was reiterated that commerce had been taxed unmercifully to pay dividends upon a vast amount of fictitious capital. Thus, the differential agreement of April 1877 and the pooling arrangement taking effect on July 1 particularly infuriated the merchants. They were convinced that the New York roads had accepted the handicaps imposed upon them by the Pennsylvania and Baltimore & Ohio roads solely to preserve their inflated capital structures.

In 1876 the rate war had held out the glittering prospect of equal rates, and a long drawn out contest had seemed inevitable if the New York roads stuck to the principles at stake. Many merchants cherished the hope that all-out trunk-line competition would eventually force the roads to squeeze the water out of their capitalization. Commerce then would be relieved permanently from the burden of paying dividends and interest on imaginary investments. True, the Erie was bankrupt, but in the worst of the depression the Central blithely continued to pay 8 per cent dividends, or, considering the amount of water involved, about 32 per cent.[94] Dividends of this nature hardly set well at a time when railroad wages were sharply slashed and the number of commercial failures reached unprecedented heights. The figures released by Dun, Barlow & Company, for example, covering the period from January 1876 to the middle of 1877, showed that 25 per cent of commercial capital had been wiped out: "Such an enormous amount of shrinkage was probably never reported before in this country during the short space of eighteen months." [95]

Charges that watered stock caused high freight rates to be levied primarily explains the roads' clinging to the distance argument as the basis for differentials. As will be seen below, railroad managers stoutly maintained that capitalization had nothing to do with rates, and angrily lashed out at mercantile demands for the erasure of fictitious securities from the books. Heating up antirailroad sentiment still higher were the large number of railroad failures in 1877 and the violent strikes of July and August. Railroad failures and labor troubles were blamed upon dishonest promotion and construction as well as on reckless and irresponsible management, and were taken to prove the necessity for closer supervision.[96]

Deeper depression, strikes of unparalleled violence, wholesale railroad bankruptcies, differential rates and pooling agreements, all combined to create an explosive agitational situation. Only a spark was

necessary to touch things off, and the perpetually hard-pressed Gran
Trunk soon struck it. The existence of the westbound pool after Jul
1877 made the other trunk lines more reluctant than ever to indulge i
rate wars. Low through rates from Europe to the West via New Orlear
had already irritated New York merchants, but in January 1878 sti
lower ones were made by the Grand Trunk from Portland and Bosto
Merchants in Boston and interior New England points were able t
ship goods at one-third to one-half less than the cost of similar shipmen
from New York. Once again the economic absurdity existed whereb
goods from the metropolis shipped by water to Boston, then back aga
through New York to the West over the Erie Railroad, cost less tha
direct shipments. Resentment, growing since the establishment of th
differential and pooling agreements, erupted with results that decisive
affected the course of railroad regulation in the United States.[97]

No longer was the fight against the railroads led by the Chea
Transportation Association, or more accurately, the Board of Trade an
Transportation as the organization now styled itself. The Chamber
Commerce, the "Commercial Senate" of the city, took over the leadersh
and threw all its weight and influence into the struggle. On January 2
1878, approximately 175 of the first business firms in New York sign
a call for a special meeting of the Chamber to consider appropriate a
tion. Among them were houses such as Low, Harriman and Compan
Phelps, Dodge & Company, Schultz, Southwick & Company, H.
Claflin & Company, and others of similar rank. The special meeting w
held on January 30 and, according to the minutes of the Chamber, a
the principal branches of trade were represented.

Probably the most significant action taken at the meeting was tl
appointment of a Special Committee on Rail-Road Transportation to de
with the subject on a permanent basis. Seven members were nam
including several leaders of the Board of Trade and Transportatio
Francis Thurber, Benjamin G. Arnold, and Benjamin B. Sherman.[98] T
chairman was Charles S. Smith, and his direction of the committee w
to be influenced strongly by respect and friendship for Thurber. Act
ally, the latter so dominated the committee that several years lat
Chauncey M. Depew of the New York Central charged that Thurb
practically controlled the Chamber's policy toward the railroads, a
had single-handedly set in motion the antirailroad, antimonopoly agit
tion throughout the country.[99]

One month passed and another special meeting was called to he
an elaborate report upon the findings of the railroad committee. Vario
"oppressive rail-road discriminations" against New York were describ
and supporting documents were offered in proof. Primary concern w
expressed over the westbound rates, thus making clear the merchandisi

rientation of the committee. Expressing the conviction that wise legisla-
on would be equally in the interests of the railroads and public, a
igh point of the committee's report was a proposal for a legislative
ommission to investigate the railroad situation in the state. Adopted
nanimously, the report and its recommendations eventually resulted in
ie famous Hepburn Committee inquiry of 1879.[100] The campaign to
ecure the investigation, the five volumes of testimony taken during its
roceedings, and the bitter conflict over the bills recommended by the
Iepburn Committee were of fundamental importance in the history of
.merican railroad regulation and will be treated in a separate chapter.
'hose developments can best be understood after the discontent making
self felt in the rural regions north of the Harlem River is considered.

New York farmers were affected by railroad development even more
isastrously than were the city merchants, and their leaders showed
ttle disposition to accept the situation passively. The once prosperous
indowners and farmers of the Empire State also attempted to cushion
ie impact of the Communication Revolution upon their prosperity, and,
i the process, sensibly influenced the course of agrarian movements
fter the Civil War.

CHAPTER IV

The Patrons of Husbandry in New York

The depreciation in the price of land is caused by the competition of the west in a great degree, but it is aggravated much
by the advantages given to the west, and what we complain of
is not the competition of the west, but we complain of the un-
equal rates; that you are carrying freights from the west often
times at a loss, and on local freights, where there is no competition, you charge us exorbitant rates, and the result is, we pay
for the advantages which the west enjoys; it is a burden on our
State as near as I can estimate it, amounting to about six millions
a year, over and above what we should be charged for our
freightage.

Frederick P. Root in the Hepburn Committee, *Proceedings*,
2:1987–1988.

In many respects the chief casualty of the bitter conflicts between
rival trunk lines and rival seaports was the proverbial innocent bystander.
Eastern farmers, and New Yorkers in particular, were hard hit as a
result of improvements in the country's transportation system. Two major
roads ran through the Empire State and the Erie Canal was a third
strong competitor for western freight. Even before the Civil War the
rapid settlement of fertile lands beyond the Alleghenies deprived New
York of the comparative productive advantages it possessed when the
Genesee Valley had been "the granary of the country." By the late fifties
the state's all-important location advantages were seriously threatened,
but the outbreak of hostilities temporarily alleviated that danger. The
rate wars of the seventies, however, produced an almost unprecedented
situation, for geographic location no longer assured economic advantage.
According to embittered New Yorkers, the railroads "load our farms
on their freight cars and carry them a thousand miles farther from our
markets without the consent of the owners (we give them credit for
doing this free of charge)." [1]

At the outset it must be stressed that in agriculture as in commerce,
industry, and finance, New York amply deserved the appellation of
Empire State. The census returns for 1870 showed it leading the country

in numbers of farms, value of farm property, and second only to Illinois in improved acreage.[2] Within the state, farm population constituted the largest single group, numbering over a million, or nearly one-fourth the total.[3]

But it is also necessary to exercise utmost caution in employing a generic term such as "farmers." The wide variety of climates within the state, its variegated land pattern, the several imprints left by Yankee, Dutch, and German stock, the disparity in dates of settlement (measured by centuries, not decades), and the marked differences in transportation facilities and distance to markets, all served to produce bewilderingly diverse systems of agriculture.[4] Careful agricultural surveys have shown that considerable variations exist in New York on county and even township levels.[5] Probably the most significant fact relative to New York agriculture in 1870, therefore, was its heterogeneous character, more pronounced perhaps than anywhere else in the country.

Like the merchants, New York farmers pose the problem of sorting out a few manageable categories from diverse economic units. One factor preventing its accomplishment is that, as a recent publication has stated in a different connection, "In some respects, nearly every locality has a climate of its own. As a result, practically all crops common to the temperate zone may be successfully grown within its boundaries." [6] Without stretching the figure too far, it may almost be said that in some respects nearly every locality had an agriculture of its own. Even if one specific type of farming is considered from among the variety then existing, it becomes evident that dairy farmers in the counties of Orange (milk), Cattaraugus (cheese), and St. Lawrence (butter), displayed significantly different patterns of production and marketing operations. Hence they were confronted by different kinds of problems which called for different and sometimes antagonistic solutions.[7]

Despite the difficulties presented by the large numbers and diverse character of New York farms, it is possible to make at least one valid, highly significant generalization. Directly, or indirectly, in terms of farming operations, the extension and improvement of transportation facilities after 1865 adversely affected the economic interests of almost every agricultural locality within the state. The generalization may appear exaggerated but the continued downward course of land values from 1870 until 1900 bears it out. Certainly York State farmers had no hesitation in pronouncing it a clear case of cause and effect. A span of time several years before and after 1865 constituted the real golden age of New York agriculture — in money terms — and thereafter economic difficulties set in at an accelerating rate. Though other factors than the Communication Revolution were present, their impact varies too much among localities to permit broad generalization. But the loss of highly

important location advantages told heavily on even the best farm land
in the state and deserves to be assigned first place in explaining it
agrarian problems.[8]

Relative to production advantages alone, New York had long since
been surpassed by the West. Close proximity to the best markets in the
country, however, had once given considerable value even to land which
would have been otherwise worthless for commercial purposes. As
result, both economically and psychologically the loss of what had
been regarded as an impregnable natural advantage disturbed farmer
throughout the state. The problem was rendered more acute because
a good deal of land under cultivation was of little agricultural value to
begin with, and an even larger area had become run-down by continued
rudimentary husbandry long after such practices were necessary or
justifiable.[9] Technological change also coincided in time with increasing
western competition and contributed much to its effectiveness. New
Yorkers could not very well complain because horse-drawn machinery
was economically more efficient in Illinois or in a neighboring locality
within their own state. They could appreciate and resent the fact that
Illinois agricultural products were shipped from Chicago to the seaboard
as cheaply, or more cheaply, than those grown 700 or 800 miles closer
to market.

Near-equality in rates tended to force New York prices down toward
the levels paid to the relatively low cost producers of the West, but the
indirect long range effects were even more devastating. Rapid expansion
of transportation facilities, coupled with long distance cheap freight
rates, powerfully stimulated cultivation of hitherto vacant western lands
Accordingly, the large increase in supply relative to effective demand
operated as a price depressant on most farm commodities, and to
greater extent than that caused directly by lowered transportation costs
Later in the century New York farmers felt the impact of the global
Communication Revolution; in the seventies the West provided almost
all the pressure. Western competition, therefore, came to be equated with
lowered prices and depreciating land values.

Attention has thus far been focused upon interstate competition a
a result of shifting location advantages; it is important to note that the
same process operated within the state. In many respects intrastate con
flicts over internal improvements were more important than those con
ducted on the interstate level. An excellent case in point was the
continued resentment expressed by Hudson River and Mohawk Valley
farmers exposed to western New York competition because of the Erie
Canal.[10] Intrastate bitterness over changes in transportation profoundly
affected the manner in which New York farmers reacted towards western
competition after 1865. With the development of a national market

taple producers tended to shift their economic attention from competi-
ors inside the state to those hundreds of miles beyond; producers of
erishable or economically bulky commodities were still concerned with
ompetitors in the next county. Hostile attitudes of Genesee Valley
wheat farmers toward Illinois wheat farmers may be compared to those
f Orange County milk producers toward Delaware County dairymen.
he Southern Tier and the North Country localities also opposed cheap
reight from the West, but their attitude toward the Erie Canal was
nore hostile and concentrated than that of producers along its banks
who were more concerned with the New York Central's rate policies.
t was a historic fact of significant proportions for this study that the
eography of the state had long stimulated intense local rivalries for
ocation advantages, created many different market centers, and effec-
ively divided the countryside into competing districts.[11]

However, all New York farmers *were* hurt by western competition
n varying degrees. If united, they comprised a large and influential
nough group to have wielded powerful political pressure to aid their
conomic interests. Although the wide diversities and deep splits sug-
ested above drastically reduced the effectiveness of rural agitation,
New York attempts to preserve location advantages set in motion a sig-
ificant trend of events.

REGIONALISM AND AGRARIAN ORGANIZATION

Possibly an acute observer surveying the countryside in 1865 might
ave detected portents of coming disaster, but the officers of the New
ork State Agricultural Society exuded nothing but optimism in com-
nenting upon the results of the year's labors. "The reports from our
ocieties show that improvement is the order of the day, and never in
he history of our Society, during twenty four years past, have the pros-
ects of the agricultural interests of our state been equal to the pres-
nt." [12] And for some time thereafter prices mounted above war levels
nd land values soared. The index number of farm prices did not reach
ts peak until 1868, and forty-cent butter and two-dollar wheat built the
garishly ornate houses that still dot the countryside.[13]

Even after the peak had been reached and passed, prices were high
nough to produce a warm glow of farm prosperity. In 1871 the well-
nformed members of the Central New York Farmers' Club calculated
he average cost of 100 acres of good dairy land in the area to be about
15,000, including suitable buildings.[14] No doubt the average price
hroughout the state was much less than $150 an acre; yet it does appear
hat land values in numerous localities ran fairly high. High land values
ead to the conclusion that despite stiff production costs commodity
rices still generated considerable optimism.

Beneath the idyllic façade, to the observer blessed with hindsight, the *Transactions* of the State Agricultural Society record telltale signs of future agrarian distress. As early as 1865, notwithstanding prevailing high prices, a speaker before the Chautauqua Farmers' and Mechanics' Union was farsighted enough to argue that local farmers could not compete with the West in cattle or grain. Increased competition was predicted because new railroads were springing up everywhere in that region of low production costs. But he foresaw a solid basis for prosperity because dairying must always be confined to its present area. Nowhere else, he claimed, did water and grasses exist capable of turning out good products.[15] This theory had considerable currency before the war and made for widespread complacency and continued resistance to change. By 1871 a leading dairy expert was sharply disputing the contention, asserting that little stock could be taken in the notion of a perpetual monopoly granted to New Yorkers by Divine Providence. According to him, improved quality was necessary if farmers were to overcome the discouragements of the past years.[16] More and more, the latter view came to predominate.

While usually couched in optimistic terms, the need to improve the quality of farming, and in some instances to shift over to new types, increasingly appeared in the *Transactions* as price levels receded from the 1868 peak. The annual executive committee reports became less uniform in their glad tidings, despite the fact that most branches of husbandry in any one year continued to do well. Perhaps as an echo of western agitation, a strong complaint was sounded in 1870 against middlemen. Farmers' clubs were hailed as organizations that might profitably engage in coöperative buying and selling.[17] Again possibly influenced by agitation in the West, town bonding to aid railroad construction also fell into disrepute. President Church denounced the practice in unmeasured language in 1871 and warned that it boded no good for farmers.[18]

Hard to pin down precisely, western hostility to railroads undoubtedly had considerable influence upon New York agrarian currents. But the motivation was distinctly different in the older region. Petitions were signed and bills introduced in the Empire State, as they had been prior to the Civil War, to secure pro rata freight laws, that is, protective tariffs against western competition.[19] On the prairies the agitation was for cheaper transportation to seaboard markets, a prospect not calculated to set easterners jumping for joy. Sharp dichotomy of interests between the two areas explains to a considerable extent New York's relatively late and numerically minor response to the Grange in the seventies. That organization had become identified with the movement to lower freight charges from the prairies, an identification which sensibly lessened its appeal for New Yorkers.

Additional explanations existed for the failure of New York State farmers, as late as 1873, to stir from their traditional rural isolation, individualism, and antagonism to coöperative effort. The rate wars of the mid-seventies had not yet broken out and a wide disparity in farm prices remained between East and West. Though in the latter region merchants and farmers carried on their famed "uprising" against the railroads, the *Transactions* of the New York State Agricultural Society reported that 1873 had been a year of more than average prosperity for farmers.[20] As evidence that before the rate wars local markets remained strong and had not yet been overly influenced by the nationalizing trend of economic activity, 1874 was also described as one of "peace, plenty, and prosperity to the farmers of New York." [21] No doubt these accounts were colored by the fact that the *Transactions* reflected the views of the wealthier agriculturists and landowners, men likely to be the last to feel the effects of hard times. An excellent study of New York farm prices indicates, however, that solid foundation underlay the *Transactions'* roseate accounts. Down from the extremely high peak of 132, the index numbers in 1873 and 1874 still stood at 104 and 103, respectively.[22]

But as the international depression intensified and cut-throat railroad and ocean freight competition developed in 1875 and 1876, farm price indices plunged to 93 and 87. As was usually the case when rural affairs did not go well, the *Transactions'* account for 1876 was considerably understated. It chose to concentrate on production results; yet its review only underscores the sad tale told by the index. "Without any actual general failure of crops, the results of the harvest have been, upon the whole, and taking the average of the different districts of the State, disappointing to the farmers." [23]

In noting that dairy farmers received "fairly remunerative" prices and "have had a tolerably good season," the 1876 account of the State Agricultural Society points up the importance of the diverse nature of New York agriculture. At the West, because meat and grain were the principal sources of income for most farmers, low prices for those two commodities tended to produce a rather uniform pattern of economic strain. It is almost axiomatic that this economic homogeneity should have resulted in greater unity of action than was possible in New York.[24] Prairie farmers in the 1870's faced roughly similar problems and had little choice in their search for solutions.

By way of contrast, New York farmers as a group, and to a lesser but still significant degree as individuals, received their incomes from widely different products. To cite one possible example, on a single farm

the profits of the 1876 dairy might well mitigate the losses of the 187
wheat field. During the seventies, diversification cushioned the impac
of financial strain upon individuals and upon the group as a whole t
a much greater extent than was the case at the West. In addition, th
wide variations in the agricultural value of New York soils produce
significant variations in income. Income variations suggested difference
in individual ability rather than group distress — an interpretation the
roughly consonant with habitual patterns of rural thought.[25]

An important consideration for the present study is that diversifica
tion did much more than cushion financial strain; it effectively limite
the degree of unity which New York farmers could attain. Butter, chees
milk, fruits, grain, beef cattle, sheep, hay, potatoes, hops, etc., wer
subject to divergent and unrelated influences. Moreover, even the sam
products in different localities gave rise to separate problems. Th
description does not quite convey the actual situation; primarily, not th
difference in kind but the difference in emphasis is what justifies stres
upon the existence of localized agricultural problems. Overarching gen
eralizations could easily be agreed upon. Adopting a common approac
towards translating them into practical terms was a harder task for th
heterogeneous group known as New York farmers.

Considering the full implications of rural isolation in literally a hors
and buggy age, their diversity meant that it was impossible to develo
simple clear-cut formulas capable of stimulating state-wide mass actio
— a clear historical difference between New York and prairie agricu
ture. It is not easy to exaggerate the role of rural isolation in retardin
the growth of the Grange in New York. Of course, a similar handica
existed in other places but intense localism, largely the result of intra
state and intracounty economic, political, and social antagonisms lon
sanctified by history, presented peculiar difficulties. More than that, a
the West common pressing problems generated strong enough pressure
to overcome isolation and localism. In the Empire State diversified agr
culture delayed such a development.[26] Possibly the point might be clar
fied by a concrete illustration.

Western competition did affect all farmers in the state adversely
but Monroe County wheat growers and Orange County dairymen fe
the impact in varying degrees. The incomes of the former were directl
affected, and they were highly conscious of it; the threat to the latte
was more indirect and less obvious.[27] Projecting this illustration furthe
it is clearly unrealistic to expect farmers from Montauk Point to th
Niagara frontier, from the North Country to the Southern Tier, to reac
identically and swiftly to the threat posed by the West. How much mor
unrealistic would it be then to expect New York and Iowa farmers t

develop similar behavior patterns during the decade? Where the types of farming in the two states were not distinctly different, they were distinctly antagonistic — a situation not likely to produce uniform and empathetic reactions. And variations in types of farming tend to condition not only economic but political, social, intellectual, and psychological, agrarian orientations.

The dissimilar attitudes displayed in New York and the West or South toward the Granger Movement, and the Grange itself, need only be explained in narrow determinist fashion if fundamental economic, social, and political realities are ignored. American farmers were not a homogeneous class and one would normally expect different sectional (or regional) responses to spring from the fundamentally different conditions of daily life. No proof can be adduced that these differences were the result of character traits attributed to frontiersmen and easterners, nor from a Social Darwinian process of natural selection drawing off rebellious souls to the "free lands." And at best, the dissimilar sectional responses can only be attributed to the uneven incidence of depression.

Aside from the obvious antagonism involved, the essential homogeneity of prairie farmers and the essential heterogeneity of their New York counterparts seem to be the basic explanation of divergent reactions in the decade. Another important but less tangible factor was the peculiarly different regional environment in which eastern and western (or southern) farmers operated. Filtering through the barriers imposed by rural isolation, the impress of urban thought patterns, urban interests, and urban influences was much more pervasive in New York agrarian areas than in other regions. Agriculture was subordinate in the East. Even in rural areas other social groups competed with it and were capable of molding the community to a much greater extent than in the West or South. An organization such as the Grange not only filled more basic needs in the latter regions, but it was far less likely to be attacked in rural areas by representatives of non-agrarian groups possessing a substantial measure of economic and social independence. Over and above the greater power of non-agrarian groups in the East, however, the urbanized regional social patterns subtly affected agrarian organization and thought.[28]

Actually, in the later seventies, as farm difficulties multiplied throughout the country and as it shook off western characteristics, the New York Grange became more militant and more influential, while in the West the power of the Order sharply and permanently declined. So thoroughly were the positions reversed that when westerners in any numbers again came to join an agrarian organization they turned to the Farmers' Alliance, which was born in New York and spread out from that state.

But the nature of the present study precludes detailed analysis of the Grange and Alliance except as part of the New York reaction to the Communication Revolution.

Chautauqua County was the site of the first regular, active Grange in the country,[29] but western agitation gave direct impetus to the establishment of the Patrons of Husbandry in New York. Testimony by leading Grangers indicates that their localities were organized when the ferment stirred up in the Old Northwest struck a responsive chord within the state. As one founder of the Grange in Steuben County later recounted its origins there: "We had heard of the farmers' movement, particularly as developed in the great agricultural States of the West. We understood that it meant combination and cooperation among the farmers; that its purpose was the improvement of the great agricultural class." [30]

Such response was not forthcoming without good reason. Apart from the growing material basis for farm discontent in New York, another set of factors was operative. As a result of the striking changes taking place in the nation after the Civil War, farmers in general became restless and uneasy concerning the new order of affairs. Lowered agricultural prestige, emergence of "great monopolies" on an unprecedented scale, shocking scandals of the Gilded Age, all these were intangible but important sources of rural discontent. In practice, if not in theory, the agricultural fundamentalism more characteristic of an older America was under devastating attack. Rapid industrialization unleashed new forces and produced new conditions to which the countryside had difficulty in adjusting, and considerable economic, social, and political displacement developed after the Civil War. At no place in the North was this more evident than in New York where farmers' sons were "lured" to the metropolis by the thousands, and Jay Gould and Cornelius Vanderbilt bought legislators by the scores. Hostile rural reaction was almost inevitable, and in the fall of 1873 it found organized expression in New York.

At the call of O. H. Kelly, national secretary, the officers of the parent body met with the masters of the individual Granges existing in the state in November 1873. A provisional organization was formed, a constitution adopted, officers elected, and plans made to push the movement.[31] Several months of activity produced results, for at the first annual meeting of the state Grange, in March 1874, the number of branches had grown from 21 to 150.[32] Optimism then ran fairly high that New Yorkers would quickly respond to the movement. According to George D. Hinckley, master of the state Grange, the aim was to secure legislation in the farmers' favor and secure protection "from the aggressive evils of concentrated capital, and monied corporations, to which the agricultural interest, the most important interest of the country, is justly entitled." But Hinckley stressed that without intending to detract from the moral, social and intellectual advantages of the Order, "I apprehend that more of our immediate success depends upon the practical use of this feature [coöperative buying] of our Order than upon any other." [33]

Heavy emphasis on coöperation in a region as comparatively well served by market facilities indicates the distinctively western influence at first permeating the organization and the widespread search as farm prices declined for an easy solution to relatively high expenses. No implication is intended here that farm prices had declined sufficiently to occasion widespread distress; yet by 1873 and 1874 the boom had ended in New York. Probably the most important result of lessened prosperity was the heightened antagonism between East and West, though it did not attain marked intensity until the later seventies. The basic antagonism existing between eastern and western farmers was a considerable handicap to the Order in New York. It was impossible to devise a program which could simultaneously satisfy farmers seeking easier access to seaboard markets and farmers angrily determined to keep them out. [34]

Resolutions adopted at the first meeting of the state Grange, and in one form or another at virtually every one thereafter, make it clear that the object sought was cheap transportation for New Yorkers and expensive transportation for all others. Thus, the meeting affirmed that the discriminations in rates for local freights were exorbitant and ruinous; that the state had full power to regulate and control railroads; and "that it is the duty of the Legislature without delay to enact a judicious *pro rata* freight law." The Grange also approved the proposed canal funding amendments which would "protect the people from taxation for the benefit of freight from the West." Still on the subject of cheap transportation for New Yorkers, stock watering and fraudulent railroad bonds were denounced and a demand was voiced for the immediate repeal of town-bonding laws. [35]

Turning to the major problem other than the transportation one, which was to occupy the Grange, legislation was advocated to equalize taxes between real and personal property and to abolish discriminations favoring the latter. Rounding out the platform, the Committee on Resolutions attacked the national banking system as a crippling monopoly, recommending in its stead free banking and adequate government currency. It reviled the liquor traffic and praised temperance, advised Grangers to exercise influence in their political parties, and, as a significant indication of rural resentment, affirmed "there is no occupation more honorable than that of farming," and urged measures "to discourage the pernicious inclinations of farmers' sons to seek employment amid the excitements and temptations of cities, and to usurp positions women are by right entitled to fill." [36]

Though as broadly conceived the program could find little agricul tural opposition throughout the state, the early air of optimism was no long sustained. Soon the practical difficulties of welding together the diverse masses of individualistic, suspicious, jealous, narrowly opinion ated New York farmers became obvious. Granger after Granger be wailed the long rural isolation which had accustomed farmers to ac alone, each for and by himself, so that they were slow to apprehend advantages to be derived from working in concert.[37] Worthy Master Hinckley's predictions turned out badly, for the business coöperative features gave the most trouble at the start. Glowing expectations of con siderable savings turned into angry disillusionment. But the poor judg ment displayed in organizing Grangers in the city of New York created greater difficulty than might otherwise have arisen. O. H. Kelly, the national secretary, had airily recommended the master of the Manhattan Grange (could anything sound more incongruous?), Robert Farley, a purchasing agent for farmers throughout the country. Unfortunately fo the Order, his firm had a grave problem in staying solvent and he promptly pocketed moneys upon receipt. So bitter was the outcry in New York that the 1875 meeting of the state Grange voted to prefer charges against Kelly.[38]

Coupled with misappropriations of funds by various local officers the Farley incident was a boon to Grange opponents. Among these opponents were local merchants, insurance agents, and townspeople who lost no opportunity to slander the Order and heap ridicule upon it. The secret features and elaborate rituals, derived essentially from Masonry made it particularly vulnerable in New York with its long history o anti-Masonic and Know-Nothing agitation. In addition, politicians and lawyers attacked by the Grange as parasites and "pettifoggers," and fear ing its potential influence upon their private preserves, attacked i unceasingly.[39]

Eventually, as the coöperative features became better understood and initial difficulties were overcome, the business aspects of the Grange came to have strong appeal for New York farmers. But these develop ments were long delayed and because initiation fees and annual dues were relatively high, skeptical farmers hung back. Many who had joined dropped out. During the seventies the high point of the numerical strength seems to have been reached about January 1, 1876, when there were estimated to be 17,000 members in 362 Granges.[40] Membership de clined to a low point of approximately 9,500 by June 30, 1877, hovered slightly above that figure for several years,[41] and then began the rapid limb which reached 140,394 in January 1922.[42] It is worth noting that the eventual success of the Patrons of Husbandry in New York stems from the paradox that despite the numerical decline, the organization actually gained in strength during the late seventies. The composition, program, and methods of work taking shape in those years provide the answer.

The Grange maintained that its members were drawn from the ranks of "the very best farmers of the State,"[43] and the available evidence tends to support that boast. It is difficult to determine the matter precisely but it seems safe to say that in general the permanent members were men owning better than average farms, using methods considerably above the norm, and with previous experience in various agricultural societies.[44] Many of the Grange leaders had business interests apart from their farms; indeed, as far as can be determined, agriculture was clearly not the main source of income for most of them. Thus they had the breadth of view, and more important, means and opportunity enough to escape the narrow preoccupation with the daily grind characterizing the average farmer.[45] Particularly after the postwar boom collapsed, the latter found difficulty in raising his sights above the level of immediate individual problems.

The largest landowners in the state did not generally join the movement but some Grangers were wealthy. At least three of this class at one time or another in the seventies and eighties were presidents of the State Agricultural Society.[46] Many individuals attracted to the Grange were also prominent in the various agricultural societies and farmers' clubs of the state. In some respects the existing bodies may be said to have paved the way for the Grange; yet on occasion it was regarded as a rival and greeted with hostility.[47]

As times grew harder in the seventies and the anticipated financial benefits failed to materialize, a rapid turn-over seems to have occurred in membership. Hard-pressed farmers, unable or unwilling to spend time and money without receiving direct benefits, dropped out,[48] and the staunch core remaining were probably men and women in easier circumstances.[49] In addition, as the organization worked out the initial difficulties, adapted itself more to New York conditions and discarded western influences, numerous solid farmers came into its ranks who hitherto had regarded it with distrust. Significantly, the New York organization increasingly revealed dissatisfaction with the parent body and a tendency to stress purely local aims and objectives.[50] Nonetheless, even as they perfected their machinery to fight western competition, Grangers paid full lip service to agricultural fundamentalism and the essential unity of all tillers of the soil.

Since its members were generally good farmers and a good many were prominent in other organizations, the Grange exerted an influence out of all proportion to its numerical strength. Just as members of the Cheap Transportation Association worked to achieve their objectives in other commercial bodies, Grangers took advantage of multiple participation in agricultural societies. At county fairs, farmers' clubs, conventions of dairymen or horticulturists, and at summer picnics, Grangers expounded their particular doctrines of agrarian salvation. The *Husbandman* claimed that the growing tendency to make summer picnics an annual institution throughout the state was directly attributable to the Order.⁵¹ Attracting hundreds and thousands of people from the countryside, these picnics made it easy for farmers to imbibe Granger arguments along with more solid nourishment — even if they were not converted to membership. Certainly the organization thought these picnics were valuable, because a constant demand was made for more and better speakers. To supplement the local talent, out-of-state orators of impressive stature and even stronger voice were imported to address the largest meetings.⁵²

The Elmira Farmers' Club is an excellent example of how Grange influence was spread outside the organization. Founded in 1869 by prosperous businessmen-farmers in Chemung County, their weekly discussions on agricultural problems attracted such favorable comment that the club rapidly gained a national reputation. The New York *Times* pronounced it "the best club of the kind in existence anywhere." Agricultural journals throughout the country joined in the praise — an even more remarkable tribute because the club's weekly discussions were the page-1 feature of the *Husbandman,* and editors were not renowned for building up competitors. Many of the club's members were Grangers who had joined together in 1874 to found the *Husbandman* as an unofficial organ of the Order. A letter from a southern farmer praised in unmeasured terms "the Elmira Farmers' Club, which feature is making your paper sought after and read and spoken of all over the United States and has rendered the *Husbandman* a household word." ⁵³

The editor of the *Husbandman,* William A. Armstrong, was secretary of the state Grange (later its master for a long period) and held the same position in the Elmira Farmers' Club. With him in the editorial chair the paper developed into an unusual farm journal. Containing a minimum of boiler-plate (as farm journals go), its wide eight pages were packed week after week with exciting discussions of contemporary and theoretical political economy, as well as virtually every argument of interest to farmers. Letters came in from all over the Union and it was a rare issue which contained no controversy. While the paper never seems to have had a paid circulation of more than 10,000, lengthy expositions of political economy did not sell many farm journals then, or now.[54]

Partly because it featured the Elmira Farmers' Club discussions, partly because it was much more than just another farm journal, the *Husbandman's* circulation was not confined to New York. To some extent this diffusion defeated the original purpose of aiding the local Grange work, even if the paper gained in prestige. Many leading out-of-state Grangers took part in the printed controversies and their laudatory letters were prominently featured. But Armstrong insisted that it was not the organ of any particular body, and it does appear to have had a considerable proportion of non-Granger readers.[55]

Its widely scattered circulation and influential class of readers made the *Husbandman* a strategic carrier of ideas. Thus, when the Grange in New York became sufficiently angry at having its legislative demands ignored to throw its weight behind the Farmers' Alliance, farm leaders throughout the country became rapidly acquainted with the newborn organization.

CHAPTER V

Railroad Rate Wars and the Farmers' Alliance

It is growing more and more apparent that farmers must assert their rights. They can no longer afford to be partisans, first, last, and all the time. The great question of transportation must by them be made a live political issue whether inside their respective parties or outside of them. Unless the producers of New York are willing to be taxed, and taxed to death, to help on Western progress, they must vote for a Legislature to represent them, and not to represent the vast corporations. The Railroad Committee of Investigation [Hepburn Committee] has developed enough, if enough were not previously known, to satisfy all thinking men how unjust are transportation rates and to show who are discriminated against . . . Next winter's legislation may be more important for New York producers than that of any in many years. The railways are carrying Western freight so low that our great Erie Canal, even, cannot compete with them.
American Rural Home (Rochester, N. Y.), August 2, 1879,
p. 263.

Political frustration and recognition by the New York Grange that tangible victories were needed if it were to grow in strength and influence were not the only reasons for the creation of the Farmers' Alliance. They were not even the major reasons. Possibly the individuals concerned might have declined the honor but a good share of the credit for the Alliance must go to the trunk-line presidents. Severe rate wars in 1875 had only been succeeded by the still more bitter conflicts of 1876 and early 1877. It was not at all accidental, therefore, that the Farmers' Alliance was born in the Rochester Court House, Monroe County, on March 21, 1877. The cattle and wheat growers of western New York, particularly susceptible to competition from the prairies, watched with growing anger as through rates fell and produce from the prairies rushed past their very farmsteads.[1] Prewar agitation against railroads had found its main base of agrarian support in western New York and developments in the seventies marked a resumption of hostilities, not the opening skirmish.

Together with through rates, commodity prices dropped, and farmers along the line of the New York Central had little doubt that the road was largely responsible for their troubles. Local rates to Rochester (and other points along the main route) were so exorbitant that, for the same quantity and kind of freight, it cost more to ship from Rochester to New York than from Chicago to New York.[2] The substantial landowners who created the Alliance were scarcely in danger of losing their property, but the large profits of former days had been reduced to the vanishing point if not to actual loss. Accordingly, land values had declined appreciably, and in this respect western New York was hard hit in the late seventies. Although the bulk of the prairie farmers suffered depression more acutely, it may be conjectured that, man for man, farmers in the Genesee Valley probably lost more money, considering their larger average scale of operations.[3] (That is, capital investment in a typical New York farm was usually higher than in a typical prairie farm.)

To indicate that substantial amounts of money were at issue, the personal impact upon F. P. Root of Brockport, Monroe County, might be noted briefly. Root, quoted at the beginning of the previous chapter, was the first provisional president of the Alliance and owned about 800 acres of excellent farm land. In 1879 he estimated that land values had declined by 25 per cent because of railroad rate policy, which, considering the nature of his holdings, cost him at least $20,000. Apart from capital losses, in his view freight discrimination amounted "to a sum of upwards of six million dollars [annual] tax upon the farmers of the State of New York," or about 5 per cent of gross income. Even if he exaggerated somewhat — and speaking broadly he was understating the case — it is obvious that such a "tax," added to real taxes, was not to be accepted without protest.[4]

Although large-scale landowners in western New York felt the effects of low through rates more directly than other areas in the state, less prosperous farmers felt the pinch of hard times more acutely. Not that severe economic distress generally prevailed. Nearly a decade of spectacular profits had preceded the decline, and agricultural solvency did not fluctuate that rapidly in New York. But farmers were not getting rich, and many were finding it difficult to meet the payments on lands or goods blithely bought during the boom. As the *Husbandman* had wryly commented early in 1876, "There is a difference of opinion upon most questions, but there are very few who are not impressed with the belief that these are hard times." [5] A year later, even in the rich Genesee Valley, F. P. Root was deploring "that spectre, which dims the vision of so many at the present, of 'hard times.' " [6]

As income declined, taxes remained as high if not higher than ever. Always a sore point, the discrimination operating against real and in favor of personal property was now felt with particular force. Given the prevailing agricultural fundamentalism, discriminations in transportation and taxation were viewed as evidence that the farmer, the creator of all wealth, was being systematically exploited by capitalist (non-landed) groups. Conflicts between personal and landed property went far back into American history, but in New York the latter had once exercised sufficient political power to protect its interests. Now corporations dominated the legislature and landowners had to get to work if they were to right the balance.[7]

Against this background of growing resentment towards corporate domination, intensified by the doleful "spectre of hard times," and the missionary work of the Grange, the origins of the Farmers' Alliance can best be understood. The "regulars" gathered at the biweekly session of the Western New York Farmers' Club were hardly poverty-stricken, but it was in their meeting rooms on Wednesday, February 21, 1877, that the movement came to life. As all too frequently happens, the drama was enacted under humdrum circumstances. Interspersed between homilies on varieties of grapes and apples, and even more earthy discussion of "manure," "how to house it," "how to use it," and "when to use it," there was talk of long overdue political action.[8]

Despite the rate wars of 1876 which had intensified resentment against low western through rates, taxation, not transportation, was the immediate occasion of the call to action. At the time there was talk in the legislature of exempting personal property and shifting the entire burden upon real estate. Animated by the traditional rural attitudes on the subject and faced with the prospect of increased money costs at a time of declining receipts, the club came to the conclusion that the time for action had come. But in answer to a suggestion that a state convention of farmers be called, the objection was immediately raised that the Patrons of Husbandry "are the proper medium through which to act." Those favoring a convention made two telling points in answering the objection. First, the Grange was pledged "not to do just what we wish to do," that is, it was pledged not to act politically. Secondly, the Grange contained only a portion of the farmers and a thoroughly representative organization was needed to protect agriculture. "If a man could appear before the Legislature and say that he represented the organized farmers of the State he would receive the greatest attention." [9]

A committee was appointed to consider the subject and their report was given at the next meeting, March 7. At that meeting the opposition of the Grange members of the club was pronounced, but to no avail. Disclaiming hostility to the Patrons of Husbandry, the advocates of the convention emphasized that the proposed organization would reach those farmers not attracted to the Grange. At the same time they stated that the movement could not succeed if the Grange did not coöperate, where-upon F. P. Root gave some tentative assurances that such coöperation would be forthcoming.[10]

Though not nearly as well known as the Elmira Farmers' Club, the sponsoring organization numbered among its members farmers wielding much influence in the state. As a result, and because the time was so obviously ripe, the call went out over the signatures of the club's officers and the presidents of the New York State Agricultural Society, the Western New York Agricultural Society, and William A. Armstrong as secretary of the Elmira Farmers' Club. The call expresses well the spirit which created the Farmers' Alliance and the purpose for which it was designed:

> In a country where laws are made and administered, often according to popular clamor, men of one class, if united, may exert a much more powerful influence than men of a much larger class, if acting in their individual character. Seeing this, all the great interests of the State, except the farming interest, have become thoroughly organized. As a result there is manifest a strong tendency, by our Legislature, to enact laws operating unjustly against farmers. Several such laws are now in force, and others still more unfair are proposed.
>
> We therefore call a convention of the farmers of this State, to meet at Rochester, on Wednesday, March 21st, to effect a permanent organization of this State and such other business as the occasion may demand. Special invitation is extended to grangers and farmers' clubs.[11]

Too little time elapsed, however, between the decision to issue the call and the actual convention of March 21 for it to have received much publicity. Nonetheless, a large number of delegates from Granges, Farmers' Clubs, and Agricultural Societies in western New York were present at the Rochester Court House. Patrick Barry, president of the state Agricultural Society, and William A. Armstrong, secretary of the state Grange had signed the call for a convention but neither they nor their organizations had any intention of creating a rival body. Hence the major discussion centered around the need for a new group and the form of work it should adopt. The chairman put it concisely upon opening the meeting: "The question before us is, Shall we organize primarily, as a mass convention, or shall we use the various associations of agriculturists now in existence as a basis, with a State organization as head?" [12]

Barry, speaking for the Agricultural Society, and James G. Shepard of Genesee County, speaking for the Grange, at first voiced opposition "to the multiplication of organizations as it increases expenses and tends to divide the farmers." Yet before the convention closed, objections along these lines had been removed and both men expressed hearty support. The constitution adopted by the Farmers' Alliance (as it was decided to call the new organization in keeping with its primary function) contained a section explicitly limiting membership to delegates from other bodies.[13]

In this respect it differed from the nativist societies so prominent in pre-war New York politics, although striking points of similarity suggest continuity between the Know-Nothings and the Farmers' Alliance.

Without pressing the issue here, it seems pertinent to indicate that the Know-Nothings had been responsible for the significant innovation of a political but nonpartisan organization to achieve a particular set of legislative objectives. It is likely that a substantial percentage of the men who were active in the Alliance had been members of the prewar nativist societies.[14] At any rate, the concept of a nonpartisan, reformist organization was not new in western New York.

According to the constitution adopted by the Alliance, each Grange, Agricultural Society, or Farmers' Club could send one delegate or such number as did not exceed 3 per cent of its enrollment. This section was "very thoroughly discussed" and apparently three considerations caused it to prevail. First, as a delegated body the Alliance would not compete for members and funds with existing groups. Second, it would act as the "mouthpiece" of all organized farmers within the state and thereby strengthen agricultural influence. Third, if the Alliance could achieve substantial victories it might stimulate unorganized farmers to join constituent societies.

Under the circumstances the decision was probably unavoidable, but eventually the Alliance was to suffer from its extremely loose form of organization. At the time none of this was obvious and a set of well-known agriculturists was elected as temporary officers to speed the work. Apart from agreeing that the Alliance should be created and that its work must be political but not partisan, little discussion was given to program. Yet discrimination in taxation and transportation was clearly the issue which confronted the new organization, and its next gathering was largely given over to it.

During the spring and summer eastbound freight rates continued abnormally low, farm prices declined steadily, and resentment against cheap western transportation and high taxes increased.[15] Although interest in the transportation problem grew, the meeting at Syracuse on September 5, 1877, was not as well attended as anticipated. Back in March the date had been objected to on the grounds that working farmers would find it inconvenient to leave at that season. However, the desire to influence nominating conventions caused the early September date to be chosen. (The landowners who dominated the Alliance were not rigidly bound to the daily routine, it might be noted.) According to the *Rural Home*, the inconvenient date did hold down attendance "but a good number of our best agriculturists were present, representing nearly every portion of the State, and their action was as definite and effective as could thus far be expected." The 125 delegates representing

26 rural counties did comprise some of the "best agriculturists." [16] Thus, the permanent officers elected at this "first annual meeting" (the Rochester convention was regarded as preliminary) included four past or future presidents of the State Agricultural Society. Five others were also present, and in all, at least thirteen men who at one time or another held that high office participated in the deliberations of the Alliance over the years.[17] It was no idle boast that the leading farmers of New York were its founders when, included in that category, with but two possible exceptions, was every president of the state Agricultural Society from 1872 through 1881. The state Dairymen's Association, Grange, leading Farmers' Clubs, and county Agricultural Societies were equally well represented.[18] Both the *Husbandman* and the *Rural Home* acted as its unofficial organs and continually publicized its activities and policies.

Other areas sent their leading spokesmen but the largest delegations came from western New York. The grain and meat growers of that section felt western competition more directly and more immediately, and Monroe, Ontario, Seneca, and Wayne led all the other counties. The fact that the Alliance was strongest in the rich Genesee Valley and Lake Counties affords a revealing insight into the nature of the movement in New York. Increasingly militant politically, given the type of men who founded and directed it, the Alliance was always an eminently conservative organization. The aims it avowed at the Syracuse meeting and persisted in thereafter can only be described as "agrarian radicalism" by a most liberal stretch of the imagination. Apart from minor issues, nothing more was desired than "equity and equality of taxation" and an end to railroad discrimination against New York farmers "in favor of those more remote from the principal markets of the continent and the world." Drastic reduction of local rates and a corresponding increase in through rates was the basic demand. Greenbacks, remonetization of silver, and similar controversial issues were ignored, for a remarkable unity of sentiment prevailed not only on what to do, but on what not to do.[19]

To secure these conservative ends it was necessary to end the farmers' "blind allegiance to party"; yet the idea of operating outside the two-party system was anathema. As a matter of fact, aside from brave words about independent action, the Alliance only tip-toed timorously into the icy waters of party politics. But the Syracuse meeting did take some halting steps in the direction of mobilizing farmers for political action and tightening the organizational basis of the Alliance. The property-conscious men who directed it naturally addressed their appeal to the "Real Estate Owners of New York."

The members of this Alliance belong to both political parties, and it is not sought to disturb their party relations, trusting that both political parties will be willing to do justice to the interests of agriculture when their attention is particularly called to these interests. We therefore advise that this organization be extended to the counties and towns of the State.[20]

The advice to institute sub-Alliances in no way implied abandonment of the original decision against a mass organization. Essentially it was a device to allow members of constituent bodies, such as the Grange, to begin the direct political action hitherto forbidden them. In theory, local Alliances would exert pressure at party caucuses and thereby affect nominating conventions; if this round-about method failed to produce good candidates, farmers were supposed to disregard party lines and vote for the best candidate. In fact, only two county units were organized prior to the 1877 election, a fairly clear indication of the difficulties involved in making political independence a reality among New York State farmers. Inherent difficulties did exist but they do not fully account for the limited successes achieved by the Alliance in its first campaign. Elaboration of this point, however, is best postponed until after a consideration of the special meeting held in December of that year.

The one-day affair in the September harvest season had been too brief to permit adequate discussion, and the executive committee therefore arranged for a special winter meeting. Held again in Syracuse in December 1877, it was deliberately timed to coincide with the state Dairymen's Association Convention — a coincidence not difficult to arrange since the president of the Alliance and the president of the Association were one and the same man, Harris Lewis of Herkimer County (also a past president of the state Agricultural Society). Attendance was larger than before, approximately 150 delegates participating from 60 local organizations in 30 counties.[21] A gratifying increase; yet perspective is gained by recognizing that only about 10 per cent of the *organized* farmers in the state were represented — a category fairly exclusive in its own right.[22]

But the two-day meeting marked a definite advance. Comprehensive papers were read setting forth the Alliance demands on transportation, taxation, and legislative action easing the requirements for mutual insurance associations. Special committees were set up and charged with the responsibility of enlightening the mass of farmers upon these subjects. The character of the meeting, as revealed to supporters, is indicated in this description: "A finer body of men we have not seen assembled; and they all appeared earnest and enthusiastic in the work undertaken — discreet, outspoken, honest . . . all that the meeting could do was done, and in most excellent temper." [23]

The *Rural Home* may have been perfectly accurate in its description but the Alliance still had a long way to go before its aims could be achieved. Basically, the problem was that its greatest source of strength was also its greatest source of weakness. By this time the Alliance had succeeded in becoming the recognized "mouthpiece" of the leading farmers of the state and the organizations they directed. Unfortunately for them, the organizations were too small and undisciplined to impress pragmatic politicians; their membership was strongly partisan; liaison between them through the Alliance was tenuous at best; and their leaders were too conservative and too inexperienced in the art to arouse mass agitation.

Proposing nothing less than to wrest control of the legislature from the omnipotent railroad lobby, they proudly proclaimed their distaste for what they pleased to call "red tape." "What the method shall be, by which this Alliance gather to itself the aggregate agricultural influence of the State, for the accomplishment of . . . [our] objects, we do not regard as very material. The less machinery in the organization, the better . . . It may be somewhat uncertain, whether the present membership fee will give the funds adequate for the necessities of the Alliance, but that can be remedied as we progress in the work before us."

Intramural rivalries may have been quieted by elevating spontaneous association to the level of high agrarian principle, but something more was needed if isolated, individualistic farmers were to become an independent political force. The Alliance was still in the never-never land where it could be supposed that vague direction and pious exhortation would overpower corporation control of the legislature and achieve pro rata laws and more equitable taxation.

THE ALLIANCE MILITANT

Given the diversified agriculture practiced in New York, hesitant leadership and loose organization were especially serious handicaps for the Alliance. In all likelihood these factors would not have been as decisive had the Alliance program been capable of really arousing the rural districts. The point at issue here is not the universality of the sentiments voiced by the organization as much as the intensity with which they were felt. High taxes were everywhere deplored and the difficulties caused by cheap western freight received increasing attention after 1876. But even the Alliance was badly split on the exact changes to be made in taxation. Moreover, taxes were essentially a local problem since county, township, and school outlays made up much the largest portion of the general property levy.[24] Relative to transportation, intrastate rivalries complicated matters, though western New York was more keenly alive to freight discrimination than other areas.

The fact that brother farmers, not railroad magnates, were the real targets of pro rata laws also tended to influence thinking on the subject. There is no intention here of overdoing the idealism and class solidarity of New York farmers, but campaigns to debar prairie producers from seaboard markets did suffer from greater restraints than uninhibited attacks on "soulless corporations." (As a matter of course the trunk lines were given top billing as villains.) In addition, due to the nature of the problem, discussions of transportation in the Empire State's rural areas tended to be abstract and negative.

In contrast to the immediate impact upon merchants, and western farmers to a lesser degree, eastern farmers felt the effects of railroad policy through a long delayed, highly involved complex of market operations. Even had the Alliance secured pro rata laws, years must have elapsed before New York agriculture could hope to receive substantial material benefits. As depression became really acute in 1878, hard-pressed farmers looked for relief to a more immediate, direct, and time-honored solution — inflation.[25] Undoubtedly, the Alliance suffered from the fact that just as it was improving its organization, economic difficulties increased to the point where its program seemed a mere palliative. The farm price index which had stood at 85 in 1877 broke to 74 in 1878, and, despite a sharp rise late in the year, measured 67 for all of 1879. Such a low point was not reached again until the really disastrous year of 1896 and indicates the severe pressures upon New York farmers.[26]

A suspiciously simple explanation can be offered for the emergence of strong Greenback sentiment among New York farmers in 1878; yet no reason exists to question it. After the Civil War large returns to agriculture were soon capitalized and resulted in high fixed costs. As prices fell, farmers with or without mortgages, facing relatively higher fixed costs, logically sought to cut expenses and improve their competitive positions. Satisfaction of the demands for cheap transportation in the West (at least on through rates), had an obvious counterpart in demands for pro rata laws in the East. Once prices reached really low levels, reforms in transportation and taxation tended to be superseded by the cry for Greenbacks and currency inflation. The crude quantity theories of the Greenbackers may have been completely erroneous but at least they were directed to the major problem confronting farmers in the late seventies. Anything less than a rapid rise in commodity prices could have only slightly relieved growing agrarian difficulties by this time, and it should be noted that in respectable circles a good deal of support then existed for paper currency and bimetallic solutions to the depression.[27]

Strong Greenback sentiment, severe price depression, and absorbing interest in financial questions during 1878 can all be documented by references to the *Husbandman*'s editorials and other features. This type of evidence is particularly impressive because the paper vigorously favored "sound money," consistently tended to play down farm difficulties before the November election, and clearly attempted to shift interest to freight discrimination and western competition as the causes of declining prices.[28]

The election returns show that a rapid growth in Greenback strength had developed in New York. Peter Cooper had been given a mere 2,000 votes in 1876; the total Workingmen and Greenback strength in 1877 was 20,000; the Greenback vote in 1878 for the highest state office (the Workingmen party had been absorbed) was 75,000, or about 9 per cent of the total. In a number of the agricultural counties the increase in Greenback strength was marked and the percentages were much above the state levels. Straight Greenback candidates for Congress received some 80,000 votes, and joint Greenback and Democratic strength amounted to 44,000 more, out of an 830,000 total. No Greenbackers were elected to Congress or to state offices but a surprising number of local contests were won in the Southern Tier.[29]

Considering the strong party attachments then obtaining, its brief organization and helter-skelter apparatus, the actual Greenback vote in all probability measurably understated the extent of sympathy for cheap money doctrines. Yet the strength of the movement was only temporary and shallow, particularly because the dominant regional forces were increasingly opposed to inflation. With resumption of specie payments for paper money beginning on January 1, 1879, the premium in gold soon disappeared and with it a strong prop of the Greenback argument. An excellent harvest, coupled with the boom in commodity prices as a result of widespread European crop failure, was of even greater importance. As price indexes rose in the later months of 1879, cheap money sentiment suffered severe deflation. The depression rapidly lifted, and for reasons that obviously owed nothing to inflationary doctrines. Under these circumstances the Greenback vote dropped precipitously to 20,000 in 1879 and 13,000 in 1880 — labor defections accounting for a good share of the decline.[30]

Not intrinsically important, the impressive 1878 Greenback vote in the state affords historical insights of considerable value. It demonstrates that hard-pressed New York farmers in various localities, despite long-time party prejudices, were willing to break party ranks when a sufficiently appealing solution was offered and their felt need great enough. Greenbackism, therefore, not only limited the strength of the Alliance by supplying a competing doctrine and organization, it also revealed the latter's basic limitations. The relative success of the Greenbackers makes it clear that the Alliance's failure to win a real mass base in 1878 was not because farmers found it impossible to desert the old parties, but because the Alliance did not offer them sufficient incentive to do so. Its limited achievements in that year of "hard times" leads to the conclusion that currency doctrines had wider and more intense appeal than attacks upon the cheap western freight rates.

Failure of the Grange to increase its membership substantially also indicates the difficulty — in the short run — of organizing New York farmers except on the basis of immediate material benefits. Conceivably, one of the reasons for the disparate success of Greenback and Granger-Alliance doctrines might have been the status of the "money question" as a prominent national issue. But the course of events in New York thereafter suggests that this factor, widespread interest and publicity concerning a specific issue, could only have been of limited importance.

Beginning in March 1879 the Hepburn Committee's investigation into New York railroads made transportation a "burning issue" from one end of the state to the other. Despite this favorable atmosphere, and despite the fact that farm prices were extremely low until late in the year (the rise did come before Election Day), the Alliance failed to win organized mass support to any significant degree. However, it was strengthened in several important respects by the Hepburn investigation. Spurred on by public attention to the issue, Alliance leaders cast aside their former timidity and became increasingly militant.

Since its formation a number of county and town Alliances had slowly developed, and these were urged to take the lead in calling mass meetings prior to the party conventions. At local meetings advisory nominations would be made for both parties "with the assurance to all concerned that these only will be supported by Alliance members and all electors in sympathy with them, upon whatever ticket they may appear." The resolution to this effect was adopted at the third annual meeting in August 1879,[31] and the extent to which the leadership had moved may be judged from the *Rural Home*'s comment: "The . . . resolution would have been a bombshell in the Alliance, two years ago; now it called out one or two [minor amendments] . . . and was finally adopted unanimously as reported." [32]

FARMER-MERCHANT *Rapprochement*

Even more significant than the Alliance's new-found militancy was the cementing of its relations with the Grange and with the New York City commercial bodies. From the outset the Grange dominated the Alliance on the local level — in fact, it probably created the county and town Alliances[33] — but the state leadership was drawn from much broader sources. Although Grangers were on the executive committee, invariably the key offices of the Alliance had been held by others. Symbolic of the growing coöperation between the two organizations on the highest levels was the joint issuance in August 1879 of "An Address to the Farmers of New York." A comprehensive analysis of the transportation question, the address pointed out that freight discrimination cost New York State farmers millions of dollars annually, and "had depreciated the value of farm lands hundreds of millions of dollars." To demonstrate that the issue now was not confined to dollars and cents, it forcefully argued that "more important than aught else, the supremacy of the people of this State over the corporations which they have created must be vindicated." [34]

As almost inevitably happens in a conflict of this nature, the basic economic drives were sublimated and emerged as ideological principles. What had begun as an attempt to achieve pro rata laws debarring western farmers from seaboard markets was now a fight to assert the "supremacy of the people." Like the New York merchants, the farmers sought to roll back the railroad revolution which was transforming the economy of the nation to their detriment. No doubt they were sincere in their identification of themselves as "the people," and railroad arrogance and control of the legislature provided a real basis for ideological contest. But it seems more accurate to assert that the basic issue was the conflict between different kinds of property groups caught up in the Communication Revolution. New York farmers would have been opposed to cheap transportation from the West whether or no railroads corrupted legislatures and dominated politics. Ideology was an instrument of agrarian policy; it did not produce that policy.

Confident of ultimate success, the Granger-Alliance *Address* admitted that a "sharp contest" would be necessary before the "arrogant . . . railway magnates" were dethroned in the legislature. One of the strongest reasons given for optimistic forecasts of victory was the aid that might be expected from New York City commercial interests. In actuality, such aid was an accomplished fact and had steadily developed since the autumn of 1876. At that time, A. B. Miller, secretary of the Cheap Transportation Association, had written a personal letter to William A. Armstrong asking for coöperation between farmers and merchants against the railroads. Armstrong strongly endorsed the proposal in the *Husbandman* and urged farmers to support the association's petition for a state Board of Railroad Commissioners.[35]

Considerable irony attaches to the *Husbandman*'s endorsement of the Cheap Transportation Association — an organization sparked by Francis B. Thurber and designed in large measure to forward the interests of New York wholesale grocers. For months prior to the endorsement of the association's petition, the *Husbandman* had been engaged in a slanging match with the *American Grocer*, a paper owned by the Thurber family and directed towards retail grocers in the interior. The *American Grocer* had warmly denounced "The Grange Co-Operative

Store Movement" and the *Husbandman* had responded in kind.[36] But, since the enemy was a common one, the *Husbandman* supported the Cheap Transportation Association's petition. So effective was its endorsement that farmers' signatures had been sent to the legislature in large numbers early in the 1877 session. From then on the *Husbandman* gave increasing publicity to mercantile activities on the transportation issue. Among other advances towards a more harmonious relationship, the Alliance bestowed a vice-presidency upon a representative of the Cheap Transportation Association at its first annual meeting in 1877.[37]

The marriage of convenience between farmers and merchants was really consummated during the following year. That railroad managers served as the agents of persuasion was stated with commendable frankness by the *Husbandman*: "The railroads themselves have done more than the Grange to make it clear to thinking people that some power must be invoked to control within certain limits the business of transportation . . . While the farmers and business men at intermediate points were the only classes to suffer and to raise objections, the press of our seaport cities had few words of sympathy to offer, and was firmly on the side of the railway managers. But now the discriminations have been made to affect New York injuriously and the press of that city threatens to advocate 'Grangerism', if railway managers do not cease their mismanagement." [38]

The union of merchants and farmers was concluded in 1878 because F. B. Thurber had come to recognize that strong rural support was indispensable for the merchants to overcome the railroad lobby. To achieve such support he had the Chamber of Commerce reverse a position taken several months before and adopt the following resolution: "That the local rates charged to citizens of this State shall bear a just proportion to those charged in through business to the citizens of other States." [39] New York merchants, in reality, opposed anything tending to raise rates from the West but the resolution was necessary to secure coöperation from the interior.

Actually, few illusions were held in the interior concerning the reasons for mercantile support of what was designed to sound like pro rata;[40] notwithstanding, cynical distrust between the two groups tended to disappear in the face of the sensational disclosures provided by the Hepburn Committee in 1879. Temporarily, the real conflict of interests was obscured by the indignation sweeping the state. Undivided efforts were necessary if the campaign against the powerful common enemy was to succeed, and cordial relations soon developed among the leaders of farmers and merchants.

Booming commodity prices late in 1879 may have had something to do with it, but the November election returns proved disappointing to the leaders of the Alliance. Both parties had been careful to insert a plank in their platforms promising redress against railroad abuses;[41] apparently farmers felt free to indulge partisan inclinations and ignored the Alliance's recommendations on candidates. The *Husbandman* berated them for ignoring the real issues of the campaign and accepting the traps laid for them by "wily political tricksters," interested only in party success to secure the spoils.[42] The failure of the Alliance to extend significantly its mass base, even when prices ruled low in the year, indicates that railroad discrimination was not felt deeply enough in most parts of the state to find organized expression. Thereafter, the impact of discrimination tended to be considerably lessened by the four-year cycle of prosperity commencing late in 1879. What the evidence suggests is that neither high prosperity nor deep depression was the proper environment for the reforms advocated by the Alliance. While unsusceptible to proof, the conjecture might be ventured that under New York conditions, drawn out mild depression would have secured optimum support for its moderate program.

Despite the obvious reluctance of farmers to depart from traditional individualism, the close working relations developed in 1879 between Grange, Alliance, and commercial leaders gave the farm groups far more strength and influence than they could have hoped to achieve unaided. Powerful New York City interests which had labored to secure cheap transportation to and from the West rang all the changes upon railroad villainy as responsible for "the impoverished and debt-burthened condition of the farmers."[43] As shown below, Simon Sterne, F. B. Thurber, and Charles S. Smith, acting on behalf of the commercial bodies, virtually ran the Hepburn investigation and they saw to it that the farmers' case was fully and sympathetically presented. Indeed, the merchants exuded such heartfelt sympathy for the noble agriculturists one is almost tempted to forget that nothing would have delighted them more than really cheap transportation east and westbound — provided, of course, that the metropolis was not discriminated against. For the moment, and for several years to come, they needed the help of the interior and had to pay the price of publicly agreeing with agrarian complaints against low through-freights.

With the farmer-merchant combination beginning to solidify, its potential strength appeared to be so considerable that minor concessions were thrown to agriculture. Politicians, hoping to forestall independent political action in the interior, finally legalized mutual fire insurance companies in 1879, granted a State Agricultural Experiment Station in 1880, and at the same session railroads and other corporations even consented to pay a slight state tax upon their property.[44] On vital issues, where important corporate interests were threatened, no such boons were forthcoming. Potential strength had to be translated into main force before the railroads consented to any regulation, and even then, what the *Times* once described as "that old acquaintance of Legislators, the *pro rata* freight bill," never came close to passage.[45]

Since the succeeding chapters are necessarily devoted to the same chronological period and cover a good deal of the material, the New York Alliance activities in the early eighties will only be treated here summarily. In spite of farm prosperity, the organization probably reached its peak influence in 1880. Large and enthusiastic crowds turned out at numerous summer meetings and the Alliance creed was given publicity through other media.[46] Freight discrimination unduly favoring through shipments no longer caused actual losses but it still limited possible profits. In addition, railroad control of the legislature was too blatant to be endured without protest. Thus a good basis existed for educating farmers on the transportation problem, and upon the socio-economic benefits of independent political action. While advances were made in the work and a greater respect for rural sensibilities developed among politicians, in September 1880 a staunch supporter conceded that "something more, not yet discovered, is needed before the mass of farmers will act intelligently and unitedly for their own interests." [47]

Paradoxically, the Alliance virtually disappeared in 1881 because public sentiment on the transportation question advanced so rapidly. The methods employed by the railroads to block the regulatory measures that were recommended by the Hepburn Committee backfired and resulted in the establishment of the National Anti-Monopoly League (discussed below). Leaders of the Alliance were prominent in the new organization, designed to unite not only farmers and merchants but the "entire people" against corporation supremacy. With the emergence of the League, the Alliance was superfluous and only existed nominally thereafter. Thus, the time span during which the Alliance may be said to have directly and sensibly influenced the thinking of New York farmers is confined to the brief period between the Greenback agitation of 1878 and the formation of the Anti-Monopoly League early in 1881. At best the program had only a limited mass appeal, winning its most enthusiastic acceptance among relatively large-scale landowners and farmers whose holdings declined in value as a direct result of western competition. Yet in the long run it made a significant contribution toward arousing farmers to defend their interests. Through its activities the Grange was able to break down the strict taboos against independent political action and achieve a limited influence upon legislation.

Apart from its immediate effect upon New York farmers, several noteworthy historical developments can be attributed to the Alliance. First, though only the rural auxiliary of metropolitan merchants, it deserves some share of responsibility for the establishment of the New York Railroad Commission in 1882. Moreover, it gave clear expression to the concept that farmers could maximize their influence by forming a single, all-embracing, permanent organization to represent them politically within the existing party structure. The independent farmers' parties springing up in the Old Northwest during the early seventies were impractical in the increasingly urban America, but a balance-of-power agrarian organization was another matter entirely. The basic concepts developed by the Alliance are extensively practiced today and find their logical outgrowth in the modern farm bloc. In addition, its activities helped to pave the way for the broader concept of the National Anti-Monopoly League, essentially an attempt to organize the "entire people" under mercantile leadership. Finally, the Farmers' Alliance, created in the Rochester Court House on March 21, 1877, began the movement bearing that name which eventually swept through the rural districts of the West and South. Notwithstanding the identity in nomenclature, marked differences in the Farmers' Alliance movement throughout the country indicate that in the age of Communication Revolution the sectional quality of American life not only remained intact but was accentuated.

NATIONAL FARMERS' ALLIANCE

The close working arrangements between New York merchants and farmers as they affected the progress of the regulation campaign within the state will be treated in detail elsewhere. But to appreciate the extent to which Francis B. Thurber's plan of 1873 to have the metropolitan merchants dominate the nation-wide movement against railroad management was realized, it is necessary to discuss briefly the organization of the National Farmers' Alliance in 1880. The metropolitan merchants were able to influence the Grange and Farmers' Alliance in their own state, and through the New York farm leaders and organizations they also were able to influence the agrarian phases of railroad agitation in the nation. Thus, clarifying the origins of the Farmers' Alliance here facilitates the task of explaining in later chapters how it came about that in March 1882 Albert Fink identified New York as the home base of "the leaders of the present crusade against railroad management." [48]

Without attempting to give a detailed account or to answer many important questions involved, it is possible to dispel some of the confusion now surrounding the early development of the National Farmers' Alliance.

Rooted in conditions deriving from the historical development of New York agriculture, the Alliance in that state was created to mobilize landowners' and farmers' political influence to cope with the particular problems confronting them during the decade of trunk-line rate wars. [49]

The detailed contemporary accounts in both the *Husbandman* and the *American Rural Home* (and other papers) leave no doubt on that score. Founded by the leading landowners and farmers of the state, the Farmers' Alliance developed a distinct program around transportation, taxation, and mutual insurance, became increasingly militant and articulate, and had at least two influential farm journals acting as its organ in all but name.[50] It was not merely the "political mouthpiece" of the Grange, it represented all organized agricultural societies in the state. As such it worked closely with New York City commercial groups, took a sophisticated approach to this relationship, and became a moderately effective instrument for the protection of agrarian interests. Never a mass organization of any size, it was a highly conscious attempt to restore to agriculture some portion of its erstwhile political power. In the process, it attracted nation-wide interest among farm leaders and led to the creation of the National Farmers' Alliance in 1880.

Leading Texas Grangers, for example, knew about the New York Farmers' Alliance from its origin in March 1877, for the *Husbandman* gave it detailed coverage — and they read the *Husbandman*. William Armstrong, its editor, was well known to Grange leaders all over the country for he attended all the national sessions as secretary of the New York Grange. In an editorial setting forth his desire to make the paper the largest agricultural weekly in the country, Armstrong stated plans to extend its correspondence and other features. Among its attractions, he claimed in November 1875, was the fact that "The Husbandman is the only agricultural and Grange paper which was represented by its editor at the National Grange in Charlestone last winter, and again this year it will give its readers fuller reports of the National Grange meeting than will be found in any other paper in the country." [51]

In line with Armstrong's plan to extend the paper's correspondence, out-of-state letters were featured and in May 1876 he printed a personal letter from R. A. Binford, secretary of the Texas State Grange: "I want to tell you how much real pleasure it is to me to read the *Husbandman*, especially your spicy articles and the proceedings of the [Elmira] Farmers' Club." [52]

Granted the propensity of farm journals to puff their wares, and the ease with which endorsements could be obtained, it is possible that Binford may have exaggerated his delight to please his fellow delegate to the National Grange. The point is, however, he received the paper. And among scores of other letters from Grange leaders throughout the country printed in the *Husbandman*, it is interesting to note one in October 1877 from R. T. Kennedy, the new secretary of the Texas State Grange. Kennedy didn't want to flatter but had to say that "yours is the *best* paper of the kind I have ever seen." [53] The key letter which explicitly indicates Texas knowledge of the New York Farmers' Alliance is dated January 8, 1878, and signed "Practicus." Whoever "Practicus" was, his previous letters to the *Husbandman* showed sufficiently detailed knowledge of the Grange in Texas to suggest official rank. Significantly, they made no mention of any Farmers' Alliance, or Alliance, in the Lone Star State.[54] The January 8 letter was unsparing in its praise:

The inquiries and discussions of the [Elmira Farmers'] Club are always interesting and of real value. But when you get intelligent, practical men, lovers of their country, on those great subjects, government and agriculture, as President [Harris] Lewis, of the Farmers' Alliance, Hon. Heman Glass, of Monroe, and other distinguished gentlemen of that great body, you make the country blaze with a character of intelligence that is calculated to give the farmers a proper estimate of their rights and a just sense of their wrongs, inspiring them with a realization of the fact of their occupation being the greatest and noblest in the land, and that they are therefore entitled to a preponderance of influence in the legislation of the country, State and National.[55]

The inspiration given Texas Grangers by the *Husbandman* points up the paper's role as the major carrier of the Alliance concept to both the South and the West. Its extensive circulation throughout the country, particularly among Grange leaders, its large list of exchanges eager to reprint the discussions at the Elmira Farmers' Club, subscriptions by ex-New Yorkers eager to keep in touch with doings in their old homes, all served to bring the new organization to the attention of farmers outside the Empire State. Flattering letters to the *Husbandman* from such leading Grangers as T. R. Allen of Missouri, T. A. Thompson of Minnesota, G. W. Lawrence of North Carolina, Lieutenant Governor Alonzo Sessions of Michigan, A. B. Smedley of Iowa, Put Darden of Mississippi, D. Wyatt Aiken of South Carolina, D. H. Thing of Maine, and many others, testify to the strategic role of the paper.[56] It could also boast by February 1878 that no less than thirty states and territories were represented in letters to the Elmira Farmers' Club.[57]

Another important medium through which the Alliance idea was spread was the annual meetings of the National Grange. Not only were Armstrong and the other New York delegates present to tell of its activities, also in attendance was the master of the powerful Pennsylvania Grange, Victor E. Piollet. An enthusiastic and highly vocal supporter of the Alliance from the start, it would have been most surprising if Piollet had failed to brief his fellow delegates concerning the Alliance.[58]

By June 1879 William J. Fowler, state secretary of the New York Alliance, could proudly inform the Monroe County branch that he was receiving letters from all over the country asking about the organization.[59] The idea had even crossed the Atlantic and the hard-pressed tenant farmers of England, also experiencing the adverse effects of the Communication Revolution, had banded together in a "Farmers' Alliance" to further the interests of agriculture.[60]

The thirteenth annual meeting of the National Grange, opening in Canandaigua, New York, on November 19, 1879, appears to have given considerable impetus towards making the Alliance a national organization. A letter from D. H. Thing, master of the Maine State Grange, printed in the *Husbandman* on the day of the meeting, is interesting in this connection. Apparently thrown into despair by the election results, Thing wrote:

> Only a few years more of this abject, servile, slavish submission to the domination of party leaders, their cringing at the crack of the party whip, and we shall be helpless tools of railroads, national banks and ring politicians. What of hope for the future of the toiling masses of my country, I see, is in the order of Patrons and the Farmers' Alliance. If the principles of these grand organizations prevail, all will be well.[61]

To encourage the spread of these principles, the report of the National Grange Committee on Transportation urged farmers "to make such alliance . . . as will enable them by their votes to elect from their own number an even handed fair share of Representatives." The adoption of this report, in view of its traditional no-politics policy, represented a long step forward by the Grange to mobilize its membership for independent political activity. It is interesting to note that the five-man Committee of Transportation included Victor E. Piollet of Pennsylvania, William G. Wayne of New York, and Colonel William W. Lang, master of the Texas Grange.[62] Lang's presence on the committee in company with the leading Alliancemen ties in with material concerning the intimate relation between the Grange and the Alliance in both Texas and New York.[63] Although after 1880 it split into northern and southern wings, in view of the intimate ties between the Grange and the Farmers' Alliance in Texas, Lang's working together with the New Yorkers is symbolic of the fact that the Alliance movement had but a single source in the late seventies, and was to a considerable extent an outgrowth of the Patrons of Husbandry.

Early in August 1880 the call for the annual meeting of the New York Alliance announced that: "At the suggestion of Illinois Farmers' Alliance men, the subject of a National Alliance organization will be presented to the meeting." [64] As late as September 15, William J. Fowler told the Monroe County Alliance that nothing further had been heard regarding the proposed National Alliance convention to be held in Chicago but "something was expected from the Committee having the matter in charge during the present week." The president of the branch was also convinced that a National Alliance would soon be instituted for "the question of transportation [was] a subject for national legislation." And as evidence that interest in the movement was mounting, Secretary Fowler reported that ten thousand copies of the New York Alliance report on transportation had been printed for distribution in the state. "Calls for as many more copies had been made by Western states and many had been sent." [65] Word must have come shortly thereafter, for Fowler was present on October 14, 1880, when the National Farmers' Alliance came into being.

It seems clear that Milton George, the new owner of the *Western Rural*, a farm journal published at Chicago, was the moving spirit behind the October 14 meeting.[66] According to his competitor, George's motive in spurring Alliance organization in the West was to boost the circulation of the *Western Rural* [67] — a charge whose accuracy would cause little surprise to anyone familiar with the practices of nineteenth-century American agricultural journalism.

Milton George was not the only man to perceive the possibilities inherent in organizing western farmers on transportation issues in 1880. By that time a close working relationship had developed between the New York City merchants and the upstate New York landowners and businessmen-farmers who led the Alliance in the Empire State, a relationship tangibly paying off in increased legislative support for railroad regulation. Yet if the New York merchants were to secure federal legislation — which they knew to be the only comprehensive solution to the railroad problem — it was necessary to create that "national constituency" so optimistically foreseen by them back in 1873. Hence, New York was not only represented at the Chicago convention in the person of W. J. Fowler (one of the featured speakers), but by a letter from the ubiquitous Francis B. Thurber. The newspaper account of the proceedings tersely summarized it:

> The Secretary read a letter from Mr. F. B. Thurber, of the New York Board of Trade, in which he reviewed the efforts made in the East to obtain a fair adjustment of the relations between common carriers and the public. The remedy, he said, could only be had through political action, and never could be obtained until representatives, both State and National, felt that public opinion earnestly demanded a remedy. The work could be accomplished through a National Farmers' Alliance. If the few continue to tax the many, within fifty years there would be a money aristocracy in this country similar to that which destroyed Rome and other Republics.[68]

Lending particular significance to Thurber's letter is the fact that he and Fowler were already engaged in activities which soon culminated in the establishment of the National Anti-Monopoly League. Apparently, in 1880 Thurber envisioned drawing the Farmers' Alliance into a national campaign to secure railroad regulation, a projection on a higher level of his increasingly successful efforts in New York. At any rate, as will be indicated below, that is precisely what happened.[69] But Thurber's proposal does not seem to have been well received at the organizing convention. Joint action between merchants and farmers was not unprecedented and the maxim "Once bitten, twice shy" apparently held good. L. S. Coffin of Iowa made some comments which throw a good deal of light upon the Granger Movement (as distinct from the Grange) in the early seventies. Possibly they were designed to forestall a reincarnation of the American Cheap Transportation Association in which Thurber had been so active:

> Mr. Coffin said they should not repeat the mistakes of the past with reference to organization. When farmers organized for protection they alone should organize. The shippers' interests were not identical with theirs. The shippers should have a society and the farmers one, and the two act in unity.[70]

After the "Farmers Transportation Convention" adjourned, the real work of the meeting began. About half of the three hundred delegates remained in their seats and proceeded to organize themselves. In short order a constitution was adopted and a set of officers elected. It was only fitting that one of the original founders of the Alliance in New York should head the organization, and, whether this was the determining factor or not, William J. Fowler, a farm journalist of Pittsford, Monroe County, became the first president of the National Farmers' Alliance.[71]

His election might be subject to any number of prosaic explanations, but it is regarded here as symbolic of the role forced upon New York farmers by the Communication Revolution. Unexpectedly deprived by railroad progress of their "isolated state" (in the sense that the German economist Von Thünen employed that concept),[72] in turn they found it necessary to deprive themselves of another kind of isolated state, that of traditional American rural individualism. In the post-Civil War world of trunk-line railroads, swift ocean steamers, and submarine cables, the mythically self-sufficient, independent husbandmen abandoned their illusions, conceded that they really were entrepreneurs of sorts — and founded a trade association.

CHAPTER VI

The Hepburn Committee Investigation

> In view of our costly experience in State management of various institutions, and the extent to which the managers and attaches of those institutions become factors in our politics, there is no doubt the State acted wisely in committing the construction of railroads to associations of citizens . . . The mistake was in not providing proper safeguards to protect the public interest and hold the roads to a strict accountability for their transactions. Thus, through the laxity of our laws and the want of governmental control . . . have crept in those abuses hereafter mentioned, so glaring in their proportions as to savor of fiction rather than actual history.
>
> Hepburn Committee, *Report,* p. 7.

The legislative investigation of Jay Gould and the Erie Railroad in 1873 provided a good deal of ammunition for New York merchants hostile to trunk-line policy; the Hepburn investigation of 1879 was a veritable arsenal — and for the country at large. Other states, notably Ohio and Pennsylvania, also produced sensational disclosures. The Credit Mobiliér Affair reverberated for many years. But it was in New York that the American railroad system was given its first real airing. As the prorailroad, conservative *Railroad Gazette* acknowledged early in 1880: "It [the Hepburn Committee] has certainly had such an opportunity of ascertaining the actual practices in the commercial operation of railroads as no other body of men ever had." [1]

A number of factors combined to make the Hepburn investigation so influential in shaping the movement for railroad regulation that it is not easy to overstate its importance. According to the biographer of Simon Sterne, the man who really conducted the Hepburn inquiry:

For twenty years after its completion, Mr. Sterne's correspondence abounds with requests for copies of the report and testimony, information as to the character of the evidence on one or other of the special subjects of investigation, and with acknowledgements of the obligations of the inquirers to the immense amount of information in regard to the practical workings of the railroad system which was then elicited . . . From many of the states of

. . . [the] Union came testimonies of the powerful interest which had been excited by the New York methods of dealing with the grievances against the railroad companies, and from senators and members of Congress of the United States comes repeated calls for the drafting of some scheme by which national control could be exercised over the railroads engaged in interstate commerce.[2]

No implication is intended here that the Hepburn inquiry was basically responsible for the establishment of federal control over railroads. Obviously, a phenomenon increasingly characteristic of industrialized countries the world over was a historic inevitability in America. As railroads progressed it became clear that they were not governed by the traditional laws of competition but, in fact, were rendering them inoperative in ever larger spheres of the economy. It also became clear that American railroads were too important to the entire community to be left to develop in anarchic fashion. Such recognition does not invalidate the thesis that the New York inquiry into railroad practices, and the developments flowing directly from it, was the single most important chapter in the direct sequence of events leading up to the Interstate Commerce Commission of 1887. Prior to 1879 national railroad regulation in America was a historic inevitability; after 1879 it was only a matter of time.

Before the Hepburn Committee went to work signs were already multiplying that the federal government must eventually begin to exercise some form of control over transportation. State railroad commissions and Representative John Reagan's continued pressure in Congress for national legislation were only twin aspects of the same trend. The trend essentially derived from the fact that the Civil War had unleashed powerful socio-economic forces which in part occasioned, in part coincided with, the even greater impact of the Communication Revolution. Their combined effect was rapidly to transform the framework of American life and society. In the postwar years the railroads played the greatest role in the process of transformation and stood out as its clearest symbols. With bewildering speed what almost amounted in economic terms to a new nation was born, and difficult readjustments were bound to ensue. Middle-class groups, primarily merchants and farmers, adversely affected by unrestricted railroad activity, came to the conviction during the seventies that some check must be put upon the "robber barons" and "oppressive corporations," to use contemporary epithets.

Not only were direct economic interests involved in the group conflicts but the pattern of events late in the decade rudely disturbed the traditional vision of a middle-class American society. Revelation in 1877 of some aspects of Standard Oil's omnipotence, the violent railroad strikes of the same year, the California "Sand-Lot" movement culminating in the "radical" constitution of May 1879 (interpreted by the New

York *Times* as "Communism in California"), these and similar developments form the setting in which the Hepburn investigation took place. Pamphlets were issued entitled "Some of the Causes of Communism," [3] editorials in leading journals warned (in terms remarkably suggestive of twentieth-century Progressives) that the intelligent, self-respecting middle class was endangered "by the double-presence of a vulgar and selfish plutocracy and a reckless, unthinking mob," [4] and letters to newspapers attacking the Chamber of Commerce's position on railroads were signed "Anti-Communist." [5]

All over the country in that decade middle-class discontent and middle-class anxiety distinctly emerged. But for reasons that have been suggested in preceding chapters these phenomena were particularly pronounced in New York. Merchants and farmers of the Empire State were afflicted by more than the fears and grievances characteristic of their fellows across the nation. Above all, they felt the threat to their uniquely valuable location advantages — threatened, they were convinced, by selfish railroad magnates. It is this feature which appears best to explain why the center of railroad hostility was again located in New York.

In sharp contrast to the 1850's, the wealthy merchants of the metropolis as well as upstate farmers and urban interests now suffered from the exigencies of trunk-line competition. The result was a combination of forces against the roads more powerful than could be assembled in any other state of the Union. Led by New York City mercantile interests, a coalition including upstate farmers, millers, manufacturers, "friends of the canal," and a variety of groups at Buffalo shakily held together long enough to challenge railroad omnipotence in the late seventies and early eighties.

MERCANTILE INDICTMENT OF RAILROAD MANAGEMENT

For the most part, upstate grievances were more the outcome of an irresistible relocalization of economic activity than the result of railroad discrimination. Place discriminations stemming from competitive low through rates and monopolistic high local charges sped the process considerably, but technological progress and transportation innovations were the real difficulties confronting Genesee Valley wheat farmers and Rochester millers. Long-time economic trends dictated the westward movement of wheat, corn, livestock, etc., and the mills to grind that wheat into flour and slaughter houses to process the meat; only the most rigid pro rata legislation could have permanently retarded the shift.

Relative to the metropolis, a considerably different set of conditions operated. She still possessed unsurpassed locational advantages, and a half century of dominance as the nation's entrepôt gave her commerce a tremendous head start. As a result, economic innovations did not necessarily pose difficulties for New York unless accompanied by strong place discrimination. So great was the magnitude of the city's interests, however, that place discrimination was only one among a number of grievances. At different times in the decade emphasis shifted from one set of problems to another but none of them had disappeared by 1879; in fact, they all continued to exist for years thereafter.

A common thread ran through the various complaints against the railroads, which, with only one exception, were given full expression in the Hepburn inquiry. The roads were run, it was charged, solely to amass fortunes for their managers without any concern for the public, and they totally disregarded the interests of the commonwealth which had legally created them. Four distinct but interrelated categories of complaints may be separated out: excessively high costs of transportation, place discrimination, personal discrimination, and railroad arrogance and corruption.[6] Though the Hepburn inquiry did not give much attention to railroad corruption of governmental processes, the committee's *Report* dealing with other categories of complaints criticized in detail the "abuses . . . so glaring in their proportions as to savor of fiction rather than actual history." Actually, even the long-time opponents of the roads professed to be stunned by what was uncovered. To cite one example, the *Commercial Bulletin* wrote after only four days of testimony:

> If the Railroad Investigating Committee were to close its sessions to-day, it would have procured abundance of evidence to prove that the New York Central does far more in the way of unjust discrimination in freight charges than has ever been charged against it or dreamed of.[7]

And several days later the books of the Central subpoenaed by the committee, and never before available, showed that since January 1, 1879, alone, over six thousand special contracts had been made to favored firms.[8] These figures were all the more sensational because a joint letter from Presidents Vanderbilt and Jewett to the committee, written on April 18, 1879, indignantly denied that even *one* special contract was in force on either of their roads.[9] It was this kind of unprecedented, unchallengeable evidence which gave such impact to the investigation's findings, and later resulted, according to President W. J. Fowler of the National Farmers' Alliance, in making "the Hepburn report . . . the bible of our movement."[10]

Perhaps it would be helpful to recapitulate briefly some material presented in a preceding chapter. The immediate impetus for the Hepburn investigation stemmed from the slash in westbound rates out of Boston by the Grand Trunk in January 1878. The rates out of New York held firm for more than a month and, coming at the depths of the commercial depression, aroused wider excitement in the city than ever before. A special meeting held at the Chamber of Commerce to consider the matter was attended by an extraordinarily large number of leading merchants and financiers.[11] Charles S. Smith, a prominent banker, presented a preamble and resolution setting up a Special Committee on Railroad Transportation, and it was this body which led the city's fight against the railroads for several years thereafter.[12]

Smith's statement reveals that the Grand Trunk incident, settled a few days later, had a more lasting impact than its intrinsic importance warranted. Merchants did not want non-dividend paying rates, but they did want legislation which would prevent future discrimination whenever New York's commercial and railroad interests happened to be particularly antagonistic.[13]

With the unanimous adoption of Smith's resolution, and the establishment of the committee he recommended, the infiltration policy begun by the Cheap Transportation Association back in 1874 paid off handsomely. Three of its leaders (the organization was now known as the Board of Trade and Transportation) were made members of the Special Committee on Railroad Transportation of the Chamber.[14] They thereupon promptly proceeded to carry out their militant program in the name of the most conservative and respected commercial body in the United States. The Chamber of Commerce, not the Board of Trade and Transportation, now led the fight against the railroads, but Francis B. Thurber and his cohorts called the shots in both organizations.

Chauncey Depew, the New York Central's chief attorney and master lobbyist, was also present at the January 30 meeting and he promised that his road "was prepared to meet the merchants at every point." [15] Despite such assurances, the Chamber's railroad committee reported at another special meeting on February 28 that a conference with the railroad presidents had proved fruitless.[16] Since little could be done through persuasion, they presented a long report which documented the discrimination against the city and contained a resolution requesting the legislature to appoint a committee to inquire "what legislation, if any, is necessary to protect and extend the commerce of our State; also to inquire into and report concerning the power and obligations of the rail-roads chartered by the State." [17] It was not a coincidence that two weeks earlier the Board of Trade had approved a petition asking Congress to appoint a joint committee to investigate the workings of the interstate railroad system of the United States.[18] Apparently it was thought best to go slow in the Chamber regarding Congressional action. The Chamber's railroad committee report confined itself to noting that wise legislation would be equally in the interest of the railroads and the public, citing Tom Scott's and Albert Fink's views as confirmation of their position.[19] (The committee neglected to point out that a slight difference in opinion existed over what constituted "wise legislation.")

To bring about a legislative inquiry the railroad committee received authority to have a concurrent resolution introduced at Albany. Losing little time, a memorial to this effect was sent to the legislature on March 5, signed by the presidents of the Chamber of Commerce, the Importers' and Grocers' Board of Trade, the Board of Trade and Transportation, the mayor of New York, the president of the Board of Aldermen, and later endorsed by the Produce Exchange at its May 8 meeting.[20]

Just two days after the memorial was presented Simon Sterne made his annual argument before the Assembly Committee on Railroads in favor of the bill to create a board of railroad commissioners.[21] Sterne cited an editorial from the *Journal of Commerce* as proof that the bill was strongly supported by mercantile groups and that public opinion now favored a railroad commission. When the bill was first drawn, he said, the *Journal* and the leading commercial organizations of the city looked askance upon it as unwarranted interference with private property. The passage of time had caused the *Journal* to reverse its opinion, and the measure was now endorsed because railroads were obviously unable to operate fairly without supervision.[22]

The April 4 meeting of the Chamber provided further evidence that the metropolis was concerned with improving its position relative to transportation. Charles Smith, chairman of the railroad committee, reported that a successful petition had been presented to the Board of Aldermen in favor of granting the railroads certain privileges hitherto denied them. Other groups had sent in supporting petitions to an extent probably never before equaled in the city. "Your Committee estimate that the signers of these petitions represented a capital of two thousand millions, and employs upwards of three hundred thousand persons." Now that these terminal facilities had been granted, Smith went on to say, the railroads were left without excuse for the freight discriminations set forth in the February 28 report. Resolutions were unanimously adopted requesting the Central and the Erie to withdraw from any combination maintaining higher rates for New York shippers, to and from the West, than were given to Boston, Philadelphia, or Baltimore.[23]

Copies of these resolutions were sent to Vanderbilt and Jewett, and the former replied in a characteristic letter dated April 18. The letter — probably written by Chauncey Depew — took high ground and accused the Chamber of "a grave error" in the assumptions upon which its resolutions were based. Far from discriminating against New York, after a desperate struggle the railroads had finally succeeded in abolishing heretofore existing discriminations. Recognizing that this interpretation of the 1877 differential agreement was, to say the least, unique, the letter attempted to justify it in the following fashion:

This result [the 1877 agreement] placed the New York shipper upon an equal footing, and gave to him the same advantages as were enjoyed by the merchants of any rival city; certainly no more could reasonably be asked. To require the New York roads to carry freight to and from the West at a rate which would disregard the excess of cost of transportation from Philadelphia and Baltimore to and from foreign ports, would give to the New York merchants such advantages as would destroy the commerce of those cities. Their roads would not submit to this, nor would these cities permit them to, until they had been exhausted in the struggle to maintain a fair equilibrium.[24]

In other words, the fact that New York rates were deliberately set above other ports did not constitute discrimination because discriminating rates were balanced by the natural and cumulative advantages of the metropolis. A good case could be made for the necessity of discriminating against New York on grounds of broad national interest — and indeed has been right down to the present — but Vanderbilt (or Depew) denied that discrimination was discrimination. The merchants perversely insisted that it was discrimination for a railroad to award differential rates nullifying New York advantages which had nothing to do with railroads. And they promptly turned Vanderbilt's letter back upon him by arguing that it only proved the necessity for a "thorough investigation of the facts by the Legislature of the State, in order to shed a full flood of light upon this important subject."

It is difficult to see how the Vanderbilt position can be characterized as anything but sophistry. The Vanderbilts themselves, both father and son, had explicitly rejected any argument which deprived New York of its "natural advantages," and merchants were hardly disposed to forget those stirring slogans enunciated in 1876. Now the position was being taken that to preserve the pooling agreement — designed, the merchants insisted, to maintain high rates and thus permit 8 per cent dividends on grossly fictitious stock — the trunk lines had the right and the power to nullify permanently any and all transportation advantages the metropolis possessed or ever could hope to possess.

RAILWAYS IN RELATION TO PUBLIC AND PRIVATE INTERESTS

Apparently Vanderbilt's letter of April 18 was timed to anticipate a public address to be made the next day by Simon Sterne on the railroad problem. If such were the case, nothing could have been better calculated to give the address maximum effect. Early in January, Thurber had the Board of Trade vote to hold a meeting at which Sterne would draw attention to the need for governmental regulation. He particularly stressed that efforts should be made to get the coöperation of the "investing interests" in securing publicity.[25] Luckily for his plan, the difficulties begun by the Grand Trunk insured coöperation beyond Thurber's wildest expectations. Over seven hundred of the great merchants and financiers of the metropolis affixed their signatures to a petition asking Sterne to address them on these subjects, among others:

> During the past few years it has been gradually becoming more and more apparent that the rapid extension of our Rail-Road system has brought with it many abuses which exert an enormous influence upon society in its commercial and political aspects; that legislation for the protection of public interests has not kept pace with that designed to serve the special purposes of great Rail-Road corporations, and that in consequence, the methods and channels of trade are fast changing, and long vested interests are suffering from this cause. These changes are of so serious a character as to threaten the continued prosperity of our city, and its natural advantages are being neutralized by artificial and removable causes.[26]

The character of the signatures is what gives this invitation its significance. Among the 700 firms and individuals were Low, Harriman & Company, H. B. Claflin & Company, Phelps, Dodge & Company, Grinnell, Minturn & Company, W. R. Grace, and James M. Brown. Sterne "consented" and fixed April 19 as the date for an address on the "Railway in Its Relations to Public and Private Interests." [27] Approximately 800 persons attended, "mostly well known merchants and bankers." [28] What they heard was a long and well thought out indictment of railroad policy which Sterne was given the opportunity to prosecute a year later in his conduct of the Hepburn investigation. His major argument was that the peculiar nature of railroad enterprise made it an exception to the general laws of competition. Once insolvent a road "runs wild" and unless restrained eventually drives solvent rivals into bankruptcy.[29]

But, Sterne continued, however much railroads gained from combination, its effect had been to divert a growing amount of trade from New York City. Vanderbilt was guilty of "pure and simple nonsense" when he denied that the metropolis was being discriminated against. "To level, by artificial regulations, a corporation, person or city, having certain natural or acquired advantages, down to the place of its rivals is to discriminate most injuriously against the one having the advantages." [30]

The logical deduction drawn from Sterne's premises — and he was certainly stating the issues accurately — was that only government interference could prevent railroad magnates from usurping the power to sacrifice other men's property to protect their own. Sterne had few illusions that it was possible to solve the problem through individual state action, although he pressed for it as a first step. In effect, he argued that only a considerable centralization of power exercised by the federal government could be expected to cope with the great centralization of economic power necessarily involved in the railroad industry.[31]

An editorial printed several weeks later in the *Nation* on "Railway Management and New York Prosperity" affords an excellent illustration of the impact of Vanderbilt's letter and Sterne's address upon public opinion. No one could possibly dispute the *Nation's* adherence to *laissez faire* but it was shocked, at least momentarily, into tacit support of the position taken by Sterne and the Chamber of Commerce. Reviewing the development of New York's commercial supremacy, the editorial declared that the canal had given New York its first advantage and that the consolidation of the Central had been viewed as a means of maintaining the city's supremacy. Over the years it had appeared as though a natural monopoly had been established in New York's favor with the result that location and accumulated advantages were capitalized into real estate values. In severe tones, the *Nation* added:

> Now, after thirty-odd years of railway rivalry, the city of New York is deliberately told by the president of its leading line of railway that the combination which he and other New York railway presidents have made with lines to cities of sister States takes away the advantages thus far possessed by New York and puts its merchants upon the same plane of commercial opportunity with rival cities.[32]

About a week before the editorial appeared the assembly passed the inquiry resolution by the heavy majority of 86 to 20, another good indication of public feeling on the subject. Whether this large favorable vote suggested to the railroad managers the possibility of hasty restrictive legislation is not clear. At any rate, despite Vanderbilt's previous assurance that he would not oppose passage of the resolution, a strong undercurrent of opposition was experienced in the Senate. According to Thurber, the genial and experienced Chauncey Depew was in Albany a great part of the time the resolution was expected to come up in the Senate and remained until after adjournment.[33] A letter from John Kelly, the leader of Tammany Hall, to Chairman Smith of the Chamber's railroad committee, indicates that Depew — or unknown railroad benefactors — must have used potent blandishments to defeat the resolution. Kelly wrote that his telegraphed appeal to "our Senators" had been to no avail and he wanted Smith to know that he was not responsible for the final result. "Let the responsibility for its failure rest with them ['our Senators'] and I assure you that I can see no excuse for their actions."[34] Apparently, as early as 1878 the perceptive Tammany leader was preparing the ground for his alliance with the merchants which flowered in the early eighties.

Charles Smith was vacationing in Europe and it was F. B. Thurber who delivered the report of the railroad committee to the Chamber on June 6. Thurber reported the failure of the resolution and listed those senators who had voted "in the railroad interest." Four Democrats from

Brooklyn and Manhattan were singled out for particular censure as having "misrepresented and betrayed the interests of their constituents," and it was suggested that they resign. Other resolutions, unanimously adopted on the motion of Jackson S. Schultz and seconded by William E. Dodge, stated that the actions of the railroads showed that their methods of management would not bear the light, and called on all citizens to work for such an investigation as had just been defeated.[35]

One of the most interesting aspects of the report is that it demonstrated the thoroughly opportunistic spirit guiding the merchants in their fight against the roads. The vote in the Senate made it clear that legislation was going to be difficult to achieve unless upstate members were brought into line. But to attain this result it was necessary to win the farmers' support. Suddenly, the merchants who had been strongly opposed to the idea of pro rata saw its merits in another light, and hastened to register their new-found wisdom publicly.[36] Their rapid conversion was probably as sincere as the roads' charge a year later that the Chamber's activities were "a communistic movement against capital invested in railroads."

A "VULGAR PLUTOCRACY" AND MIDDLE-CLASS AGITATION

The cynical opportunism displayed in regard to pro rata points up one of the most difficult problems involved in analyzing the movement for railroad regulation, i.e., the motivation of its leaders. Material interests certainly were involved, but it is as certain that more than material interests were involved. There is little doubt that if Thurber agreed to call off his crusade against the roads he could now have easily secured highly favorable rates for himself, as other erstwhile militants had done. Moreover, in spite of the general depression, his own firm was making more money than ever and rapidly becoming one of the largest wholesale grocery houses in the world. Thurber's partners, particularly an older brother who headed the firm, were unhappy about his activities as a railroad reformer; not only was he unable to give full attention to business, but his health suffered from the strenuous regime of mixing groceries with agitation.[37]

Nor is Thurber the only example which might be mentioned in this connection. Thurber was called upon to take charge of the Chamber's railroad committee late in the spring of 1878 because the chairman, Charles S. Smith, suddenly retired from business and departed for London. Thurber feared that the railroads had forced his retirement and wrote a letter to this effect. Smith thanked his "Dear Friend" for expressing concern, but assured him that "the RR^d men had no part in this matter." The truth was that he had been in New York for 32 years without a vacation, that one of his family was in ill-health, etc.

But the final and controlling reason was that I have money enough well invested to live on just as well as I am now living without business, and I had determined to gratify some tastes which I have been nursing for years. I certainly gave up a magnificent business [private banker] with the regrets of all my partners. Perhaps I made a mistake but I am now enjoying my new-born freedom. *Bravo Bravo* for your work (RR[ds]) when I come home I will work with you as well, and as hard as I know how to do.[38]

A tentative line of speculation might be that the leaders of the New York antirailroad management campaign in the seventies were men more aroused to activity by abstract considerations of railroad ruthlessness and arrogance than by direct self-interest, men who felt that the traditional structure of American institutions was threatened by a "vulgar plutocracy," men who received greater satisfaction from thwarting the designs of railroad magnates than they did from more humdrum business activities. This is not to deny that their material interests were involved, either directly or indirectly, but it would seem to account for the dissimilar responses to railroad policy exhibited by individual New York merchants and business leaders. Such speculation is encouraged by the lack of widespread mercantile reaction to another letter written by Vanderbilt on June 25, 1878. Obviously unimpressed by the storm of criticism raised against his previous letter, and alert to ominous signs of an impending rate war, he strongly urged a policy of pooling as the only salvation of the roads.[39]

But a *Times* reporter interviewing merchants on the chorus of trunk-line statements clamoring for pools after Vanderbilt's letter quoted one (possibly Thurber) to this effect: "A grocer, who has a large business was full of indignation at the apathy evinced by merchants toward the railroad corporations." [40] Not one to content himself with denouncing apathy, Thurber had just founded an organization to do something about it. In June 1878 a number of gentlemen met at the Fifth Avenue Hotel and created the "Commercial and Industrial League." Declaring itself in favor of "Co-Operation for Self-Preservation," the League was intended to do "the purely political work" which would not legitimately come within the scope of action of the principal commercial bodies.[41] The Board of Trade and Transportation, originally conceived of in this light, had by now become a more orthodox mercantile organization, patterned after the Chamber of Commerce.

Apparently, the direct impetus for the League's creation was the defeat of the proposed legislative inquiry into railroad abuses. Corporate interests of the country acted as a solid force, Thurber maintained, and thereby influenced legislation to benefit themselves. Something had to be done to enable businessmen, property owners, and citizens generally to pool their influence in favor of men and measures favorable to their interests. In an age of organization and centralization of economic and political power, the public could no longer afford the luxury of individual action or inaction.[42]

For the most part, the men gathered at the Fifth Avenue Hotel had also participated in the founding of the Cheap Transportation Association five years before. There were some recruits, such as the leading merchants Jackson S. Schultz and C. C. Dodge of the Chamber of Commerce railroad committee who had become actively involved in railroad reform during the agitation earlier in the year. Nonetheless, the League apparently found it impossible to arouse the mass of merchants from what the *Times* called "the apathy of the 'respectable' and intelligent voter." [43] Just as the prominent agriculturalists pushing the Alliance had difficulty in convincing farmers that neglect of politics cost them dear, mercantile leaders were unable to make the "Commercial and Industrial League" a going concern — at least in their first attempt. In fact, it seems to have disappeared shortly after creation only to re-emerge several years later as the far more successful National Anti-Monopoly League.

CHAUNCEY DEPEW AND RAILROAD PUBLIC RELATIONS

The inability of mercantile and agricultural leaders to overcome public lethargy at a time of deep depression indicates that something more was necessary before a successful protest movement could be launched to challenge corporate power. Something more *was* provided in 1879 in the form of the Hepburn investigation. Interestingly, though it originated in depression, the investigation reached its climax after prosperity had returned late in the year. As the *Journal of Commerce* had pointed out back in 1878, Vanderbilt's reckless disregard for public opinion and public rights was heading him for a most extensive fall. "While Mr. Vanderbilt holds his high revels, there is a handwriting on the wall!" [44]

Part of the message was spelled out at the Chamber of Commerce meeting of February 6, 1879. Again a memorial was unanimously adopted setting forth the grave abuses existing in railroad management and requesting a thorough investigation.[45] This time the merchants showed more flexibility in their tactics. It soon became clear that the state Senate — afterwards judged to be "the worst that ever sat in Albany" [46] — was still not disposed to intrude on the privacy of railroad management. Accordingly, the assembly alone was asked to set up an investigating committee and a resolution to that effect passed on February 28. Having concentrated their efforts on the small number of senators, the roads were outmaneuvered and the Hepburn inquiry officially launched.[47]

But the resolution was drawn in such general terms that the committee felt its first task was to determine the extent and manner in which to carry it out. A letter addressed to commercial organizations and local officials throughout the state asked them to prefer charges against the railroads in Albany on March 26.[48] Since the Chamber of Commerce was recognized to have brought the inquiry about, it was the first group called upon to present suggestions. On behalf of the Chamber, Thurber read a prepared statement containing five specific areas of complaints: place discrimination, personal discrimination, excessive rates, disregard of stockholders' rights, and "general lack of that publicity and responsibility to the public which properly belong to organizations exercising a great public function like that of operating public highways." [49]

Although the Chamber's statement formed the essential basis around which the inquiry was conducted, the Board of Trade and Transportation felt some points had been overlooked and presented 28 specific subjects for investigation. In addition, statements were received from the Buffalo Board of Trade, the Oswego Board of Trade, the New York State Millers Association, a representative of Orange County milk producers, the Onondaga Farmers' Club, the Kings County Milk Exchange, and a representative of the Albany Lumber Dealers.[50] The Produce Exchange sent a revealing letter, which, as the committee later commented, "plainly expressed on the part of a powerful body of merchants, an unwillingness to disclose abuses they know to exist, because there is no power permanently to stand between them and the railroads with whom they must deal and who would doubtless make them pay for their disclosure by increasing their rates or by cancelling special contracts." [51]

The railroads were not represented at the hearing, but on April 18, 1879 — exactly one year after the Vanderbilt letter telling New York it had to accept the pool — Presidents Vanderbilt and Jewett of the New York Central and Erie railroads, respectively, replied in a joint letter to the charges made against them by the Chamber of Commerce.[52] (It was commonly understood that Chauncey Depew was the real author of the 48-page letter.) Thus, the issue was specifically joined as a contest between the roads and the Chamber, a rather bad blunder on the roads' part. It is also of some importance in the history of railroad regulation that Depew in this letter — and in other public statements — employed obvious untruths and unpleasant innuendos which only served to put the railroad case in its worst possible light and appeared to be proof of railroad arrogance and deceit.[53]

Emphasis is warranted that in important aspects of the controversy the roads were clearly right and the merchants and farmers clearly wrong. In an era of Communication Revolution it was really impossible to cling to the illusion that trunk lines were dedicated to the service of certain local interests in their war against all other local interests. Neither merchants nor farmers even remotely attempted to present a program designed to cope with the problems of *all* the groups vitally affected by railroad development. And merchants and farmers were unreasonable in simultaneously calling for free railroad competition and protesting against the discriminations which inevitably accompanied unrestricted competition. (The fact that the railroad managers had no workable proposals either, and were equally indifferent to the general welfare, is true but irrelevant here.)

The joint letter made these points, but its general tone and much of its content did something more than nullify them; it played directly into the hands of Thurber and his co-workers. They could quote conservative papers such as the *Evening Post* and *Journal of Commerce* to the effect that the letter "offensively impugned" the intelligence and motives of the Chamber, was "impertinent," and made "sneering objections." [54] As a result, the valid opposition of the roads to the policies advocated by metropolis and interior could be ignored and attention centered on the weak aspects of the railroad case.

Merchants and farmers were not merely interested in having the roads operated in the public interest generally; they wanted them operated in their interest almost exclusively. The Communication Revolution had resulted in the sharpest kind of competition between New York merchants and those in Boston, Philadelphia and Baltimore, and between New York farmers and those at the West. Under these conditions, Empire State interests looked to the Central and Erie for aid. With a global economy rapidly developing, however, the roads could hardly be expected to play the role of local carriers and subject their operations to the resultant handicaps. Notwithstanding, upstate interests insisted that their earlier "natural location" advantages be preserved at all costs and a protective tariff of stiff pro rata adopted; the metropolis sought to maintain and extend its near-monopoly of the country's commerce and protested vigorously against port differentials. Yet the difficulties inherent in the port differentials, for example, are best indicated by the fact that the controversy is carried on to this day and that New York commercial interests are still denouncing them.[55]

RAILROADS ARE PUBLIC ESTABLISHMENTS

The most interesting aspect of the joint letter was its denial that the state could in any way regulate railroads so as to diminish the earnings allowed them under their original charters. Without mentioning the Dartmouth College case by name, the doctrines laid down there were echoed and charters were held to be perpetual contracts. "The citizens building the railroads have . . . a strong claim to all the profits that may come to them under their contract with the State. This contract cannot be violated by the State." [56]

That the roads should have believed this to be a tenable position in 1879 is remarkable. After the Supreme Court's Dartmouth College decision of 1819, various states took alarm and either by general laws, or by constitutional amendment, provided that the legislature should, at all times, have the power to alter, amend, or repeal the rights or privileges conferred upon corporations. Having had a law to that effect for many years on its statute books, in 1846 New York embodied such a provision in its constitution. The western states, on their organization, substantially followed the New York lead. Subsequently, in the famous Granger cases of 1876, the Supreme Court upheld the right of states to pass legislation altering charter rights or privileges of railroads. (Other legal decisions to the same effect, however, were cited by advocates of regulation before and after *Munn v. Illinois*.) Thus, in 1879, the Central and the Erie took a position which disregarded the Supreme Court decision, the New York constitution, and the real facts of economic life in the late nineteenth century. They claimed that the original charters granted under entirely different economic conditions were fixed and immutable. In reality, despite lip service to the contrary, they went further. As the *Evening Post* commented two months later regarding attempts by Depew to keep railroad books secret:

The ground of this mistaken attitude is a false notion of the nature of railroads and their business — the notion that they are private establishments, and their affairs are and ought to be matters of secrecy. Railroads are public establishments.[57]

Not content with having set themselves above governmental "interference," the roads went on to issue a blanket denial of any and all abuses charged to them by the Chamber of Commerce. They even went so far as to maintain that they had not opposed the legislative investigation and were not guilty of personal discrimination.[58]

The charge which roused Vanderbilt and Jewett to greatest indignation, however, was that liberal quantities of "water" existed in the capitalization of their roads and that rates were kept up to pay dividends and interest on such fictitious capital. First of all, they insisted, there was not any watered stock in the Central or the Erie. The Chamber was challenged to prove that increases in stock did not represent profits plowed back into the enterprise. Speaking on behalf of the two most notoriously watered roads in the country, they asserted:

As a fact, the ordinary dividends earned, instead of being paid to the stockholders, were used by the company, and paid out for new construction and equipment, and the stock was issued to represent such construction and equipment.[59]

Moreover, Vanderbilt and Jewett continued, they had a perfect right to keep up rates to pay dividends on unrestricted issues of stock if they chose to do so.

As to rates being kept up to pay dividends on 'watered stock' it may be said that so long as the law exists permitting a railroad company to make certain charges for the transportation of freight and passengers such company would have the right to fix the charges at the highest rate permitted by their charter irrespective of the question of the amount of stock issued and there is no power that can alter the contract without the assent of the railroad companies.[60]

Here they not only disregarded the Supreme Court, the New York constitution, and the changes in the economics of transportation since their charters had been issued, they disregarded the charters themselves. As the merchants never tired of pointing out, Section 33 of the General Railroad Act of 1850 — the Act which governed the issuance of charters and applicable to charters already in existence — explicitly limited profits to 10 per cent "upon the capital of the corporation actually expended" in construction.[61] Watering stock may not have been illegal but paying dividends on such stocks plainly violated the law. Therefore, the question of the amount of stock issued was quite pertinent to the amount of profits permitted to railroads. The legal 10 per cent limitation, it deserves to be noted, destroyed any argument for increasing capitalization on the possible basis of replacement costs, increased earning power, superior management, good will, etc.[62] But the above considerations were purely theoretical, according to the railroad presidents, and had nothing to do with rates.

Competition fixes rates without regard to the amount of any company's stocks or bonds. The five lines from Chicago bid for traffic, and no line can procure any part of it except at the price made by the cheapest route. Thus the sum which the company can net from the business is the same, whether its capital is large or small; if too great, it is the sufferer in diminished dividends.[63]

On this page of the letter trunk-line competition was held to ensure reasonable rates; the public would be protected and only stockholders damaged if watering were liberally employed. Several pages later, however, the warning is found that trunk-line competition was an unmitigated calamity to them and to everyone else! So disastrous, in fact, that pools had to be resorted to in order to protect all interests.[64] The Nickel Plate and the West Shore were soon to teach William H. Vanderbilt an expensive lesson concerning the benefits of pools, but here the relevant point is that pools obviously abolished competitive rates. Without competition every inducement existed to set rates high enough to pay profits on watered stock — an inducement, the merchants charged, to which the railroads succumbed. This situation, together with differentials designed to maintain such rates, was the heart of the mercantile objection to pools. A reasonable objection, the Chamber's statement on the subject had nonetheless provoked Vanderbilt and Jewett to denounce its "destructive, communistic characteristics," and to cite it as an example of the "growing tendency to socialistic principles . . . [which] if not checked, will produce scenes of disaster that would now appal [*sic*] the country." [65]

What the eminently conservative Chamber had said to bring on these charges of subversive activity was that railroad capital contained about 50 per cent water, and, since pools were the only method by which rates could be kept up to pay returns on such fictitious securities, if it were decided that these rates were unfair to the public, prohibition of pooling would be the most direct way to lower them. [66] The Chamber had also charged that pools to pay profits on fictitious capital led to discriminatory rates diverting trade from New York City. Attempting to justify differentials and pools, Vanderbilt and Jewett were forced into the awkward position of defending differentials on the basis of distance from the West — a position Vanderbilt had managed to avoid in his 1878 letter. Overlooking the cost factors actually involved, they meekly accepted the views of the Pennsylvania and the Baltimore & Ohio managers "that in justice to the exporting cities they represent" the difference in mileage to Philadelphia and Baltimore entitled them to lower rates than to New York. [67]

Such terminology was particularly unfortunate because it led to the inference that New York roads did not represent *their city* as the more southerly lines did — precisely the charge made against them by the merchants. This interpretation was hardly softened by the admission that since the other roads would not yield, Vanderbilt and Jewett felt that they must do so in order to avoid widespread railroad bankruptcy. And to make an exceedingly untactful letter even more unpalatable, they went on to assert that New York would not be affected by the "small difference" if "the present race of merchants have the energy and business wisdom that has characterized their predecessors." [68]

Since the presidents accepted the distance argument as justifying increased costs to New York merchants, how could they refuse to accept the same argument made by New York farmers and millers demanding pro rata freights? Here they reversed their ground entirely and called upon the upstate areas to suffer so that the commerce of New York City would benefit. If the New York State legislature adopted some form of pro rata and Pennsylvania and Maryland did not, the Central and Erie could not compete for western produce and trade would be diverted from the metropolis. To avoid such a calamity the people of the State of New York were urged not

to prevent the railway companies in the State from carrying through freight from beyond the western boundaries of the State to its chief city at less rates per ton per mile than they charge to the people within the limits of the State, even with the acknowledged fact that through such rates the people of the State cannot compete in prices with the productions thus brought within their State, and that great interests are thereby sacrificed and that the cultivation of many acres of good ground must be abandoned, the great mills which once converted the grain into flour must be abandoned, and many other interests suffer greatly.[69]

All this in the interests of the commerce of New York City — and in the same letter telling New York City to accept differentials based on distance, which diverted trade to Baltimore and Philadelphia. Gleefully, the merchants leaped upon the contradictory arguments and Sterne later taunted the roads with the charge that whenever their interests made it necessary for them to talk of distance "they are more ultra *pro rata* freightists than any member of the granges of the interior of the State of New York." [70] The frank plea for self-destruction to the upstate farmers and millers confirmed their worst possible fears and gave them every incentive to side with the metropolis against the roads. Obviously, it obliterated the position that only a small group of selfish merchants were opposed to railroad policies and that no real cause existed for other citizens to fight F. B. Thurber's grocery battles. Chauncey Depew continually attempted to present the question in this guise, as his statement some weeks later illustrates: "If F. B. Thurber should die to-night this inquiry would stop." [71]

But the joint letter provided the best possible proof that the interior of the state was to be sacrificed in the interests of the railroads, and a parade of farmers, millers, lumber dealers, etc., was staged by Sterne during the hearings to underscore the point again and again.[72] Commercial papers of New York supporting the merchants were mournful when they contemplated the sad plight of the farmers. Railroad managers unfairly discriminated against them, and western farmers located on cheap, fertile lands were able to drive them out of their home markets. Even the strongly prorailroad *Commercial Advertiser* warned that the Farmers' Alliance was composed of solid Republicans who "are earnest men, with an old grievance, and mean business." Significantly, in the light of later events, it also pointed out that "the country has been flooded with documents by the Board of Trade and Transportation intended to 'fire the hearts' of every farmer against the railroads." [73]

and personnel possessing the knowledge, training, experience, and judiciousness to do the job well were non-existent. Perhaps the best perspective to adopt in regard to the Hepburn inquiry is that it represented a pioneering attempt to deal with some key problems of modern political economy; problems posed by a dynamic industrial society which necessarily engenders conflicts of interest between different economic groups in the course of its operations.

Despite nominal control by the Hepburn Committee, Simon Sterne, chosen by the commercial organizations to expose what they regarded as railroad malpractices, actually directed the course of the entire proceedings and was given almost a free hand. The merchants could not have asked anything more. Sterne was their legal representative and also, in effect, the state's attorney to prosecute the indictment his co-worker Thurber had drawn up. Every question the merchants had wanted answered by the roads they would now have to answer, and under oath. All the books and evidence they wanted to examine could now be subpoenaed. All the witnesses they wanted to summon could be summoned, and at times and places calculated to have the greatest effect. Little wonder that the merchants "accepted" the responsibility and agreed to assume the expense of employing counsel to conduct the investigation. What is puzzling is that the roads agreed to the procedure.

At the start it was expected by the merchants that the hearings would not take more than two or three weeks and that expenses would be insignificant. But the blanket denial of the roads concerning the existence of abuses, and their insistence that only a small group of selfish individuals were interested, dictated a different course. It resulted in the investigation's taking the better part of eight months, with hearings held from one end of the state to the other.[2] Nothing could have better suited the purposes of the merchants, although they apparently had not planned it that way. Instead of only achieving intense but short-term attention, the long months of testimony built up a cumulative force that could not have been matched otherwise. The scope of the investigation was so wide and the disclosures so startling that interest never lagged. Practically every journal in New York City (and a good many upstate ones) covered the hearings day by day so that it was almost impossible for newspaper readers to remain unacquainted with the evidence.[3] The Greenback fever was dying out, no presidential canvass was in progress, and the indictment of the Standard Oil Company in Pennsylvania only added spice to the legislative inquiry in New York. In sum, no overpowering competition existed for newspaper space, and public attention was not distracted from the case built up by Sterne.

Apart from the nature of the evidence, the sources from which it was drawn contributed greatly to the impact of the investigation. By late August the roads were definitely on the defensive and assuming the unaccustomed pose of "martyrs and victims" of legislative persecution.[4] Embarrassment among railroad managers was profound, for one of the inquiry's striking features was the extent to which Vanderbilt claimed to be ignorant of his own road's operations in particular, and the facts of economic life in general.[5] Mercantile objections to railroad policy had always been met with the taunt that they were the vaporings of "dreamers," "theorists," "doctrinaires," that is, men who had no "practical experience" in railroading. Now the chief target of these gibes, Sterne, had William H. Vanderbilt, the president of one of the great railroad systems, on the stand. Vanderbilt could not have been as ignorant as he made himself out to be, but the damaging effect upon claims of railroad omniscience was the same. Bitingly sarcastic editorials could take as their text "What Mr. Vanderbilt Does Not Know."

For example, Vanderbilt did not know that six thousand special contracts existed on the Central; that ocean rates were the same from the various ports but that differentials were granted, based on the assumption that they were cheaper from New York; whether the Central's traffic had increased or decreased; how much traffic was local and how much through; the actual costs of carrying freight (operating costs); what rates were profitable to the road; how railroad grades or density of traffic affected cost; what rates Standard Oil paid on his road; why some people got special rates and others did not; and a long list of other gaps in his knowledge of his railroad could be given.[6]

THE MERCHANTS VINDICATED

Vanderbilt may not have known the answers to vital questions but a steady parade of witnesses were summoned who did — or thought they did. The three phases of the investigation which probably raised the loudest tumult and the deepest indignation were discriminatory rates, stock watering, and Standard Oil. On the first two the presidents of the roads were particularly vulnerable because they had explicitly denied any such practices had ever taken place. As Sterne took keen pleasure in pointing out at the close of the inquiry, considering the real state of facts, "Nothing short of fatuity or an absolute and blind reliance upon this committee's not doing its duty ever could have induced men, situated as Messrs. Jewett and Vanderbilt then were, to sign that document." [7]

Sterne could afford to gloat. The freight agent of the New York Central had conceded that fifty per cent of the local traffic was carried at special rates — rates so low that their recipients had marked advantages over smaller competitors not similarly blessed. Substantial depreciation of the value of farm land, due largely to the wide disparity of through and local rates, was shown again and again, and the harmful effects upon Rochester millers and Buffalo commission men received full attention. Relative to New York City, Vanderbilt was forced to concede that if ocean rates were not cheaper from the metropolis — the theory he had used in part to justify differentials — as the evidence showed they were not, then the merchants had a legitimate cause for complaint.

Inquiry into stock watering enabled Sterne to rake up every financial skeleton in the Erie and Central closets — and there were enough skeletons to fill a good-sized cemetery. No two estimates drawn from the evidence presented at the hearings agreed upon the combined total; they ranged from a minimum of $100,000,000 to $180,000,000 of fictitious securities. Even the latter figure may have been an understatement.[8] And in flat contradiction to the claim that all stock represented "construction and equipment," Edwin Worcester, secretary of the Central, coolly and explicitly explained how $45,000,000 of water had been added during the 1869 consolidation of the New York Central and the Hudson River railroads.[9] The Hepburn Committee was charitable in its report and accepted the estimate that only $9,000,000 of water had been pumped into the two roads before consolidation; that is, it found that a total of $53,500,000 in the New York Central and Hudson River Railroad stock (bonds were not touched upon) represented nothing except imagination and audacity. But the report avowedly was not concerned with determining the exact amount of fictitious securities because it took the position that their "validity is beyond the power of courts or legislature to attack." [10]

Since the Erie was bankrupt, at least the public was spared the necessity of paying interest and dividends upon its fictitious securities. The Central was a different matter. Vanderbilt's leading idea, repeatedly expressed, was that railroads were entitled to earn a fair profit on the capital invested.[11] By fair profit he meant 8 per cent on stock, and by capital he meant stock of $90,000,000 (in round figures) and funded indebtedness of $40,000,000.

Disregarding the bonds — also largely fictitious — the Central paid regular annual dividends of over $7,000,000.[12] This amount was paid on stock which even Secretary Worcester conceded was 50 per cent water. As noted above, the Hepburn report also found that $9,000,000 had been added to the stock upon the original consolidation of the New York Central in 1853. But it assumed that the $23,000,000 capital of the roads consolidated in 1853 represented real investment. Six years earlier, George O. Jones had demonstrated to the Windom Committee that only about $6,000,000 was actually spent in the construction of the several roads combined into the Central in 1853. Accepting Jones' argument that the Hudson River Railroad had been free of water in 1869, at best

The Iron Hand

$20,000,000 of the New York Central and Hudson River Railroad's stock represented actual cash investment, but Vanderbilt insisted on the right and necessity to pay 8 per cent dividends on $90,000,000.[13]

Sterne seized upon an argument made by Depew to emphasize the huge "tax" paid upon such stock by New York State. Depew in his closing statement to the committee stated that the rate wars on through traffic between 1875 and 1877 had cost the New York roads from four to five million dollars — a sacrifice, he coolly declared, suffered only to preserve the metropolis' commercial advantages. And he berated the merchants for ingratitude in not helping the roads to sustain such loss.[14] Unfortunately for Depew, Sterne could point out that the New York Central — even while losing huge sums of money on its through traffic according to its own attorney — paid dividends amounting to $14,500,-000 during the two-year rate war. Thus, the local traffic had made up all the deficits resulting from trunk-line competition, and the Central had paid the regular 8 per cent dividend on heavily watered stock. The extent of this "tax" upon New York could best be judged, Sterne trumpeted, by remembering that both the Pennsylvania and the Baltimore & Ohio had been forced to pass their dividends during the rate war.[15]

Shocking as was the proof of stock-watering and discrimination in general, the favoritism shown Standard Oil in particular may well have had the greatest effect upon public opinion. Hundreds of pages of testimony were taken — mostly from the railroad officials directly involved — which thereafter constituted an almost inexhaustible supply of ammunition against railroad management and corporate monopoly. The interpretation placed by Sterne upon the significance of Standard Oil is extensively reproduced here as an illustration of the reasoning by which erstwhile strong supporters of *laissez faire* became committed to government intervention in the late nineteenth century, and of the emotional language in which they couched their arguments.[16]

This chapter of American railway history exhibits the most shameless perversion of the duties of a common carrier to private ends that has taken place in the history of the world. It exhibits more clearly than any other example could have exhibited the fact that railway charges are in the nature of taxes and the description given by the Supreme Court of the United States of the power of taxation, that it is the power to destroy, is absolutely true of railway tariffs . . .

Except in so far as the railway officers who have an actual interest in, and honestly mean to manage in that interest their railway, may be taught a lesson by the results of their Standard Oil arrangements, which may, at least, deter them from attempting to repeat their experience again, what is there to prevent the creation of like monopolies in any other product of our country? . . .

The railway charge is so important an element in the price of every commodity that is carried from a distance in the United States and intended for export, that it is within the power of our railway magnates to become partners in every special line of occupation, and it is this power to destroy and to build up which no community can allow to roam and exercise itself unchecked, which must be restrained, curbed and rendered subservient to the general public weal through the instrumentality of wise legislation rigidly enforced.[17]

VANDERBILT BOWS TO PUBLIC OPINION

In the absence of a rigorous methodology upon which there is consensus, the state of public opinion is almost always subject to such widely varying interpretations that it is difficult to "prove" the result of the Hepburn Committee's work in 1879. Any researcher who so desires can appear to find "evidence" to support almost any position he wants to take. Nonetheless, the reactions displayed by politicians, merchants, and William H. Vanderbilt to the impact of the investigation makes it clear that they, at least, held similar opinions on the subject.

Politicians' views are evident from the party platforms adopted in September 1879. Cynics may hold to the belief that party platforms do not necessarily express the fervent convictions of their architects; no one can deny that they reflect their architects' convictions on what the voters want to hear. It is therefore instructive to sketch briefly the history of the railroad regulation plank from 1876 on.

In that Presidential year none of the major parties felt it necessary to pledge their sacred word to curb transportation abuses; more significantly, neither did the Greenbackers think it worth mention. In fact, as late as February 1878 the national platform of the Greenback party was silent on the subject. However, the National Greenback Labor Platform adopted at Syracuse on July 24, 1878 (in reality, the New York organization under a more grandiose title) called for a railroad inquiry similar to that proposed by the New York Chamber of Commerce. In September 1878 the Democrats confined themselves to noting that "corporations chartered by the state [are] always subject to State supervision in the interest of the people," and the Republicans ignored the topic.[18] What a difference a year meant! In 1879 both parties went unequivocally on record that, in the words of the Republicans, "it is the clear province and the plain duty of the State to supervise and regulate . . . [moneyed and transportation] corporations as to secure the just and impartial treatment of all interested . . ."; the Democratic version, "the railroads prohibited by law from unjust discrimination, and from favoring localities or individuals." [19]

Strong planks promulgated by politicians cheered the merchants and, together with other indications of progress, filled them with buoyant optimism. Thurber was then in England recuperating from his labors, and private letters to him leave no doubt of the real feelings of the

merchant leaders. A. B. Miller, who in Thurber's absence was running
the Board of Trade and Transportation, jubilantly reported early in
September:

friend Sterne has sustained our cause nobly. Literally placed the RR Kings
'hors du Combat'. You will notice by the printed reports of the investigation
[enclosed] which convey but a feeble impression of the investigation — that
Mr. Vanderbilt as well as Jewett *claim to be in* favor of Governmental regulation [federal not state] which is certainly a great change of tune.[20]

Ten days later, after the political conventions, with John Kelly of
Tammany Hall running as an independent, Miller drew these optimistic
conclusions:

We now have three tickets or rather four nominations for Governor &
three State tickets . . . which each have pronounced for Railway supervision
on the part of the State. I think therefore that we have occasion to feel that
our efforts have not been without results, which in the near future must be
productive of fruits.[21]

Charles Smith, chairman of the Chamber's Committee on Railroad
Transportation, was even more unrestrained:

Depew and Jewitt [*sic*] treated me with *respect* in Saratoga [at a hearing
there]. *Entre nous* they are on their knees. We *shall* get all *we want*. The
two political platforms *have endorsed* our action —[22]

We are not as fortunate in being privy to William H. Vanderbilt's
inner thoughts. He may have exaggerated in stating that he owned 87
per cent of the Central stock, as he has been quoted as saying, but there
can be no doubt that he owned an unusually high proportion, high
enough to make it in effect a "one-man road." [23] By way of contrast, the
Erie's securities had passed on to thousands of "innocent holders," including of course the traditional "widows and orphans." Attacks upon
the Erie, therefore, were inhibited to some extent by these considerations, but attacks upon the Central received particular impetus from the
realization that one man virtually owned, controlled, and profited from
its heavily watered stock. The action of both major political parties —
parties that could not in any sense be regarded as radical — was a
significant sign of the times.

According to the later recollections of J. P. Morgan's son-in-law,
Depew warned Vanderbilt that New York was tired of having its main
road controlled by one man and advised him to sell part of his holdings.[24]
Though memoirs are notoriously unreliable, this fits in with Vanderbilt's
contemporary public statement that he desired "to get other people to
help him bear the brunt of popular criticism and legislative inquiry." [25]
In that depression year, it might be remembered, "Communism" had

won out in California, and even the conservative Chamber of Commerce took a position favoring the destruction of a good share of railroad capital.

A pamphlet entitled "Some of the Causes of Communism," almost certainly written by F. B. Thurber, may have been a factor influencing Vanderbilt's final decision to sell. Distributed in the midsummer of 1879 under the signature of "Average Citizen," it was an elaboration of an earlier pamphlet bearing the same title. Drawing upon the evidence turned up by the railroad investigation, and sprinkled liberally with quotations from leading papers such as the New York *Times,* Albany *Journal,* etc., it is an excellent analysis of the discontent then stirring the American people. One quotation vividly illustrates the symbolic role assigned William H. Vanderbilt by men attempting to organize that discontent into effective channels. The pamphlet which contains the quotation deserves special attention since Thurber was generally conceded to be the "chief promoter" of hostility toward railroad power, and appears to be the leading figure in the middle-class movements against corporation domination during the late seventies and early eighties.[26]

The means which Mr. Vanderbilt has to perpetuate and extend his power are yearly increasing . . . [details of Vanderbilt's interests and income]. With such a capital and such an income, there is practically no end to Mr. Vanderbilt's power, and the time must come in the near future, when a limit shall in some manner be placed upon it, or it will dictate to the agriculturist, manufacturer and merchant what share of the profits they shall derive from their various vocations, as it now does to the laborer the compensation which it will award for a given service.[27]

Thurber's concluding paragraph effectively deflates sensational treatments of economic discontent after the Civil War, and accurately reflects the conservative nature of those movements against corporate domination of American life.

The American Republic has survived the storms and troubles of a hundred years. Whether or not it will exist for another century will depend largely upon the making and execution of our laws. It is, perhaps, not strange that legislation for the protection of the public interest should have failed to keep pace with the enormous changes which steam, electricity and machinery have wrought — all within a half-century, and it is the abuses attending the employment of these great forces which have caused the manifestations popularly known as 'Communism,' but which to a great extent, is simply the well grounded dissatisfaction of the 'Average Citizen'.

With this type of sentiment growing as the Hepburn investigation unfolded, Vanderbilt and his advisers faced unpleasant prospects. Even if the pool were not broken by government action, the Hepburn Committee's views to the contrary, steps might be taken to repeal the Consolidation Act of 1869 legalizing the late Commodore's midnight watering operation; or George Jones' plan of 1872 to reduce railroad capitalization to the amount actually expended "in good faith" might be revived. Vanderbilt's concentrated holdings would be the chief target of such plans, as well as their chief inspiration. Railroad officials and attorneys certainly dwelt upon the immorality of legislative "confiscation" of property strongly enough in 1879 to suggest that they really were concerned with the possibility.

Other reasons have been suggested for Vanderbilt's taking the advice supposedly given by Depew; yet it is difficult to believe that desire to disarm public hostility heightened by the Hepburn investigation was not a controlling factor. If a goodly number of "innocent holders," "widows and orphans," etc., owned a large interest in New York Central, a much better basis would exist for protesting against the destruction of thousands of "happy homes." Vanderbilt may well have been reluctant to part with stock that had paid dividends in and out of rate-war season, but on November 26, 1879, he concluded negotiations whereby J. P. Morgan took 250,000 New York Central shares from his burdens. That he was not pressed for funds to carry out any plans he might have been considering is clear because the $30,000,000 he received for the stock was invested in government bonds.[28]

Morgan's handling of the Vanderbilt stock sale further paved the way for one of the more important developments in modern American history — the active domination by the financier of large-scale corporate enterprise in general, and railroads in particular. Later it will be necessary to consider the impact of this development upon railroad regulation; here the point is that the Hepburn investigation played a definite part in speeding up the process after the rate wars of the seventies had intensified bankers' distrust of railroad officials' ability to manage the properties "soundly."

LEGISLATION IS MORE DIFFICULT THAN EXPOSURE

J. P. Morgan's son-in-law may have been correct in stating that Depew advised the sale, but the latter's closing statement before the Hepburn Committee a day after that event reveals that he, at least, kept up a bold front in public. Depew's richly imaginative style is impossible to recapture by paraphrase or by illustration, and only a reading of the original does full justice to his talents. Some hint of it may be conveyed by noting that he insisted the testimony showed no proof of watered stock or proof of railroad discrimination, and claimed that the people of New York had demonstrated during the course of the hearing that they were perfectly satisfied with railroad management.[29] Not to be outdone by his colleague, Judge Shipman representing the Erie praised the roads' conduct, denied that there was anything in the New York

Constitution or in the findings of the Supreme Court which permitted the state to regulate them, and warned darkly against "the paternal theory of government."[30]

Practicing politicians, possibly more experienced at diagnosing the public temperature than Depew and Shipman, and whose business interest was politics, not railroads, thought the situation called for large doses of soothing syrup. The new governor, Alonzo B. Cornell, a stalwart of the Roscoe Conkling stripe of Stalwart, made it clear in his first annual message that he believed some legislative action, or at least some legislative attention, was necessary. Although he confined himself to generalizations, his message indicates the experienced politician's awarness that it was no longer possible to ignore the question, or to deny the state's power to regulate railroads.[31] The Republican convention of 1879, dominated by Stalwart professionals, had written a platform far more attuned to the popular clamor than the notes struck by Chauncey Depew in opposition to state "interference." And in the judgment of the *Times* the railroad lawyers were making a serious mistake in lecturing, in effect, "that the management is perfect, and that evidence which has called forth indignation from one end of the State to the other is unworthy of attention."[32]

Having taken more than 4,000 pages of testimony, the Hepburn hearings officially closed on December 19. The committee's report was given to the Assembly in January 1880, just two years after the original flurry of agitation in the Chamber of Commerce. It was not completely valueless to the roads for it cleared up some erroneous impressions in relation to alleged abuses. Thus, the Albany Bridge, the Fast Freight Lines, the Sleeping Car Companies, the Express Companies, and several leased roads were absolved of the "parasitic" charges formerly hurled at them. The early "inside rings" that fed on railroads, the committee found, had been generally done away with, except for stock yard companies and grain elevators. Aside from these two categories, the committee sustained the managers' claims to honest and efficient operations of subsidiary organizations.[33] On every other count, however, the *Report* strongly supported the indictment drawn by the Chamber of Commerce.

Watered Stock, Standard Oil Company, Proxies, Annual Report to the State Engineer and Surveyor, Discriminations (place and personal), all were headings under which glaring need was found for correction. The position taken by the railroad attorneys that the state had no power to intervene was found to be wholly without merit. On the contrary, "the legislature has not only the power to regulate the transportation of freight and passengers upon our railroads, but it has the power to regulate the charges of all other persons or corporations whose functions are, by lease or contract with the railroads, made a necessary link in the chain of transportation." [34] Holding to such views, the Hepburn Committee recommended a series of seven bills to remedy the proved abuses. Briefly, they were to this effect (although different language was employed):

1. Amendment of the General Railroad Act of 1850 to regulate the manner in which capital stock could be increased.

2. Regulation of the consolidation of railroad companies (particularly to prevent repetition of Commodore Vanderbilt's financial feats).

3. Regulation of voting by proxy to insure that only actual owners issued them, and forbidding the sale of proxies.

4. Regulation of the freight transportation by railroads, usually spoken of as "The Anti-Discrimination Bill."

5. Creation of a Board of Railroad Commissioners similar to the Massachusetts Act but with even less power.

6. Provision for a detailed description of the form of the Annual Report by the railroads to the state engineer and surveyor.

7. Closure of the legal loopholes by which the elevated railroad stocks had been inflated.

With the introduction of these seven bills on January 22, 1880,[35] the first phase of the Hepburn investigation may be said to have closed. The next phase, the struggle to achieve such legislation, can be dated from the Chamber of Commerce meeting on February 5. There, the railroad committee gave its report on the results of the railroad inquiry and submitted several resolutions which were unanimously adopted.[36] Both political parties were called upon to redeem their pledges and enact the Hepburn bills without delay, though these bills were judged to be more conservative and less thorough than the evidence warranted. Moreover, national laws to secure equality and publicity in railroad management "cannot be too soon enacted." [37] The railroad presidents had insisted that only national legislation — if constitutional — could solve the problems inherent in trunk-line development. The merchant reformers, therefore, while concentrating upon state action, did not overlook any possibilities and had the Chamber go on record regarding interstate commerce. (They were also then engaged in a national campaign to support John Reagan's bill on that subject.)

The Board of Trade and Transportation meeting several days later also indicated dissatisfaction with the mild tenor of the Hepburn bills but resolved to go along with them. It was already obvious that the railroads were prepared to put up a stiff fight and the board called upon farmers and merchants to give more attention than in the past to political duties.[38] Such admonition was in order. As a concession to public opinion, bills listed above as 1, 2, 3, and 6 were permitted to become law. The major fight at the session centered around the "Anti-Discrimination Bill," and to their aid the railroads summoned literally trainloads of "special-raters," that is, interior merchants and manufacturers enjoying preferential rates. These men poured into Albany and besieged the legislature, but they were followed by an equally determined group of non-special-raters. The bill was relatively mild and, according to Chairman Hepburn, it had been deliberately patterned after the Massachusetts antidiscrimination act then in effect.[39] Without going into details, it was designed to abolish personal discrimination — the carload entitling the shipper to the lowest rate and thus pleasing the merchants — and contained a moderate long-haul, short-haul clause pleasing to the farmers and upstate millers, lumber dealers, manufacturers, etc.

Like its action on the resolution ordering an inquiry into railroad practices, the Assembly overwhelmingly passed the bill 81 to 32. After a bitter and drawn out fight, the Senate killed it.[40] If the New York *Times* was any judge, and the Assembly's vote indicates that it was, the Senate had acted in defiance of the popular will.[41] The Senate chose to disregard the popular demand for antidiscrimination legislation, but merchants refused to believe that it acted solely out of regard for right and equity. Bluntly stating that the upper house was almost entirely controlled by the railroads, the Chamber of Commerce called upon all good citizens to agitate for reform until the principles of equality and publicity were embodied in law. The Board of Trade and Transportation echoed these resolves and the merchants set to work to translate public indignation into political power.[42]

PRELIMINARIES TO ORGANIZATION

Apparently as early as February 1880 the possibility had been foreseen of the Senate's defeating the major Hepburn bills. Thurber had called a special meeting of the Board of Trade and Transportation to consider possible action in that event. The high point of his report was that a pledge be sent to millers, Grangers, merchants, members of Farmers' Alliances, etc., for signatures so that a nucleus might be created "around which to form in the future, if necessary, a body pledged to reform." [43] Several weeks later the *Times* reported that the board was flooding the state with a compact stating that the signers would consider themselves released from all party ties if the legislature defeated the railroad bills. The paper's reporter had been shown a pile of signed and returned documents, six inches thick, and told that the board expected the aggregate number of signatures to exceed 40,000. Open statements had been made indicating the Hepburn bills would be "stifled in the Senate" and the organization was determined to prevent their defeat by making party managers understand the forces they would alienate.[44]

A sarcastic editorial in the *Commercial and Financial Chronicle* indicates that the arguments and tactics employed by the board were receiving increasing attention. Entitled "Our Farmers Ruined by Railroads," it denied that discrimination was causing hardship to New York agriculture. It went on to point out that the difficult problems involved in railroad rates called for wise and dispassionate handling, and then queried: "And yet is not the discussion of late largely settling down to a commiseration for our poor State Farmers (each has a vote) ruined by the rich Mr. Vanderbilt?" [45] The Central, it might be noted, was far more committed to "special rates" than the Erie, and it led the fight against the antidiscrimination bill. In fact, the Erie seems to have reacted only passively to the idea of regulation and allowed its rival to carry the brunt of the fight against it. Editorial comment by the *Commercial Advertiser* several weeks later testifies to the successful agitation among the farmers:

By a vote of yeas 81, nays 32, the Anti-Discrimination Bill passed the Assembly yesterday. The majority for the bill is unusually large, considering how clearly its dangerous features were brought out, and among the few clear headed men who supported it were all the blatherskites, communists and strikers in the House. The farmers of course favored it. They have been taught to believe that the railroads and not the natural laws of trade . . . are responsible, because they, no more than the English farmer, can compete with the agriculturists of our Western States.[46]

At about the same time, the *Husbandman* reported that allegiance to political parties was broken to a marked degree among many thousands of voters in the state; [47] to speed up the good work it concentrated on the transportation issue as never before. And New York was so closely balanced politically that a small percentage of ticket-splitters could sway the result, particularly if attention were concentrated on the single issue of transportation, and national politics were ignored.[48] A not atypical example in this respect may be given from a letter to the *Husbandman* in July. The author, a self-proclaimed "dyed in the wool Republican," stated that he would vote for Garfield for president, but in the Assembly transportation was the issue and he would act accordingly. Moreover, State Senator Mills from Herkimer County had sold out to the railroads, "and his vote against the interests of his constituents will not soon be forgotten, or forgiven." [49]

Since the senators were not up for re-election in 1880, it was impossible to do more than say "wait until next year" in their case. To organize the resentment effectively, however, and because the Assembly had not proved sufficiently amenable on the railroad commission bill, a meeting of agricultural and commercial interests was held at Saratoga on August 5. Back in 1873 the Cheap Transportation Association had catechized prospective legislators on their views regarding transportation, and the technique was revived in 1880. Apparently the mercantile leaders were convinced that the groundwork had been sufficiently laid for them to get into politics (as indeed Thurber seems to have always desired), and at Saratoga a platform was drawn up and three questions adopted for presentation to Assembly candidates. They were asked to pledge their vote for laws compelling railroads to base charges upon "the cost and risk of service, instead of upon the new theory, enunciated by railroad managers 'what the traffic will bear' . . ."; to prohibit discriminatory rates; and to establish a board of railroad commissioners.[50]

Soon after the Saratoga meeting, William J. Fowler wrote Thurber that the platforms and questions had been unanimously adopted by "several thousand Grangers . . . after an able address by Gen. Diven of Elmira." [51] Diven was doing an extraordinary amount of speaking for the Farmers' Alliance that summer and was having considerable success in rousing the rural areas. A gentleman farmer, a past president of the state Agricultural Society, and a highly prosperous lawyer, the General was peculiarly well-qualified to discuss the railroad question. For many years, including most of the Jay Gould regime, he had been an important official on the Erie. His testimony before the Hepburn Committee had been especially damaging to the roads because it was impossible to dismiss him as lacking practical experience. It was Diven who had revealed the details of how, in the fifties, the first New York railroad commission had been bought off, and he provided other titillating proofs to justify the claim that he was a "practical" railroad man.[52]

Why Diven should have suddenly been converted to the cause of railroad reform is unclear and only vague speculations suggest themselves. But, in any event, during the summer of 1880 he denounced railroad discrimination against New York agriculture from one end of the state to the other. According to the *Husbandman,* unprecedented crowds of farmers turned out at meetings to cheer him on, and attendance figures such as 4,000 and 6,000 were common. Other orators such as General E. F. Jones of Binghamton (several years later lieutenant governor of New York), and Victor Piollet, master of the Pennsylvania Grange, stumped the countryside and proclaimed Alliance doctrines. Neighborhood talent was also employed,[53] but despite all the agitation the Alliance did not greatly increase its organizational strength. Nonetheless, there was more ferment than ever before and Thurber sent a message to the Alliance convention on August 25 saying "that the farmers were the hope of the State in protecting it from corporations." A. B. Miller, present as a delegate from the New York Board of Trade, was quoted to this effect: "Their hearts are with the Alliance. They had been to the Legislature dozens of times to obtain justice but in vain. The farmers have the power to crush the monopolies if they use it." [54]

The Alliance convention was almost entirely given over to the transportation question and Diven became the new president. Both Miller and Thurber were re-elected as vice-presidents, the bonds of union between merchants and farmers were drawn closer than ever, and it was freely charged by the railroads that Thurber was paying the expenses of the organization.[55] Some credence is lent to this claim by an interesting, if vague, statement made in 1880. A leading Allianceman noted that "of late the State Alliance had received money from generous men to go ahead with its work." [56] The reference may have been to Diven, but it would have been like Thurber to have given solid evidence of his encouragement.

However that may be, the New York Board of Trade and Transportation was clearly interested in stirring up other organizations on the transportation issue, and its efforts were not confined to the Empire State. Thurber's letter to the National Farmers' Alliance in October has been mentioned in a previous chapter, and the Board had also strenuously propagandized on a national scale in favor of the Reagan bill to regulate interstate commerce.[57] The inspirational results of these activities, and those carried on by the Chamber of Commerce, are evident from the address of the master of the National Grange in November 1880 praising the valuable work of the New York merchants in "enlightening the people upon the great wrongs committed by the railroad companies against the public interest . . ." [58]

One concrete step taken by the Chamber to keep agitation alive, and to raise it to an even higher pitch, was the preparation of a lengthy questionnaire on the railroad problem. Drawn up in August and distributed after the November elections, it had the object of stimulating discussion of the "principles governing the relations of railroads to the public, and thus endeavor to arrive at an equitable adjustment of same." With this end in view it was circulated widely to newspaper editors, congressmen, governors, officers of commercial organizations, college presidents, railroad presidents, etc. The enterprise was notably successful. Approximately 100 replies were received, almost unanimously in favor of remedying abuses by proper legislation, and praising the Chamber's initiative in "calling the attention of the country to the necessity of regulating the transportation question." [59] But the most important answer was the one sent in by Judge Jeremiah S. Black of Pennsylvania.[60]

Black, attorney-general of the United States during the Buchanan administration, a former judge of the Pennsylvania Supreme Court, and still a powerful figure in the Democratic party, replied in a long letter which produced exactly the kind of controversy necessary to the Chamber's campaign. Strongly supporting governmental regulation of railroads, the letter took the extreme position (at least for the time) that they were mere "public highways" belonging to the state.[61]

Judge Black also spelled out in detail the harmful practices of unrestrained railroad managers, pointed to their adverse effects upon the national economy, and warned that "It will require a strong organization and much labor to reduce them." [62] Released by the Chamber for publication on December 2, the letter became an overnight sensation. The New York daily press gave it wide circulation and editorials poured forth on the theme.[63] Clearly concerned with the letter's impact, the railroads obtained an opinion from George Ticknor Curtis on the subject of the legal relation of the railroads to the state, in the form of a reply to Judge Black.[64] Curtis' position was so thoroughly uncompromising, and so thoroughly out of touch with the popular temper, however, as to stir the *Times* to editorial indignation:

> In short [according to Curtis] the State, in granting a franchise for building and operating a railroad, brings into being a power to whose mercy its citizens are subject, and has left itself no authority to regulate or control it for their protection. This doctrine is simply monstrous, and therefore we submit that it cannot be public law in any civilized country.[65]

Black's letter and the reply it elicited from Curtis put the subject squarely before the American people. Jay Gould, in his own fashion, was helping to see that it remained there. The year 1880 was marked by an increased tendency toward the consolidation of railroad lines. Gould was busily uniting and plundering roads in the West and the Southwest, and other men were engaged in similar work throughout the country. Railroad prosperity, largely due to the extraordinary export of agricultural commodities beginning late in 1879 and continuing thereafter for several years, stimulated not only physical expansion but organizational combination and unity. What the *Times* called a "great confederacy of railroads" was visibly shaping up, week by week. Thus the debate in New York over railroad regulation was taking place in a setting increasingly designed to make it a matter of national concern.[66]

The response to the Chamber's questionnaire had indicated that leaders of opinion throughout the nation were vitally interested. Black's letter and Curtis' reply, coming on top of a wave of consolidations, stirred wide public interest, and the New York transportation reformers faced the imminent problem of getting legislation past a railroad-controlled Senate. Nearly a decade of agitation by merchants and farmers was now on the verge of bearing fruit. The time was ripe to attempt once more that "Non-Partisan Political Movement, for the Protection of our Material

Interests" of which Francis B. Thurber had drawn the blueprint in 1878. Accordingly, the National Anti-Monopoly League came into being, the first nationally significant movement of its kind; that is, politically active, open to members of all ethnic groups and religions, and organized on nonpartisan lines. Corporate domination of the American party system after the Civil War had been virtually unchallenged except by professional politicians; now it was proposed to create an independent political pressure group on behalf of the "people." Adverse economic consequences of the Communication Revolution had been most visibly present in New York, and appropriately enough, the Empire State was also the scene of one of its more significant political consequences.

CHAPTER VIII

The National Anti-Monopoly League

> The work of the Anti-Monopoly League is taken up none too soon. It is quite time that organized action on the part of the people against the tremendous organization of corporate power was begun. The League sets out with definite purposes. It proposes to arouse public attention and to inform the popular mind with a view to securing State and national legislation which shall bring the vast interests of transportation under the control of law and into subservience to the rights and interests of the people. The period for discussing the necessity of action and the authority to act has passed. The necessity has been amply demonstrated, the authority of the Government in the premises rests on an impregnable basis . . .
>
> While the corporations have . . . been strengthening and consolidating their power, the people have been almost unconscious of what has been going on or have regarded it with a sort of helpless apathy. Bodies of commercial men have been cognizant of the facts and have endeavored to awaken public interest and to promote legislative action . . . the work of the Anti-Monopoly League is not only practical, but necessary, in order to secure results whose importance grows more pressing with every month of delay.
>
> Editorial, "The Anti-Monopoly Crusade," New York *Times*,
> February 23, 1881.

The first major counterattack against corporate power after the Civil War was formally christened on January 6, 1881, in a private room at the long famous Knickerbocker Cottage restaurant on Sixth Avenue. In that appropriate setting, the National Anti-Monopoly League was organized by merchant reformers, old-style "Jeffersonian democrats," labor leaders, Greenbackers, and socially conscious ministers. Francis B. Thurber and Peter Cooper, the two leading figures of the movement, held different opinions on monetary doctrine but they were united in resisting "The Encroachments of Corporate Monopolies upon Public Rights." Together with a small band of kindred spirits they subscribed to succinctly worded tenets which clearly derive from prewar Loco-Foco agitation.

A Nightmare of the Future

Our principles: Anti-Monopoly.

We advocate, and will support and defend, the rights of the many as against the privileges for the few.

Corporations, the creations of the State, shall be controlled by the State.

Labor and capital, allies, not enemies — justice for both.[1]

The diverse composition of the League's founders symbolizes the range of discontent resulting from increasing corporate ascendancy after 1865. Merchants and industrialists such as Thurber and Cooper, labor reformers such as John Swinton, humanist ministers and philosophers typified by the Rev. R. Heber Newton and Professor Felix Adler, all were stimulated to action by the rapid changes making themselves evident in American life. The vision of a middle-class society, traditionally (if perhaps inaccurately) linked with the name of Thomas Jefferson, was fast disappearing, and the men gathered under the banner of Anti-Monopoly were determined to halt its march toward oblivion. But to preserve Jeffersonian social ideals amidst the centralizing tendencies of the Communication Revolution, it was necessary to stand Jeffersonian and Loco-Foco laissez-faire political economy on its head. As they saw it, not freedom from government but control by government was indispensable if a small number of corporations were to be prevented from becoming dominant and "the rich richer and the poor poorer." The economy had developed to the point where it was no longer capable of assuring the good society unaided and the Anti-Monopoly League was created to bring the machinery of government to bear upon the problem.[2]

A major difficulty confronted the League at the outset. So long as corporations were politically omnipotent, the powers of the state were used to accelerate rather than to halt the rate of economic concentration. Obviously, before the government could be employed in the interests of the people, it had to be controlled by the people. Thus the Anti-Monopoly League was conceived of as an independent pressure group within the framework of the two-party system. In theory this device would avoid the difficulties of a third party at a time when partisan ties were extremely rigid, and the League would achieve sufficient strength to wield the balance of political power. With such leverage, it was supposed, the League could force through the necessary legislation to end economic concentration. In practice, despite amazing temporary success, the League was unable to fulfill either its plan to control the party machinery, or its dream of reverting to a simpler economy.

Viewed in perspective, the National Anti-Monopoly League is judged to be humanist in sentiment, modern in political methodology, and essentially reactionary in economic outlook. The League was the major seed bed for the notions of "trust-busting" characteristic thereafter of middle-class reform groups in the United States, and its doctrines influenced the subsequent history of American protest movements to a considerable degree.

JUDGE BLACK LAUNCHES THE NATIONAL ANTI-MONOPOLY LEAGUE

According to Chauncey Depew, the Anti-Monopoly League derived its inspiration from the favorable rates granted New York interior wholesalers. As Depew told the story in March 1882, Thurber had warned him back in 1874 that the metropolitan merchants would no longer tolerate rates more favorable to interior rivals than to themselves. To put pressure on the railroads, Thurber and his "clique of merchants in the metropolis" organized the Cheap Transportation Association, succeeded in turn by the Board of Trade and Transportation. That organization was employed to create antirailroad agitation all over the country and a printing office in the rear of Thurber's establishment sent out tracts "by the million a year." As the Board of Trade and Transportation could not go into politics under that name, Depew continued, it established a branch called the Anti-Monopoly League. Thurber called the first meeting, prepared its constitution, made speeches in its behalf nearly every night for almost a year, and was the author or director of every tract it ever issued. Then he made an alliance with John Kelly of Tammany Hall and "the movement became a practical political force in the politics of our State." [3]

Depew's purpose clearly was to discredit the League, but in spite of such left-handed compliments there is little reason to doubt that Thurber was the real leader of the movement. Commenting on the considerable influence of the League in 1882, the Central's attorney declared:

> There is no man living in the United States who could have created, set in motion and kept in motion an organization which has grown to proportions such as this, except with the ability, energy, intelligence and large capital and fortune of my friend Thurber. When I state that he is the bottom and the top, the rind and the core of the anti-monopoly movement he objects, and yet it is not an assault upon his character, and nothing but a compliment to his ability.[4]

The *Nation's* estimate coincided with Depew's,[5] and friends as well as opponents paid tribute to Thurber; so close a student of the railroad problem as Joseph Nimmo, Jr., hailed him as "the chief apostle of reform." [6] In other sympathetic eyes he was "the Ajax of this whole movement in the Chamber of Commerce and the Board of Trade and Transportation." [7]

Something like the Anti-Monopoly League was bound to have emerged in the United States, Thurber or no Thurber, but the specific form it took probably did derive, as Depew suggested, from the problems of New York merchants. Nonetheless, numerous other groups and individuals were sympathetic to the purposes of the League. Its president, Lucius E. Chittenden, a prominent New York lawyer, was one of the five men who had founded the Free Soil party and had been the first Register of the United States Treasury under Lincoln. Like John Henry, Chittenden represented the antislavery elements in the Republican party, and it was no accident that parallels were continually drawn between Anti-Slavery and Anti-Monopoly. By way of contrast to Thurber, a wealthy merchant holding "sound money" views, another founder of the League was Peter Cooper, an even wealthier industrialist and the outstanding apostle of Greenbacks in the nation.[8] (The "money question," however, was to play no part in the Anti-Monopoly movement for some time.)

Once the preliminary organization had been effected early in 1881, a name and constitution adopted, and officers elected, steps were taken to publicize the League and win a mass following. The emphasis on railroad regulation can be seen in the specific "objects" of the organization as defined in its first "Address to the People." [9] Anti-Monopoly meant:

1. Laws compelling transportation companies to base their charges upon "cost and risk of service."

2. Laws to prevent pooling and combination.

3. Laws prohibiting personal discrimination on "public highways."

4. Establishment of railroad commissions or courts, state and national, to enforce legislation.

5. Laws compelling public officers to defend a citizen's rights "against injustice by powerful corporations."

6. Laws prohibiting taxation of the public to pay dividends on watered stock.

7. Stringent laws against bribery, including a prohibition of free passes.

8. National legislation fixing maximum railroad rates.

9. A liberal policy toward waterways to prevent exorbitant railroad rates.

10. "Laws providing for the restriction within proper limits of corporate powers and privileges generally, and for the protection, education and elevation of the masses."

As outlined in the "Address," state, county, and Assembly district Leagues were to be organized in order to influence the nomination by existing parties of candidates "who will support our principles." If both parties nominated good men, the League would allow its members to exercise individual preferences. If only one good candidate was chosen, all party affiliations were to be laid aside and a solid vote cast for the man endorsed by the League. If neither party presented a suitable candidate, independent nominations were to be made. All "reputable citizens" in accord with these purposes and methods were invited to become members. No entrance fee or annual dues were charged, "the organization relying upon the patriotism of its members to support it by voluntary subscriptions." (Thurber and Peter Cooper were the foremost patriots.) Despite its national title, the heart of the movement was in Manhattan, and the National Executive Committee located there maintained a tight rein on the entire apparatus. From the New York headquarters, literally millions of tracts and documents were sent to every state in the Union during the first year of existence alone.[10]

On February 8, 1881, copies of the "Address to the People," together with Judge Black's letter to the Chamber of Commerce and a book in which to record the signatures of new recruits, were sent to the 300 members then enrolled.[11] Several days later, literature explaining the purposes of the League went out to potentially sympathetic editors and their support was requested.[12] The response to these mailings must have been favorable for a mass meeting was scheduled at an unusually early date. Organized in January, the League was able to fill every seat in the Great Hall of Cooper Union on February 21, with prominent businessmen of the city largely comprising the audience. Invitations had been sent to leading figures throughout the country to attend the meeting and to permit the use of their names as vice-presidents of the League. The response indicates that the *Times'* editorial approving the League reflected a widespread sentiment, for 500 names, including that of Henry George, were secured in this fashion.[13]

As a result of the Cooper Union meeting, the League was launched with enough publicity to satisfy a press agent's dream. The featured speakers were Judge Black (Dem.), Secretary of the Treasury William Windom (Rep.), Congressman John Reagan (Dem.), and William J. Fowler, president of the National Farmers Alliance. Unable to attend, Windom sent a strong letter warmly supporting the League and stressing the need for such a movement. But the sensation of the night was Judge Black's address. Black delivered a blistering attack on railroad abuses and warned that the democratic structure of America was severely endangered by corporate monopolies. Referring to a recent increase of freight rates on grain shipments, he charged that the trunkline managers were guilty of unconscionable exploitation. By a peculiar compilation of statistics he "proved" that $675,000,000 annually was stolen from the people on through freights alone.[14]

Black's figure was nonsensical and the friends of railroad management immediately seized upon his statement as proof of the over-all inaccuracy of the Anti-Monopoly indictment. Albert Fink, the pool commissioner, effectively ridiculed Black's statistics in a letter to the *World* several days later[15] which was quickly republished in newspapers throughout the country. The extent of the controversy may be indicated by the *Railroad Gazette's* editorial praising Fink's reply. Such refutation was important, the *Gazette* observed, because Judge Black's speech and his earlier letter to the Chamber of Commerce "were very widely circulated and the extravagant statements made in them were just what strike the public mind and are remembered." [16]

The *Nation* soon leaped into the argument with a harsh attack on "The Fallacies of the Anti-Monopoly League," concentrating almost exclusively upon Black's $675,000,000 figure.[17] Thurber replied in a letter which maintained that the judge had inadvertently repeated a figure shouted by someone in the audience, but stressed that there was no disputing the general accuracy of the attack upon railroad abuses.[18] The controversy dragged on for several issues and the magazine steadfastly clung to the $675,000,000 statement, pointing out that it was being spread "far and wide" and consequently doing much harm. Judge Black, Secretary Windom, Thurber, and the Chamber of Commerce were all blamed for the growing hostility to railroads. Charles Francis Adams, Jr., now a paid employee of the trunk lines, also got in some licks at Thurber,[19] and the latter jogged that erstwhile reformer's memory with quotations from his earlier writings in reference to stock watering.[20] Whatever else may have been the result of the heated arguments over Judge Black's statement, it thrust the Anti-Monopoly League into national prominence virtually overnight.[21]

WHEN POLITICIANS FALL OUT, ANTI-MONOPOLISTS MAKE HAY

Publicity was gratifying but the New York merchants still had the practical problem of pushing legislation past the tightly controlled state Senate. Despite solemn pledges made by both parties and the strong sentiments expressed by Governor Cornell in his annual message to the legislature, little expectation apparently existed of any such achievement in 1881. A report made to the Board of Trade and Transportation in February stated that "A majority of the present Senate having been elected in the interest of the railroad companies, it is safe to say that no action which will be just to the mass of the people can be expected from that body." [22] But with an eye to the forthcoming state senatorial elections in November, the Hepburn bills were reintroduced. Possibly to disarm some of the opposition from interior wholesalers, and (because it was a more moderate measure) to attract conservative support, emphasis was shifted towards obtaining a Board of Railroad Commissioners instead of an antidiscrimination bill.[23]

Again Chauncey Depew made his annual pilgrimage to Albany, and again he warned of the dangers of communism and anarchism: "Brother Sterne wants the Commission bill; anti-monopoly wants a dozen other bills, and Schwab wants the life, by assassination, of the railway presidents. That's the culmination." [24]

Although the Assembly ignored Depew's gloomy prophecies and overwhelmingly passed the commission bill, the upper house showed little inclination to go along.[25] On May 3, the *Times*, still a staunch Republican journal, warned that killing the bill might have serious consequences for the party because "the majority of the Senate is composed of Republicans, whom it behooves to consider somewhat seriously the enormous load that is just now being packed upon the party, and to hesitate before they add to the burden." Here the *Times* was referring to the celebrated outbreak of hostilities in 1881 between the Stalwart and Half-Breed wings of the Republican Party.

The clash between Stalwarts and Half-Breeds was more than a mere factional fight over which deserving politician got what patronage plum. Stalwarts might be termed the pure (*sic*) professionals, the politicians whose vested interests were the spoils of office and political power, power dependent upon their control of patronage and their ability to move with popular currents. In contrast, the Half-Breeds possessed larger visions, more specific vested interests associated with railroads and industrial enterprises, and were more partial to the whims of "Big Business" than responsive to the popular mood.[26]

Based on the record, it is doubtful whether any Half-Breed leader would have been likely to subject the secretary of the New York Central to the sharp going over that Senator Conkling gave him before the Windom Committee in 1873 when railroads were the popular objects of disfavor.[27] Contrariwise, James G. Blaine, the national leader of the Half-Breeds, was scornful of men like Conkling who could not see "beyond a custom house or a post-office";[28] and Chauncey Depew, chief counsel and vice-president of the New York Central, ran Half-Breed affairs in the Empire State.

Depew's lieutenants were such men as State Senator Wagner of the Wagner Drawing Room Car Company (Vanderbilt was a partner), State Senator Dennis McCarthy of Syracuse whose business interests received the special rates awarded favorites of the New York Central, and State Senators William Robertson, William Woodin, "Lo" Sessions, and other members of the legal profession serving as counsel to railroad companies.[29] Thus, when the newly elected President Garfield, dominated by Blaine, Whitelaw Reid, Depew, and the Half-Breeds, hurled the now famous "thunderbolt" against the Stalwarts, it was not only Roscoe

Conkling who protested the nomination of William Robertson for collector of the New York Custom House.

The unofficial organ of Henry George's movement in New York, *Truth,* forcefully commented on the protest to the Robertson appointment by two thousand of the prominent merchants of the city early in April 1881. *Truth* hailed the protest as another sign that the nation was rising to defend itself against this "new encroachment of the monopolists." [30] According to the paper, Robertson was one of the Vanderbilt agents in the state Senate and had "steadily and openly defended his master's interests and executed his master's commands whenever they existed to be defended or carried out." Even better evidence of mercantile alarm at the Robertson appointment is found in a personal letter from Francis B. Thurber to Roscoe Conkling. The letter, written immediately after the nomination was made public, is couched in terms suggesting that it was designed to reinforce the independence of Stalwarts towards their railroad-supported opponents. Robertson was depicted as the tool of the railroad power "which aims to obtain supreme control of the affairs of our government. A power which dictates to all production and commerce what share of the profits shall go to producers and the public and which dwarfs all statesmanship by declaring war upon any public man who is too independent or patriotic to bow to its will." [31]

If Thurber's letter was designed to insure a serious public breach in the Republican party, he must have been pleased by Conkling's subsequent course of action. The Stalwart leader decided to fight the nomination and quickly precipitated a contest which was of interest to the entire country, or, more accurately, to those of its people interested in politics. Traditional senatorial courtesy and Conkling's position as chairman of the committee having jurisdiction over the nomination seemed to give him the upper hand. His position was also reinforced by metropolitan mercantile support against the replacement by a railroad "henchman" of what was then a startling rarity in public life, an honest collector of the Port of New York. But encouraged by Blaine, Whitelaw Reid, Depew, and other Half-Breeds, Garfield refused to withdraw his nominee and the quarrel's dimensions grew.[32]

Allegedly at the suggestion of Tom Platt, the junior senator from New York, both he and Conkling dramatically resigned in the middle of May. Since the New York legislature which had elected Platt in January was still in session, and the Stalwarts were in considerable strength, they expected quick re-election, and with it, a mandate to oppose Garfield. Something went wrong. To their evident surprise, the legislature experienced a radical change in sentiment; instead of an easy victory they found themselves fighting for their political lives. Moreover, Governor Cornell, apparently bent on redeeming his reputation after long years of service as a Stalwart, stayed aloof and did not attempt to use the power of his office to force their return.[33]

It seems likely that Depew had been largely responsible for Conkling's unexpected difficulties. Depew was the Half-Breeds' leader in New York and he was also the chief attorney and lobbyist extraordinary of the New York Central. Conkling had been a machine politician of long standing; yet there is little or no evidence that he had been subservient to the corporations, or quick to respond to the dominant interests' wishes on issues which really aroused the people and upon which professional politicians might best be cautious. For example, when cheap money sentiment was rapidly growing in 1877–1878, he was subjected to severe attack by the *Nation*: "Have the bankers observed that their 'Senior Senator' has not once opened his mouth about the danger with which the country is threatened by schemes of repudiation and adulteration, or given the smallest sign either in public or private of knowledge of or interest in them?" [34] And Conkling's sympathetic biographer was forced to agree with the *Nation's* comment upon this curious silence and his failure to take part in the debate over the Bland-Allison silver act: "He remained a hard-money man, like [President] Hayes himself, but he did nothing about it except vote at the proper times."

Among Conkling's other failings, as seen from the viewpoint of certain business interests, he had successfully disputed control of the Republican party with Blaine and Depew, both closely associated with railroads. It may well have been that Depew decided to take this opportunity to perpetuate Conkling's retirement and thereby end the era of independent politicians. In the struggle, besides the ample resources of the New York Central's treasury, Depew could count upon the support of the upstate businessmen who received favored treatment from the railroad. Many of these were influential in local politics and were working closely with Depew in 1881 to defeat the railroad commission and antidiscrimination bills pressed by the merchants and farmers. The fight between Depew and Conkling must be viewed against this background, and it would seem to explain why the legislature underwent so marked a change in sentiment from January to May.[35]

In any event, the attorney for the New York Central did lead his special-rate warriors into battle against Conkling, shouting "Down with the Machine" — and, incidentally, to win a senatorship for Depew. The benefits accruing to Anti-Monopoly from the bitter fight between the machine politician (Conkling) and the corporation politician (Depew) were not overlooked by thoughtful observers. The Brooklyn *Daily Eagle,* edited by Thomas Kinsella (a leading Democrat and a vice-president of the League), carried a prophetic editorial entitled, "Conkling's Resignation and the Anti-Monopoly Movement." Whatever Conkling's purpose had been in resigning, the editorial argued, the effect was to persuade a great many people that "the inevitable struggle between the plain manhood of the country and the powerful moneyed corporations for the control of our government is a much more immediate affair than they thought it was." [36]

Solid evidence to substantiate the *Eagle*'s prophecy was soon forthcoming in the contest to elect new senators in the New York legislature. On June 9, S. H. Bradley arose in the Assembly and announced that he had been paid $2,000 the night before to vote for Chauncey Depew. Bradley declared that Senator "Lo" Sessions, a notorious railroad lobbyist, had been the agent of corruption and called for a committee of investigation. Conkling supporters seized upon this opportunity and the *Commercial Advertiser*, a staunch Stalwart organ, attacked Half-Breed lobbying and corruption with an impressive show of moral outrage.[37] The paper's position is all the more interesting because in former years it had saved its indignation for railroad reformers and opponents of corporate control of legislation. Given this opening, Conkling swung into action and countered Depew's "Down with the Machine" slogan with a strong attack upon corruption and the power of monopolies.

On June 21, the Stalwart leader was reported to have delivered to his followers a speech that might well have been made by a charter member of the Anti-Monopoly League:

> After dwelling upon the growing power of monopolies in this country he spoke of the various corporate influences that have been arrayed against the Stalwarts. He said it was almost inevitably a severe task to fight wealth, but more especially was it difficult to do so when the millions were unscrupulously used by corrupt agents . . .
> The power of railroad corporations has grown immensely in the United States, and it is mostly to be feared when it undertakes to debauch sworn legislators . . .
> If this condition of affairs is to continue where will the country go? Where will the party be? . . . Where can the citizens of the State of New York find a party to fight their battles against corporate monopolies and against bribery and corruption in every form, whether in Albany or elsewhere? . . .
> Mr. Conkling dwelt further upon the topics of corporate monopolies and the official corruptions which they induce. He desired that his words should produce the most profound impression of which they were capable.[38]

Details of the continuing fight between victorious Half-Breed and defeated Stalwart would only belabor the issue. The point is that the struggle for dominance in the Republican party, and the abortive attempt to make Depew a United States senator, produced fertile soil for Anti-Monopoly doctrines to take root. In addition, it engendered a feud between Conkling and his erstwhile follower, Cornell, which contributed to a veritable "political revolution" in 1882.

While Stalwart and Half-Breed exposed each other's blemished past, present corruption and future menace to the Republic, during the spring and summer of 1881 Anti-Monopolists made hay. Numerous meetings were held and large quantities of literature were distributed with excellent results. The response was so encouraging that the editor of the Brooklyn *Daily Times* had no hesitation in declaring early in May that "It is safe to say . . . that the next great movement of people of the United States will be the movement against monopolies." In addition to vigorous support by the Board of Trade and Transportation, Thurber claimed that the majority of the city press supported the movement, and the League was estimated to have 20,000 members in New York alone.[39]

THE CHAMBER OF COMMERCE SPREADS "COMMUNISM"

Not as active in mass educational work as the Board, the Chamber of Commerce under Thurber's guidance also did its subtle best to provide ammunition for Anti-Monopoly orators. One of its questionnaires on the railroad problem, together with Judge Black's answers to these questions, had been sent for comment to Leland Stanford, president of the Central Pacific Railroad. He replied in a letter dated January 20, 1881, but it was not discussed until the April 7 meeting of the Chamber. The railroad committee then reported Stanford's views and subjected them to scathing analysis. Considering the state of public opinion the Californian had really taken a bold stand. His letter denied any obligation to run a railroad in accord with the public interest, justified the practice of charging what "the traffic will bear," exhibited a profound contempt for the decisions of the Supreme Court, and frankly admitted that railroad companies spent large sums to control nominations or elections.[40] In other words, Stanford had openly proclaimed views which were precisely those the Chamber had claimed were typical of railroad managers but had not been able to prove conclusively.

In the discussion that followed at the Chamber, only one hardy soul (Elliot Shepard, William H. Vanderbilt's son-in-law) dared to defend Stanford's position, and the meeting enthusiastically voted to print a thousand extra copies of Stanford's letter and the railroad committee's report thereon.[41] Through such publications, and through resolutions demanding regulatory legislation, the Chamber contributed to the ever increasing public awareness of the crusade against "railroad monopolies." Thurber's remarks at the meeting which discussed Stanford's reply illustrates how sophisticated the merchants had become in their approach to the railroad problem. The man who had once fervently believed in "competition" and exclusive freight trunk railroads as the solution for transportation ills now proclaimed:

> By its very nature a railroad is a monopoly. Capital is not readily gathered to build competing lines. The pooling of the trunk lines proves that competition cannot be relied upon for maintaining reasonable rates, and the discrimination in rates by which one man is made very rich and others kept poor, shows that, if we would preserve the principles upon which our Government is founded, there must somewhere be lodged a superior power to protect the people.[42]

The fact that Thurber was successful in getting such doctrines approved and circulated by the Chamber of Commerce, the oldest and most influential body of its kind in the United States, is a benchmark of first-rate importance in measuring the progress of regulatory concepts. So alarmed by their evident progress was Henry Poor that in 1881 he wrote a long preface for his annual railroad manual, the famous "Sketch of the Rise and Progress of the Internal Improvements, and of the Internal Commerce, of the United States; With a Review of the Charges of Monopoly Made Against Railroad Corporations." After acidly reviewing the history of the prewar Clinton League, he declared that the same class of agitators had now captured the Chamber of Commerce and found in it a fine field for their activity, "one in which respectability and credulity are very nicely matched." [43] And then Poor tore into the Hepburn investigation,[44] but claimed that its attack upon railroads was only the prelude "to one of far wider scope, going to the foundation of their [railroads'] right to property." What he referred to in this alarmed fashion was the Chamber's questionnaire designed to heighten interest in railroad regulation.[45]

That the Chamber should have endorsed Judge Black's position on railroad matters was shocking to Poor. Black's opinion in 1881 concerning railroads was compared to his opinion as U.S. attorney-general in 1860 that the federal government had no power to prevent the South from seceding — a comparison not without propaganda value in the days when waving the Bloody Shirt was a major form of athletics. What agitated Poor was not Judge Black's "infamous" and "destructive doctrines"; the latter's personal views on railroads or any other subject were dismissed contemptuously.

> But it is of vast importance what the Chamber of Commerce of the City of New York says. That body published Mr. Black's letter, gave it the widest circulation, commended it in its annual report for 1881, as embodying 'the best thought of the country upon the subject,' and that, too, after its misstatements, absurd on their face, had been publicly and wholly refuted. It continues to reiterate Mr. Black's assertions that the railroads of the country belong to the public, not to their shareholders; that when their charters expire

by lapse of time, the shareholders have no more interest in them than an out-going Collector has in the building he recently occupied.[46]

Summing up the impact of the events and activities since the founding of the League on January 6, the Anti-Monopoly leaders might well have taken pleasure in their accomplishments by midsummer of 1881. The state of public opinion was crystallizing in favor of anti-monopoly principles and a renewal of savage rate cutting had even brought Albert Fink, certain railroad journals, and others in the railroad interest, to advocate some form of legislative regulation.[47] Yet the League had a long way to go before its objects could be attained. Despite increasing agitation, despite a "monster petition" in its favor signed by over 2,000 business firms in New York City,[48] despite pressure exerted by branch leagues in 22 out of the 24 Assembly districts in Manhattan,[49] the state Senate adjourned late in July without having passed the Railroad Commission Bill.[50] Clearly, the next order of business for the League was to administer a political rebuke to the senators who had voted in the "railroad interest."

TAMMANY HALL DISCOVERS ANTI-MONOPOLY

As might be expected, the League had not done nearly as well in organization as in agitation. Drawing up the blueprints for an inde-pendent balance of power group and propagandizing in favor of anti-monopoly principles was much easier than translating them into effective political strength. The League had made a good start in Manhattan and Brooklyn but throughout the rest of the state little or no machinery existed to back up its demands. Though the Farmers' Alliance was get-ting considerable response to its continuing denunciation of railroads and was coöperating closely with the League — in fact its officers were almost without exception leading members, and the Alliance had really become the rural wing of Anti-Monopoly — it too had made only halting strides towards developing organized political influence. The difficult task remained of coalescing the antimonopoly sentiment in the state and putting the movement on a practical operating basis.

The New York Senate adjourned on July 25 and a week later a call went out for a conference of all organizations interested in "the com-mercial and industrial welfare" of the state. The Utica Conference, as it came to be known, was an effective device to weld together politically the various organizations opposed to railroad policy in New York. Fairly impromptu arrangements betrayed the movement's organizational weaknesses,[51] but an impressive array of delegates assembled represent-ing the leading associations of farmers, merchants, millers, canallers, etc., from New York to Buffalo. Before the day was over (August 18) they had all been committed to the Anti-Monopoly cause and had agreed to set up the preliminary machinery to make the movement statewide. Thus, an "Address and Resolutions" were adopted which, word for word, embraced the League's principles and objects. In addition, a resolution was tacked on to the effect "that the water ways of the State should be enlarged and made free of tolls." [52] While the "friends of the canal" may have been pleased, identification with a free canal was to limit severely the Anti-Monopoly appeal among New York farmers.

Taking the unusually bold step for those days of specifically denouncing by name nineteen senators "usually found voting with the corporations," the conference called for the organization of Farmers' Alliances or Anti-Monopoly Leagues in every district of the state to defeat them. Misgivings were expressed over the propriety of commercial and agricultural organizations (the Grange for example was supposed to eschew politics) participating so directly in elections, but, as one delegate put it: "How can the people know who these men are [railroad senators] if we are afraid to call them by name?" [53]

To carry out the work of the conference a set of officers was elected headed by General Diven of the Farmers' Alliance. Vice-presidents to flank him were chosen from every organization represented at Utica and four secretaries were named to take care of the paper work, distribution of documents, etc. Among them was Frank S. Gardner, a full-time employee of the New York Board of Trade, then concentrating its efforts on spreading Anti-Monopoly doctrines. In addition to the regular officers, provision was made for a state committee to consist of one delegate from each Congressional district. Creation of this body secured an organizational nucleus throughout the state and constituted a real advance.[54]

The *Times*, which then supported the League (with reservations), hailed the Utica Conference as "Practical Anti-Monopoly Work." [55] To make the work even more practical, a meeting of the state committee was held at Albany on October 12. An executive committee was chosen and charged with the responsibility of circulating an address to the people. Accordingly, an abstract of the proceedings at Utica was distributed under the revealing title, "Shall Railroads Be Servants or Masters?" Members of the state committee were given the assignment of organizing their Congressional districts, and all groups favoring anti-monopoly principles were urged to get written pledges from candidates to support those principles. Moreover, "where candidates will not do so, then all honorable means should be used to prevent their election and in such cases all party affiliations should be disregarded." [56]

It may have been a coincidence but also meeting at Albany on October 12 were the delegates to the state Democratic convention. No doubt the Democratic delegates were aware that the Republicans had gathered a week earlier with the Half-Breeds, led by Depew, in full control.[57] As a result of Depew's dominance, in contrast to 1879 when Stalwarts held sway, the original Republican platform had only contained a feeble plank on "monopolies." But the Anti-Monopolists present had introduced a supplementary resolution in favor of a railroad commission. The fact that the Republican convention accepted the resolution, even with Depew as chairman, indicates the extent of popular feeling on the subject. If the *Daily Graphic* was correct, the obvious Republican distaste for railroad regulation subsequently helped to convince the Democratic leaders to place their party "squarely upon an anti-monopoly platform." [58] Whatever the reason, the Democratic platform was strong enough to have been dictated by F. B. Thurber — right down to railroad rates "limited to the cost of service with a reasonable profit, instead of the mercenary exaction of 'all the traffic will bear.' " [59]

Sudden conversion to antimonopoly by John Kelly, the leader of Tammany Hall, may have provided another reason for the enthusiastic adoption of reform principles by the Democratic bosses at their convention. Kelly was not even represented, but the Tilden-Manning group which controlled the convention apparently was determined to undercut his new line. Not only had there been a falling out between Republican Half-Breed and Stalwart in 1881, Tammany and the "regular Democracy" had also indulged in a factional display. To punish Kelly for straying from the path of party regularity, a rival group had been organized in Manhattan, the "County Democracy." The County Democracy made common cause with the Tilden-Manning group and John Kelly seemed to be out in the political wastelands.[60]

But Kelly had quickly recognized the strategic possibilities of riding back to power on the Anti-Monopoly bandwagon. When Tammany met on August 30, 1881, he had it adopt resolutions declaring war on "corporate monopolies." The legislature of 1881 was severely castigated for having voted against a railroad commission, and the people were exhorted to elect men who would see that it was made into law.[61]

After this meeting Tammany Hall and John Kelly's two newspapers, the *Star* and the *Express*, had a new and popular war-cry, "Opposition to Monopolies." A large mass meeting was held on October 3, 1881, just a week before the state Democratic convention. The enthusiastic crowd packed Tammany Hall to capacity and furnished an audience for two simultaneous outdoor meetings. Kelly flatly laid down the line for his braves: "The time has now come to openly espouse the cause represented by the Anti-Monopoly League." Responding to .this heart-felt declaration of alliance, Thurber was quoted as saying that he had been told Tammany was not sincere in its antimonopoly stand but refused to believe it. " 'For one,' said the speaker, 'I say all honor to Tammany Hall for thus early recognizing this issue. We hope all other parties and sections of parties will do so as well. If they do, then the Anti-Monopoly League will not take sides; if they do not it will support the candidates of Tammany Hall and see that they act up to their professions. This is what the League has come for, and it has come to stay until the people's rights are obtained. It will affiliate with no one's party; it will trade with nobody, but it will watch everybody.' " [62]

The *Christian Union*, commenting upon the October 3 mass meeting, regarded Kelly's conversion as highly significant: "the fact that an astute political leader like Mr. Kelly beats the anti-monopoly tattoo upon his drum indicates the existence of a wider feeling on the subject than the bulk of our hand-to-mouth politicians imagine." [63] Once Kelly took to the drum and appeared to be rallying significant numbers around him, the Manning-Tilden-County Democracy forces apparently felt compelled to set up an even louder clamor for railroad regulation. Perhaps this explains why the Democratic platform was so eloquent on the evils of "chartered monopolies" and the need for a railroad commission.

ANTI-MONOPOLY ROLLS ALONG

As the 1881 election campaign progressed, the League's balance of power strategy appeared to be working well. President Chittenden was able to announce to a mass meeting on October 26 that of the nineteen "monopoly senators," only three had been renominated outside New York County and two within the city. [64] Five had actually been renominated outside Manhattan, but Chittenden was on the right track. And the two city senators, Hogan and Seebacher, were the particular targets of an intense and successful campaign by Thurber.

To oppose Hogan, elected by a large majority in 1879, the League nominated John Boyd, a member of its County Executive Committee. Thurber paid almost all the expenses and ran the campaign, and Boyd had Tammany support as well. Yet as William Whitney of the County Democracy was quick to point out, the defeat of its candidate, Hogan (who had a Republican endorsement to boot), was essentially due to the Anti-Monopoly League. [65] Senator Birdsall of Queens and Suffolk was also defeated, and the three "corporation senators" re-elected out of the original nineteen won by considerably reduced majorities. For the first time in many years, the Republicans lost control of both branches of the legislature, and James W. Husted, a Depew Half-Breed and a prime Anti-Monopoly target, was badly defeated for state treasurer. [66] Tammany Hall, which had seemed headed for disaster, elected three senators (counting Boyd) and eight assemblymen. In addition, many of the successful candidates had pledged adherence to Anti-Monopoly principles: not unnaturally the leaders of the movement claimed a considerable victory and their prestige rose. [67]

Two months after the election the annual meeting of the Board of Trade and Transportation celebrated its most successful year of existence. John F. Henry pointed to the rapid addition of 150 prominent firms to membership as proof that the business community appreciated its efforts on behalf of the commercial interests. Henry also congratulated the members of the Board on their pioneer work in arousing the nation to the "overshadowing power of the consolidated railroad corporations," and their leading role in creating the American Board of Transportation and Commerce (Cheap Transportation Association). From this latter body, according to Henry, "went forth the influence that has extended and grown until it has covered the whole land, and resulted in the great issue of anti-monopoly; through which the people of the State of New York have elected a majority of its legislature, which it is believed will sustain the great doctrine of equal rights by voting for measures that will protect and benefit the public at large, instead of a favored few." [68]

Striking confirmation of Henry's boasts relative to the board's influence, direct and indirect, is afforded by J. J. Woodman, master of the National Grange. During his annual address to the Grange in November 1880, he had expressed gratification that both the Chamber of Commerce and the Board of Trade and Transportation were doing such valuable work in the struggle for railroad regulation. [69] And a personal letter from him in reply to one from Thurber suggests that their working relationships were fairly close. Like Thurber, Woodman also deplored Stanley Matthew's elevation to the United States Supreme Court and his letter resolutely continued: "But let us not despair but continue to 'agitate,' and keep the 'Anti-Monopoly' Ball rolling." [70]

Six months later, at the next annual Grange meeting, Woodman did his best to keep the " 'Anti-Monopoly' Ball rolling." He called the Order's attention to Judge Black's letter to the Chamber of Commerce, cited Secretary Windom's letter to the Anti-Monopoly League, declared that "decided progress had been made during the past year," and went on to reveal how closely the Grange was working with the League:

> By request of the National Anti-Monopoly League, Judge Black drafted a petition to Congress, praying for the legislative regulation of inter-State commerce of railroads. The League kindly offered to furnish copies of it to our Order for circulation for signatures by Subordinate Granges; and I directed them to be sent out, under the endorsement of the National Grange. I submit this action to you, and trust that you will take the necessary steps to encourage patrons everywhere to interest themselves in circulating them and carrying out the recommendations of the League. [71]

Since at the time the chairman of the National Grange Committee on Transportation was William A. Armstrong of New York, the worthy master's words found appropriate echo in its report. Armstrong passionately urged farmers to take organized independent political action "for the protection of natural rights against the monstrous greed of corporate power that riots in the chaos of principles overturned and confused by its wanton assumptions." [72]

Although the rate wars of the mid-seventies had resulted in the registering of a distinct slump in interest on the transportation question in the *Proceedings* of the National Grange, a rapid revival had occurred with the accession in 1878 of two staunch Farmers' Alliancemen to its Committee on Transportation, Piollet of Pennsylvania and Wayne of New York.[73] Year by year the committee reports became bolder,[74] and the positions taken by Woodman and Armstrong in November 1881 indicate the intimate ties then enjoyed by the National Grange, the New York Alliance, and the Anti-Monopoly League. When it is recalled that William J. Fowler, the first president of the National Farmers' Alliance was also an enthusiastic Anti-Monopolist, it would seem that credence must be given to John Henry's claims regarding the dominant position of New York merchants in the campaigns for railroad regulation.

A NEW YORK RAILROAD COMMISSION AT LAST

John Henry of the Board of Trade was not the only one to come up with an interpretation of the 1881 election results in New York flattering to his organization. John Kelly of Tammany Hall was equally certain that they meant the Hall had a mandate from the people to enjoy a leading place in the legislature. What Tammany really wanted was to be taken back into the party and given a large share of the legislative patronage. Daniel Manning, the Democratic state boss, was determined to prevent such a renaissance of Tammany's power; yet the peculiar composition of the Senate and Assembly put him in a difficult position. The Democrats controlled both houses and were charged with the responsibility of organizing them, but they needed Tammany's votes for that purpose. Manning wanted those votes but did not want to pay Kelly's price. The shrewd Kelly, loudly proclaiming his antimonopoly loyalties, took the position that the Democratic machine was defying the popular will, that is, excluding Anti-Monopoly (read Tammany Hall) from influential positions.[75] Delighted Republicans would not get Manning off the hook and the legislature was unable to function effectively for weeks. One result of this maneuvering was that the Anti-Monopoly League received a gratifying amount of attention from both sides and reaped reams of publicity.[76]

As long as Tammany could claim that it was defending the interests of Anti-Monopoly, from the point of view of propaganda the Democratic machine was at a tactical disadvantage. To remove this handicap a meeting was arranged on February 1, 1882, between the Democratic caucus representatives and those of the League. The result was the election of Charles Patterson to the speakership and the end of the impasse in the Assembly. But an editorial in Manning's organ, the Albany *Argus*, made it clear that the League had become a power in state politics and was not dependent any longer upon Tammany's benevolent interest.[77]

If further proof of the League's political power is required, Chauncey Depew can be called upon to supply it. His tactics in previous years had been to denounce all regulation and to dismiss its advocates as a small band of visionaries and selfish metropolitan merchants. Apparently afraid that his opponents had enough strength in 1882 to achieve really drastic legislation if no compromise were made, Depew adopted a different course. The Massachusetts railroad commission was now seen to be a model for New York to follow. The shifting balance of power explains Depew's conversion as it does Thurber's raising the ante. When the merchants' influence in the legislature was inconsequential, their representatives had lauded the Massachusetts commission and Depew had scoffed at it. By 1882 the Anti-Monopoly League had made rapid gains and it was Thurber who no longer saw much point in mild measures. With him to lead the way, the Chamber of Commerce now gazed longingly upon the authority granted to the Georgia railroad commission, a body way to the left of the conservative old Bay State Board of Commissioners. Accordingly, after the fashion of pragmatic American politicians, Depew took the position left vacant by Thurber and the cause of progress was served.[78]

Possibly Depew had been most impressed by the fact that the *quid pro quo* to break the legislative deadlock was a definite promise on the part of the Democrats to carry out the platform pledges favoring railroad regulation.[79] As a telegram to Thurber from one of Manning's followers nicely phrased it: "Will the election of Jacobs be satisfactory upon the understanding that the pledges of the Democratic State Convention are to be honorably fulfilled answer immediately." [80]

To understand why Thurber agreed to support Jacobs for presiding officer of the Senate — the same Jacobs attacked by the Anti-Monopoly League a few days earlier as "one of the most efficient agents of corporations in the State" — it is necessary to recognize the fundamental differences between convention "pledges" designed for public consumption and the same "pledges" made by politicians acting in a personal capacity. Thurber's affirmative answer, however, had not set well with all League officials. Henry Nichols, the national secretary, flatly declared when appraised of the move that Thurber "was incapable of such action" and was dismayed to learn the truth.[81] Two weeks later he was warning Thurber of demoralization setting in throughout the organization, and that "the hold we have been making on the whole state is slipping away from us." He was particularly bitter because Thurber had dropped everything to concentrate on a special election to replace the recently deceased Senator Wagner, or, as Nichols sarcastically suggested, "While you are exerting yourself to reinforce Mr. Jacobs with another vote . . ." [82] But the outcome of the election was significant enough to make Nichols reverse his judgment, and further explains Depew's conciliatory position a week later.

Several weeks prior to the by-election, the New York *Times* printed an interesting editorial on the "Symptoms of Political Change." Though it noted a growing spirit of independence among the people, it declared that the demagogic war cries of antimonopoly such as John Kelly had been sounding would not find significant response.[83] Probably Thurber saw this editorial and its implied slap at the League for associating with Kelly; in any event the election to replace State Senator Wagner offered a good opportunity to impress the legislature with the strength of the Anti-Monopoly movement. Wagner had been the head of the Senate railroad committee which killed the railroad commission bill in 1881, and had been re-elected in the fall by a margin of nearly 7,000 votes. Another spur to Thurber may have been that during the fight over the legislature's organization Tammany representatives were openly contemptuous of Anti-Monopoly claims to voting strength.

As Thurber later recounted the story, the Anti-Monopolists persuaded the state Democratic organization to put up a candidate for the vacancy. Then they went vigorously to work, made the only active canvass, formed seventeen branch Leagues in the district, held forty meetings, distributed thousands of documents, and, to the astonishment of the Democrats, elected their man.[84] The *Saratogian*, a Republican paper in the district, granted "that it was Anti-Monopoly that did the business," [85] but the *Times* preferred to blame it on the Stalwart-Half-Breed feud [86] — a lame explanation by the *Times* because the feud had been as strong, if not stronger, in the fall when Wagner won his overwhelming victory. Considering Nichols' sarcasm of two weeks before, a private letter to Thurber from him seems to reveal the victory's true dimensions:

I wish to congratulate you on your success in the 18th district; for to you alone is due the credit of Mr. Baucus' election. You have taken a weak man, and without assistance from his party have made him overcome a large majority.
No better illustration has occurred since the inception of the Anti-Monopoly movement of the hold it has taken on the public than this gives.[87]

After the stunning upset in the eighteenth senatorial district, the Anti-Monopoly League was riding high. It could point to the acknowledged fact that in the fall it had elected a political unknown, John

Boyd, over Senator Hogan in a strongly Democratic district in Manhattan. Then late in the winter, to show its versatility, Thurber had wrought an even greater political miracle in an upstate Republican district. Moreover, both Democratic factions had bid for the League's endorsement in organizing the legislature, and the Tilden-Manning wing had specifically promised to fulfill hitherto not so sacred platform pledges.

With success crowning the organization's efforts, and in order to press existing advantages, invitations aimed at forming a state League were sent out in March.[88] The activities of the Utica Conference had paved the way, as had speaking tours by several paid organizers employed by the national committee. The well-known Samuel F. Cary (Peter Cooper's 1876 running mate on the Greenback ticket) had stumped the state for several months in the winter of 1881–82, apparently with considerable success. To achieve optimum audiences Frank S. Gardner had gone out as his advance man, but N. B. Kilmer, secretary of the Kings County Milk Exchange and a long time railroad opponent, had also done well on a solo circuit.[89] In addition, the League appears to have employed a full-time office manager, who, in the brief period between December 22, 1881, and February 2, 1882, saw to the writing of 1,116 letters, 95 postal cards, and the distribution of 4,724 wrappers, circulars, envelopes, etc.[90]

As a result of this burst of activity, and the prestige now attached to the Anti-Monopoly movement, the meeting at Albany in April 1882 was even more successful than the Utica conference of the past August. Reports indicate that about 400 prominent men came from most sections of the state, and among other things, listened to a long speech by John Kelly supporting virtually every reform then current.[91] Yet the most significant aspect of the affair was not the tenor of the speeches or that well-known merchants, farmers, millers, etc., attended; it was that the men gathered at Albany were not formal delegates to a regular convention but individuals attending a conference. No set of permanent officers were elected and the temporary appointees were only given the power to prepare for a delegated convention at a future date. In other words, despite the considerable agitational stir, no real Anti-Monopoly machinery existed in the state.

Together with his co-workers, Thurber had succeeded in banding together the leaders of numerous commercial, agricultural, milling, canal, and other associations nursing grievances against the trunk lines. But an organized mass basis of any significance was still lacking. The explanation seems to be fairly clear, if perhaps oversimplified. Lofty generalizations setting forth the Anti-Monopoly creed were able to win popular endorsement; they were too abstract to overcome the difficulties of creating a disciplined, efficient, mass organization. Although the concrete proposals of the League regarding transportation could also win popular endorsement, they only affected the day-to-day interests of the masses in a round-about fashion. Reflecting certain property conflicts, they were most attractive to certain property owners; they hardly constituted a program of vital impact to people whose only contacts with the "robber barons" were vicarious encounters via newspapers, pamphlets, or speeches. Moreover, in one important respect the League's proposals clashed directly with the interests of the overwhelming majority of New York farmers, the only sizeable group much interested in transportation.

Many of the men active in the Anti-Monopoly League were intimately concerned with the success of the Erie Canal and favored all measures to improve its operations. Another group viewed the canal as a weapon to use against the railroads. Still others were willing to go along with the "friends of the canal" solely to get their support for proposals of particular interest to themselves. Thus, after the Albany meeting, the League came to be strongly identified with, in fact, the chief proponent of a "free canal." [92] The legislatures of 1880 and 1881 had approved the constitutional amendment permitting such a step and it now had to be submitted to the people in the 1882 elections. The amendment abolished tolls and henceforth the state would be obligated to pay for all maintenance and improvements.

Notwithstanding the arguments of the Anti-Monopoly leaders of the Alliance and Grange, as the large majority of New York farmers saw it, they would have to pay taxes so that western rivals might get to market more cheaply. Nothing could be better calculated to antagonize New York farmers, and advocating free canals killed whatever possibilities existed of the League's taking root in the rural areas.[93] (Support for a free canal also tends to explain further the failure of the Farmers' Alliance to grow.)

To no one's astonishment, the railroads opposed the canal amendment, and they took full advantage of the opportunity it afforded them to weaken the League. Free canals were a "burning issue" during 1882 and although the urban vote along the canal route passed the amendment, the *Husbandman*, its lone agricultural exponent, admitted that the overwhelming mass of farmers opposed it.[94] Moreover, to the considerable cost of the League's popularity, the roads had effectively linked agrarian antagonism to free canals with agrarian antagonism to oleomargarine. Thurber was the most prominent figure in the League's drive for free canals, and his grocery firm was also the most prominent distributor of oleomargarine. Rapid displacement of butter by oleo in the late seventies and early eighties hit dairy farmers hard, and opponents of the League took pains to see that they were made aware of Thurber's connection with the new product.[95]

"Oleomargarine Thurber," as the New York *Tribune* was wont to tag him, certainly hurt the League to some extent, but free canals were much more important in sapping its potential strength in the rural areas. However, in the spring of 1882 the split in the rural-urban coalition was not yet deep enough to weaken its effectiveness. In fact, Thurber, the League, and the New York merchants were then approaching their biggest legislative triumph. Various bills had been introduced creating a railroad commission, including one by Senator John Boyd of Anti-Monopoly persuasion. His bill, modeled after the Georgia commission, was strong, far-reaching, and gave the commissioners elaborate rate-fixing powers. Though the Anti-Monopoly League had influence and the people favored railroad legislation, the League did not have the kind of influence nor was the public sufficiently aroused to win a bill patterned on such lines in Chauncey Depew's New York. A milder measure, similar to one recommended by the Hepburn Committee, and based on Massachusetts' experience, had also been introduced. As indicated above, Depew evidently believed the railroads' best strategy was to let it go through since it essentially only gave the commissioners power to investigate and recommend action.

That the merchants had come a long way since the first bill for a commission had been easily pigeonholed in 1874 is suggested by the size of the vote in 1882; the Assembly passed it, 75 to 39, and the Senate by 30 to 1. Yet the vote gives an exaggerated impression of the legislators' "reform" sentiments. Public interest had been aroused to the point where some sort of a commission was certain to be established. The Republicans, however, because of internal party dissension were determined not to let Governor Cornell name the three-man board. A compromise bill was finally worked out giving appointive power to the governor to be elected in November and the Republicans then abandoned opposition.[96] This development accounts for the overwhelmingly favorable Senate vote.

The law creating a railroad commission contained an odd provision compelling the governor to name one Republican, one Democrat, and one man chosen by the Chamber of Commerce, Board of Trade and Transportation, and the National Anti-Monopoly League. To say the least, such a provision was unusual and gave the merchants a flamboyant feather to grace their political caps. But rejoicing was by no means universal and papers such as the *Evening Post* took a dim view of the proceedings. It objected to the three organizations named in the bill because they bore "no legitimate relation to the State," and, apparently referring to legal incorporation, acidly observed: "One of them, the Anti-Monopoly League, although well known to the newspapers, is, we believe, not known to the law at all." [97]

CHAPTER IX

Justice for All

Intelligent self-interest on the part of capitalists should lead them to support the Anti-Monopoly movement. The Anti-Monopolists are trying to lift the safety valve and prevent an explosion which will surely come, if the great financial free booters of the country are allowed to go on corrupting our elections, controlling legislation, debauching our courts, and riding roughshod over public rights. Capitalists who honestly earned their accumulations are as much interested in the success of anti-monopoly as any other class. *Justice for all* is the only thing which will insure the permanency of our form of government.

Editorial in *Justice*, September 9, 1882, p. 2.

Considerably milder than Francis Thurber had desired, the 1882 bill setting up a railroad commission in New York nonetheless was a singular personal victory for him.[1] But if Thurber took satisfaction from the creation of a Board of Railroad Commissioners,[2] he was extremely dissatisfied with the legislative session in general. Most of the "honorables" pledged to Anti-Monopoly principles before election had promptly forgotten them after election.[3] John Boyd had been faithful, but even Senator Baucus, a man whom Thurber had practically put into office singlehandedly, proved a weak reed once the votes were counted. Although the railroad commission issue had been well enough publicized to force the legislative lobby to be prudent, on more obscure measures it ran wild. In those halcyon days of low prices and modest standards of living, it must be remembered, an eager legislator could earn a competency or pay off a mortgage in a single season. And Jay Gould, active that year in behalf of elevated railroads, could always charge expenses to his "India Rubber Account," as he once designated $900,000 spent in the Erie battle.

ANTI-MONOPOLY OUT ON A LIMB

Disillusionment was a characteristic sentiment among Anti-Monopolists as they surveyed the results of their tactics after the 1882 legislative session ended. They had been able to buy verbal support for reform

principles by granting endorsements to eager candidates. Keeping successful legislators in line was another matter. To cope with the flagrant
corruption of the "Black Horse Cavalry," or "the Forty-Thieves" as one
group in the Assembly was known, the Anti-Monopolists adopted new
tactics in 1882 and brought forth a document which was claimed to be a
unique departure in the history of American reform movements.

During the summer they issued a pamphlet bordered in black and
bearing the title, "The Anti-Monopoly League Presents with Sorrow the
Following Concerning the Record of the Legislature of 1882." Hailed by
the Lowville *Times* as "the first of the kind ever published," [4] it consisted primarily of a detailed analysis of every legislator's voting record
on key issues. Its publication had been heralded by a mass meeting at
which the legislature as a whole, and for the most part as individuals,
had been censured.[5] The *Times* heartily approved: "It will be a genuine
service to the public to place before it in legible form that can be preserved for remembrance and reference the record of the votes of those
who betrayed the interests of the people to serve those of the corporations or private schemers." [6] Presumably, such a handy reference work
would enable the people to keep track of their representatives and warn
senators and assemblymen that their over-all record would be common
knowledge. This would bring about a change for the better in government, a change urgently required according to the League:

> The United States cannot afford to become a nation of millionaires and
> tramps, and this has been the direct tendency of legislation during the past few
> years. It is to the interest of the people to send honest men to make laws; it is
> to the interests of the monopolists to have dishonest ones elected.[7]

But more than a compilation of legislative votes was necessary to
purify Gilded-Age politics, and conviction grew during the summer of
1882 that an independent party with independent candidates was the
only answer. Towards that end, and to push the Free Canal Amendment
which formed a rallying point for urban and canal interests all along the
water route from the Buffalo Board of Trade to the New York Produce
Exchange, Thurber and Peter Cooper put up the money to found *Justice*.[8]
The first issue was dated August 5 and featured a strong but anonymous
front-page letter calling on Anti-Monopoly to go it alone. While the
issue did not editorially commit the paper to such a course, broad hints
were dropped that little possibility existed of winning reforms through
the old parties. In private there was no such hesitation.

A letter to Thurber from O. J. Smith, editor of the *Saturday Express*,
a midwest Greenback paper, indicates that the New Yorker had written
to him urging a plan to bring about "a great party" of "all anti-monopoly
clans and factions." Smith agreed with Thurber and proposed a secret
conference soon after the November elections to pave the way for "an

open conference or convention to organize the new party." The former added that "Gen. [James B.] Weaver favors it." [9] Interestingly, soon after the 1881 elections the New Yorker had rejected as premature a suggestion by General Weaver along the very lines he (Thurber) now proposed. As Thurber then had put it: "The principal reason why I opposed our organizing in the beginning as a party was that I wanted to command the support of the party press to educate the people on these issues. This has to a considerable extent been accomplished, but I do not think that the time has quite arrived to lance the ulcer." [10]

At a meeting of the state committee of the Anti-Monopoly League on August 16, 1882, Thurber expressed an opinion to the effect that it now *was* quite time "to lance the ulcer." [11] These views had also been voiced by others, but Thomas Kinsella (editor of the *Brooklyn Eagle*) urged caution. In rebuttal, President Chittenden of the national League made an eloquent speech charging that not a single political issue was left to divide the Democratic and Republican parties, and that their leaders could be "bought and sold like cattle by the non-partisan robber chiefs of monopoly." [12]

While supporting the move for an independent party, Thurber claimed that the state committee was not representative enough to take such decisive action on its own, and urged a full convention to sound out the Anti-Monopoly sentiment in the state. But he warned that it was important to meet before the old parties did because they would demagogically enunciate "principles" designed to steal the "anti-monopoly thunder." By a vote of 28 to 10 the committee adopted a resolution to hold an early convention at Saratoga on September 13.[13] The resolution, in effect, put the League on record as favoring a new party.

Significantly, from the start of publication, and increasingly thereafter, *Justice* featured articles and letters aimed at securing labor votes for Anti-Monopoly. Such a tendency was predictable, for if the League was to step out in the direction of independent action, it was necessary to stir up mass enthusiasm. As a case in point, the Anti-Monopoly leaders were quick to support the freight handlers' strike then in progress against the railroads, and took a militant stand for the abolition of laws curbing trade-union activity.[14] This leftward course of action eventually alienated many conservative merchants and farmers attracted to the League by the transportation issue, but in no other way could the organization have hoped to win a mass base.

By the fall of 1882, the League had already advanced much beyond its original absorption with railroads. It now advocated civil service reform, reservation of public lands for actual settlers, a mild financial plank calling for government issue of all currency ("metallic or paper"), and postal savings banks, telegraphs, and telephones, that is, government telegraph and telephone systems. Moreover, railroads were no longer viewed as the only corporations threatening the American Republic. "The Standard Oil Company, The Hawaiian Sugar Monopoly and The Steel Rail Manufacturers Combination, are sufficient illustrations of the direction in which we are drifting." [15] Verbal pyrotechnics aside, however, it would be a mistake to think of the League as a radical organization — if radical is taken to mean going to the root of a problem, or making a sharp break with the past in the structure of society.

Thurber may have understood as clearly as any of his contemporaries the revolutionary impact of steam and electricity; yet he persisted in the belief that it was possible to harness the new forces within the framework of an older society.[16] Reading the passionate speeches of the Anti-Monopoly leaders in 1882 it is difficult to avoid the conviction that nostalgia was the dominant note of the movement — nostalgia for the allegedly good old days of a simpler, more or less middle-class America when Labor and Capital were "allies, not enemies," and there had been "justice for both." The very name of the paper, *Justice*, was designed to embody that concept, and the first issue harked back to the Declaration of Independence as the foundation of antimonopoly principles, sardonically terming it a "Socialistic Manifesto — The Declaration of a Band of Red Handed Communists." [17]

In that year, financiers such as Rufus Hatch, journalists such as Henry D. Lloyd, socially conscious ministers such as Lyman Abbott, Henry Ward Beecher, and R. Heber Newton, and numerous other individuals, newspapers, organizations, etc., warned of a great explosion to come if corporation excesses were not curbed.[18] The Anti-Monopoly League published a pamphlet called "The Impending Crisis" consisting of statements along these lines from leading papers throughout the country, and quotations from leading politicians such as David Davis of Illinois, Governor Isaac P. Gray of Indiana, Secretary Windom, Judge Black, and others. The New York *Evening Post* saw "a real, a menacing, a present danger"; the *Times* warned that railroads must be legally controlled or "sooner or later a conflict will come between their power and the might of the people which will shake the very foundations of law and order"; Governor Gray opined that "the republic cannot live long in the atmosphere which now surrounds the ballot box." According to the pamphlet, a volume might be filled with similar utterances.[19]

Apparently the League became convinced during the summer of 1882 that an independent political movement was not only necessary but, more to the point, feasible.[20] And a major stimulus towards independent action had been coming for some time from the direction of Tammany Hall. Still very much outside the regular Democratic reservation, its votes were counted upon as part of a potential coalition against the old parties. Before the state committee of the League met on August 16, its leaders had been encouraged by John Kelly to call a convention and nominate an independent ticket. At that date it seemed certain that Tammany would again be excluded from the Democratic convention and Kelly's paper haughtily maintained it would not go even if invited.

But with the flexibility so characteristic of American politicians, by September 6 the Tilden-Manning machine had decided to forget the past and Tammany suddenly announced itself back in the regular Democratic fold. As reported in the New York *Sun*, the Anti-Monopolists were thoroughly dismayed by Kelly's reversal of plans. An unnamed leader was quoted as admitting that the League had little actual machinery in the rural districts and had been counting on Tammany for both organization and votes in the city.[21]

While Tammany was carrying out its unwelcome surprise, an even greater political bombshell was in the making to relieve the Anti-Monopoly League's embarrassment. For reasons best known to himself, Alonzo B. Cornell, as governor, turned his back on erstwhile bosom companions and, to the surprise of all who knew him, demonstrated some measure of political independence. In 1881 Cornell had refused to aid Conkling in his hour of need, and he had also antagonized Depew by supporting railroad legislation. Moreover, he angered upstate "special-raters" entrenched within the Republican party by refusing to veto the railroad commission bill in 1882 despite their threats of revenge.[22]

The final blow to his political career was his failure to sign the Elevated Tax Bill of the same year. Jay Gould had procured the measure from the legislature at no little expense, and Cornell's refusal to sign it was said to have cost him a cool $200,000. The Pacific Steamship Mail Company bill involving some $90,000 for Gould had been similarly treated. In addition, the vetoes constituted a direct slap at Conkling — now out of office and bent on securing a lucrative private practice — who had been engaged by Gould because of his political influence in New York. Conkling's failure was a damaging blow both to his legal reputation and legal assets.[23] By these unorthodox actions Cornell had raised a powerful coalition against his renomination, and after the "plot" leaked out surprisingly little effort was made to conceal the details of the hatchet job in preparation by Gould and Conkling.

Early in August an enterprising reporter dug up the story of a meeting in Gould's mansion at which ways and means were discussed to punish Cornell for his intransigence.[24] Soon the story was out in the open. Fanned along by a series of charges, counter-charges, and a spate of angry interviews with all concerned, it excited increasing speculation as September 20, date of the Republican convention, approached. Thus the entire first page of the September 9 issue of *Justice* was devoted to the Gould-Conkling-Cornell vendetta, and the paper declared that "All the monopoly elements seem to be massing against the renomination of Governor Cornell." An adjoining editorial noted that it remained to be seen whether the Republican party would permit his defeat.

With Cornell now cast in an antimonopoly role, and the Republican convention pictured as the future site of a battle between good and evil, much of the pressure for independent action was removed from the Anti-Monopoly meeting of September 13. A logical reason now existed for postponing important decisions until the old parties gathered later in the month and an easy way out of an otherwise embarrassing situation appeared — and was taken. The state committee was given stand-by powers to handle the problem and decided to send observers to both conventions. After their reports were in, it reasoned, the League would be in a better position to know which way to jump.[25]

GROVER CLEVELAND AS ANTI-MONOPOLIST

The Anti-Monopoly League's convention presented some interesting aspects in its own right.[26] Every county in New York was represented,[27] with the rural delegates predominantly made up of Grangers and Farmers' Alliancemen long active in the fight against railroad management. A long platform was adopted, including the references to "steam and electricity" certain to be found in any document Thurber had anything to do with. After an incisive indictment of the old parties it gave them but one more opportunity to nominate good candidates and press for needed reforms. As the *Times* dryly commented upon the list: "If they have not covered the whole ground of needed reform it is because something escaped the memory of their platform makers. Their ringing arraignment of corporate power and its evil designs may be somewhat colored, but it has a basis of actual wrongs and abuses and of real danger to the State."[28] The section addressed to labor was particularly strong and points up Anti-Monopoly's recognition of the need to widen its base beyond merchants and farmers. And incorporated into the first plank was the popular distrust of large fortunes so characteristic of the several decades after the Civil War.[29] Over and over again the League was to recite as proof positive of its arguments the fortunes of Gould, Vanderbilt, Huntington, etc., and query, "How Did They Get It?"

After September 13 the New York League was on an organized basis throughout the state, was armed with a platform directed at broad sections of the people, and, in addition to the *Husbandman*'s support, controlled a newspaper spreading its message nationally. But it had to await the actions of the regular party conventions before deciding on its future course. As seen by the League, their results were pithily summed up in *Justice*:[30]

THE NEW YORK REPUBLICAN CONVENTION
CAPTURED BY MONOPOLY INTERESTS

A Governor who Dared Veto a Bill of Jay
Gould's Stricken Down, and a Machine
Man Nominated in His Stead

Jay Gould Leads the Republican Horse
To Water, But Can He Make
Him Drink?

THE NEW YORK DEMOCRATIC CONVENTION
A GREAT GATHERING OF THE CLANS

The United Democracy

ANTI-MONOPOLY A LEADING FEATURE

Candidates of Unknown Views On a
Distinct and Specific Platform
Will They Maintain Its Principles?

As predicted, the Republicans discarded Cornell, and even strong GOP papers such as the New York *Times, Evening Post*, Buffalo *Express*, Utica *Herald*, etc., bitterly acknowledged that "Jay Gould had triumphed." The Albany *Evening Journal* (Rep.) reported that "weak-kneed delegates were assured that Gould would elect the ticket 'if it took a million dollars,'" but the paper doubted that sum was enough to sell the deal to the people.[31] As a result of his recent operations in railroad consolidations and other forays, Gould then qualified strongly as the most hated man in the United States.

Meeting two days after the Republican nominations, the Democrats had been quick to take advantage of Gould's obvious role in the GOP convention. For once all the power-hungry factions in the party united, enthusiastically proclaimed what amounted to an antimonopoly platform, and greeted the League's observers with the strong clasp of kinship. Though the Anti-Monopolists had good reason to rejoice, they nonetheless cast a wary eye at Grover Cleveland's nomination for governor.[32] Previously, in analyzing prospective candidates, *Justice* had been less than complimentary toward Cleveland in calling him "a highly respectable railroad attorney." [33] It was also disturbed by the fact that "the man who first travelled through the State setting his name afloat in the various newspaper offices was a notorious Albany lobbyist, whose residence is at Buffalo, and who has been one of A. D. Barber's trusted lieutenants. Query. — Why do they want Mayor Cleveland?" [34] Not in time, that is, after election, *Justice* was to find out to its sorrow, but his endorsement now was certain.

The state committee of the League met on October 3 and a subcommittee drew up an address to the people analyzing the party conventions from an antimonopoly perspective. Pulling few punches, it noted that the secret power of corporate monopoly was active in both parties and in all factions of both parties. But in the Republican convention corporate monopoly had triumphed and openly struck down a governor who incurred its hostility. Although the same influence had manifested itself among the Democrats, it had not been permitted to control. The slate presented by the "railroad manipulators" was broken; antimonopoly principles requested by the League were embodied in the platform; and "candidates were named who, we have reason to believe, will live up to them in good faith." It therefore seemed to be the clear duty of all antimonopoly Republicans and Democrats "in the present instance, and without prejudice to future political action" to support the entire Democratic state ticket — and the address urged them to do so in unmeasured terms.[35] Yet how could such recommendation be squared with the previous criticism of Cleveland as a "railroad attorney?"

In a late issue we stated that Mr. Cleveland, the Democratic nominee for Governor, was a railroad attorney. Our assertion was founded upon information deemed trustworthy, but we have since learned that the only foundation for the statement was that Mr. Cleveland's law firm was for a time counsel for a branch road some forty miles in length, which has since been leased by the Erie Road for 999 years, and that they then lost their client. While Mr. Cleveland's firm does a general law business, they are not, nor is any member thereof counsel for a railroad company; and we, therefore, take pleasure in correcting the impression which our previous article conveyed. We are glad to be able to state that the interview which the committee of the Anti-Monopoly League had with Mr. Cleveland was considered a satisfactory one, and that his fellow-citizens in Buffalo, both Republicans and Democrats, are so enthusiastic over the man that it has removed any prejudice we had against him.[36]

The correction can hardly be said to have been correct. Apparently Cleveland's assurances to the League members interviewing him on his stand concerning railroad regulation and other leading issues had been so forthright and unequivocal that they were accepted at face value. Had they checked carefully, it is hardly likely that a correction would have been printed in *Justice* — although the Anti-Monopoly League was opportunistic enough to have endorsed his candidacy notwithstanding.

A sympathetic biographer has noted that among Cleveland's clients in the late seventies, and at least as late as 1881, were "the Standard Oil Company, the Merchants' and Traders' Bank, the Buffalo, Rochester, & Pittsburgh Railroad, and the Lehigh Valley Railroad." Moreover, in

September 1881 Cleveland had been offered the opportunity to become the chief counsel for the New York Central in western New York. "Chauncey Depew, now vice president of the road, besought him to take the place, saying that it would add $15,000 a year to his income. He was strongly tempted and tried a number of Central cases. Yet after prolonged deliberation, he refused. He knew that Laning [the recently deceased incumbent] had been compelled to rush for trains, stay in bad hotels, and prepare cases under pressure for hurried presentation. He told his friends that having saved about $75,000, he did not need the money, and that acceptance would restrict his personal freedom in the choice of his work and the control of his time more than he could endure." [37] Had these facts been generally known at the time it would have had to have been an extraordinarily tough minded group of pragmatic Anti-Monopolists who publicly withdrew the epithet "railway attorney"; Cleveland was precisely the type of lawyer who, they insisted, was a major source of railroad political power.

Some objection was offered to the wholesale endorsement of a particular party at the meeting of the State Executive Committee, but the recommendations of the subcommittee were overwhelmingly adopted by a vote of 39 to 2, with a few abstentions.[38] In truth, the turn of events had been much more favorable than the League had any reason to expect after Tammany left it in the political lurch.[39] The League's reversal of the original plan to go it alone, however, was sharply criticized by O. J. Smith, editor of the *Saturday Express*. In direct contradiction to the views Thurber had expressed previously to Smith, *Justice* frostily informed the latter that the League would have thrown its power away if it had resorted to independent action.[40] Given the opportunist orientation of the New York merchants, and under the circumstances then obtaining in New York, it is difficult to see how any other decision could have been taken. But the reversal of plans gave western anti-monopolists grounds for suspicion which were to cause future difficulties for the reform movement and split its ranks.

THE VANDERBILT CONCEPT OF PUBLIC RELATIONS

Among the more interesting aspects of the over-all election campaign that year was the wholesale desertion of party by newspapers and prominent individuals. Never before, and seldom thereafter, was the issue drawn so sharply between the corporations and the people in terms of major party politics. Henry Ward Beecher, of impeccable Republican lineage, leaped into the fray, and to the loud plaudits of his congregation passionately declared: "On the day that Governor Cornell was set aside, Avarice and Revenge met and kissed." [41]

Another highlight of the campaign was Jay Gould's threat to the

New York *Times*. Through various newspaper properties Gould nearly controlled the Associated Press, and he let it be known that if the *Times* continued to attack him on the Cornell issue he might "take it into his head some day that the *Times* shall have no more news, and in that way retaliate its assaults." Such a blatant threat to freedom of the press stirred up a loud clamor against "corporate monopolies" and provided juicy material for use on the hustings that fall.[42]

Notwithstanding Gould's claims to the honor, it is to William H. Vanderbilt that the prize must be awarded for the worst public relations "boner" of that year. Late in September it had been asserted that Gould, Vanderbilt, assorted satellites, lieutenants, etc., met several times to pool their talents and resources to elect the Republican ticket. Naturally all the changes were rung upon these meetings as proving the existence of "a desperate struggle between the People and the Corporations for the possession of the State." [43] Vanderbilt, however, had other problems than politics to bother him at the moment, and probably irritated by these, he let slip the phrase forever linked with his name.

The Nickel Plate railroad had been deliberately built to parallel his Lake Shore so that Vanderbilt would have to buy it. After its completion in the fall of 1882 he faced the gloomy prospect of having to pay the blackmail price its promoters were demanding. On October 8, Vanderbilt and party arrived at Chicago to survey the situation and were greeted by two reporters. In the course of the subsequent interview he used the phrase which was thoroughly in context, thoroughly characteristic of him, and one which he had frequently employed before. But given the heated situation at the time, his immortal "The public be damned" was political dynamite.[44] In all probability, under other circumstances it would have passed unnoticed; its intrinsic importance derives from the setting, not the phrasing or even the sentiments. Numerous railroad officials had voiced the same kind of opinion from time to time — Leland Stanford, for example, in writing — and the Hepburn testimony is replete with the concept. So blatant in fact had been Vanderbilt's statements on the subject that the Hepburn *Report* took this notice of his freely avowed views: "The claim recently put forth through the press by Mr. Vanderbilt, that in case of a commission, the commission must either own the railroads or the railroads own it, presupposes an absolute hostility between the interests of the railroads and the interests of the public, which in the judgment of this committee, does not, or, at least, should not exist." [45]

As if to make his disregard for public opinion unmistakable, Vanderbilt in the 1882 interview expressed himself even more candidly on the relationship between railroad presidents and the "representatives of the people."

Q. What do you think of this anti-monopoly movement?
A. It is a movement inspired by a set of fools and blackmailers. To be sure there are some men interested in it whose motives are good, if their sense is not. When I want to buy up any politician, I always find the Anti-Monopolists the most purchasable. They don't come so high.[46]

Obviously the latter statement was much more revealing and important than the one upon which Vanderbilt's fame rests, but it failed to gain as much notoriety. "The public be damned" had everything that could be desired in a catch phrase — pungency, simplicity, and brevity. Brief enough in fact to be emblazoned on campaign badges and worn with great ostentation before the election.[47]

It is not clear whether Gould, Vanderbilt, Depew, and others, really were overconfident enough to believe that with the Stalwart aid of Conkling and the President of the United States, Chester Arthur (a Conkling disciple), they could push any slate through, or whether they decided it was worth losing to warn future rebellious politicians of the fate in store for them. Certainly they could not have been prepared for the extent of the disaster that occurred on November 7. The *Evening Post,* then edited by Carl Schurz and E. Lawrence Godkin, and hardly open to the accusation of harboring Anti-Monopoly sympathies, commented:

The defeats of the Republican party in New York, Pennsylvania, Indiana, Connecticut, New Jersey, and even in Massachusetts, following upon that in Ohio are phenomenal. The anti-Republican majorities in some of those States have scarcely any parallel. The so-called tidal wave of 1874 was only a lively ripple compared with this overwhelming flood . . .

The Republican leaders should indulge in no delusion about it: the people have begun to become tired of the Republican party as it has been for some years — tired of its boss rule and its machine methods, tired of its constant professions of reform without performance.[48]

The *Times* hailed the results as "The Work of Retribution," and to support its analysis pointed out that "The majority by which Mr. Cleveland is elected Governor of this State over Judge Folger is absolutely unprecedented in the history of State elections." [49] Such an analysis is also borne out by the fact that though some decline in prices and business activity set in shortly before November, the country was still near the peak of a remarkably prosperous four-year period; there was nothing like the panic of 1873 which probably had accounted to a large extent for the Democratic victory of 1874. Finally, the sheer magnitude of Cleveland's plurality, 192,854, in a state as evenly balanced as New York, is a fact of impressive historical significance.

The plurality dwarfed any previous landslide in New York history and it also towered far above the results in every other state in 1882. Comparing the results in six states singled out by the *Evening Post*

(New Jersey had only local elections) underscores the importance of New York developments in the Democratic victories throughout the nation in 1882.[50]

	Dem. Gov. or Sec. of State, 1882		Rep. Pres., 1880	
	Pluralities	*Percentage*	*Pluralities*	*Percentage*
N. Y.	192,854	58.47	21,033	50.27
Pa.	40,202	47.79	37,276	50.83
Ohio	19,115	50.12	34,267	51.13
Mass.	13,949	52.22	53,245	58.48
Ind.	10,684	49.68	6,642	49.32
Conn.	4,161	51.05	2,656	50.50

No contention is made here that the Gould-Cornell feud in New York, and the events directly preceding it, fundamentally explain the election results throughout the country. On the contrary, it is viewed as merely the catalytic agent precipitating the political explosion building up since 1865. Labor Reformers, Liberal-Republicans, Grangers, Railroad Reformers, Greenbackers, Anti-Monopolists, Independents of multiple stripes and kinds, all had registered angry dissent at various times during nearly two decades. Seen in perspective, 1882 appears to register their cumulative triumph — a triumph, moreover, which shattered the strict ties of party regularity even beyond the repair of the Bloody Shirt and the awful memories of Andersonville. For in that year the issue was sharply drawn as never before between the corporations and the people, with the Republicans representing the "monopolies" and the "money power," and the Democrats on the side of the angels.

In such an atmosphere, even men who were almost religious in their approach to the party of the Union and the "Martyred Lincoln" voted "against the corporations."[51] Depew had successfully led the attack on the Stalwarts in 1881 under the slogan of "Down with the Machine." In 1882 the opponents of what Depew and Conkling together represented went into battle trumpeting, in effect, "Down with the Corporations — And the Machine."

But once the party ties which had copper-riveted postwar American politics were sundered they could never be quite as fast again. The subsequent emergence of third parties and ticket-splitting as a permanent feature of American politics indicates that the country never again sank back into *quite* the blind partisanship bequeathed it by the Civil War and Reconstruction. In this respect, 1882 serves as a significant landmark in the history of American politics. The situation whereby the Republicans represented evil and the Democrats good was obviously fantastically unreal and could not last for long. In New York disillusionment speedily set in, a bare three months after election being enough for Grover Cleveland and the Democratic legislature to do the job. The crucial point is that the campaign of 1882 made it a virtue to defy the strict taboos of the party gods. Like Humpty-Dumpty, after the fall of 1882 the pieces could not all be put back together again.

CLEVELAND DIDN'T PUT IT IN WRITING

The Anti-Monopolists would have been uncharacteristically reticent had they not claimed a large share of the victory, and even the *Times* was disposed to go along with them to some extent. It pointed to the significance of the fact that of 128 Assemblymen only 39 had been re-elected. Ordinarily a large proportion of incumbents were elected and the paper credited the Anti-Monopoly *Record of the Legislature of 1882* as having contributed to the result. The *Record* had listed 40 Assembly-men (the "Forty Thieves") who had voted against the public interest, and the *Times* gave the box score on them as follows:

Of these 40 Assemblymen 28 failed of renomination; and of the 12 re-nominated 6 were defeated at the polls . . .

A separate list of 10 members from this city was prepared containing the names of those who were regarded as specially deserving of defeat, either in the nominating conventions or at the polls. Four of the 10 were nominated, but Col. Murphy of the First District, had the distinction of being the only one re-elected.[52]

Since the three incumbents who had been defeated were all Dem-ocrats — in the year of their party's unprecedented victory — it might be conceded that the "political earthquake" which struck in New York City was fairly selective in its victims. Nor did the Anti-Monopolists confine their boasts to Manhattan, where, by election time, they were fairly well organized. In a triumphant post-mortem Thurber pointed to the Assembly results, and noted also that the League had sent out 300,000 sets of Cleveland-Hill ballots and free canal ballots to 50,000 Anti-Monopolists on its mailing list. The wide disparity between the Cleveland-Hill plurality of 200,000 and the rest of the Democratic ticket's mere 100,000 was assigned by Thurber to the League's activity and in-fluence. It is highly doubtful that Thurber's explanation was all embrac-ing but the margin of the gap does provide substantiation for some part of his claims.[53] Moreover, he continued:

In other States the Democratic majorities were comparatively small, and these I attribute largely to the dissemination of anti-monopoly literature by the Board of Trade and Transportation for several years past, and the exten-sive work in the same line done by the Anti-Monopoly League during the past eighteen months.

Probably the millions of pamphlets sent out by these organizations and the work done by sympathizers had contributed, directly or indi-rectly, to the election results of 1882. But the extent of their contribution is something else again. The key point here is that the election results undoubtedly elated members of the various reform movements in the country and provided them with the kind of victory necessary to raise their sights still higher.

Thurber's analysis was printed in the *Husbandman* in November and had been prompted by a letter from its editor, William Armstrong. Apparently the latter had become convinced by the unprecedented "complete political independence" displayed on November 7 that the time was ripe for a new party and informed the New Yorker of these views. Thurber replied that it did not make much difference to him how the results were achieved, so long as they were achieved, but went on to warn that continued organization on the part of the people was necessary if both the Democrats and the Republicans were to be kept in line.

The Anti-Monopolists' worst suspicions were rapidly confirmed by Grover Cleveland after he took office on January 1, 1883. As noted above, their early doubts about Cleveland's railroad connections had been allayed by an interview with him shortly after the Democratic convention. That he then gave definite assurances regarding his position on key issues was not only asserted by Anti-Monopolists after his inauguration,[54] but seems apparent from the endorsement of Cleveland in *Justice* on October 14, following the interview. Unfortunately, as a leading Anti-Monopolist who had warned against supporting him subsequently pointed out, the League had failed to get any statements in writing. After his nomination, the letter maintained, the "monopolists" entered into negotiations which led to their offering no opposition to Cleveland's election. And the writer pointed to the significance of the fact that Cleveland delayed his public letter of acceptance which generally straddled the issues until *after* he received the Anti-Monopolist endorsement.[55] According to those who had interviewed him in Buffalo, however, Cleveland had assured them "that the railroad commission bill ought to be executed in the spirit in which it was adopted." He was also quoted as having said in reference to the bill that "the time had gone by when principles could be put in platforms with mental reservations." [56]

The first hint that Cleveland was going to break his promises and ignore the pledges in the Democratic platform came when he failed even to mention the transportation question in the governor's annual message to the legislature. When his nominations for the Board of Railroad Commissioners came out some days later, Cleveland's future course was fairly plain. The law made it mandatory for him to accept the nominee of the commercial organizations; hence John O'Donnell, an Anti-Monopoly leader who had been active in the fight for the commission, was put on the board. Cleveland, however, saw fit to give him the shortest term.

And it can not be said that the governor's two appointees demonstrated that they showed the "spirit in which it [the bill] was adopted"; nor were they distinguished by outstanding technical qualifications or free from political attachments.[57]

John Kernan, a rising lawyer of Utica, was the son of a former U.S. senator, Francis Kernan. The Kernans were a powerful family in New York politics and closely allied with former Governor Horatio Seymour of Utica. According to the *Times*, the latter exercised great influence with Grover Cleveland.[58] John Kernan had never held any political office, but he had several times been chairman of the Democratic Committee in Oneida County and had frequently taken the stump during election campaigns.[59]

Young Kernan also had been the legal counsellor of an interesting organization suddenly come to life in New York in 1882, the "Merchants, Manufacturers, and Farmers' Union." Hastily formed by the specially favored shippers along the line of the New York Central, the "Union's" objective had been to defeat the railroad commission bill. After its passage in the legislature they had brought heavy pressure upon Cornell to veto the bill but were turned down. Shortly before the meeting of the Republican convention in 1882, one of its leaders, Dennis J. McCarthy, Jr., made this frank avowal of the group's aims: to defeat Cornell because he signed the railroad commission bill, and to work for its repeal.[60] To employ understatement, Kernan's position as the legal counsellor for a "Union" of this type did not suggest that he would carry out the Railroad Commission Act "in the spirit in which it was adopted."

Cleveland's other appointee was also looked upon with suspicion by railroad reformers, and after the board had been in operation some eighteen months the record was said to have justified it.[61] Among other reasons for the original distrust, William E. Rogers was the son-in-law of Hamilton Fish, a potent force in Republican circles, and had been recommended for the post by General Grant, John J. Astor, Samuel Sloan, Edwin D. Morgan, and similar Wall Street figures.[62]

Several days after Commissioners Kernan and Rogers were named (to the surprise of everyone but Cleveland's intimates),[63] the *Times'* Albany correspondent reported that some Democrats were angry over the governor's appointments in general, and that there appeared to be a rift between Boss Manning and "the Seymour-Kernan crowd." The selection of Kernan, Jr., as railroad commissioner had caused the first mutterings since it had been widely supposed that William Purcell of the Rochester *Union and Advertiser* was to have the job.[64] The *Times'* dispatches during this period, therefore, tend to support the heated charges brought against Cleveland some months later by James G. Shepard, a long-time Democrat, prominent Granger, Farmers' Allianceman, and

Anti-Monopolist. Shepard charged Cleveland with deliberate bad faith in his appointments and maintained that his betrayal of promises to the Anti-Monopoly League in this and other matters would be answered by the people at the polls.[65] (The election results of 1883 and 1884 in New York make him appear to have been a fairly good prophet.)

Bad as Cleveland's appointments were in the eyes of Anti-Monopolists, his vetoes were worse. The most famous, and the one which aroused the most ill will, particularly among railroad reformers long active in the movement, was the veto of the five-cent fare bill. (The bill set the fare on the elevated roads at five cents for the entire day rather than only at rush hours.) By this time, Jay Gould and Cyrus Field (of Atlantic Cable fame) controlled the New York City elevated railroads, and the watered stock, that is, their recent additions plus the past infusions by Samuel J. Tilden, amounted to approximately half the capitalization. Legislation fixing the elevated fare at five cents throughout the day had been agitated for years and had come before the 1882 legislature only to be defeated by the lobby. In fact, it was one of the chief issues upon which the group in the Assembly known as the "Forty Thieves" had won its dubious reputation. During the election campaign the bill had received much prominence, and, as the *Times'* Albany correspondent put it, "When the Democratic delegates to Syracuse last fall and those to Albany the year before endorsed the platforms which had been cheerfully drawn up by their leaders, they had in mind the elevated roads, and they howled themselves hoarse over the planks that were directed against monopolies in general and this one in particular." [66]

Upon assembling in 1883, after winning victory under a reform banner, one of the earliest acts of the Democratic legislature was to pass the five-cent fare bill with substantial unanimity. However, the attorneys for the roads, headed by David Dudley Field, drew up elaborate briefs against it, and on March 1 an extraordinary petition was sent from New York City to Governor Cleveland. Prayers offered for the veto of the bill were signed by one of the greatest array of financial names ever put to any petition and represented approximately a billion dollars of capital.

> The undersigned residents of the city of New York beg leave to represent to the Governor that the bill now before him, known as the five cent fare bill, is regarded with great apprehension as a breach of faith on the part of the state and an attack upon the rights of property, injurious to the holders of the stock and bonds issued and held, *based upon the chartered rights of the corporations of this state* [italics added].[67]

Among the names on the petition were Drexel, Morgan & Company, E. D. Morgan & Company, Jesse Seligman & Company, Brown Brothers

& Company, Morton, Bliss & Company, Hamilton Fish, Hugh J. Jewett, William H. Vanderbilt, David Dows & Company, etc. To appreciate the significance of the petition, and the quality of its signatures, it is necessary to indicate the railroad developments then taking place. Only against the background of growing national sentiment for government control of railroads and other major segments of the economy does the significance of Cleveland's veto of the five-cent fare bill emerge. Without the perspective gained by placing the veto in context, the furor over its passage seems disproportionate. But in context it appears both as an excellent illustration of the leading question of political economy then agitating the country, and a key development in the conflict over its resolution.

The cycle of booming prosperity, beginning late in 1879, had been a tremendous stimulus to railroad expansion, consolidation, and promotion, particularly in the West and Southwest. As in the late sixties and early seventies, this activity had been accompanied by a wave of financial plundering which was to lead to the stock-market crash of 1884 and to an even more painful reckoning in 1893. Though the techniques were more refined than in the earlier period, hostility to railroads throughout the nation, for some years quiescent, was again growing. The Board of Trade and the Anti-Monopoly League flooded the country with pamphlets, and branch Leagues, particularly in Nebraska and Kansas, had scored notable successes in 1882.

In many cases the men signing the petition to Cleveland were the men financing, promoting, and speculating in the western roads. Whether the elevated fare was five cents all day or not would scarcely have called forth such an array of great names. It was the doctrine proclaimed by the petition which made it significant. For if the doctrine prevailed and the bill, overwhelmingly passed by the legislature, was defeated on constitutional grounds, an important victory would have been gained against the tendency towards altering "the chartered rights of . . . corporations" — a tendency which renewed railroad free booting was visibly accelerating. Thus, after Cleveland answered the prayers of a "Billion Dollars and the Corporation," Jay Gould's paper (the *World*) printed a full column of statements from various financiers singing the governor's praises in this key:

Mr. O. D. Baldwin, the President of the Fourth National Bank said:

Governor Cleveland in vetoing this bill has done a good and wise thing. He has virtually stepped in between the capitalists in the State and the Communistic element in the Legislature. This latter element has been growing in strength during the past few years and has exercised a depressing influence upon all securities, especially of late, while this bill has been pending in the Legislature. It is to be hoped that this check may exercise a wholesome effect.[68]

Considering the publicity attached to the bill, the hostility to Gould and everything he stood for, and the solemn pledges made by the Democrats, Cleveland's veto would have been certain to provoke anger in any event. But it was the accompanying message that brought on the harshest criticisms. Cleveland might easily have taken various grounds if his intention simply had been to defeat the reduction in fare, but he chose to meet the underlying issues involved. To be more accurate, he practically adopted the brief submitted to him by David Dudley Field. Under the circumstances Cleveland's message led to the conclusion that he was eager to proclaim his agreement with the dominant financiers and railroad entrepreneurs of the land.

The major contention embodied in his message was that the original charters of the elevated roads and the General Railroad Act of 1850 constituted a firm and irrevocable contract precluding subsequent regulation. In effect, he fell back on the doctrine enunciated in the Dartmouth College case of 1819:

The constitutional objections which I have suggested to the bill under consideration are not, I think, removed by the claim that the proposed legislation is in the nature of an alteration of the charters of these companies, and that this is permitted by the State Constitution and by the provisions of some of the laws to which I have referred. I suppose that while the charters of corporations may be altered or repealed, it must be done in subordination to the Constitution of the United States, which is the supreme law of the land. This leads to the conclusion that the alteration of a charter cannot be made the pretext for the passage of a law which *impairs the obligation of a contract* [italics added].

To make the cloak of legal immunity as tight-fitting as possible, Cleveland added this dictum:

If I am mistaken in supposing that there are legal objections to this bill, there is another consideration which furnishes to my mind a sufficient reason why I should not give it my approval. It seems to me that to reduce these fares arbitrarily at this time and under existing circumstances, involves a breach of faith on the part of the State and a betrayal of confidence which the State has invited.[69]

Apart from the implications of the message,[70] one factual point is pertinent in considering Cleveland's position. No basis existed for his contention that the five-cent fare bill violated an "obligation of contract" because the acts relating to the roads expressly gave the legislature the right to amend or repeal them at its pleasure. As Railroad Commissioner O'Donnell was later to show, "the entire system of elevated roads is by express words under the contract of the Legislature to change or repeal at pleasure." And the claim that the New York Common Council in 1875 had approved certain rates of fare — and thereby entered into an implied contract — was equally spurious since the record showed that it had only approved the routes recommended by the commissioners of Rapid Transit.[71]

The paper which attacked Cleveland most mercilessly for his veto message was James Gordon Bennett's *Herald* — a paper, it might be noted, thoroughly out of sympathy with the Anti-Monopoly League on most issues. The veto was made public on March 2 and the *Herald's* editorial the next day was headed: "Which Are the Stronger, the Corporations or the People Who Created Them?" [72] After commenting on the fact that Cleveland copied his "smoothly reading verbiage" from the briefs of the railroad attorneys, it observed that the governor had often been urged to test its alleged unconstitutionality by signing the bill and letting the courts, the proper agency, decide the issue. Concerning Cleveland's anxiety over good faith, the editorial continued:

he has left something out of sight in his veto. He has omitted to take notice of the many and gross breaches of faith committed by these corporations toward the State and the people . . . We may justly say that, being the chief executive guardian of the rights of the State and the people, Governor Cleveland is unfaithful to his official trust when he argues the case of the elevated railroads as if they are clear of frauds upon popular rights . . . He knows, as every lawyer knows, that it is a fundamental maxim of the common law that 'fraud voids every contract tainted with it,' and yet he alleges that any restriction of fares, on these roads, will be a 'breach of faith.' The faith for which Governor Cleveland argues, as if he were one of the very attorneys whose brief he follows is not a 'pure and simple faith,' but a faith which would bind the people to one side of the bargain and release Mr. Tilden, Mr. Gould, the Field family and the rest of the six years' series of elevated road tricksters from any obligation on the other side to the people and the State.

Then the *Herald* went on to discuss the more basic question involved, and the politics surrounding the veto.

Governor Cleveland has made his choice as a lawyer, as a public officer, and as a politician. He has cast his lot on the side of the great corporations and corporate manipulators, and staked his chances for future political preferment on their favor. He has done it boldly, with no attempt at disguise. We respect him for that. We expected as much from him. The political and legal principles to which he has given his adherence in this veto are of much broader application than to the elevated road fare question. They relate to every railroad corporation in this State and probably to every one in the United States, and there are many other classes of chartered interests to which they apply. They have a direct bearing upon the great political issues which are taking shape in the national arena. Monopolies of all kinds, whether fostered by a State Charter or a federal tariff, have many political theories in common, the servants of one are as a rule easy to become servants of the other, and it is quite touching to witness a hopeful Presidential candidate choose his side in the coming struggle between them and the people for the control of the powers of government.

Adding the final twist to the knife, the editorial pointed both to the Democratic platform, directly antithetical to the gubernatorial veto, and to Cleveland's letter of acceptance giving it his "hearty approval." Several days later the *Herald* returned to the attack. It argued that the position taken by Cleveland was in flagrant contradiction to repeated rulings of the highest state courts and the Supreme Court, and that the principle of state control had been judicially affirmed or recognized in a long line of decisions.[73] But although the *Herald* emphasized the constitutional issue involved, it was the *Times* which best described the political maneuvering accompanying the veto.

In January the *Times*' Albany correspondent had already called attention to the rift between the Manning machine and "the Seymour-Kernan crowd," and concluded that the latter group had gotten the upper hand.[74] Late in February the Albany dispatch predicted that it would create no surprise if Cleveland vetoed the five-cent fare bill. According to the *Times*, C. S. Cary of Cattaraugus County, a bosom companion of the governor, his recognized representative in the Assembly, and a railroad president by vocation, had discussed the bill thoroughly with Horatio Seymour and was now satisfied that the Democratic legislature had made a mistake in its treatment of the New York elevated roads. Cleveland was pictured as an ardent admirer of Seymour, and, during the few weeks that he had occupied the Executive Chamber was said to have paid close attention to the "sage of Deerfield's" views upon matters of state and party policy. And Cleveland's deference to Seymour was described as one of the circumstances creating jealousy and anger among the members of Boss Manning's machine who had assumed from the outset that they were to have exclusive control of the Democratic administration.[75]

The *Times*' correspondent's accuracy in predicting both the internal Democratic quarrels and Cleveland's veto indicates that he had excellent sources and supports his later account of its reception in the legislature. The effect of the veto was said to have coupled the name of Jay Gould with the word Democracy "in a way that grated harshly on the ears of sensitive Democrats." It also recalled incidents of the last campaign when Gould had sent his "Boodle" to Saratoga and defeated Cornell, and then sent it hurriedly to Syracuse to secure "the nomination and election of a Democratic candidate for Governor who was perfectly acceptable to Gould and his hirelings." The topic was eagerly dwelt upon by both Republicans and Democrats after the message was read, and the correspondent ventured an observation which takes on particular importance because the *Times* had abandoned its Republican heritage to support Cleveland in the 1882 campaign.

Whether he [Cleveland] or his friends derived aid and encouragement from Jay Gould or not will perhaps never be clearly proved. In the absence of any proof to the contrary, however, a great many voters of both parties will continue to believe that the sharp, unscrupulous Wall Street operator has captured the coterie who constitute the leaders of the Democratic party, and that, in the language of the 'Street', he is 'working them for all they are worth'. On one point there can be no doubt, however, and that is that the Governor's veto is predicted upon the theory that his party would lose caste with the moneyed concerns of the State if the Five Cent Fare bill was signed, and the history of the politics of the last few years is to create the impression that moneyed concerns are the ones to patronize, because of the financial support which they can render in a hotly contested campaign. This idea is known to be endorsed by some of the Democratic leaders, who think they see a rapid return of their party once more to power by currying the favor of men of Gould's stripe.[76]

Both the *Times'* and the *Herald's* interpretations of the controlling reasons for the veto are reinforced by a private letter sent to Cleveland by an upstate lawyer while the bill was on his desk. "The better class of both parties," the Oswego lawyer wrote, were alarmed by the bill and regarded it as a triumph of the "communistic element," and the first step in the destruction of corporate rights and investments. "This feeling seems to be *so general and deep rooted* that I thought it my duty to drop you this note, — as it is well sometimes to know the public pulse. I may add that all of our political friends hereabouts believe (as I do) that a bold, ringing veto of this bill would reassure the capitalists of the country, inspire confidence everywhere, and achieve for you a *national popularity* that would not 'go down' at the bidding of any rival in 1884." [77]

Cleveland's bold, ringing veto probably did help him to become President but the hostile reaction to his railroad commission appointments and the veto of the five-cent fare bill, along with similar appointments and vetoes, significantly affected the future pattern of the campaigns for railroad regulation. For one thing, Anti-Monopoly dreams of achieving a balance of power status were eventually shattered, and the demand for a new party soon proved to be irresistible. For another, Cleveland's nomination by the Democrats for the Presidency in 1884 was taken as proof that the party had sold out to Jay Gould. Finally, his New York railroad commission appointments, thoroughly raked over in 1884, strengthened the supporters of the Reagan bill in their opposition to a National Board of Railroad Commissioners. New York was viewed as a clear example of the ease with which such an agency would be taken in camp by the roads; and since Cleveland was President when the Reagan and Cullom bills were up for serious consideration, he would name the commissioners if the latter measure were enacted.

ANTI-MONOPOLY DRIFTS TOWARD INDEPENDENCE

Although the New York Anti-Monopolists were disillusioned by Cleveland's disregard for Democratic pledges, the major third party impetus came out of the West. In that section the antirailroad movement had won impressive political victories in 1882, and the locus of power now began to shift away from the Empire State. Early in 1883, upon western initiative, a call was circulated for the antimonopoly forces to convene at Chicago on July 4 "for the purpose of organizing a new political party to espouse the cause of legitimate industry in the irrepressible conflict already entered upon between the confederated monopolies and the people." The enthusiasm of the westerners was easily understood. No less experienced a politician than Representative S. S. Cox of New York believed that antimonopoly was "to be the great issue of the future." Writing to John Reagan in April 1883, he recited the signs that pointed towards its future prominence. "That future is appreciated with your bill. It cannot be set aside." (If Reagan wasn't going to run for speaker of the next House would he lend his support and prestige to Cox?)[78]

Signs of the times notwithstanding, the New York Anti-Monopoly leaders regarded a third party as premature and *Justice* indicated its disapproval. Ironically, it took the form of an open letter to Jay Burrows, secretary of the Nebraska Farmers' Alliance, and a leader in the movement for a third party.[79] Ironically because a letter from Burrows to Francis B. Thurber in May 1882 indicates that the original impulse for the creation of an Anti-Monopoly League in Nebraska had come from the East.[80] (Burrows, incidentally, was a native New Yorker and had grown up in Chautauqua County.)

Burrows had enclosed with his 1882 letter a confidential circular from him to Nebraska Alliancemen urging them to attend the meeting to organize a state Anti-Monopoly League.

This meeting has been called at the instigation of the National League, and is an honest effort to organize those classes of the people of the State who are sincere Anti-Monopolists, but who are ineligible to membership in the Alliance.[81]

Thurber had been asked by Burrows to send a message by way of encouragement to the new organization, and was informed of the Alliance's plan of action.

We intend to keep in the background, lest the Monopoly papers will pronounce the League as a bantling of the Alliance. But we will see that the organization falls into proper hands.

Apparently the "proper hands" had done an excellent job in Nebraska and the 1882 campaign went well for the Anti-Monopolists. Flushed with victory, the Nebraskans now were out to smash the old parties and the open letter printed in *Justice* was designed to cool their enthusiasm.

The major argument advanced against an independent party was that the basic issues were not yet sufficiently understood by the people to overcome the practical difficulties involved. One of the difficulties cited was that even the *organized* reform elements were not in agreement upon the proper measures to stress. Thus, the call for the Chicago conference was strongly "free trade," a position criticized as introducing "an element of discord at the start, which will split the convention to pieces, as it now splits both the parties."[82] *Justice's* position was that the convention should be utilized to perfect the Anti-Monopoly organization on a truly national basis and that the new party project should be filed for future reference. Despite the severe strain put upon the doctrine by a governor such as Cleveland, the paper still expressed faith in the balance of power concept.[83]

Aided by the campaign waged by *Justice,* the New York leaders of Anti-Monopoly still retained sufficient influence to direct the movement. Contrary to the expressed purpose of the call, the Chicago conference did not form a new party. Instead, after protracted debate a resolution offered by N. B. Kilmer of New York was adopted. His resolution provided for a national organization with a president, a vice-president for each state and territory, and other officers. Branches would be established in every state in the Union and, unlike the original National Anti-Monopoly League, annual dues of $1.00 collected to finance the work. In deference to the western majority at the conference, Kilmer stressed that "His resolution did not prevent the Anti-Monopolists of any State from running a separate ticket if they believed they could by so doing, more rapidly advance the cause which we had at heart." [84]

John F. Henry, one of the small group of men who had founded the New York Cheap Transportation Association back in 1873, was elected president of the new National Anti-Monopoly Organization. Kilmer was chosen assistant secretary, and Indiana and Illinois furnished the secretary and treasurer, respectively. To indicate the creation of a new body, the word "League" was dropped out of the title.[85]

If an easterner was chosen president, and eastern advice was taken in the matter of a third party, western views prevailed in the matter of a platform. Despite New York protests, a strong preamble and platform were adopted; railway, banking, tariff, and land monopolies were denounced, and a long list of measures advocated to break their power. Special emphasis was given to railroad regulation and a Congressional committee was called for to investigate the cost of construction, as well as the cost of transportation, and thereby insure appropriate legislation. But these measures were only the beginning. The platform demanded a postal telegraph, forfeiture of 105,000,000 acres of land by corporations and states, prohibition of non-resident alien acquisition of land, abolition of the National Banking system, a graduated income tax, postal savings banks, prohibition of speculation in commodities, amendment of patent laws to prevent monopolies, direct election of all public officials "as far as practicable" including the President and Vice-President, and the free trade plank so ardently desired in the West.[86]

This wide-ranging platform may have prepared the way for the Populists to follow in the next decade, but in the 1880's it served to disrupt the Anti-Monopoly movement. Several indications of the underlying sectional cleavage cropped out at the conference. For example, the resolution offered by New Yorkers to eliminate the tariff plank was defeated with some display of emotion. "Mr. Crews said the East couldn't tell the West any longer 'Protection is for your interest', because the West had found that that was a falsehood (applause)." [87] The most significant exchange occurred during the debate over the form of organization. Until this conference, despite the impressive title, the National Anti-Monopoly League had been largely a New York affair. Though other states had branch Leagues, organizationally they were autonomous. Only the prestige, experience, influence, and legislative success of the founders, Thurber, Henry, L. E. Chittenden, Peter Cooper, etc., and the existence of *Justice,* had enabled the New Yorkers to dominate the movement. But Cleveland's desertion of the antimonopoly principles contained in the Democratic platform had been a cruel blow to New York prestige. Its vaunted balance of power concept, so triumphant in November, was thoroughly deflated by July. One of the speeches in opposition to Kilmer's resolution against a third party was reported in this succinct fashion:

Mr. C. O. Dixon, of Illinois, said the claim was made that there were two hundred thousand Anti-Monopolists in New York; they elected a governor, and at the first opportunity he betrayed them. Out West, in Nebraska, they acted with horse sense, and they had twenty-eight members of the State Legislature and a well organized party. Judging by results, which plan was best? [88]

Kilmer's resolution prevailed, but thereafter the West increasingly controlled the movement. The original National Anti-Monopoly League was dissolved in August and New York took its place as merely one of the state leagues.[89] *Justice* continued to preach the balance of power concept, but Cleveland's repudiation of antimonopoly placed the New Yorkers in a dilemma. To exert the balance of power it was necessary to support one set of politicians against another; yet in the 1883 campaign the Anti-Monopolists were hard put to work up enthusiasm for either ticket. On the one hand, the Republicans, chastened by catastrophe, had nominated respectable men and adopted an improved platform; no disposition existed to take it seriously. On the other, there was the dismal record of the Democratic "reform" legislature of 1883 and the even more dismal reality of Cleveland, the "reform" governor praised by his party's 1883 convention.

Anti-Monopolists leaned to the Democrats but the distinction was extremely fine — certainly nothing to make it possible to wage a spirited canvass.[90] Moreover, no major issues on the state level appeared to take the place of the railroad commission and the free canal which had served as excellent rallying points for the campaigns of 1881 and 1882. To be discussed more fully in the next chapter, railroad construction had led to severe rate wars on local as well as on through traffic, an almost unprecedented situation in New York, and one which softened upstate hostility towards roads which obviously were no longer "monopolies." The pool fell apart, differentials were ignored, and railroad managers were far less arrogant than in former days. Finally, the merchants had failed to support the farmers' demand for pro rata before the railroad commission that summer, virtually ending the alliance between the metropolis and the upstate rural areas. Some Alliance and Grange leaders continued to show interest in Anti-Monopoly, but there was nothing left to make rank and file farmers forget or forgive the free canal and "oleomargarine-glucose-Thurber." [91]

ANTI-MONOPOLY AT THE CROSSROADS

Justice's editorial policy reflected the essentially negative position to which the New York Anti-Monopoly leaders had been reduced in 1883. Opposed to a third party, distrustful of the major parties, disillusioned by the turn of events, lacking major issues upon which to carry on an independent canvass, the League contented itself with attacking the worst of the legislators up for re-election and calling for their defeat. Another record of the legislature was published — indeed, in many ways an improvement over the previous one — and Anti-Monopolists were urged to reward friends and punish enemies. But a close reading of *Justice* suggests that by this time the earlier vigor and spirit had gone out of the antimonopoly movement in New York. Notwithstanding, when the election returns were in, the paper was quick to claim an important victory.

In marked contrast to the Democratic sweep of 1882, the Republicans recaptured the legislature and elected the Secretary of State, the top office in the contest. Only 6 of 25 state senators singled out for punishment survived, and the organ of the New York League saw the election results as proof of "the rising tide of public opinion against corporate aggressions." The striking reversal in the state was attributed to "Cleveland's violation of his pledges and his disregard of Democratic principles." In post-mortem fashion, the governor's course of action was reviewed and a warning sounded that unless he and his supporters were deposed from leadership the Democrats faced gloomy prospects in 1884.[92]

Justice was not alone in finding the election results proof of a growing spirit of political independence. The New York *Times* drew similar conclusions from the returns, asserted that the tendency of public opinion was strongly in the direction of reform, and flatly maintained that the "reform idea . . . is the controlling force in American politics." [93]

One significant difference, however, marks the election post-mortem of 1883 from the two preceding it. Anti-Monopolists could find proof of the acceptance of their ideas but they could not point to any specific victory as a result of their work. No real effort had been made in 1883 to take an active role in the campaign, and the League had become almost moribund other than through its publications. In many ways the resignation of Francis B. Thurber from the chairmanship of the State Executive Committee symbolizes the changed status of the movement in New York. Personal considerations dictated the resignation, but his letter of explanation avowing continued interest in reform is revealing. According to Thurber, the Anti-Monopolists need only maintain a position of observation and keep the people informed because "the agitation for the reforms we advocate is already so far advanced that it cannot be stopped. All classes of citizens now admit that the corruption and aggressions of corporate power not only unjustly oppress labor, but are endangering legitimate property rights and undermining the very foundations of the Republic." [94]

If Thurber was satisfied and willing to retire to the sidelines, at least two other founders of the original National Anti-Monopoly League were not. In October 1883 John Swinton, a journalist and labor reformer, published the first issue of the paper bearing his name. His major contention was that all the divergent reform groups were drifting in the same direction, "toward the practical assertion of those rights of man proclaimed in our revolution, which are now being undermined in an alarming way." The need of the hour was to forget differences and to unite the scattered strength of Anti-Monopolists, Greenbackers, Farmers' Alliancemen, Free-Soilers, Social Democrats, Knights of Labor, Central Labor Unionists, Trades Assemblymen, etc. Together, these forces could make an impressive showing, and Swinton hammered away at the idea that they take to the field in 1884 as a unit.[95] In sharp contrast to Thurber, who symbolized entrepreneurs striving to right the balance of power thrown askew by the Communication Revolution, John Swinton symbolized the tiny, quasi-radical minority in the United States preaching mild class conflict.

Another charter member of the League, John F. Henry, also disagreed with Thurber, and, as president of the national Anti-Monopoly organization, was in an excellent position to insure independent action. In response to the call he sent out for a conference to nominate a Presidential ticket, some 160 delegates representing 21 states and territories assembled at Chicago on May 14.[96] In spite of the New York League's forceful opposition, a third party was formed and Benjamin F. Butler of Massachusetts nominated as its candidate for President. Hardly a man to inspire confidence in a crusade for "the rights of man," Butler's long and unsavory career included allegiance to both major parties and flirtations with the Greenbackers. In fact, for some months after his nomination it was uncertain whether Butler would actually run, and his eventual decision to do so, as he later admitted, was only motivated by a desire to draw off votes from the Democrats and elect James Blaine.[97]

Why Butler was selected by the Anti-Monopolists and Greenbackers to challenge the "robber barons," and the details of the 1884 campaign per se, are not relevant here. What is relevant is that with the nomination of Grover Cleveland by the Democrats and Blaine by the Republicans, the New York Anti-Monopolists reconsidered their decision and joined in the third party movement. With all their old time fervor, Thurber and numerous other pioneers of the movement for railroad regulation attacked the major parties for nominating candidates "identified with monopoly interests," and succeeded in forcing "social questions" into greater prominence than would otherwise have been the case.

Two aspects of the 1884 campaign are particularly pertinent to the present study for they suggest the atmosphere in which the Interstate Commerce Act was passed and the relationship of the Communication Revolution to late nineteenth-century American protest movements. In June, *Justice* launched an unrestrained attack on Cleveland as a tool of corporations and a hand-picked Gould candidate. Letters were published from James Shepard, William J. Fowler, L. E. Chittenden, and various other Anti-Monopolists mercilessly raking over his record as governor. Even the New York Farmers' Alliance was temporarily resurrected to issue an address to the people denouncing him. Cleveland's appointments to the railroad commission, and his veto of the five-cent fare bill were stressed in the attacks, and anti-Cleveland papers all over the country soon picked up the refrain.[98] (In addition, Cleveland was vulnerable on other counts, including his veto of a bill limiting street car conductors to a 12-hour day on the interesting ground that the men were being deprived of their freedom by such legislation. Labor in fact was even more virulent in its denunciation of him than were advocates of railroad regulation.)

Judging from the innumerable extracts printed each week in *Justice,* reform groups were far more concerned with Cleveland's failings on the major issues of the day than they were with his alleged lack of personal morality. They were opposed to him politically, not because he had fathered a bastard but because they thought he was one. By the fall of the year, A. M. Pence, a well-known western lawyer, was writing to the Chicago *Tribune* that Cleveland's election would jeopardize the entire movement for transportation regulation. The next President was bound to appoint a number of Supreme Court justices, he noted, and Cleveland was "the most prominent representative of the theory that railroads and other monopolies were beyond the control of the States." Pence did not think Cleveland had been bribed to veto the five-cent fare bill — instead his honest convictions were viewed as deplorable.

Gov. Cleveland is evidently a thorough-paced monopolist, and is a graduate, taking the highest honors, in that college of political science presided over by the editors of the *Nation* and the New York *Evening Post,* who for many years held up to scorn and contumely, and who scoffed and jeered at the granger legislation of the 'rowdy West'.[99]

Evidence that the attack upon Cleveland was taken seriously by his supporters is seen by the fact that both the *Nation* and the New York *Times* — apparently the *Times'* editors did not believe consistency to be a virtue in this case — felt compelled to defend his veto of the five-cent fare bill and the numerous other vetoes and appointments cited to his discredit.[100] General Edward F. Jones, a prominent New York Democrat, Granger, and Farmers' Allianceman, attempted to answer the Alliance's address attacking Cleveland's record. He stressed Cleveland's personal honesty, but admitted: "It is not my object to defend Gov. Cleveland from these criticisms, for frankly, I agree to a very great extent therewith." [101]

Echoes of the widespread publicity given to Cleveland's record as governor failed to die down after his election as President. As the campaign for national railroad regulation grew in intensity, a split developed in the ranks of reformers. One group supported the Reagan bill which essentially depended upon the courts to carry out its provisions; the other preferred the Cullom bill which provided a national railroad commission appointed by the President to administer appropriate legislation. Among the most determined opponents of the Cullom bill was the National Grange. The Grange insisted that "The people want no board of Railroad Commissioners to stand between them and the transportation companies." It claimed that state commissioners had worked badly and failed "to enforce the law of the Common Carriers." And it would appear to be more than a coincidence that New York was singled out by name to prove the dangers of such a form of regulation.[102]

The New York commission came in for especially sharp criticism by James F. Hudson in his famous book of 1886 on the railroad problem. Like the spokesmen for the National Grange, Hudson thought it significant that the railroads preferred commissions to all other types of regulation. And he suggested that the New York commission's "extraordinary tenderness" for the roads was a potent factor inducing such preference. Without mentioning names, he suggested that its "extraordinary tenderness" stemmed from the fact that the all powerful influence exerted by railroad companies had "reached the members of the commission." [103] Distrust of the commission form of regulation on precisely these grounds had been expressed before Cleveland became governor of New York, but to note that his regime did nothing to dispel the distrust is to resort again to delicate understatement.

In one other important respect the third party movement of 1884 impinges upon the present study. Before the campaign was over, virtually all discontented groups to whom the names of Blaine and Cleveland were equally distasteful joined in the People's party. The result was that the forces using Butler as a rallying point represented nearly every panacea for social ills then afloat in the United States. Thus, despite its having a candidate like Ben Butler, the 1884 third party movement was essentially aimed at men who, to repeat John Swinton's formulation, were drifting toward "the practical assertion of those rights of man proclaimed in our revolution, which are now being undermined in an alarming way." In other words, it was a fairly broad based campaign designed to prevent the Communication Revolution from destroying the relatively middle-class structure and egalitarian philosophy of mid-nineteenth century America. Holding forth the vision that the new forces of steam and electricity could be harnessed for the benefit of all within the framework of American institutions, when the men participating in the 1884 campaign talked of "the people" they did not only mean specific property groups. In a certain sense the 1884 campaign can be taken as the ideological culmination of the agitation which New York mercantile groups had been waging since the early seventies. Almost in spite of themselves some of their leaders briefly came to enunciate concepts and slogans which were much less conservative than those originally impelling them to action.

The Anti-Monopoly League did not die with the campaign of 1884 but slowly faded away. The fading process, however, is not an integral part of this study and can be disregarded. The purpose here has not been to present a history of the League but to trace the process whereby the Communication Revolution forced the merchants and farmers of the

Empire State to take the lead in the reform movements of the seventies and eighties. Building upon the concepts inherent in the Farmers' Alliance, the merchants of the metropolis expanded them to include the political union of the entire people against the "corporate monopolies." Railroads headed the list but no disposition existed to ignore telegraph, telephone, and public utility corporations in general. The result was the prototype of the independent mass pressure group, which, in one form or another, has been an important feature of American politics ever since.

CHAPTER X

New York and the Interstate Commerce Act

It is noticeable that there are more advocates of Government interference than heretofore, and that the applicants no longer represent one single interest . . .

Thus the curious spectacle is presented of friend and opponent alike pleading for redress at the hands of the Government. The mercantile community ask that violent fluctuations in rates be done away with, that drawbacks and rebates be made impossible, that no more be charged for a long haul than a short one, that discrimination be abolished, that diversion of freight be no longer permitted, and that various other grievances, real or imaginary, be attended to. The railroads too, now look to the Government to help them out of their difficulties. They want to see to it that no road does business for less than cost, that minimum rates be fixed by law, that pools and combinations be legalized, that the building of parallel and competing lines be prohibited in the future, and that solvent roads be in some way protected against the competition of bankrupt roads. Finally, there come the investors in railroad property — stockholders and bondholders — who ask for much the same thing, but in addition want a remedy against speculative directors and managers, some provision against an impairment of their investment either by parties without or within, statutes enforcing their rights and privileges, protection of the minority against the majority, a guarantee against unfair leases or leases or other arrangements made by directors without the consent of stockholders, and so on *ad infinitum* . . . In a word, merchants want to be protected against the railroads, the railroads want to be protected against themselves, and investors against both. And they all cry for the same soothing syrup — legislative enactment.

Editorial, "Government Control of Railroads," *Commercial and Financial Chronicle*, 17:666–667 (June 6, 1885).

As might perhaps be expected, the theoretical bases of American railroad reform essentially derived from the experiences and experiments of the more mature European economies. Reading the contemporary literature after the Civil War one is struck by the decisive impact of

European doctrines and debates. For example, Josiah Quincy, Jr., probably the most prominent figure in the reform movement during the late sixties and early seventies, delivered an address to the Boston Board of Trade in October 1867 entitled "Public Interest and Private Monopoly." Emblazoned on the cover of the pamphlet is this revealing quotation from the English Parliamentary debates of the 1840's: "We Have to Say to the Railway Companies 'You Shall Not Have a Permanent Monopoly Against the Public' — Sir Robert Peel." In this address, and in another subsequently delivered to the Boston Social Science Association, Quincy freely referred to European experiences and particularly praised William Galt's "admirable work on Railway Reform" — an influential English book published in 1865.[1]

The views of Charles Francis Adams, Jr., Quincy's young Boston contemporary, also display the marked influence of European thinking upon the subject. Writing in 1867 on "Railroad Legislation," he observed that throughout Europe and America railroads were the subject of increasing attention, and demands for change were prevalent. But he regretted that America continued to blunder away without benefiting from European investigation and experience.[2] The article, and his subsequent writings, were designed to correct that state of affairs, and in them Adams' debt to European influences is marked.[3]

Probably the work which made the most profound impression upon Adams and other American students of the "Railroad Problem" was the famous report in 1872 of the English Select Parliamentary Committee on railway amalgamation.[4] The major conclusion of this comprehensive inquiry was the *impossibility* of maintaining competition between railroads. "Committees and commissions, carefully chosen, have for the last thirty years, clung to one form of competition or another. It has, nevertheless, become more and more evident that competition must fail to do for railways what it does for ordinary trade, and that no means have yet been devised by which competition can be permanently maintained." Accordingly, the committee recommended, and Parliament created in 1873, a railroad commission with judicial powers to regulate the roads.[5] Adams, while accepting the conclusion that railroad competition was impossible, did not accept the recommendation that a strong railroad commission was the solution. Instead, he turned to Belgium and found the answer in its system of mixed state and private enterprise. Competition worked its beneficial results, he argued, only if the state was one of the competitors. As was true thereafter of his numerous, if contradictory, proposals for railroad salvation, he soon abandoned the "yardstick" theory. But the impress of European influence upon him was evident at all times.[6]

Despite Adams' claims to the honor, Simon Sterne was probably the contemporary student of the problem who made the most elaborate and purposeful use of European experience to argue the case for American railroad reform. In his pilgrimages to Albany, lectures to the businessmen of New York, conduct of the Hepburn inquiry, in a scholarly analysis of the "History and Political Economy of Railways," and in an official report to President Cleveland in 1887,[7] Sterne painstakingly examined Old World developments for light upon New World problems. Like Adams, he concentrated on English railroads because they were privately owned, and drew support for American regulatory measures from the views of James Morrison, Robert Peel, William Galt, numerous Parliamentary debates and Royal Commissions, and the actual working out of English legislation. In his closing argument to the Hepburn Committee, Sterne emphasized that the provisions of the New York General Railroad Act of 1850 (the Act which many states imitated) followed the lead of English and Prussian legislation.[8]

Since Sterne later was asked to write some of the essential provisions of the Interstate Commerce Act, he was in a good position to put the results of his study into practice. In major respects the American legislation closely followed Lord Cardwell's Act of 1854 which compelled railroads to adopt a uniform system of accounts, give shareholders access to the companies' books, prohibit unjust discriminations, and perform like treatment under like circumstances for all freighters. The parallel between English and American legislation is even clearer when one considers that the Interstate Commerce Commission was created to administer statutory provisions concerning railroads, just as the English Railroad Commission of 1873 was given judicial powers to enforce Lord Cardwell's Act of 1854.[9] Sterne's summary comment in his 1887 report to President Cleveland, just prior to the passage of the Interstate Commerce Act, makes the intimate relationship between English and American legislation clear. He stressed the point that mistakes concerning railroad legislation in both the United States and England had a common source, that is, in laissez-faire doctrines, and that "the tendencies of remedial measures are on parallel lines, with the difference only that England in its course of legislation on the subject and recognition of such mistakes is about a generation in advance of this country." [10]

That such a transfer across the Atlantic should have occurred is not remarkable when consideration is given to the impact of England and Europe upon American intellectuals and scholars in the nineteenth century. The contemporary literature demonstrates that the Atlantic Ocean was a sea-going highway for ideological interchange, not a moat cordoning off the United States from the more mature economies of Europe.

If Europe exported the fruits of her railroad experiences along with capital to build American railroads, again, as was only to be expected, it was easterners who transmitted them to the country at large. The merchants of New York, Boston, Philadelphia, Baltimore, etc., were in closer touch with the intellectual currents of the Old World than the farmers around Oshkosh, Peoria, Kankakee, or Portage, and the seaport merchants were also in the best position to appreciate the revolutionary effect of railroad development upon internal and foreign commerce. But interest in the transportation question cannot be regarded as the property of one section. Due to vast geographical expanse, tremendous economic potential, and the particular conditions governing American history, communication was always a national problem affecting all parts of the country, directly or indirectly. Dependent upon circumstances the center of interest tended to shift from time to time, but the shifts are susceptible to rational explanation. Notwithstanding, this catholic position does not invalidate the view that the seaports — particularly New York — were the first to take the lead in questioning railroad policy and, broadly speaking, supplied the basic thinking on the problem. The fact that they did so is historically important and must be recorded if the course of American railroad regulation is to be properly understood; such recognition, however, does not imply inherently superior wisdom, virtue, or devotion to the nation.

Intellectual location placed the eastern merchants (and fellow citizens) in the best position to profit from European experience and to be influenced by European debates; economic location forced them to grapple most intensely with the problem of cheap transportation as a factor in commercial operations. And cheap transportation in the United States became important during the early seventies because international competition added to the difficulties of disposing of the increasing American agricultural surpluses. Given the emerging real world pattern, it would have been surprising if the beginnings of the Communication Revolution and the creation of an international economy had not been better appreciated along the Atlantic Coast than along the banks of the Mississippi River.

NEW YORK MERCHANTS IN SEARCH OF A BANDWAGON

Prior to the severe rate wars of the mid-seventies, the chief objective sought by railroad reformers and agitators was cheap transportation. Even in New York City, increasingly concerned with place discrimination, major interest centered upon the absolute level of rates — the rubric, Cheap Transportation Association, adequately sums up the situation. If cheap transportation was the prime object, competition was the prime solution offered by agitators everywhere. Rate regulation was advocated — and actually carried out in several western states — but as the Windom Committee hearings of 1873 indicate, most stress was placed upon lowering transportation costs through the development of new and improved facilities. No dichotomy existed between the two types of remedies and the Windom Report concluded that Congress had the right to legislate in favor of either or both. However, its major emphasis was given to expanded facilities, particularly improvement of the country's waterways. Despite such senatorial endorsement, a considerable number of contemporaries shared the conviction that exclusive freight railroads afforded the best prospects for securing low cost freight rates.[11]

Railroad enthusiasts must be broken down still further between narrow gauge and standard gauge partisans, and advocates of government or private ownership of the proposed roads. Virtually everyone who looked to exclusive freight railways to lower transportation costs was a firm believer in federal power to regulate interstate commerce. Those who favored private enterprise wanted national charters to prevent the individual states from blocking the construction of new roads. (State legislatures were on occasion zealous in behalf of vested interests or the preservation of local monopolies such as the Camden and Amboy Railroad.) The other group went even further in their claims for national power and urged a government owned and controlled road to provide additional facilities and to serve as a regulator of existing lines. Still another category favorable to the assertion of federal authority comprised those men taking a dim view of state rate fixing.[12] Thus, delegates from the New York Chamber of Commerce and Produce Exchange supported a resolution before the National Board of Trade in 1874 to assert national control of interstate commerce so that "Granger legislation" would be blocked and capitalists induced to invest in new roads.[13]

In the early seventies, then, a variety of individuals and groups, for a variety of reasons, championed the cause of federal regulation of railroads. Apart from the theoretical opposition stemming from constitutional or laissez-faire views (the importance of which frequently tends to be exaggerated but some weight must be assigned it), Democratic politicians were particularly averse to anything hinting of "centralization" during Reconstruction days. Moreover, sectional conflicts of interests, wide diversity of opinion among reformers, strong belief in the benefits of improved waterways, and the influence of railroad lobbyists in Congress, all these prevented any but the most innocuous measures from passage. In addition, one of the more important considerations affecting the course of railroad regulation during the early seventies was the fact that so few people were equipped to handle it with any skill.

It cannot be overstressed that the American railroad system after the Civil War presented new economic problems incapable of solution by reference to previous "practical" experience or orthodox political economy. Hit-or-miss opinions were commonplace while serious students of transportation were rare.[14] Not until 1877 when Joseph Nimmo, Jr., began to issue his official reports on internal commerce was anything really known about its volume, let alone the conditions which affected it.

European precedents could be liberally drawn upon for basic ideas and legislation, but the considerable disparity between American and Old World economic, political, and social developments militated against the success of mere imitation. Even across the Atlantic, England, Germany, France, and Belgium employed significantly different regulatory systems. Working one out suitable to the particular requirements of the United States presented many difficulties. Other complications aside, the dynamic pace and continuous expansion of the post-Civil War economy delayed the formulation of a regulatory measure comprehensive enough to insure passage. It is only necessary to observe the continuous, rapid, and contradictory shifts in position of such diverse commentators as Charles Francis Adams, Jr., and Francis B. Thurber to appreciate the tenuous state of knowledge concerning the railroad problem in the seventies and eighties. Two basic factors seem to have been operative: the pressure of events rather than the logic of theory basically shaped the varying approaches to the railroad problem; different interpretations of the same events stemmed fom the different interests of the onlookers, rather than their different capacities for observation and understanding.

The problem was not so much to recognize that the federal government had to exercise some degree of control over the railroad system as to determine the precise manner in which control would be exercised. Under the pressure of events the various proposals were subject to frequent and drastic alterations which necessarily impeded the creation of a stable body of opinion supporting a given measure. The extremely diverse nature of the economy, added to its dynamic pace, militated against such a development. With the coming of the rate wars in the mid-seventies, and the trunk-line pool which followed, New York interest in railroad regulation steadily grew. On the other hand, despite intensified depression, western concern with the transportation problem evaporated with startling rapidity, the Granger Movement virtually collapsed, and not until the eighties did that section again display much concern with railroad regulation. Although definitely an exaggeration, the Massachusetts railroad commissioners' observation late in 1877 suggests the country's changed mood: "The discussion [of the railroad problem] has now almost wholly lost its hold on the public attention and is confined to a few persons." [15]

Iowa presents a good illustration of the sudden turnabout in western sentiment. Its Railroad Act of 1874, forced through the legislature by overwhelming popular pressure, had attracted international attention. Four years later the railroad companies had the situation well in hand again, and demonstrated their old-time influence by practically repealing the 1874 Act. The same lack of sustained interest was shown in the field of national regulation. In January 1874 Representative McCrary of Iowa introduced a bill in Congress which provided for a railroad commission and prohibited extortion and unfair discrimination by railroads engaged in interstate commerce. Although the bill soon passed the House, it was killed by the Senate.[16] But after low through rates were achieved, the West's interest in the movement for national regulation sharply declined. Thus, in the mid-seventies the New York merchants enrolled in the Cheap Transportation Association found themselves in the unenviable position of holding a near-monopoly on agitation. And generals without privates rarely win wars, political or otherwise. Displaying characteristic flexibility, the New Yorkers shifted tactics and their trumpet blasts were no longer sounded in support of drastic remedies. Since they recognized from the start of agitation that the problem called for national solution, activities were never confined to New York.

Taking stock of the situation, the leaders of the New York Cheap Transportation Association were able to congratulate themselves upon the fact that their work had forced an unprecedented sense of responsibility to the public upon railroad officials, and had led to the recognition of vital distinctions between common carriers and industrial corporations. Such progress was viewed as encouraging, but little disposition existed to rest upon their accomplishments. Though they did not analyze the problem in these explicit terms, four major courses were open to the New Yorkers if the strategic objective of national regulation was to be gained. They could continue to "educate" the public (city, state, and national) through pamphlets, meetings, and other media; arouse such intense interest in the New York campaign for state regulation that the effects would be contagious elsewhere; create new organizations to regain a national vehicle for their program after the American Cheap Transportation Association dissolved in 1876; finally, they could work through established bodies other than their own.

Previous chapters have discussed the New Yorkers' lavish expenditures upon publications for national circulation, their success relative to state legislation in the New York Chamber of Commerce as well as in forging a coalition between metropolitan and upstate groups, in developing harmonious relations with the Farmers' Alliance and Grange (state and national), in bringing about and exploiting the Hepburn investigation, and in creating the National Anti-Monopoly League. It is now appropriate to focus attention upon their activities in the National Board of Trade and in the campaign for federal railroad regulation.

THE NATIONAL BOARD OF TRADE AS BANDWAGON

In many respects the National Board of Trade provided the hardest test for the New Yorkers' agitational talents. Unlike the American Cheap Transportation Association, the Board of Trade was exclusively made up of mercantile delegates from rival cities, men not precisely eager to form a constituency so that "the commercial interests of New York may be looked after and fostered" — the avowed purpose animating the metropolitan militants. Capturing control of the National Board of Trade from sophisticated mercantile rivals must have appeared more formidable than deftly guiding the Cheap Transportation movement born in the hectic days of 1873. But since rate wars were accomplishing the objectives of the latter organization its dissolution was foreshadowed, and in June 1875 the New York Cheap Transportation Association made successful application for membership in the National Board of Trade.[17] Losing no time, Francis Thurber promptly set about the task of providing direction for the board at the very meeting which admitted his organization to membership.

In compliance with previous decisions, the president of the board had prepared a report on transportation for distribution in printed form to the delegates. Thurber announced that he approved of it but suggested that it was not comprehensive enough in some respects. He therefore moved that a committee be appointed to draft resolutions for submission to Congress. With a neat display of teamwork, Thurber's co-worker, John Henry, seconded the motion, and a committee was named.[18]

When the Committee on Transportation brought in its report, the spokesman was none other than Francis Beatty Thurber — a familiar function for him to perform. Not surprisingly, the preamble and resolutions were much in advance of anything the National Board of Trade had hitherto approved, and strenuous objections were raised against their adoption. The major dispute centered over a resolution calling upon the federal government "to prescribe and enforce such regulations as will insure substantial justice to all concerned [in interstate transportation]." His persuasive abilities notwithstanding, Thurber was unable to carry it. But he did succeed in getting the board to adopt a modified preamble and set of resolutions. Among other things, certain defects in the transportation system were deplored, establishment by Congress of a Department or Bureau of Internal Commerce was urged, state legislation was called for to prevent stock watering, provide a uniform method of railroad accounts, and require "railroads to receipt for quantity, and to deliver same at its destination."[19] (Railroads then refused to give such receipts.) Under the circumstances, Thurber and associates had turned in a creditable performance. They had made their mark at the board, put it on record in favor of specific legislation, and paved the way for further missionary work.

The 1875 session of the National Board of Trade set the general pattern which was to hold true until the passage of the Interstate Commerce Act a dozen years later. The New Yorkers would introduce propositions considerably in advance of prevailing sentiment, forcefully argue the case, and settle for something less. Usually, the "something less" was an advance over previous action. Their persistence, resourcefulness, and steady progress in pushing the National Board of Trade towards an advanced position constitutes a remarkable performance. Together with numerous other efforts by them on behalf of the cause, it warrants the conclusion that New York merchants constituted the single most important group behind the passage of the Interstate Commerce Act. But no implication is intended that they actually directed the final stages of the campaign, or that national railroad regulation was the product of their creation.

As the quotation beginning this chapter indicates, one of Jimmy Durante's lines might be borrowed to note that in time almost everybody wanted to get into the Act. Representatives of the New York merchants did play a significant role in framing it, and their association was more active in securing support for its passage than any comparable body, or perhaps, all other comparable bodies combined — a claim made by them which is supported by their dominant role in the National Board of Trade. Such considerations, however, are secondary. The crux of the matter is that the doctrines which had been agitated and popularized since 1873 by New York merchants, above all other groups, came to fruition in the economic setting of the middle eighties.

LEAN YEARS FOR AGITATORS

Considering their success at the 1875 meeting of the National Board of Trade, the delegation from the New York Cheap Transportation Association naturally was enthusiastic in its report upon returning home. The board was praised as a most useful and important institution, "the Commercial Senate of the Country," in which was condensed the wisdom of its constituent bodies throughout the United States. While its deliberations possessed no legislative power, they "were most important in shaping and directing the legislation of the country in proper channels." [20] So that its deliberations might have the benefit of experienced guidance counsellors, when the National Board of Trade next met in June 1876, it was asked to consider a proposition submitted by the New York Cheap Transportation Association. The proposition consisted of a preamble and resolutions stating that the railroad revolution had created conditions which made mandatory the devising of means "by which our present inadequate, incongruous and chaotic system of transportation can be regulated, the extreme fluctuations in rates avoided, the disastrous so-called 'railroad-wars' prevented, and certain general rules (including a uniform classification of freight) adopted, which will be binding throughout the United States." [21]

That not everyone shared the New Yorkers' concern about the effects of rate wars, and that hostility against railroads in the country diminished with declining freight charges, is evident from the mild tone of the only resolution making a specific recommendation for legislative consideration. A drastic retreat even from Thurber's watered down proposals of a year before, it merely asked for the compilation of information and statistics by state and national commissions of inquiry "upon which can be based just principles of action." Answering objections to this mild resolution, the New York delegates found it necessary to affirm that the object was simply to get commissioners, "not with power to interfere with the running of the roads, but commissioners who will recommend legislation."

The resolution was finally adopted but the *Proceedings* of the board are further evidence that federal regulation of railroads was hardly a burning question when rate wars satisfied the demand for cheap transportation in the seventies.[22] A similar sentiment prevailed at the next meeting of the board. As was true of the National Grange in the same year, the 1877 session saw no propositions forwarded on interstate commerce and the board didn't even meet in 1878.[23] National disinterest concerning transportation in the mid-seventies was reflected in Congress; a sharp decline took place in the number of bills introduced on the railroad question.[24] Evidently, severe depression also meant hard times for New York merchants in their campaign to educate the country on the necessity for federal regulation.

Tactical considerations seem to have been responsible for the New Yorkers' failure to introduce a railroad resolution at the 1877 session of the National Board of Trade. Certainly they had not lost interest in the question, nor had they concluded that their campaign was hopeless.[25]

Despite the bleak picture painted above of agitational prospects, several developments tended to keep the railroad issue alive in other places than New York, and encouraged the metropolitan merchants. Sensibly aiding their educational campaigns were the adverse reactions in Pennsylvania to the operations of Standard Oil, the beginning of the drive for railroad commissions in the South, the Sand-Lot Movement in California which made the Central Pacific a target for popular attack,[26] the violent railroad strikes of 1877, the wave of railroad bankruptcies in that year, and the creation of the New York Farmers' Alliance. Indeed, following the failure of the 1874 McCrary bill, Standard Oil can be credited with providing direct impetus for the next important Congressional development.

A speech by James Hopkins, the representative from the Pittsburgh district, delivered in May 1876 in support of his bill to regulate interstate commerce, indicates that railroad discrimination rather than cheap transportation was now the prime source of Congressional concern — such as it was. Hopkins emphasized that the grievances which he recited were not peculiar to Pittsburgh but were felt everywhere. As proof of "the fact of favoritism, and of uncertainty which is in itself an incubus upon business," he cited the support for his bill by "representative men" from various eastern cities.[27] Hopkins' bill failed to pass even the House; although amended and modified considerably, it was the basis of the later measure usually associated with Representative John Reagan of Texas.[28]

REAGAN OF TEXAS AND THE MERCHANTS OF NEW YORK

It is against the background of growing hostility toward railroad discrimination and arrogance, especially marked in New York after the trunk-line pooling agreement took effect in July 1877, that the Reagan bill to regulate railroads needs to be considered. Why John Reagan of Palestine, Texas, former Postmaster-General of the Confederacy, took up the cause of federal control of interstate commerce is not clear at the present writing. Excessive subsidies and land grants to railroads in his home county some years before — the only local abuses cited by him in the *Congressional Record* — hardly appear to explain Reagan's ten-year campaign.[29]

But certain impressions and facts stand out from the Congressional debates. First introduced in 1877, the bill was conceded by Reagan to have been "framed by a skilled lawyer, not by my skill." The lawyer was never identified further by the Texan other than that he was from Buffalo, New York.[30] In reality, this was George B. Hibbard, then serving as counsel to the Petroleum Producers' Union fighting Standard Oil. Hibbard's pamphlet on the subject of Congressional power to regulate interstate freight rates had so impressed Reagan that he incorporated it into his handwritten report on the bill to the speaker of the House.[31] Years later Representative Hopkins claimed in effect to have begun the Congressional movement to check railroad discrimination and the record largely bears out his contention.[32] (The 1874 McCrary bill was more concerned with the level of rates than with the personal and place discrimination central to the Texan's measure.) Discussing Reagan's bill in May 1878, Representative Thompson of Pennsylvania flatly asserted "that it was the discrimination in the freight of oil to the seaboard which gave rise to this bill." [33]

Of greater significance than the authorship of the bill is the fact that it was designed to abolish place and personal discrimination. As Reagan's arguments in its favor indicated, these topics were much dearer to the hearts of merchants than of southern or western farmers. Reading his remarks in the Congressional debate of 1878, it is obvious that the plight of the latter scarcely figured in his thoughts. Some brief reference is there, but essentially he was concerned with the effect of discrimination upon commercial and industrial interests. To support his stand, he cited resolutions favoring national regulation passed by the Pennsylvania and New York legislatures, Chambers of Commerce in New York, Pittsburgh, Milwaukee, and "boards of trade and chambers of commerce of a number of leading commercial cities of the United States." [34] And of particular interest, in view of Reagan's subsequent close association with the leaders of the New York Board of Trade and Transportation, is his reading into the *Congressional Record* that organization's report and resolutions adopted in April 1878.

The following are the proceedings of the Board of Trade of the city of New York which I read in full on account of their valuable suggestions, adding that it may become necessary to have such a board of commissioners as is recommended. But that should, if proper, be the subject of a separate bill. I also notice that this board of trade seems to have fallen into the same error with reference to the pending bill that members of this House fell into, that the bill provides for *pro rata* rates of freight. This doubtless arose from a misunderstanding of the fourth section of the bill. It contains no such provision.[35]

Here Reagan was referring to the long-haul short-haul clause almost unanimously opposed by those western representatives voicing opinions in Congressional debate. Their opposition to the clause was pronounced and even one of Reagan's supporters, Townshend of Illinois, admitted that the West was against it and desired its deletion.[36] The Congressional debates on the regulatory measure reveal a definite sectional split; spokesmen claiming to represent eastern farmers favored the bill on the ground that it restored their natural advantages; westerners charged that the long-haul short-haul clause "would prevent one bushel of grain from going from the western producer to the eastern seaboard. You virtually shut the market to him." [37]

In answer to a question as to whether the railroads would not simply raise through rates if his bill passed, Reagan admitted much logic attached to such a supposition. His reply reveals that little basis exists for picturing the foremost Congressional champion of railroad regulation as the voice of the West — particularly of the western farmer:

One great object of the bill is that it shall aid in preventing those railroad wars which have hitherto been so disastrous to stockholders and so injurious to the country by the fluctuations in the prices of transportation. The object is to prevent pooling, to prevent discrimination between shippers and between places, to prevent rebates, and to compel the railroads to pursue their business in an honest and legitimate way.[38]

As Representative Bragg of Wisconsin had stressed earlier in the year, rate wars, and the low through rates accompanying them, were precisely what western farmers wanted.[39] To say the least, Reagan's concern for stockholders' dividends was not fully shared at the West, and this affords another indication of the slight influence that section's agriculturists — or any others — had upon him.

Reading the *Congressional Record* of the late seventies and early eighties without preconceptions about the inherent "nationalizing" tendencies of the West or its paramount role in the movement for railroad regulation, one tends to arrive at somewhat different conclusions. The impression which emerges is that commercial considerations, above all those affecting the major cities of the East, dominated the arguments in favor of regulation. Apart from the fact that States' Rights' arguments against "centralization" were not foreign to western representatives when it suited their purposes, the long-haul short-haul clause clearly motivated much of the opposition to the bill stemming from that section.[40] Even conceding the diversity of views making up "western" opinion, it seems correct to assert that the sentiments expressed by Representative Henderson of Iowa were not atypical in the so-called Granger states — and beyond.

I am led to believe, Mr. Chairman, that the proposed fourth section [long-haul short-haul] has grown out of complaints that railway lines are discriminating in their freight charges in favor of the West. In New York it is made a matter of complaint that the New York Central and the New York and Erie Railroads discriminate against the people of that State and charge them more proportionally than they do the people of the West. It is the same thing in Pennsylvania with the Pennsylvania Railroad, and perhaps the same charge may be made against the Baltimore and Ohio Railroad. Mr. Thurber, an intelligent gentleman of New York connected with the board of trade and transportation of that city, who takes a deep interest in the passage of the . . . [bill] proposed by . . . [Reagan], is reported to have said in speaking of the great wrongs which have been perpetrated upon the people of the State of New York by railroads that —
'It is wrong that the farmers of this State [New York] should be charged for transporting their produce a rate proportionally three or four hundred per cent higher than those of the Mississippi Valley.'
The same complaint is made by many others [in the East].

Henderson's pointed reference to Thurber's "deep interest" in the Reagan bill was not misplaced. Early in 1878, in an attempt to stir up sentiment favoring national legislation, the New York Board of Trade and Transportation circulated a petition calling upon Congress to appoint a joint committee to investigate the workings of the American railroad system.[41] When the House Committee on Commerce reported out the Reagan bill, the New Yorkers immediately took it up. Though their endorsement was tempered by its failure to provide for a Board of Railroad Commissioners and its inapplicability to shippers of less than carloads, they now had a specific measure meeting most of their requirements. Accordingly, they concentrated upon gaining support for Reagan's bill,[42] and in the process developed such close working relationships with him that it was eventually modified to meet their wishes regarding less than carload shipments.

The New York Board of Trade and Transportation worked hard on behalf of the Reagan bill in 1878, but neither their agitational efforts nor any others attained sufficient response to explain its passage in the House that year. Pending an intensive study of Congressional sentiment towards Reagan's bill, the question of why it did pass the House can not be answered here. But the Senate apparently was less inclined to strike attitudes against "railroad kings," and it pigeonholed the bill with little fuss despite a memorial in its favor by two hundred and fifty of the "most respectable merchants" of New York City.[43] Undaunted by the Senate's lack of action, Thurber's organization reaffirmed the necessity of federal legislation and vowed to continue the fight. Resolutions thanking Reagan for reintroducing his bill in 1879 no doubt encouraged him.[44] More tangible support was given in the form of the Hepburn investigation. If Congress did not choose to expose transportation abuses, New York could provide an object lesson whose effects would hardly be confined to the Empire State.

State legislation was the immediate objective of the Hepburn investigation but its direct and indirect results were much more encompassing. That ultimately the shortest way to federal regulation was through action on state levels was a concept appreciated by the New Yorkers. An editorial discussing the inadequacies of state control in the *American Grocer* (Thurber's paper) made the point explicitly:

> Doubtless regulation of interstate commerce by Congress will also be found necessary, but we must have *both* State and national legislation; neither can do it alone. If the State of New York leads off, other seaboard States will follow, and national legislation will come in due time.[45]

AGITATION BEGINS TO BEAR FRUIT

Attention has been repeatedly drawn to the impact of the Hepburn inquiry but a brief reference is appropriate in connection with the campaign for national control. During Albert Fink's testimony in 1882 against the Reagan bill he took considerable pains to impugn the Hepburn Committee's procedures, qualifications, and recommendations, and pointed to it as the kind of legislative inquiry that had to be avoided. "The New York committee, for instance, has done the greatest harm by bringing out and spreading broadcast over the country incorrect reports in regard to railroad management and the relations of the railroads to the people." [46]

If the Hepburn revelations were still fresh in 1882, they were even more blooming in December 1879, when the National Board of Trade resumed its annual deliberations at Washington. The heightened prestige acquired by the New York delegates as a result of the inquiry, the national attention it attracted, the documentary exposure of railroad abuses it provided, all were skillfully employed. Two rather general proposals for national legislation were on the formal program of the board — including one submitted weeks earlier by the New Yorkers — but Thurber offered a more specific resolution from the floor. It came as close to endorsing the provisions of the Reagan bill as the New Yorkers thought tactically sound.

First, to raise a special commission or tribunal to secure uniformity and publicity of railway contracts and transactions; Second, to enforce provisions securing uniformity of rates and classifications under like circumstances, and relative equality where circumstances differ; Third, to secure publicity of rates and prohibition of sudden and arbitrary changes; Fourth, to secure the prevention of extortionate charges and of personal or local favoritism.[47]

During the course of discussion Thurber emphasized that his resolution "was purposely framed in as conservative a form as possible," [48] and Simon Sterne took pains to emphasize that point in a lengthy address supporting the resolution. Instead of making the main effort on behalf of his resolution, Thurber cannily handed the oratorical ball to the now nationally famous Simon Sterne. With pardonable pride, the latter noted that his conduct of the Hepburn inquiry well qualified him to speak on the matter.[49] Once launched, Sterne took the delegates on a comprehensive guided tour of the railroad question in Europe and the United States, demonstrated the urgent need for the passage of legislation recommended by Thurber, trusted "that this Board is at one with the Board of Trade and Transportation in New York" upon the question,[50] and wound up by recommending the appointment of a special committee to press for the resolution at a Congressional hearing. Dominating the discussion which followed, the New York delegates, both from the Chamber of Commerce and the Board of Trade and Transportation, also took the most advanced ground. Attention was focused largely upon Thurber's resolution and together with the more general propositions it was approved overwhelmingly.

Not one to lose sight of basic objectives amidst the joys of victory, Thurber moved to implement Sterne's recommendation and a committee was appointed to go before the Congressional Committee on Commerce then in session. Thurber and President Fraley of the Board were its spokesmen. Thus the House Committee not only had the benefit of the New York Board of Trade and Transportation's views from its own delegation, it also had a somewhat milder version in the name of the National Board of Trade.[51]

The House Committee on Commerce chose to ignore recommendations from any source in favor of Reagan's proposal and substituted in its place the "Henderson bill." Written by Charles Francis Adams, Jr., it provided for a National Board of Railroad Commissioners, recognized the existence of pools, rebates, drawbacks, etc., and was antithetical to Reagan's measure in every sense. Alarmed by the erroneous impression that "the Reagan bill is practically abandoned, and pains have been taken to make the impression general," the New Yorkers launched a strenuous counter-offensive early in 1880. A public letter was drawn up and sent to "Grangers, leading newspapers, and prominent influential men who are in accord with our work," which subjected the Henderson bill to critical analysis; it was described as "a cunningly devised scheme to defeat real legislation in the public interest and more fully protect the railroads in their practices." A call to arms was sounded:

> It is not the intention to let the 'Reagan Bill' die in Committee, and we learn from Judge Reagan that he has the consent of the Comm to report his bill with the 'McLane' and 'Henderson Bill,' and a day will probably be appointed for their consideration by the House. While the appointment of a Board of Commissioners is necessary to guard the interest of the people, it is of greater importance that they should be first protected by the positive requirements of law as provided in the 'Reagan Bill.'
> It is important therefore that the friends of the bill should persist in urging its passage by both *letters and petitions.*[52]

Little over a week later, Reagan was informed that the New Yorkers had already received copies of newspaper editorials "fully stating the situation of this bill and urging their readers and the public to send in petitions for its passage." [53] And as proof that their intense campaign for state antidiscrimination laws worked in favor of his bill, he was sent clippings demonstrating that "in order to defeat state legislation they [railroad supporters] have been obliged to place themselves upon record favoring national legislation which should be greatly in aid of your bill." [54] The Board of Trade and Transportation was hardly content to allow the railroads to seize the initiative on national legislation in order to stave off local regulation; by June 1880 it announced that more than 6,000 copies of the Reagan bill had been printed, and accompanied by a report thereon, sent throughout the country to all public and commercial bodies. Moreover, it had mailed "during the few months just passed," no less than 300,000 documents on various subjects, principally the railway question. And their organization, it was further claimed, "had done much to incite action on the part of other Bodies and interests throughout the country." [55]

Apart from their activities at the National Board of Trade, the New York militants were then working closely with the leaders of the Grange and the Farmers' Alliance on both state and national levels, and dominated the New York Chamber of Commerce. All this would be enough to justify their claim to having incited action by other groups and interests but a large number of petitions preserved in the National Archives further documents their case. Identical printed petitions signed in 1880 are found there from "citizens" throughout the country, as well as printed petitions specifically designed for Boards of Trade and bearing the endorsement of various associations and individuals from Bangor, Maine, to Belton, Texas.[56]

A report submitted to the New York Chamber of Commerce is a neat illustration of the New York mercantile militants at skillful work. Presented by Thurber for the Special Committee on Railroad Transportation, it described in alarmed tones the measures employed by the railroads to defeat key bills proposed by the Hepburn Committee. A favorite Thurber quotation from Senator David Davis on the impending struggle between corporate power and the people was included, and sharply worded resolutions calling for state and national railroad regulation were proposed and unanimously adopted in the name of the most powerful body of merchants, bankers, railroad presidents, and others, in the United States.[57]

Armed with such unanimous mandate, the Special Committee on Railroad Transportation promptly proceeded to agitate for national action. The lengthy questionnaire discussed in a previous chapter was drawn up in August and had the desired effect. As the *Milwaukee Sentinel* noted in November: "The New York Chamber of Commerce is taking the initiative in calling the attention of the country to the necessity of regulating the transportation question . . . It looks somewhat as if the railroad question would before long become a decidedly active one. It has of late served as a fertile topic in magazine and review literature; and if there is not a systematic effort behind it all, it is being pushed forward by the weight of its own importance." [58] When Judge Jeremiah Black's response to the questionnaire hit the nation's press and periodicals in December 1880, the efforts of the New Yorkers bore their heaviest fruit since the Hepburn investigation.

Presumably no need exists to jog the reader's memory concerning the widespread effects of Judge Black's contribution towards the people's enlightenment. The New Yorkers, however, were disposed to caution at the subsequent National Board of Trade meeting. But signals were switched at the last minute apparently, or one of their delegates got carried away, for when the Board of Trade and Transportation's perennial proposition on "Inter-State Traffic" came up, he moved the creation of a special committee to urge Congress to enact a law similar to the Reagan bill. Thurber and other New Yorkers immediately acted to forestall argument on the resolution — premature action might boomerang and put the board on record *against* the bill — by suggesting that normalcy (*sic*) be allowed to prevail, that is, the adoption of the proposition already on the program. The proposition reaffirmed Thurber's resolution approved in 1879, and declared that the experience of each recurring year proved the more urgent necessity of regulation of interstate commerce via railroad. And so it came to pass.[59]

Obviously the Reagan bill was still deemed medicine too stiff for the National Board of Trade to swallow, but the New York Chamber of Commerce had been labored with longer and stronger — and represented interests more desirous of preserving the supremacy of the Port of New York. Stating that they made no apology for again asking the Chamber to consider the question, early in January 1881 the Special Committee on Railroad Transportation reported on the subject of railroad regulation, with particular reference to the Reagan and Henderson bills then pending in Congress. Public opinion was declared to have rapidly advanced to an intelligent comprehension of the question, and the press of the metropolis and leading journals throughout the country were said to "have supported, with great unanimity, the principles advocated by this Chamber . . ." In the committee's opinion, the time had arrived "when the public should justly insist that the relations of railroads to the public shall be defined by appropriate legislation." And the near unanimity expressed in favor of legislation remedying railroad abuses by approximately 100 respondents to their questionnaire was cited in support. The "Adams Bill, or as it is known in Congress 'The Henderson Bill'," was compared most unfavorably to the Reagan bill; one was in the interest of the railroads, the other served the community. Naturally, the Chamber endorsed the community service bill, but it also called for a National Board of Railroad Commissioners "to see that all laws of the United States relating to railroads are duly executed, and generally to supervise the operation of inter-State railroads." [60]

DIVISION IN THE RANKS

The Chamber of Commerce's action on the Henderson and Reagan bills points up important features of the campaign for railroad regulation — features important enough to justify interrupting the chronological sequence of events. As will be discussed below, by this time the trunk lines favored national legislation but only in the form of a relatively powerless Board of Railroad Commissioners. One effect of the Henderson-Adams bill was to compete for Congressional favor and make possible the claim that some attention was being paid to the transportation problem. Though neither it nor its railroad-sponsored successors ever passed, they at least had the effect of seriously hampering the Reagan bill. Moreover, the spectacle of railroads pressing for a national commission caused Reagan and numerous other supporters of regulation to shy away from this kind of proposal.[61] At least as early as the summer of 1879, the Texan and Thurber were corresponding upon the subject, and the former placed high value on the suggestions made to him by the New Yorker. He granted that a national commission probably "will ultimately have to be created; but we were deterred from providing for it in the bill because we were apprehensive it would cause the defeat of the bill if we provided for it, by enabling its enemies to say, as they did successfully of a former bill having that object in view, that it placed important and dangerous powers in the hands of a few persons, which were liable to be abused." [62]

After the railroad-inspired campaign for a commission got rolling, Reagan's reluctance and suspicions measurably increased. Drawing upon the common law and English and American precedents, his bill permitted individual shippers to sue in the courts for damages when railroad companies violated its provisions against personal and place discrimination. Simultaneously, mercantile convictions grew that the statute was not really self-enforcing and that a strong commission was indispensable.[63] Thus, whenever they were successful in getting the Reagan bill endorsed or discussed, they conceded its inadequacies and invariably sponsored an additional resolution favoring a commission. At the 1884 meeting of the National Board of Trade, for example, Simon Sterne explicitly drew the parallel between Lord Cardwell's Act of 1854 and the Reagan bill, and the necessity for an American supervisory body after the model of the English Railroad Commission. The 1854 Act had been a dead letter until the tribunal was created in 1873, he noted, and the same fate would befall American legislation unless the lessons of English experience were learned.[64] On the other hand, Reagan, and men of his persuasion, pointed to American experience as proof that the commission device was liable to abuse and could easily serve as an instrument of the railroads rather than one to control them.

Inevitably, Reagan's position created serious difficulties for mercantile and other non-railroad advocates of government control. Instead of achieving a substantial degree of unanimity on specific measures, a division of opinion existed in the reform ranks which grew more pronounced. The Texan cannot be charged with having created the division

— in all conscience, particularly after Grover Cleveland's regime gave reformers pause, abundant evidence existed to justify his fears — yet it remains true that the division of opinion served to dissipate the force behind the railroad regulation movement. Nonetheless, though it was an important consideration, the internal division of opinion does not appear to have been the basic reason for failure to achieve regulation in the early eighties.

Had there really been a strong national demand for legislation capable of expressing itself in political terms, the Reagan measure could hardly have been pigeonholed in committee for half a dozen years. As the passage of that curious combination of ambiguous provisions known as the Interstate Commerce Act was to demonstrate, when the demand for legislation grew strong enough, divisions of opinion could delay and partially stultify enactment; they could not prevent it. However, the process of stirring up agitation requires attention before further discussion of its 1887 outcome.

ANTI-MONOPOLY TO THE FORE

Organization of the National Anti-Monopoly League early in 1881 has been previously discussed in terms of the metropolitan campaign for state legislation; it was also designed to serve a similar purpose on the second front of national regulation. The New Yorkers were aware that the railroad problem was incapable of local solution, and they were also alert to the possibility that the Supreme Court of the United States might be converted to the view that state laws violated federal jurisdiction over interstate commerce. The League's *Address to the People* cited Leland Stanford's reply to the Chamber of Commerce's questionnaire as proof that "railroad monopolists" were engaged in a campaign to free themselves from any form of control whatsoever.

> We charge upon these monopolists the intent to increase their gains and perpetuate their power by organized resistance to appointed authority, and treason against their government. They intend to control our Judges, and to disobey such judicial orders as they do not approve until they can reverse them.[65]

Making good use of Stanford's claim that the railroads were not common carriers, and his demand, as they accurately put it, that government "let us alone," the *Address* called upon the people to organize in defense of traditional institutions before it was too late.[66]

In view of Reagan's continued stress upon the endorsement given his bill by commercial organizations, the strenuous efforts made by the New Yorkers to save it from oblivion in 1880, and the close working relations already existing between them, it was appropriate that he become active in the National Anti-Monopoly League. With Secretary Windom, Judge

Black, and President Fowler of the National Farmers' Alliance, Reagan was a featured speaker at the February 21, 1881, meeting successfully launching the League.[67] Soon his name was added to its letterhead as vice-president, a distinction shared only by Peter Cooper and the "radical" governor of Maine, Harris N. Plaisted. Fragmentary correspondence preserved in the Reagan papers indicates that relations continued on an intimate basis between him and the officers of the League despite differences over the best form of railroad regulation.[68]

Possibly the best evidence that the campaign for railroad regulation was really gaining momentum by the spring of 1881 is the behind-the-scenes story of Edward Atkinson's famous article, "The Railroads and the Farmer." Atkinson, a well-known if non-professional political economist of the time, had been requested by the editor of a new agricultural journal to write an article on that subject for its first issue. In January 1881 he was only willing to revise a former pamphlet;[69] by March, after Judge Black's speech at the Anti-Monopoly League and Albert Fink's reply had heated the question up, Atkinson's interest had grown considerably. His letter accepting the editor's request for an article also indicated that Fink might be interested in placing a large order for copies of the issue: "The question of State interference with railroads is likely to come up in a serious way, and I rather think the article will be a strong card on the railroad side of that question." [70] In reply, the editor noted with much satisfaction "your hope that the article can be made to do us good with certain people, and I beg to say in this connection that we need it." [71] The publication needed it, Atkinson wanted to get the widest possible circulation for the article which, in his opinion, was "the most important one" he had ever written,[72] and the railroads were anxious to play this "strong card" against Judge Black and the Anti-Monopoly League.

A series of letters and personal calls thereupon ensued, involving, among other railroad figures, Fink on behalf of the trunk lines, John Murray Forbes, Collis Huntington, and Charles E. Perkins. As a result, funds were provided to send copies of the *Journal of the American Agricultural Association* containing the article to 2,000 newspapers throughout the country, to large numbers of influential figures in America and abroad, and to those individuals on a "select list of 100,000 names in New York State" responding favorably to a circular offering it for just the postage; in all, various major railroads paid for nearly 32,000 copies of the magazine.[73]

A letter from Charles Perkins of the Chicago, Burlington, and Quincy to Atkinson is particularly revealing of late nineteenth-century methods of ideological warfare. Atkinson had indicated that he planned to follow up the first article with another in the same journal:

It seems to me the course you suggest is a good one and I hope you will carry it out. I believe you would reach more people, however, if you could use the Atlantic or Harper [*sic*], or Scribner, or the North American, than through the Agricultural Journals. The public is going to take its tone largely from the newspapers, and the newspapers are pretty sure to see what is said in the popular monthly journals. Then too, the anti-railroad people like Mason in the North Atlantic, Thurber in Scribner, and Lloyd in the Atlantic go to these magazines and it would be well to put the other side in the same place. I do not hope to reach the *masses* with the truth upon the transportation problem until it has filtered through the more intelligent business public. Today the ignorance upon the subject among business men and lawyers and legislators is as dense as it is among the farmers.

If the intelligent people can once be made to see that the let-alone policy as regards railroads is the safe one and that any other policy is full of danger, if the *property* interest can be made to see this, we shall have a great many men helping to educate voters. Men who are dead set the other way.[74]

At the January 1882 meeting of the National Board of Trade, the New York militants successfully labored to make what Perkins called the "dense ignorance" of the "intelligent business public" even denser. Towards this end, the Board of Trade and Transportation submitted a proposition considerably in advance of the one approved a year earlier. Discussion was extensive and the New Yorkers — both from the board and the Chamber of Commerce — took bolder stands than before in meeting objections to the proposition.[75] Ambrose Snow openly declared in favor of the Reagan bill but John Henry, claiming to speak for Reagan and other congressmen, was content to press for adoption of the resolution as submitted. Its key demand was: "That a permanent commission or tribunal should be established, whose business it would be to supervise and control in the interest of the public all common carriers doing an interstate business, and make such recommendations to Congress from time to time as may seem necessary for the public interest." [76]

McLaren of Milwaukee said that Thurber's resolution of 1879 had deliberately been made less "radical" because the Reagan bill could not win approval. He argued against the current one because "The resolution of 1879 went as far as the members of this Board were prepared to go." [77] After further discussion, the resolution quoted above was unanimously adopted but with a qualifying clause inserted: "That a permanent commission or tribunal should be established, whose business it would be, *under suitable regulations and restrictions* [italics added], to supervise . . ." [78] Since other parts of the proposition were junked in order to achieve this degree of unanimity, it cannot be said that the New Yorkers scored an unqualified victory.

At the National Board of Trade it was necessary to make haste slowly; when it came to writing petitions for mass circulation some of the stops could be pulled out. At the request of the National Anti-

Monopoly League, Judge Black drafted a petition in 1881 to Congress praying the legislative regulation of interstate commerce by railroads. The Reagan bill was not mentioned specifically but its essential features were included in the recommendation to Congress. One feature of the campaign was noteworthy: in contrast to former years when separate forms directed towards different groups were employed, Black's petition served as the sole focus of concentration. Use of this tactic explains an otherwise puzzling fact about the flood of petitions signed by individuals pouring in upon Congress during the winter of 1881–82; though the petitions originated in 35 states every one preserved in the National Archives is identical! [79]

Because a favorite line of railroad argument against restrictive legislation was that the people generally were satisfied and only agitators discontented, the petitions were most useful to Reagan. As proof of popular support, he could assert proudly in March 1882, "I think it is safe to say that a greater number of petitions have come to Congress asking for action on this subject [railroad regulation] than on any other ever before it for action . . ." [80] Two weeks earlier Albert Fink had paid tribute of another sort to the effectiveness of the Anti-Monopoly campaign. His testimony before the House Committee on Commerce is replete with sarcastic comments directed against the New York merchants and all their works. The introductory remarks made by him have been previously quoted but they are revealing enough to warrant reiteration and fuller statement.

Fink was attempting to demonstrate that the railroad problem was a difficult one everywhere and that the "evils" encountered in American transportation did not result from the greater wickedness of American railroad managers but were inherent in the system of railroad transportation itself. In France, for example, though the state had almost absolute control over railroads, the people were by no means satisfied. "In fact, if you were to read the articles that are published in the French press, particularly in the *Republique Française*, the organ of Gambetta, you could readily imagine that they were written in New York by the leaders of the present crusade against American railroad management." [81] In Albany, the week before, Chauncey Depew had been even more specific; he identified Francis B. Thurber as the individual most responsible for creating "the anti-monopoly and anti-railroad agitation all over the United States . . ." [82]

Fink acknowledged the existence of certain evils of American railroad management which needed correction; however, he contended, these constituted an exceedingly small proportion of the total volume of complaints. Either Reagan was eager to make the point at every possible occasion or he misunderstood Fink, for he answered the latter by emphasizing the great number of petitions received by Congress praying for relief.[83] Representative Washburn then chimed in with the observation that not too much stock need be taken in those petitions: "Somebody, I don't know who, but some power, has caused such petitions to be drawn and distributed broadcast over the country, and people, in many instances, have signed them without the slightest idea of what they were doing." [84]

Reagan met this line of attack by citing unmistakable evidences of state action relative to railroads and challenged Fink to answer the complaints reported by the Hepburn Committee. Here Fink took a leaf from the book used by Chauncey Depew before that committee; he dismissed the charges by Boards of Trade since they evidently represented a "class interest that would like nothing better than to get control of the railroads and reduce *their* earnings so as to increase their own. The producers do not come before you and complain; the consumers do not come before you and complain; but the merchant, who wishes to cut down the railroad to the lowest point of compensation in order that he may fill his own pockets, comes before you and represents himself as 'the people' and makes his complaints, and under the delusion that he does represent the people, the country has been entirely misled." [85]

The trunk-line pool commissioner's preoccupation with New York merchants who cast themselves in people's clothing is evident from his numerous allusions on that occasion to Judge Black; the Anti-Monopoly League; Edward Atkinson's refutation of the "harangues" made by Anti-Monopoly leaders; the erroneous doctrine that "cost of service" determines rates around which the League was "specially organized"; the distorted use made by the Chamber of Commerce and Board of Transportation of the slogan that railroads charge what the "traffic will bear"; the harm done by the Hepburn Committee; and the real lack of genuine grievance by "these very people in New York who make all this fuss and scatter this misinformation and misrepresentation all over the country." [86] In subsequent appearances before Congressional committees, Fink continued to bear down heavily upon the Anti-Monopoly League and its leaders as agents of discord dangerous to the common weal.[87]

Further evidence that Fink was correct in regarding New York as the home of the leaders of the antirailroad "crusade" was soon offered when the same Committee on Commerce gave part of one day to the friends of railroad legislation. Together with delegations from other cities, representatives of the New York Board of Trade and the National Grange appeared.[88] Significantly, the two delegates appointed by the National Grange master, J. J. Woodman (an Anti-Monopolist), were W. G. Wayne and J. G. Shepard of New York, both Farmers' Alliancemen,

Anti-Monopolists, and faithful allies of the metropolitan merchants.[89] And Judge Reagan's argument before the same committee sounded like an Anti-Monopoly League tract. In fact, a number of its quotations were taken directly from various *Documents* of the League, and when printed it bore on its title page the "Modern Barons" quote from President Garfield prominently featured in Anti-Monopoly literature.[90]

At the risk of seeming to belabor the issue, a brace of illustrations may be cited to reinforce and point up the thesis that New York merchants rather than western agrarians led the campaign to restrict free enterprise in American railroading. The first is a comment by the *Railroad Gazette* in March 1882 concerning the fact that "The Nebraska Farmers' Alliance has endorsed the New York Anti-Monopoly League principle that railroad rates shall be based on 'cost and risk of service.'" The *Gazette* expressed surprise that such endorsement had been forthcoming of a principle, which, if applied, would prevent Nebraska from shipping its products and reduce its land values to less than fifty cents an acre.[91] It is difficult to conceive of a higher tribute to the persuasiveness of New Yorkers bent upon improving their competitive position than the endorsement by Nebraska Alliancemen of a principle handtailored to metropolitan needs and diametrically opposed to their own. Albert Fink provides the second illustration. Testifying before a Senate committee in 1883, he conceded that the plank "in the platform of the Anti-Monopoly League" accusing railroads of charging "all the traffic will bear" had passed into general currency.[92] The wide acceptance of the New York Anti-Monopolists' key slogans, "cost and risk of service" and "all that the traffic will bear" (the slogans abound in the contemporary literature), assiduously spread through speeches, tracts, *Justice*, etc., appears to sum up adequately their leading role in the reform movement.[93]

CONGRESSIONAL ACTION AT LAST

In spite of increasingly successful Anti-Monopoly propaganda and the direction given by New Yorkers to once uncoördinated protests against railroad "oppression," little visible progress was made in 1882 towards the achievement of national legislation. The report Shepard and Wayne made to the National Grange concerning their reception by the House Committee on Commerce stressed two points: the committee was packed "solid in the railroad interest," and the people were not yet "fully aroused." [94] The conviction that lack of sufficient popular pressure explained the slow rate of progress against the "despotism of monopolies" was more distinctly emphasized by the National Grange master, J. J. Woodman, at the same session in November 1882. According to him, "The apathy of the masses and seeming indifference of businessmen towards the growing power and arbitrary exactions of these huge organizations cannot be explained by any system of logic, and savors more of fiction than reality." [95]

Woodman's caustic comments were a little too harsh on the American people. Granted the history of intense partisanship characterizing the decades after the Civil War, the diverse American socio-economic environment, the general prosperity of 1879–1882, the differences among reformers, and the extremely complicated nature of the railroad problem, it would have been a cause for wonder if progress on a national scale had been rapid. As Joseph Nimmo, Jr., pointed out to his friend, Thurber, the practical difficulty in drawing up legislation was that "while regulating the railroads you incidentally regulate trade, and this regulation of trade, although incidental would be by far the most important result of the measures which might be adopted." [96] Each city, each section, and each group looked to regulation to aid its specific interests; considerations of abstract justice were barely given more than lip service. Forging a coalition strong enough to overcome the power of the railroad lobby in Congress was complicated by the need to reconcile divergent, and frequently antagonistic, sectional and group interests. Contrariwise, although fiercely quarreling among themselves, railroads found little difficulty in mustering a solid front against legislation they considered hostile.

In 1882 New York merchants were especially concerned with national legislation because port differentials involving interstate commerce had come to the fore, but in that year their major political concentration was upon a state railroad commission, carrying the free canal amendment, and wresting control from the "corporations" in the New York election campaign. Once these objectives were attained, they assumed, the metropolis would have stronger bargaining power with which to fight the differentials. (Understandably, the latter aspect was not stressed by the leaders of the Anti-Monopoly League in national agitation.) [97] Yet the very incentives driving New Yorkers towards action on the national level tended to make their objectives more difficult of attainment. Differentials tended to divide seaboard commercial groups, and interior and coastal merchants hardly saw eye to eye over the special rates granted wholesalers in Syracuse, Rochester, Cincinnati, Chicago, St. Louis, etc., which acted to keep interior retailers close to home. Moreover, to the extent that either group retained interest in the railroad question, eastern farmers tended to favor long-haul short-haul statutes protecting their location advantages, and western farmers tended to look askance at legislation adding to their locational disadvantages.

Aware of the obstacles to be overcome in winning national regulation, the New York militants deliberately concentrated upon state legislation as a necessary preliminary. The "political revolution" of 1882 in the Empire State, and elsewhere throughout the country, hardly added up to "apathy" and "indifference." And the flood of petitions that year to Congress further indicates that Woodman was overstating the case against the American people's political intelligence. Translating public resentment against "railroad oppression" into a stable coalition mustering substantial numbers of Congressional votes necessarily was a drawn-out process. Eventually, reverberations of various state campaigns against "monopolies" and "railroad kings" grew sufficiently loud and threatening to politicos. Then regulatory campaigns began to move in march time.

In fundamental respects 1882 marked the peak year of agitation on the part of New York merchants. After that date, it seems more accurate to say that the near anarchy characterizing the American railroad system (discussed below) rather than the activities of individual organizations or groups forced the country to adopt regulation. As railroad managers continued to demonstrate their inability to provide a stable, non-discriminatory, remunerative rate structure when let alone, the conviction grew among virtually all interested parties that something else had to be tried.

Justice continued to proclaim Anti-Monopoly doctrines and the New York merchants by no means retired from the field. Nonetheless, after the creation of the New York Railroad Commission induced the roads to take a more accommodating line, and after the breakdown of the trunk-line pool in the early eighties, the push went out of their erstwhile militancy. The Chamber of Commerce returned to its more normal passivity,[98] and although the New York Board of Trade and Transportation actually increased in strength and prestige, its tone became more moderate and agitational activities less strenuous. Reference here is to mass activities; at the National Board of Trade its delegates continued to press for advanced resolutions.

To forward the cause of regulation at the 1883 session of the National Board of Trade, the New York Board resubmitted its original resolution of the previous year which had finally been passed in watered-down form. But after sensing the temper of the delegates, John Henry retreated and only asked reaffirmation of the resolution as adopted in 1882. Thurber did not share his co-worker's tactical views and held out for stronger action. However, he took the occasion to justify his currently less militant position: "I have fought so long and so strongly for some regulation of corporations, to find out whether the corporations control the country or the country has the right to control them, that I have in my own State, acquired the reputation of being radical; during the last year I have been trying to correct that by trying to become conservative." Henry's analysis proved to be more realistic and the final action taken by the National Board was simply to reaffirm its 1882 stand.[99]

During 1883 the New Yorkers continued to decelerate their pace, and even Secretary Burrows of the Nebraska Farmers' Alliance — the most militant and successful in the West — found that "the farmers are apathetic and the number of voters who are bought and sold seem to be increasing everywhere . . ." [100] Yet the onset of economic depression, and the less than impressive demonstration of managerial ability by railroad managers, led to a kind of self-generating momentum for federal control. Suiting action to what seemed to be the changing climate of opinion, the New York ex-militants introduced their boldest proposal to date at the 1884 session of the National Board of Trade. At last the "Commercial Senate" of the country was asked to endorse the Reagan bill.[101] Again Simon Sterne was brought forward to give the delegates the benefit of long years of study and experience; the disastrous conditions of the nation's railroads, he argued, proved the failure of the "let well enough alone" policy.

Analyzing Reagan's bill in detail, Sterne urged endorsement of its principles. But he conceded that it had some defects — chiefly the failure to provide for a railroad commission — and opponents seized upon these admissions to fight the resolution's adoption. Philadelphia, Chicago, and Boston delegates led the opposition, and the *Proceedings* indicate that only New Yorkers supported their resolution favoring Reagan's bill. Delegate Frost of the Boston Merchants Association successfully moved to amend the resolution by having it merely read:

That a National Board of Railroad Commissioners should be established by Congress as an executive and supervisory body to study the transportation problem and see that the laws relating thereto are complied with.[102]

Somewhat chastened by the rebuke administered to them in 1884, but with the national demand for regulation visibly rising in extent and pitch, the New Yorkers returned to the fray a year later. Their resolution on the program of the National Board included the one quoted immediately above but with this preface:

Resolved, That Congress should without delay, enact a law for the regulation of interstate commerce; that acknowledged wrongs should be prohibited and remedies provided so simple and practicable that the individual citizen in any part of the country can avail himself of them; that a National Board of Railroad Commissioners . . .[103]

Thurber made it plain that tactical considerations alone dictated New York's decision not to ask the National Board to endorse the Reagan bill recently approved by the House of Representatives. He did desire, however, to put the organization on record as affirming the necessity to define wrongdoing and to secure remedies for individuals in every part of the country. A Board of Railroad Commissioners was also needed: "But to have such a Board without specific statutes defining the cases of acknowledged wrongs and prohibiting them, would be something like having a police force without laws to guide them." [104]

Unlike the previous year, the New Yorkers succeeded in 1885 in getting their proposition through unamended. This action marked their last positive victory at the National Board of Trade. In 1886 and 1887 they were forced to fight rear-guard battles to prevent passage of resolutions opposed to any long-haul short-haul and anti-pooling clauses. By this time Congressional legislation of some kind was almost inevitable and the basic conflict was over whether it should include those two provisions. No longer in control of the New York Chamber of Commerce delegation, Thurber and Company also found their ability to influence the national board sensibly reduced. In 1886 they were unable to stave off adoption of resolutions which endorsed the Cullom bill but recommended that the long-haul short-haul clause be stricken out.[105] A year later, just before Congress finally acted, although they could not pass their own resolution, they did defeat the Chicago Board of Trade's proposal which again attacked that clause. (Actually, the majority of delegates favored the Chicago proposal — the vote was 25 to 16 — but a two-thirds rule was in effect at the national board.)[106] Pending a more thorough study of the complicated maneuvers behind the final passage of the Interstate Commerce Act, the question must be left open as to how it came to include the long-haul short-haul and anti-pooling clauses strongly opposed by leading commercial organizations (and others) in the country. But that neither eastern nor western farmers were responsible for their inclusion seems clear.[107]

RAILROAD POOLS AND WATERED STOCK

If farmers played a minor part in the national regulation movement during the eighties, another group not usually thought of in this connection must be assigned more weight. In 1879, while John Reagan was writing to Francis Thurber about the difficulties inherent in securing a railroad commission from Congress, some surprising recruits were being won for such a course of action. The recruits were leading trunk-line officials gradually coming around to the idea that such a commission might actually prove of considerable value to them. Clearly, the road by which they arrived at this conclusion was different from the one taken by Thurber or Reagan, and their objectives were equally dissimilar. No doubt a desire to head off state legislation, particularly in New York, was an important factor but more fundamental considerations also existed.

Railroad Competition
[William H. Vanderbilt Learns a Lesson]

By the late seventies it had become plain that railroad competition was a luxury too expensive to be indulged in much longer. Under the pressure of events, the desirability of the trunk-line pool was increasingly appreciated. At least one major difficulty, however, confronted the pooling enthusiasts. Despite the appointment of Commissioner Fink in 1877, the establishment of a Joint Executive Committee representing the trunk lines and the western roads in June 1879, and the formation of an eastbound pool at about the same time,[108] no real guarantee existed that the agreements would not be broken at any moment. Even the more manageable westbound pool was always threatening to break down, and as Vanderbilt and Fink were later to reveal, it had never been carried out faithfully.[109] The *Railroad Gazette* put the problem succinctly:

> If there is more complaint of broken agreements in the railroad business than in most other affairs, it must be remembered that in the railroad business the agreements which are broken are primarily those which the law does not compel the companies to keep.[110]

Though a generous interpretation of railroad policy and practice, the *Gazette*'s observation does point up the fact that no legal machinery existed to force managers to keep their word in regard to traffic agreements. Furthermore, unlike most other businesses, in railroading so strong a temptation existed to break agreements that little stigma attached to it. But if a commission could be set up to compel the observation of contracts and transform the pooling agreements into legal obligations, then, it was believed, American railroading would enter upon the Promised Land of no rate wars and highly lucrative, uninterrupted dividends.

Charles Francis Adams, Jr., Albert Fink, and George R. Blanchard (an Erie vice-president) were probably the three men most responsible for developing the concept of using national control over railroads to strengthen the pooling machinery. Adams had been drifting in that direction since at least 1876,[111] and his 1878 book vigorously advanced the idea of a "confederation" of railroad corporations which would be legal, public, and responsible.[112] About that time Adams' diary contains entries in this vein: "Took Col. Fink out to dinner and drove him out in afternoon, having a railroad talk with him." Several months later: "To Putnams' and much relieved to find that they had already disposed of an edition of my 'Railroads'. An interview with Col. Fink . . ." After other interviews, breakfasts, etc.: "Got notice of my appointment as r. r. arbitrator." [113] Having become one of the members of the Board of Arbitration set up by the Joint Executive Committee to settle disputes, his enthusiasm for the "confederation" grew accordingly.

Fink and Blanchard were also thoroughly convinced that pooling was

the answer to the problem (the former probably influenced Adams'
thinking on the subject), and during 1879 and 1880 both vigorously supported the idea that now was the time for all good governments to come
to the aid of the railroads.[114] High fixed costs and excess capacity had
proved themselves to be potent educators regarding the merits of
laissez faire when the Communication Revolution really hit its stride
after 1875. Far from repudiating the idea of "government interference,"
as railroad managers had been quick to do only a few years earlier, the
keenest thinkers in the industry now understood that only through the
use of governmental power could they hope to keep it under control.
For example, in January 1880 Commissioner Fink presented a long argument to the House Commerce Committee in opposition to the Reagan
bill which provides an excellent exposition of his views upon "The
Railroad Problem and Its Solution" — views reported to his employers,
the Joint Executive Committee, a month earlier. In his argument he
claimed to be in sympathy with the objects of the bill but declared that
his plan would actually accomplish them, whereas Reagan's was doomed
to failure. After examining the railroad question in detail he voiced this
sweeping opinion:

> I hope that my reasons are now better understood why I ask Congress to
> sanction, under the supervision of the general government, the agreements
> made between railroad companies, for the purpose of settling all questions
> that may lead to a war of rates and to a disturbance of the properly established
> transportation tariffs of the country. It is time that the antiquated notions that
> have taken such a strong hold of the legal minds of the country — that all
> agreements between railroad companies, in regard to transportation tariffs,
> are against public policy, and are in the nature of conspiracies — should at
> last give way to a proper understanding of the true nature and objects of
> these agreements, and to a conviction of their necessity and of their highly
> beneficial results upon public welfare; and instead of prohibiting such agree-
> ments — as it is intended to be done by the bill under your consideration —
> legal force should be given to them by the general government, and its power
> should be exercised in carrying out these agreements.
> *This is all that is required on the part of Congress to settle this vexatious
> railroad problem* [italics added].[115]

As did virtually everyone who proposed legislation concerning American railroads, Fink cited a European precedent for his plan. He emphasized that it was along the same lines as the English Clearing House
Act of 1850 authorizing a number of railroads to combine activities
and conduct their business as one road.[116] Appropriate legislation to put
Fink's formula into practice was drawn up by Adams and introduced in
the same session of Congress as the Henderson bill. Several years later
Adams wrote to a Massachusetts congressman and related his unsuccessful efforts to have it introduced as the "Reagan Bill" in place of the
Texan's original proposal.

I did my very best, four years ago, to induce him to incorporate the less harmful of its features with a proper commission bill, which would render an intelligent investigation possible, and to introduce the whole of it as the 'Reagan Bill', into the House. I assured him, and I was authorized to do so, that such a bill should encounter no opposition from the railroad companies in its passage. The bill that I submitted to him was as conscientiously prepared by me, as any bill could be. It was modelled after the Massachusetts bill, and went just as far in the direction of meaningless or harmful legislation, as it was possible, in safety, to go . . . [Reagan refused] The result has been that no bill at all has been passed, up to this time, and I greatly doubt if any bill will be passed.[117]

To the trunk-line managers plagued by increasingly bitter rate wars after 1875 a railroad pool had seemed to be the answer to railroad prayers. Not enjoying the legal sanction which would have made rate agreements firmer contracts, however, pools were far from a solid guarantee of peace and plenty. (Reagan at least scored a negative victory in preventing such legislation.) When enough traffic existed to keep all the roads reasonably busy a pool tended to operate most successfully. In dull times the agreement was honored more in the proverbial breach. The boom in commodity exports late in 1879, and the prosperity accompanying it, would seem to have provided an ideal setting to insure the success of the trunk-line pool. Yet, as events were to prove, pending government assistance neither prosperity nor depression was conducive to sustained harmonious operation. Prosperity caused ambitious managers within the pool to dream of building new lines or extending old ones, dreams which tended to upset the existing traffic pattern when acted upon. But an even greater threat to stability came from without.

As the New York *Commercial Bulletin* emphasized early in 1881, remunerative operation led to a heavy flow of capital into railroads (the inducement, it might be observed, was particularly strong in areas where roads paid high dividends on watered stock). Since the trunk-line pool stood committed to the necessity of taking in new lines, the *Bulletin* asserted, "It will thus be seen that the direct and inevitable effect of the pool is to bring into the field an overwhelming flood of new companies." Eventually, as new roads demanded and received a share of the existing traffic, rates would have to be jacked up to maintain profit margins to the point where an outraged public opinion would ruthlessly smash the pooling system. The *Bulletin*, while predicting that such a development was comparatively distant, noted that the completion of arrangements for two new trunk lines between Buffalo and New York indicated the process was well under way. "The device that was intended to extinguish competition is thus increasing it ten-fold." [118]

It also became apparent in the summer of 1881 that the stability of the trunk-line pool was subject to attack from within. The attack stemmed from William H. Vanderbilt's refusal to consider amending the pooling agreement in the event that new lines were built or existing ones extended, a provision strongly desired by other trunk lines. The Baltimore & Ohio especially yearned to expand at the New York Central's expense and the conflict between John Garrett and William H. Vanderbilt was not long concealed.[119] Vanderbilt's lucrative properties also provided the inspiration for the major assault upon the pool by non-participants. The "Seney Crowd" of Wall Street financiers built the Nickel Plate to parallel his Lake Shore road from Buffalo to Chicago. The promoters of the West Shore, directly paralleling the New York Central itself, included John Jacob Astor, George M. Pullman, General Horace Porter, and other leading capitalists.

Not only did the prospect exist of eventually forcing Vanderbilt to buy both roads to maintain rates on his lines, huge profits could be (and were) made in the construction. The West Shore, for example, cost about $29,000,000 to build and was capitalized at $76,000,000.[120] Nor were the Nickel Plate and the West Shore the only lines projected in what railroads call "Official Territory." By late 1881 six distinct sections of roads were being built under separate organization and it was anticipated that January 1, 1884, would see seven trunk lines operating between the seaboard and the West.[121] Truly, the pooling system was bearing a stranger kind of fruit than had been expected by its enthusiastic promoters.

Since most of the assaults were leveled at his properties, Vanderbilt was understandably disillusioned with the pool's operation. Other factors may have existed, but as the railroad war beginning in the spring of 1881 continued, assertions were freely made that Vanderbilt had deliberately provoked it in order to discourage the construction of competing lines.[122] By August conflict had developed on such a scale that the *Railroad Gazette* could comment: "The extent of the railroad war is now greater than at any other time in the history of our railroad system." [123] Threatened on almost every side, and in need of whatever support he could get, Vanderbilt, or whoever really made policy for the New York Central, decided that the time had again come to denounce the port differentials. Accordingly, he permitted himself to be "interviewed" by the New York *Tribune* and unloosed an unrestrained attack upon John Garrett of the Baltimore & Ohio; the latter was accused of attempting to divert trade from New York by giving cut rates contrary to the trunk-line agreement. Garrett replied in kind a month later, flatly charging that Vanderbilt's course of action was designed to "make railway property so unprofitable that the building of lines parallel to his will be stopped through the inability of parties connected with them to raise the money for their construction." Vanderbilt's suddenly developed opposition to seaport differentials was subjected to withering scorn as both hypocritical in spirit and untrue in facts.[124]

Despite Garrett's incisive attack upon Vanderbilt's sincerity, and the latter's previous desertion of the city in 1877, wishful thinking caused hope to exist in New York that this time the metropolis could depend upon the solemn assurances of the Central's president. Editorials in the *Commercial and Financial Chronicle* afford a good insight into the evolution of metropolitan public opinion. Shortly after Garrett's blast against Vanderbilt was delivered the *Chronicle* asserted that it had boomeranged. Misgivings existed concerning Vanderbilt's sincerity, the paper noted, but the vast majority were willing to take him at his word. "New York's commerce has of late years been harmed, and anyone who rises in its defense will receive the cordial support and co-operation of the entire community." [125]

Skepticism concerning Vanderbilt's intentions, however, had by no means disappeared, as the *Chronicle's* editorial two weeks later indicates. It maintained that the public was willing to accept the necessity for the railroad war, "if it is carried on in the interest of New York commerce as Mr. Vanderbilt asserts. But using this old property as a football in Wall Street is something of which even the suspicion should be avoided." [126] Contrary to expectations, the war continued after the canals closed for the winter, and Vanderbilt's unfaltering opposition to differentials was taken to indicate his sincerity.[127]

Disillusionment was not long delayed. Instead of fighting to the end, Vanderbilt experienced a rapid change of heart.[128] C. F. Adams, Jr., seems to have suggested the way out of the impasse. "In the afternoon, just as I was going home, a most extraordinary letter from Vanderbilt — my head ought to turn." And on the last day of 1881 this notation appears in his "Diary": "found a letter from Cassatt of Penn-road accepting my basis of settlement of R. r. war. Wrote to Vanderbilt." [129] As announced publicly by the latter, the proposal was that the railroad presidents leave the differentials tb be settled by a board of arbitrators before whom the various Chambers of Commerce would argue the question. Thus, the famous Advisory Commission of 1882 was set up in January. To the disgust of metropolitan interests, Vanderbilt thereby absolved himself of any responsibility for the differentials against New York and the railroad war soon came to an end.[130]

But the appointment of the Advisory Commission had an explosive effect upon the *Chronicle* and it laid down a fierce ultimatum on behalf of the metropolis. The long quotation below serves as a useful summary of New York's position and takes on considerable significance when the paper's past opposition to the mercantile efforts on behalf of railroad regulation is remembered, together with its fundamental conservatism.

We believe we do not overstate the case when we say that our people will never again quietly submit to what are called differential rates. Commissioners may report in favor of them and Presidents may agree upon them, and bind themselves through a pool to an observance of the agreement, but if needs be a power higher than they will sooner or later break it.

We speak more strongly than is our wont because we know that there is a feeling existing here which will brook no compromise, and at base it is right in principle. It has, to an extent, shown itself in the past, for it has been the power behind every movement proceeding from this city against railroads. Our business men are not tainted with communistic ideas, but they have of late years been lending their aid to schemes that savor strongly of communism, being thrown into that attitude through the disregard of their rights and interests by corporations. This discrimination, for instance, is imposing upon our commerce a burden it cannot bear; and if it is continued the people are sure to take the remedy into their own hands, until this popular feeling finds expression in legislative action. Demagogues of course take advantage of the spirit the wrong incites, and so the movement ends in legislation not alone forcing New York roads to carry as low as the lowest, but jeopardizing vested rights and interests . . .

In this era of close figuring and small profits, shall . . . [New York] quietly acquiesce in granting . . . [rival] cities an advantage that can have and does have but one effect? That is the whole issue. Everybody can see its importance to each merchant in this community, for it does not require argument to prove that a three cent higher rate will eventually turn a large portion of the export trade, and with it the import business, through the more favored port. It is only a question of time, and of how long a time merchants who have already been compelled to establish branch houses or make business arrangements at Baltimore on account of this discrimination can perhaps best answer. Peace between railroads is of course desirable, but if communities and their business connections must be sacrificed to attain it, better, we say, a hundred times better, that the war should continue. And this is in the stockholders' interest as well as our merchants', for one can prosper only as the other prospers.[131]

The New York *Times* echoed the sentiments expressed by the *Chronicle*,[132] and the same strong line was taken by the commercial organizations in their arguments to the Advisory Commission.[133] Notwithstanding, the commissioners failed to be impressed. After months of hearings in which the rival cities argued their case, they turned out a report leaving the situation precisely where it had been — the differentials which had existed under the agreement of 1877 were nominally still in force.[134] With remarkable candor, Albert Fink admitted almost in so many words that the issue had already been settled *before* the hearings took place.[135]

ANTI-MONOPOLY DOCTRINES BECOME RESPECTABLE

Railroads sensibly contributed to the progress of national legislation in ways other than Vanderbilt's broken promises and warped sense of public relations. In part they accomplished this through the economic disturbances and dislocations caused by rate wars, personal and place discrimination, stock watering, fraudulent promotion and construction, etc. But they also made a more positive contribution, for the idea of national legislation to strengthen the pooling system did not disappear with the virtual breakdown of the pool in 1881 and the continuous strain upon it thereafter.

Probably impressed by the popular opposition to legalized pools, Albert Fink and C. F. Adams, Jr., soon came up with another plan for federal regulation designed to secure the same objective. Trunk-line officials hastened to announce their public approval and according to the New York *Times* it attracted considerable attention.[136] Whatever the motivation, every declaration in favor of regulation added momentum to its coming. In fact, so clearly inevitable was the movement that even the *Commercial and Financial Chronicle*, a journal firmly dedicated to *laissez faire*, was forced in 1882 to admit that "the tendencies of the times seem to be slowly carrying us towards federal intervention of some sort, whether we will or not. The fact is that the railroad has revolutionized everything." [137] Thus the *Nation's* prophecy of 1873 to that effect was echoed as an accomplished fact less than ten years after it was made, and like the *Chronicle*, the *Nation* now viewed unrestricted railroad operation as not long for this world.[138]

The difficulty plaguing the trunk lines was that no sooner had one new line been disposed of than another took its place as a trouble maker. Without going into the details, non-stop rate wars were the order of the day in the early eighties. However, an important difference marked the rate wars of the seventies from those of the next decade. Through rates were slashed between West and East but the no-holds-barred competition between the four New York trunk lines for local traffic also drove those tariffs down to even more extreme levels.[139] Differentials were also disregarded and the Empire State benefited directly, whereas it previously had paid high local charges during rate wars. This feature tended to mitigate the charge that New York roads favored "foreigners" unduly and farmers, in particular, were less hostile than before. Yet the very instability of rates was a factor tending to perpetuate mercantile dissatisfaction.

A further contribution to demoralization in trunk-line territory was the onset of economic depression. Crops were poor during 1882 and 1883, and traffic sharply declined just at the time when facilities, stimulated by the boom after 1879, expanded rapidly. Here again was the classic formula for trouble and American railroading went from bad to worse, the stock market panic of May 1884 adding heavily to the strain.[140] The trunk-line area affords probably the best illustration of the virtual breakdown of the railroad rate system but the process was at work everywhere. Overexpansion, as well as fraudulent promotion, construction, consolidation, and manipulation of railroads, brought on a heavy wave of defaults late in 1884. According to an investors' journal such as the *Commercial and Financial Chronicle,* those defaults emphasized "the absence of responsibility to the public either in money or in business reputation among the projectors and organizers of railroads." [141]

Investors were not the only group hit hard by the near-anarchy characterizing the railroad system in the eighties. Cut-throat competition necessarily resulted in discrimination and rebates on a grand scale. George Blanchard charged that upon completion the Delaware and Lackawanna, and the West Shore, made over two thousand special contracts to attract business; no reason exists to doubt his statement.[142] Especially in a period of depression, favoritism hurt those merchants not similarly blessed. Fluctuating rates also tended to disrupt normal commercial operations and contributed to the demand for regulation. Areas not served by competing roads were spared the difficulties of fluctuating rates only to suffer from extortionate charges. Although in New York local traffic no longer paid for the losses suffered on through freight to pay dividends on watered stock, other places were not as fortunate.[143]

With the break-down of the pooling system in the mid-eighties, New York merchants continued to support national regulation but for different reasons than before. While the roads fought among themselves the New York merchants as a group did not suffer long from any specific grievance; judicious pressure on their part or the natural state of disequilibrium saw to that. However, if specific grievances no longer led to elaborate campaigns for correction, the uncertainties and disturbances surrounding railroad operations generated ever-increasing sentiment in favor of national regulation. Railroad disorganization unsettled the entire economy, and merchants, along with other businessmen, experienced the adverse effects. Moreover, in New York and elsewhere, merchants were particularly sensitive to transportation developments, anxious for stability, and keenly alive to the problems of personal discrimination. Thus, when the House was finally forced to reconsider Judge Reagan's bill in December 1884, he could argue that Chambers of Commerce and Boards of Trade the country over had gone on record as favoring its principles — among them the New York Chamber of Commerce, Board of Trade and Transportation, and Produce Exchange.[144]

Mercantile complaints may have led all the rest; yet even his opponents conceded that the reason Reagan could now get his bill considered and passed was that the country had been thoroughly awakened to the question. President Arthur in his message of 1883 called upon Congress to take appropriate action,[145] and the Republicans campaigned in 1884 upon a platform which included this plank:

> The principle of the public regulation of railroad corporations is a wise and salutary one for the protection of all classes of the people, and we favor legislation that shall prevent unjust discrimination and excessive charges for transportation, and that shall secure to the people and the railways alike the fair and equal protection of the laws.[146]

When the Republican party, headed by James G. Blaine, campaigned upon a platform hailing the principle of the public regulation of railroad corporations as a "wise and salutary one," then Anti-Monopoly sentiments indeed had taken deep root. For the real heart of the Anti-Monopoly creed was that "Corporations, the creation of the State, shall be controlled by the State." Francis B. Thurber expressed the concept late in 1885 in this prophetic fashion:

> Corporations performing delegated functions of the State, which can only be carried on by exercising a public franchise, must be controlled by the State and as fast as possible these delegated functions reassumed by the State. The time for a *laissez faire* policy is past. Our civilization is constantly growing more complex and the forces which now control it must themselves be controlled and directed or disastrous collisions will surely result.[147]

CONCLUSIONS: RAILROAD REGULATION
IN THE ERA OF COMMUNICATION REVOLUTION

Though numerous factors contributed to its development, successful enunciation of the regulatory concept in the United States was basically a product of the Communication Revolution. As a result of technological and organizational innovations after the Civil War, the men controlling major rail networks rapidly found themselves in possession of virtually unprecedented economic power. Nothing was more natural than that they use this power to further their own interests and those of men allied with them. In a country as dependent upon transportation as the United States, it was equally natural that in the process they had to affect adversely other powerful vested interests. Since those interests were unable to protect themselves according to the old rules of the economic game, they proposed to rewrite the rules.

The disproportionate power enjoyed by the "railroad kings" could only be matched if the non-railroad segments of the economy banded together to use the machinery of the state in their own behalf. Hence the replacement of the old battle-cry *"laissez faire,"* by the Anti-Monopoly slogan, "Corporations, the creation of the State, shall be controlled by the State." For reasons that perhaps have been reiterated too frequently, New York merchants led the counterattack designed to thwart the excesses of the railroad revolution. Necessarily, the movement took on a definite ideological character but if the interpretation presented here is correct, speaking broadly, the basic aims were to restore a more equal division of the profits of American enterprise and permit the continued functioning of the private enterprise system.

Rapid expansion of the rail network in the United States and rapid growth of the national economy meant that the centralization of railroad power had to be met by a centralization of government power if it were to be curbed. In other words, the power of the nation had to be exercised, not that of the individual state. This fact was recognized from the start of serious agitation in the seventies. But because the incidence of railroad pressure upon different property groups was felt at different times and in different ways, the necessary unity of purpose to accomplish federal regulation was impeded. Such a development could only take place when economic relationships became so intimate that the various injured groups were affected more or less simultaneously.

After years of fruitless effort, the passage of the Reagan bill in the House and the Cullom bill in the Senate, both in January 1885, indicates the rapid progress of events since late 1882 when J. J. Woodman had deplored "the apathy of the masses." Reconciliation of divergent methods of exercising governmental control and the divergent purposes of various groups and sections took two more years. The trend, however, was irresistible.

Because it seems to be a contradiction in terms, it deserves to be reiterated that leading railroad officials had made important positive contributions towards making the regulation trend irresistible. The pooling system which had once seemed a tidy device to institutionalize the railroad managers' disproportionate economic power proved otherwise in practice. Hence astute railroad officials came to promote the proposal that the government legalize pools. In no other way did it seem possible to maintain agreements and avoid cut-throat competition. Developed during the late seventies, strong impetus was given to the concept by the burst of railroad construction in the early eighties. Parallel roads, whether built for speculative purposes such as the Nickel Plate and the West Shore, or actually designed for long-time operation, such as the Delaware and Lackawanna, threw the railway world in continuous uproar. Other sections of the country experienced the same phenomena. Under these conditions, the relations between railroads and merchants changed sharply and the following statement by Thurber to the Cullom Committee in 1885 has no counterpart in the seventies.

Professional promoters have overloaded our railway system with watered stock, and have imposed upon the practical railway men of this country, who operate these great highways, the impossible task of earning dividends upon this mass of fictitious capital and at the same time satisfying the public. Having thus over-capitalized our transportation system they endeavored by combination to enforce rates which would yield dividends upon the entire capital. This in turn has stimulated the building of parallel lines, which in many cases were not needed, and in times of commercial depression, like the present, their pools and combinations break down and they appeal to the National Government for legislation to enforce their agreements upon each other and enable them to tax the commerce of the country to sustain these fictitious values.[148]

The struggle between the West Shore and the New York Central serves as an excellent illustration of both the chaotic state of railroading in the mid-eighties[149] and the powerful forces thereby set in motion on behalf of a durable peace. Apart from larger considerations, J. P. Morgan's role in the sale of Central stock in 1879 gave him a direct interest in the restoration of "order" out of chaos; the House of Morgan's reputation with investors was damaged when the road's dividends were cut sharply in 1884 and 1885. Moreover, his firm handled the financial operations of the Pennsylvania Railroad and that company was intimately involved in the quarrel between the New York roads. Behind the scenes the Pennsylvania was supporting the West Shore in its fight against the Central. In turn, Vanderbilt had joined with John D. Rockefeller, Andrew Carnegie, and others, in the construction of the South Pennsylvania, a parallel road aimed at crushing the Pennsylvania. The ramifications went even further but enough has been indicated to suggest the tangled web of capital interests involved and the compelling reasons inspiring Morgan to take a hand.[150] In his words, he came to the decision that "something should be done to bring more harmony among the trunk lines." [151]

The details of Morgan's endeavors to establish "harmony," including the purchase of the West Shore by the New York Central, are not germane, but his recognition that matters could no longer be allowed to drift underscores the tendency of the times. The American economy had reached the point where railroad demoralization could no longer be permitted to continue without attempts at restraint. Forceful intervention by a financial giant like Morgan expresses one facet of the situation; attempts to secure government intervention, another. Nor does any dichotomy necessarily exist between the two forms of control. Little reliable evidence exists at present to substantiate the view; yet it seems appropriate to raise the question as to whether Morgan did not favor the use of federal power to end the near-anarchy characterizing railroad management and promotion.[152] Certainly, the events of the early eighties had caused various railroad officials to take a fresh look at the possibilities inherent in Anti-Monopoly slogans concerning the nature of relations between the state and corporations.

Even before the completion of the West Shore, the New York Central's managers had seen the handwriting on the wall and attempted a reconciliation with their mercantile opponents in New York. Gone were the days when Chauncey Depew would ridicule the demand for a state railroad commission, or brand the attempts to regulate railroads as "communistic," or insist that railroad managers would not tolerate "interference." If the quotation below is compared with his annual lectures to the legislature prior to 1882, or his closing argument to the Hepburn Committee, it clearly was a more conciliatory Depew who addressed the New York Chamber of Commerce banquet on May 8, 1883.

There is no reason why we should have any dispute — you who handle the commerce, and we who carry it — no reason why we should have any dispute that we cannot settle by ourselves; and if we cannot settle it a tribunal has been established in this State which ought to be broad enough, honest enough and courageous enough, to settle it on the one side or the other, without regard to the cry of communism or monopoly. And it should be our common aim (and in saying that, I believe I speak the sentiment of the whole transportation interest of the United States) to have a national tribunal which shall accomplish two things — hold equally the reins of impartial justice between the shipper and the carrier, and at the same time, while this tribunal controls in a measure the property invested in corporations, and subjects it to restrictions and regulations imposed upon the money used in no other business, they should grant to it, so long as it properly serves the public within the territory it traverses, protection against being pirated, by being unnecessarily harassed and paralleled. If they are to govern the management of existing lines, they should have the power to determine whether new ones are needed, and to permit or prohibit their construction. [Cheers] [153]

When in trouble the Central had always shown a disposition to stress the community of interest existing between it and the New York merchants; the extent of the troubles its managers foresaw can be judged from the sacrifices it was offering to make. In effect, Depew was proposing a *quid pro quo*. If the merchants helped the road to achieve exemption from competition, it in turn would agree to a certain amount of state and national regulation. Hence his conciliatory words, and more important, the generally conciliatory course of action taken by the New York roads thereafter. This was made abundantly clear by John O'Donnell, the merchants' nominee to the state Board of Railroad Commissioners who continued to act on their behalf. "I believe our Commission act would be like a rope of sand were it not for the fact that the principal railroads of the State of New York have cheerfully obeyed our recommendations." [154]

Probably the best explanation of the Central's generally cheerful obedience (there were notable exceptions) rests in the commission's recommendation soon after its creation to amend the General Railroad Act in order to prevent "unnecessary" railroad construction. According to James

F. Hudson, "This . . . [was] the first official enunciation of the doctrine that the railways have a proprietary right in the traffic of the localities which they serve." [155] And it is indicative of the less hostile relations between railroads and merchants — who frequently were stockholders as well — that by the spring of 1885 even the Board of Trade and Transportation endorsed the recommendation.[156] Relations were not precisely cordial and a wide gap still separated their views concerning the best method to attain economic salvation, but at least they were both agreed on the need for regulation of some sort. Furthermore, the activities of the state railroad commission and the nature of its recommendations caused even the *Commercial and Financial Chronicle* to praise it. After three years of operation the paper stated that it had been of service to all interests. The very railroads which once opposed it so strenuously now recognized that it had been useful to them. "In fact, some railroad officials have no hesitation in saying frankly that the wisdom of the Board's creation has been amply demonstrated." [157]

The picture that emerges in the mid-eighties is a growing recognition on almost all sides that "interference" by the government was necessary to set the railroad system in order. No intention exists of overlooking the basic differences in opinion over how the power was to be exercised, nor the frequent reversals in judgment under the pressure of events. Nonetheless, repeated endorsement of the principles of government regulation by railroad officials, as well as by journals speaking for them or for the financial and investing community, was an important factor in speeding its enactment into law. Many of the realities of contemporary American national politics, above all, many of the realities of American economics, have to be ignored if the Interstate Commerce Act of 1887 is viewed as primarily the result of a victory by the "people" over the "corporations."

The stress placed on the railroads' general acquiescence to regulation is not vitiated by the fact that the final act contained two provisions which they had bitterly opposed: the prohibition on pooling and the long-haul short-haul clauses. Once a sufficient head of popular steam had been allowed to be built up — the Supreme Court decision in October 1886 denying the states all power to regulate interstate commerce explosively augmented the pressure — it would have been fairly dangerous to attempt to cap it tight. Affairs had reached the point where the crude tactics employed by Commodore Vanderbilt, Jay Gould, Tom Scott, and others to kill unfavorable legislation were obviously unwise.

But it is at least suggestive that the construction given the long-haul short-haul clause by the Interstate Commerce Commission, according to the *Commercial and Financial Chronicle* which strongly opposed the provision, soon almost did away with the necessity to suspend it.[158] And the prohibition upon pooling can hardly be said to have interfered with

J. P. Morgan's attempt to bring "order" into railroading.[159] Once the façade of regulation had been accepted, the roads, at least for considerable time thereafter, found little difficulty in doing just about what they pleased in the matter; it is true that to a certain extent the force of public opinion inhibited their pleasure.[160]

Simon Sterne's role in drafting the provisions of the Interstate Commerce Act rounds out this study of the part played by New York merchants and farmers in the movement to subject railroads to government control. After his testimony before the Cullom Committee, Sterne was requested by its chairman "to put in Bill form your view of a proper law." [161] Evidently "the great respect" expressed by Senator Cullom did not diminish for by June 1886, he was addressing Sterne as "Dear Friend," instead of "Dear Sir." [162] The account given of the New Yorker in the *Dictionary of American Biography* credits him with having "drafted essential provisions of the federal Interstate Commerce Act of 1887." Additional evidence of the regard in which Sterne was held by Cullom and the other members of the committee is their recommendation to President Cleveland that he be chosen to make a report "on the relations of the governments of nations of Western Europe to the Railways." Cleveland accepted the recommendation,[163] and the report's emphasis upon the lessons to be learned from English experience points up the derivative nature of American railroad regulation.

It appears an appropriate comment upon the far-reaching changes ushered in by the Communication Revolution that Simon Sterne, confirmed disciple of the classical political economists and first secretary of the American Free Trade League formed in 1864, some two decades later should have helped to write the Interstate Commerce Act which, on the national level, formally marked the first major challenge to *laissez faire* in the United States.[164]

NOTES

Chapter I. Early Movements for Railroad Regulation and Cheap Transportation

1. "Communication Revolution" is the term employed throughout this study to connote the significant changes in transportation and communication that took place in the late nineteenth century. For a more extensive treatment of the term, see Lee Benson, "The Historical Background of Turner's Frontier Essay," *Agricultural History*, 25:59–62 (April 1951).
No inference is intended that the amount of space devoted to various phases of the developments prior to 1873 centering about railroad regulation and demands for cheap transportation is relative to their intrinsic importance. Among other considerations, the particular focus of the present study, the extent to which developments have been treated in existing secondary accounts, and the relative obscurity of significant antecedents have determined the chapter's proportions.

2. *Report of the Industrial Commission* (Washington, 1901), 9:901–915; Simon Sterne, *Railways in the United States* (New York, 1912), 35–36, 41; Caroline E. McGill, ed. *History of Transportation in the United States before 1860* (Washington, 1916), 292–293, 316–317, 320–321, 355–356, 383–384; Charles F. Adams, Jr., *Railroad Legislation* (Boston, 1868), 3–8. Adams' pamphlet was originally printed in the *American Law Review* of 1867–1868 but contains an interesting appendix not found there.

3. *Report of the Industrial Commission* (Washington, 1901), 9:906–907; Edward C. Kirkland, *Men, Cities, and Transportation* (Cambridge, Mass., 1948), 1:267–284, 2:230–240.

4. David M. Ellis, *Landlords and Farmers in the Hudson-Mohawk Region, 1790–1850* (Ithaca, New York, 1946), 181.

5. *Letters to the Rail Road Companies, and to the People of the State of New York, on the Propriety of a Permanent Reduction of Rail Road Fare, or of a Purchase of the Rail Road by the State: Together with a Form of a Petition to the Legislature on These Subjects* (Utica, New York, 1843), 3, 4, 13. The author styled himself "H * * *," and the pamphlet consisted of articles originally published in the Utica *Gazette* and Oneida *Whig*.

6. For a convenient summary of the major changes made by the convention on such important issues as "State Aid to Private Enterprise," and "Corporations," see Charles Z. Lincoln, *The Constitutional History of New York* (Rochester, N. Y., 1906), 2:91–101, 179–182, 184–195. The sections on "Canals" and "Limiting State Debts" describe the reactions against an expansive program of internal improvements and the victory of the advocates of retrenchment. *Ibid.*, 2:45–58, 165–179.

7. A. B. Johnson, "The Legislative History of Corporations in the State of New York," *Hunt's Merchants' Magazine*, 23:613 (December 1850).

8. *Ibid.*, 23:610–614; Sterne, *Railways in the United States*, 41–42.

9. *Hunt's Merchants' Magazine*, 23:610, 613.

10. Lincoln, *Constitutional History*, 2:91.

11. Article 8, Section 1, reads: "Corporations may be formed under general laws; but shall not be created by special act, except for municipal purposes, and in cases where, in the judgment of the legislature, the objects of the corporation cannot be attained under general laws. All general laws and special acts passed pursuant to this section may be altered from time to time, or repealed."

12. *Hunt's Merchants' Magazine*, 23:613.

13. "Of the Committee on Railroads, in Relation to a General Law," New York State *Senate Document*, No. 64 (1847), 3–5.

14. *Ibid.*, 5–9.

15. *Laws of the State of New York, 1848*, ch. 140.

16. "Railroad Legislation of New York in 1849," *Hunt's Merchants' Magazine*, 21:163 (August 1849).

17. *Laws of the State of New York, 1850*, ch. 140. A valuable copy of the law, containing all amendments to 1860, is found in Henry V. Poor, *History of the Railroads and Canals of the United States of America* (New York, 1860), 325–352.

18. Sterne, *Railways in the United States*, 41–42.

19. *Laws of . . . New York, 1850*, ch. 140, sec. 28, 31, 33.

20. Simon Sterne's criticisms of the 1850 act stemmed from his belief that it represented a misapplication of the generally sound principles of political economy. An important reason for the errors in early legislation, he held, was the dominance of *laissez faire* at the inception of the railroad system in both England and America. See his *Railways in the United States*, 34–35, 41–43, 89–90.

21. Henry V. Poor, "Sketch of the Rise and Progress of the Internal Improvements, and of the Internal Commerce, of the United States," in his *Manual of the Railroads of the United States for 1881* (New York, 1881), xlviii–xlix.

22. "Annual Report of the Railroad Corporations . . . 1849," New York State *Assembly Document*, No. 92 (1850), 1–2; "Annual Report of the Railroad Commissioners . . . for the Year Ending September 30, 1855," New York State *Assembly Document*, No. 12 (1856), 2:ix.

23. *Ibid.*, 2:ix; "Report of the Committee on Railroads on Bill to Repeal Act Establishing the Board of Railroad Commissioners," New York State *Senate Document*, No. 96 (1856), 1–4.

24. *Laws of the State of New York, 1855*, ch. 526.

25. New York State *Assembly Document*, No. 12 (1856), 1:xix–xlvi.

26. *Ibid.*, pt. 1:xlv–xlvi.

27. New York State *Senate Document*, No. 96 (1856), 4.

28. New York State *Assembly Document*, No. 12 (1856), xlvi.

29. New York State *Senate Document*, No. 96 (1856), 1–7. The quotation is from p. 2.

30. "Report of the Railroad Commissioners in Reply to Resolution of the Senate," New York State *Senate Document*, No. 156 (1857), 1–3.

31. New York State *Senate Journal* (1857), 809. The senator who reversed himself was Frederick P. Bellinger of Herkimer County.

32. *Laws of the State of New York, 1857*, ch. 633. The legislative history of the bill is found in New York State *Assembly Journal* (1857), 583, 1070, 1278, 1367, 1416, 1472; New York State *Senate Journal* (1857), 809, 839–840, 967. The bill passed the Senate unanimously; the Assembly recorded only two negative votes.

33. *Argument of Hon. Chauncey M. Depew Before the Assembly Committee on Railroads in Opposition to the Bill, "An Act to Create a Board of Railroad Commissioners and to Regulate Their Powers," March 28, 1878* (Albany, 1878), 4–5.

34. Hepburn Committee, *Proceedings*, 3:2723–2725.

35. David M. Ellis, "Rivalry Between the New York Central and the Erie Canal," *New York History*, 29:275–284 (July 1948).

36. The New York and Erie reached the Great Lakes in 1851, the short lines running from Albany to Buffalo were consolidated into the New York Central in 1853, the Baltimore and Ohio reached the Ohio River in the same year, and the Pennsylvania Railroad had an all rail route from Philadelphia to Pittsburgh in 1854. Not until 1857, however, did it actually own the entire line. Poor, *History of Railroads and Canals*, 272, 280, 471, 579.

37. "Report of the Majority of the Committee on Ways and Means in the Special Message of the Governor Respecting the Imposition of Tolls on Railroads," New York State *Assembly Document*, No. 107 (1855), 1–16.

38. See Clinton League, *Proceedings of the New York State Conventions . . .* This lengthy document was first printed in November 1859; another edition of 13,000 copies was put out in December. It was issued as No. 77 and No. 151 of the *Documents* of the Clinton League, and printed in New York. The contents included much more material than the title indicates and it constitutes the best single

source upon the pro rata and tolling movements in New York. Cited henceforth, as Clinton League, *Proceedings*.

39. "Report of a Majority of the Select Committee on Petitions for Regulating the Freight Tariffs on Railroads," New York State *Assembly Document*, No. 178 (1859), 3–10.

40. "Report of a Majority of the Select Committee on Petitions for Regulating Freights on Railroads of This State," New York State *Assembly Document*, No. 47 (1860), 3–8.

41. New York State *Assembly Journal* (1858), 216, 246.

42. Thomas Parson's bill was not the first of its kind in New York. In 1853 there had been an attempt to write a pro rata clause into the act authorizing consolidation of the New York Central, and in 1855 the Buffalo Board of Trade had sought to get legislative approval for the pro rata principle. Clinton League, *Proceedings*, 59–60, 96. As early as 1852 and 1853 a pro rata measure had been proposed in the Ohio legislature. New York State *Assembly Document*, No. 60 (1869), 12.

43. Ansel Bascom of Seneca Falls led the fight for railroad tolls. For his position see Clinton League, *Proceedings*, 30, 50–52, 66–67, 68–70.

44. Carlos Cobb of Buffalo was the chief spokesman for the upstate merchants and millers. His views are found in *ibid.*, 39–45, 56–57, 58–59.

45. Henry O'Reilly was the spokesman for the metropolis. See *ibid.*, 17–20, 61–62, 68.

46. This conclusion is derived from a study of the correspondence between Carlos Cobb and Henry O'Reilly, the reports of various legislative committees, proceedings of the canal conventions, and the public appeals made to farmers to support the positions advanced by the conventions. Cobb to O'Reilly, October 4, 9, 13, 19, 25, November 1, 2, 7, 8, 23, 25, December 2, 10, 1859; Cobb to Hugh Allen, November 17, 1859; Daniel Mann to O'Reilly, September 21, November 8, 1859. All O'Reilly correspondence is from the Henry O'Reilly collection at the New York Historical Society, Miscellaneous Box #22.

47. *Address to the People of the State of New York Concerning the Canal and Railroad Policy of the State* (Buffalo, 1859?), 3. Cited henceforth as Syracuse Convention, *Address to the People*.

48. *Ibid.*, 3–13.

49. The committee consisted of Henry Fitzhugh, Oswego, Sanford B. Hunt, Buffalo, Thos. G. Alvord, Syracuse, John T. Lacey, Rochester, Henry O'Reilly, New York. *Ibid.*, 14.

50. *Ibid.*, 14.

51. The trunk-line rate wars of the late fifties and the railroad conventions to deal with them are concisely treated in Rolland H. Maybee, *Railroad Competition and the Oil Trade, 1855–1873* (Mount Pleasant, Mich., 1940), 89–99. According to Freeman Hunt, the 1858 convention held at the St. Nicholas Hotel was the first great movement of the kind. *Hunt's Merchants' Magazine*, 39:621 (November 1858). Contemporary reaction in New York to the rate wars and differential agreements is found in New York State *Assembly Documents*, No. 166 (1859), entitled "Report of the Committee on Railroads, Relative to the Classification Tariff of Prices, etc., on All Freight Transported on the Railroads of This State," 2–6; also see New York State *Assembly Document*, No. 180 (1859), entitled "Report of the Minority of the Select Committee on the Pro Rata Freight Bill," 4–10; New York, *Legislative Restrictions on the Carrying Trade of the Railways of the State of New York: Viewed in Connection with Outside Competition . . .* (New York, 1860), *passim*.

52. Syracuse Convention, *Address to the People*, 5,13.

53. New York State *Assembly Document*, No. 178 (1859). In all, the report was 29 pages long and contains some elaborate statistical material on the extent of discrimination and the competition between railroads and canals. It was not accompanied by a copy of the bill but one is included in the report of the Committee on Railroads, together with a typical petition. New York State *Assembly Document*, No. 166 (1859), 6–10.

54. For the residence of both men, George Opdyke and J. H. Mallory, and their organizational attachments, see New York Chamber of Commerce, *Annual Report . . . for the Year 1859–60* (New York, 1860), 100; Clinton League, *Proceedings*, 2. Mallory was a member of the Clinton League and one of its delegates to the Utica Convention of the "Friends of the Canal System." His firm opposition to pro rata in the spring of 1859 and his support of it in September 1859 — the convention adopted pro rata unanimously — is indicative of the pressures upon New Yorkers interested in the preservation of the Canal system to go along with upstate demands for pro rata. The unanimous vote for pro rata is stated in the account of the meeting in *ibid.*, 62. The minority committee report is New York State *Assembly Document*, No. 180, (1859), cited in full in n. 51 above.

55. *Ibid.*, 1–2.

56. *Ibid.*, 2–3.

57. *Ibid.*, 5. Another legislative report strongly adverse to pro rata on much the same grounds is New York State *Assembly Document*, No. 166 (1859), 1–6.

58. Clinton League, *Proceedings*, 23–24.

59. B. Brockway, "Our Canals and Our Railroads," *Hunt's Merchants' Magazine*, 41:164–165 (August 1859).

60. J. E. Bloomfield, "Suggestions and Statistics of Railroads and Canals," *Hunt's Merchants' Magazine*, 37:251–255, 372–377 (August, September 1857); "The Public Works of the State of New York," *ibid.*, 37:692–700 (December 1857).

61. Clinton League, *Proceedings*, 5. Editorials were reprinted from the New York *Times, Herald, Tribune, Courier and Enquirer*, and *Daily News*, warning against the "plot" to sell the canals, and upholding the course of the Clinton League in fighting to preserve them. *Proceedings*, 5–6, 15–16, 112.

62. *Ibid.*, 18–19.

63. *Ibid.*, 30, 38, 46–47, 68–70.

64. A letter from Cobb to O'Reilly, dated October 28, 1859, is evidence of both the accuracy of the charge that the State Executive Committee deliberately subverted the principles of the convention, and his cynical contempt for the rural masses.

65. Cobb was generally acknowledged to be the key figure in the antirailroad agitation in New York and his correspondence with O'Reilly testifies to his dominant role. More importantly, it indicates that the agitation for pro rata in New York State was led by upstate merchants and millers, particularly those at Buffalo who were losing out to rivals in Chicago and other Western cities. See Daniel Mann to O'Reilly, September 21, 1859; Cobb to O'Reilly, October 19, November 8, December 10, 1859.

66. See the manuscript minutes of a "Canal Meeting" held at Buffalo, September 13, 1859. Signed E. H. Walker, and found in the O'Reilly collection.

67. Many of the original replies, as well as several of the printed ones, were found in the O'Reilly collection.

68. For the movement's significance, as the leaders viewed it, see Cobb to O'Reilly, October 9, 1959; O'Reilly to the former governor, Washington Hunt, September 20, 1859 (a copy).

69. The printed replies are found in Clinton League, *Proceedings*, 8–13.

70. The 77th document was the November edition of the *Proceedings*. The edition dated December 1, 1859 was No. 151 of the Clinton League documents; the first one had been published in September. O'Reilly had faith in the power of the printed word and was a great believer in sending documents to key individuals. For example, the 112-page edition of the *Proceedings* was sent to every county supervisor in the state.

71. On Election Day, November 8, the New York *Herald* editorially congratulated itself upon its sagacity in predicting the reaction to the Rochester convention of September 1 (quoted in Clinton League, *Proceedings*, 112). The shrewd emphasis upon the "railroad conspiracy" to destroy the canals helps to explain the success of the agitation.

72. The pro rata bill barely squeaked through the Assembly at first, 65 to 61.

The final vote several months later was 70 to 20; apparently "the people" had been heard from in the interim. The legislative by-play between Assembly and Senate on pro rata — the Senate passed a bill ostensibly in concurrence with the Assembly, which in reality was meaningless — is concisely shown in New York State *Assembly Journal* (1860), 1135–1139, 1383. The early vote is found on pp. 459–461. The majority report of the Assembly committee on pro rata is New York State *Assembly Document*, No. 47 (1860), 1–24. It pointed out that the agitation against railroad policy was not confined to New York; similar policies of railroad discrimination had led to similar reactions in Pennsylvania, Ohio, and Maryland. In the prewar movements no proposal was found to solve the question through Federal regulation.

73. The legislative deadlock is shown in the majority report of the Senate conferees of the joint committee of conference on railroad tolls, which includes the minutes of the joint committee. New York State *Senate Document*, No. 90 (1860), 1–27. The economic, legal, and moral arguments against tolls in the face of trunk-line competition, the Constitution of 1846, and the Federal power to regulate commerce are treated in New York State *Senate Document*, No. 35 (1860), entitled "Report of the Minority of the Select Committee, on the Petitions and Bills for Imposing Tolls on Certain Railroads," 1–18, and in New York State *Assembly Document*, No. 119 (1860), entitled "Report of the Minority of the Committee of Ways and Means, on the Petitions and Remonstrances Relating to the Imposition of Tolls upon Property Transported upon the Several Railroads of This State," 1–8.

74. "Remonstrance of the Chamber of Commerce against the Passage of 'An act in Relation to Transportation of Freight on the several Railroads of This State,' etc., New York State *Assembly Document*, No. 59 (1860), 3–4.

75. Frederick Merk, "Eastern Antecedents of the Grangers," *Agricultural History*, 23:7–8 (January 1949).

76. Emerson C. Fite, *Social and Industrial Conditions in the North During the Civil War* (New York, 1910), 48; Frederick Merk, *Economic History of Wisconsin During the Civil War Decade* (Madison, Wis., 1916), 309–323; Henrietta M. Larson, *The Wheat Market and the Farmer in Minnesota, 1858–1900* (New York, 1926), 40–43; Frank L. Klement, "Middle Western Copperheadism and the Genesis of the Granger Movement," *Mississippi Valley Historical Review*, 38:683–689 (March 1952).

77. A decade ago Chester Destler advanced the thesis that "western radicalism" is best understood if one traces the migration of concepts and movements originating in the East. "Western Radicalism, 1865–1901: Concepts and Origins," *Mississippi Valley Historical Review*, 31:335–368 (December 1944). An intensive study of the personnel, ideas, and slogans of the western agitation from 1863 to 1866, and again in the early seventies, would serve to test the thesis further. Certainly its validity is consonant with the findings of the present study.

78. Merk, *Economic History of Wisconsin*, 322–327; Fite, *Social and Industrial Conditions*, 49–54; Larson, *Wheat Farmer in Minnesota*, 46–49; Klement in *Mississippi Valley Historical Review*, 38:689–694; Bessie L. Pierce, *A History of Chicago* (New York, 1940), 2:64–66; Earl S. Beard, "The Background of Railroad Regulation in Iowa," *Iowa Journal of History*, 51:17–19 (January 1953).

79. *Ibid.*, 19–21; Merk, *Economic History of Wisconsin*, 327–328.

80. Fite, *Social and Economic Conditions*, 48–54; New York Chamber of Commerce, *Fifth Annual Report* (New York, 1863), 24–25. The resolutions adopted by the Chamber at the April 3, 1862, meeting led to the appointment of a commissioner by the governor of New York to study the question. The lengthy report by Samuel B. Ruggles, a leader in the Clinton League's campaign to preserve the canals, provides an excellent picture of the various interests attempting to shape wartime transportation improvement. *Report of Samuel B. Ruggles, Commissioner Appointed by the Governor of the State of New York, under the Concurrent Resolution of the Legislature, of April 22, 1862, in Respect to the Enlargement of the Canals for National Purposes* (Albany, 1863), 1–105.

81. Fite, *Social and Economic Conditions*, 51. The call was issued over the

signatures of many senators and representatives and especially sought the coöperation and aid of boards of trade, chambers of commerce, agricultural societies and business associations. *Report of Samuel B. Ruggles . . . in Respect to the Enlargement of the Canals for National Purposes*, 93–94.

82. *Proceedings of the National Commercial Convention, Held in Boston, February, 1868* (Boston, 1868), v–vi.

83. Dexter Perkins, "Henry O'Reilly," *Rochester History*, 7:7–9, 13–15, 21–22 (January 1945); National Cheap Freight Railway League, *Grand Rally in Behalf of the Producing Interests* (New York?, 1868), 3–4; *The Great Questions of the Times, Exemplified in the Antagonistic Principles Involved in the Slaveholders Rebellion Against Democratic Institutions as well as Against the National Union; as Set Forth in the Speech of the Hon. Lorenzo Sherwood, Ex-Member of the Texan Legislature, Delivered at Champlain, in Northern N. Y., Oct. 1862 . . . Arranged for Publication, on Request from the Democratic League and Other Friends of the Union, by Henry O'Rielly* (New York, 1862). The information concerning O'Reilly is found in Perkins; Sherwood's history is given in an editorial reprinted in the *Grand Rally* from the Hamilton (New York) *Democratic Republican*. ("O'Reilly changed the spelling of his name to O'Rielly, and that form is on his tombstone, but the name appears more commonly in the usual spelling." *Dictionary of American Biography*.)

84. Miscellaneous documents of the League are bound together in the New York Public Library under the rubric, National Anti-Monopoly Cheap Freight Railway League, *Monthly Circular Document 5, September 1867*. Publications 6 nos. 1867–68. The contents will be cited individually henceforth. The library also holds a *Memorial by Lorenzo Sherwood to the Congress, for an Atlantic and Pacific Freight Railway Com'y* (Washington, March 4, 1867), and the *Grand Rally* pamphlet cited above in n. 83. Columbia University has the *Monthly Circular* of the League for October and November 1867. The title used in the text of the present study is from the cover page of the October *Circular*. O'Reilly's style was, to say the least, highly erratic and cover pages, titles, etc., show considerable variation. Apparently he never brought together all the publications of the League in one omnibus edition, as he had those of the Clinton League. The *Grand Rally* pamphlet seems to have been the last one he was responsible for and a note on the last page suggests that the League had run out of funds in 1868.

85. An autobiographical statement by O'Reilly claimed that "He originated, in 1867, an organized movement for reforming and cheapening the operations of the Railroad System of the United States." Reprinted in Edward R. Foreman, "Valuable Source Material of History: The Henry O'Rielly Documents," Rochester Historical Society, *Publication Fund Series* (Rochester, New York, 1930), 9:125. Although Sherwood conceived the plan upon which the League was based, O'Reilly probably was accurate in his claim to having originated the organization. For his troubles, however, according to Foreman, he received a remuneration too small to meet his living expenses. *Ibid.*, 143.

86. Chester Destler's observation that a definite connection probably existed between the prewar Loco-Foco agitation and the postwar National Anti-Monopoly Cheap Freight Railway League is borne out in the personal history of Lorenzo Sherwood and Henry O'Reilly. Destler, in *Mississippi Valley Historical Review*, 31:336–339.

87. Information which dates Sherwood's plan as having originated in 1866 is found in an editorial from the *American Railroad Journal*, reprinted in *Opinions of the Press in Various Regions Concerning the Anti-Monopoly Cheap-Freight Railway Policy* (New York? 1867?), 20.

88. Apparently the plan was first advanced in the columns of the *Great Republic*, a journal published in Washington, D. C., where Sherwood was residing. The continual references to the paper in various pamphlets suggests that Sherwood had some interest in it, or was on excellent terms with its editors. *The Development of Our Industrial Resources. What to Do, and How to Do It. By Lorenzo Sherwood , . . Reprinted From the Great Republic* (Washington, D. C.?, 1867?), 8.

89. *The Cheap Freight Railway. Mr. Sherwood's Speech at Chicago* (Chicago?, 1868?), 2; *Proposed National System of Cheap Freight Railways . . . Letter from the President of the National Cheap Freight Railway League, and Others, to Citizens of Texas* (Washington, D. C.?, 1867?), 6.

90. Descriptions of the plan, in varying degrees of detail and emphasis are found in Sherwood, *Development of Our Industrial Resources*, passim; National Anti-Monopoly Cheap Freight Railway League, *Document VI*, October 1867 (New York, 1867), 78–80, *Document VII*, November 1867, 104–105.

91. *Regulations of the National Anti-Monopoly Cheap Freight Railway League* (New York?, 1867?), 1.

92. National Anti-Monopoly Cheap Freight League, *Document VI*, October 1867, 72. The same page contains editorial expressions of approval from several New York papers; the *Evening Post, Daily Times, Tribune, Express.*

93. National Anti-Monopoly Cheap Freight League, *Document VI*, 94–95.

94. *Ibid.,* 94.

95. *Document VII*, November 1867, 103.

96. *Ibid.,* 105.

97. All the pamphlets cited above contain tributes from a wide variety of sources, but see in particular the *Documents* for October and November 1867. Among the important figures associated with the movement, three in particular are worth singling out because of their later activities concerning railroad regulation: Josiah Quincy, Jr., Charles Francis Adams, Jr., Shelby M. Cullom.

98. Sherwood, *Proposed National System of Cheap Freight Railways,* 1–3, *B. F. Wade and the Cheap Freight Railway* (Washington, D.C.?, 1867?). The names of the "co-operators" are found in the first item cited.

99. *The Cheap Freight Railway. Mr. Sherwood's Speech at Chicago,* 4.

100. Evidence that the decline of the movement was well advanced early in 1868 is seen in, *Grand Rally of the Producing Interests,* 16.

101. *The Cheap Freight Railway. Mr. Sherwood's Speech at Chicago,* 7.

102. The most comprehensive account of Vanderbilt's efforts to win control of the New York Central, and the public reaction to it, is found in Wheaton S. Lane, *Commodore Vanderbilt* (New York, 1942), 207–225. See also Maybee, *Railroad Competition,* 142–147.

103. See the Memorial of the Chamber of Commerce to the Legislature, adopted March 26, 1868, in its *Tenth Annual Report* (New York, 1868), under "Reports of Special Committees," 1:80.

104. *Tenth Annual Report,* 1:46.

105. *Ibid.,* 1:46–48, 75–80.

106. *Ibid.,* 1:77. See also the editorials in the *Commercial and Financial Chronicle,* 6:295–296, 326–327 (March 7, 14, 1868).

107. Maybee, *Railroad Competition,* 101–139, 226–238; Chamber of Commerce, Memorial, 1:76–78.

108. Boston Board of Trade, *Fourteenth Annual Report* (Boston, 1868), 58–61, 100–101; *Proceedings of the National Commercial Convention,* 80–92; *Proceedings of the First Annual Meeting of the National Board of Trade, Held in Philadelphia, June, 1868* (Boston, 1868), v–ix.

109. *Proceedings of the National Commercial Convention,* 58–77, 102–103, 111–119, 121–124, 130, 150–157; National Board of Trade, *Proceedings,* June 1868, 35–38, 133–139, 149–153; *Proceedings,* December 1868 (Boston, 1869), 164–171, 238–255, 260–278, 281–306, 311–318; *Proceedings,* December 1869 (Boston, 1870), 56–57, 67–73, 74–145, 209–255, 350–351; *Proceedings,* December 1870 (Boston, 1871), 38–61, 88–160, 230–278, 290–302; *Proceedings,* December 1871 (Boston, 1872), 44–140; *Proceedings,* October 1872 (Boston, 1872); *Proceedings,* October 1873 (Chicago, 1873), v–vi, 86–186, 247–267; *Proceedings, Adjourned Meeting,* January 1874 (Chicago, 1874), 122–156.

110. National Board of Trade, *Proceedings,* December 1869, 5–6. The various delegations to the annual meetings described the actions of their organizations and the measures they proposed to solve the transportation question. In 1869 the board

was composed of thirty-seven constituent bodies "and these include upwards of sixteen thousands of the business men of the country." *Ibid.*, 7.

111. Lane, *Commodore Vanderbilt*, 227–234; Maybee, *Railroad Competition*, 155–164, 188–191; Charles F. Adams, Jr., *Chapters of Erie* (Boston, 1871), 380–413; Josiah Quincy, Jr., *Cheap Food Dependent on Cheap Transportation. An Address Delivered Before the Boston Social Science Association, Jan. 14, 1869 by Josiah Quincy Its President* (Boston, 1869), 10–20; *Commercial and Financial Chronicle*, 8:614–615, 677–678, 711–712 (May 15, 29, June 5, 1869); "Report of Special Committee Appointed Under a Resolution of the Assembly Adopted Feb. 2, 1869, to Investigate the Facts Connected with the Increase of Stock of Certain Railroad Companies," New York State *Assembly Document*, No. 142 (1869), 1–59; "Report of the Committee on Railroads in Relation to Alleged Increase of Capital Stock of the Hudson River, New York Central and Erie Railway Companies," New York State *Senate Document*, No. 58 (1869), 1–17.

112. *Proceedings of the State Canal Convention Held at Rochester, January 19th, 1870 . . .* (New York, 1870), *passim.*

113. Edward H. Mott, *Between the Ocean and the Lakes: The Story of Erie* (New York, 1899), 180–200; Gustavus Myers, *The History of Tammany Hall*, 2nd ed. (New York, 1917), 222–249. The most significant account of Tweed, Erie, assorted rings, pro rata bills, classification bills, stock watering, etc., is the remarkably candid report of a legislative committee and the lengthy record of its proceedings — approximately 800 pages in all. See "Report of the Select Committee Appointed by the Assembly, March 11, 1873, to Investigate Alleged Mismanagement on the Part of the Erie Railway Company, Together with the Testimony Taken Before Said Committee," New York State *Assembly Document*, No. 98 (1873), xvii–xviii 119–131, 156–157, 269–274, 346–351, 534–539, 552, 624–625, 629–639, 769–771.

14. Ida M. Tarbell, *The History of the Standard Oil Company* (New York, 1904), 70–145; Maybee, *Railroad Competition*, 313–391.

115. Kirkland, *Men, Cities, and Transportation*, 2:237–246.

116. George H. Miller, "The Granger Laws: A Study of the Origin of State Railway Control in the Upper Mississippi Valley" (Ph.D. dissertation, University of Michigan, 1951), *passim;* Robert T. Daland, "Enactment of the Potter Law," *Wisconsin Magazine of History*, 33:45–54 (September 1949); Robert McCluggage, "Joseph H. Osborn, Grange Leader," *ibid.*, 35:178–184 (Spring 1952); Beard, in *Iowa Journal of History*, 51:1–36 (January 1953); Mildred Throne, "The Repeal of the Iowa Granger Law, 1878," *ibid.*, 51:97–130 (April 1953). Miller's study is comprehensive and enlightening but I am inclined to the opinion that the political potential represented by the western farmers was a more important factor in securing legislation than he appears to suggest. Without agrarian agitation, mercantile campaigns would have had much greater difficulty; indirectly, at least, farmers contributed to the passage of laws which Miller has shown originated with commercial groups.

117. "Report of the Senate Select Committee on Interstate Commerce," 49 Congress, 1 Session, *Testimony* (Washington, 1886), 99.

118. William Z. Ripley, *Railroads: Rates and Regulation* (New York, 1912), 460–626.

119. Pierce, *History of Chicago*, 2:77–87.

120. Paul Wallace Gates, "Large-Scale Farming in Illinois, 1850–1870," *Agricultural History*, 6:24; *Husbandman* (Elmira, N. Y.), April 17, 1878, p. 4. For biographical articles giving details of the landholdings and economic interests of other well-to-do leaders of farmers' movements, such as Dudley Adams (Iowa), J. A. Thompson (Minnesota), John S. Armstrong (Illinois), see *Husbandman*, September 3, December 10, 1879, p. 2, November 11, 1880, p. 2. McCluggage, in *Wisconsin Magazine of History*, 35:178–184, discusses the varied career of Joseph Osborn, Wisconsin Grange leader and civil engineer, merchant, manufacturer, real

estate operator, etc., born in 1822, son of a professor of classical languages in Columbia College. One need only read Flagg's address to the Northwestern Farmers' Convention in 1873 to appreciate that he was not a dirt farmer (reprinted in Windom Committee, *Transportation Routes to the Seaboard*, 2:659–666). In reading the contemporary sources I have received the distinct impression that the spokesmen for the farmers were not working farmers in the customary sense of the phrase. Either they were large-scale landholders employing laborers or renting to tenants, or agricultural editors, produce merchants, real estate dealers, scale manufacturers, seedsmen, insurance agents, etc. who may have owned farms as well. In addition to other wares, agricultural-service industries furnished leadership.

121. Joseph Nimmo, Jr. "First Annual Report on the Internal Commerce of the United States . . . 1876," *Executive Document 46*, 44 Congress, 2 session, Part 2, serial 1761 (Washington, 1877), Appendix, 93–95.

122. See Merk, *Economic History of Wisconsin*, 329–343. The discussion here needs to be read in conjunction with Professor Merk's later researches cited above in n. 75.

123. The first reaction of leading eastern newspapers and periodicals was not adverse to the western agitation; on the contrary it was hailed as long overdue. Only after the panic late in the year and the passage of regulatory legislation did easterners undergo a change of heart. New York *Times*, March 28, April 12, September 1, 5, 1873; *Nation*, 16:249–250, 377, 381–382, 397–398 (April 10, June 5, 12, 1873), 17:69 (July 31, 1873); *Commercial and Financial Chronicle*, 18:4–5, 204 (January 3, February 28, 1874); *Railroad Gazette*, 5:263 (June 28, 1873). Possibly the best illustration of the eastern reversal of opinion is provided by Charles Francis Adams, Jr. In 1871 he praised Illinois regulatory legislation highly; in 1875 he wrote the article which is invariably cited as evidence of eastern hostility to western railroad regulation. Compare, *Chapters of Erie*, 421–429, and "The Granger Movement," *North American Review*, 120:394–424 (April 1875).

124. The rapid drop in commodity prices is best seen by consulting the statistics compiled by the New York Produce Exchange. See its *Annual Report, 1879* (New York, 1880), 404, for a monthly wheat price index from 1863 to 1879 inclusive. Prices began to fall in June 1868, and went into an accelerated decline thereafter.

125. Hepburn Committee, *Proceedings*, 3:3171–3172.

126. New York *Times*, December 3, 1874.

127. By the summer of 1876 the *Railroad Gazette*, 8:332 (July 28, 1876), was pointing out that "The charge for transportation is now so low that the Northwestern farmer is as well situated as one within a hundred miles of New York."

Chapter II. New York City and the Pattern of Transportation Change

1. New York *Tribune*, September 10, 11, 12, 1873; New York *Times*, September 10, 11, 1873.

2. *Ibid.*, September 11, 1873.

3. Charles Francis Adams, Jr., "Boston," *North American Review*, 106:1–25, 557–591 (January, April 1868).

4. *Arguments of the New York Cheap Transportation Association . . . Made Before the Committee on Railways, of the Senate, March 28, 1876* (New York?, 1876?), 15; New York Produce Exchange, *Annual Report, 1882* (New York, 1883), 82.

5. The topographical conformation of the Atlantic Slope meant that New York's hinterland, that is, the area in which transportation costs were least to the seaboard via New York, included important areas in southern New England and New Jersey.

6. An excellent illustration of the blighting effects of the New York land system upon settlement is found in the detailed study by Edith M. Fox, *Land Speculation in the Mohawk Country* (Ithaca, N. Y., 1949).

7. *Thirteenth Census of the United States, Population,* 1:30–31, 80.

8. Calculated from data presented in the *Census,* 33–34, 80–81. The state of New York was growing at a much faster rate than Massachusetts, Pennsylvania, or Virginia until the 1830–1840 decade when Pennsylvania took a narrow lead. The Erie Canal now tended to encourage migration into the Old Northwest, a process which retarded population growth in New York city's immediate hinterland but greatly increased growth in the entire region tributary to it. Population increase in the city reflected the expansion of its hinterland; New York City's rate of growth in the 1840–1850 decade, the high point, was 78 per cent. It appears to be significant that the growth rate dropped sharply for several decades after the Civil War, a period when railroad development sharply diminished the transportation advantages enjoyed by the port of New York.

9. Robert G. Albion, *The Rise of New York Port* (New York, 1939), 8; Noble E. Whitford, *History of the Canal System of the State of New York* (Albany, 1906), 1:829–830, 909–913; *Report of a Committee of the Chamber of Commerce of New York on Canal Navigation by Steam, December, 1858* (New York, 1858), 9–14; *Address by Hon. William J. McAlpine, Before the Chamber of Commerce . . . May 8th, 1873* (New York, 1873), 5–12; "Report on the Canals of the State of New York," in New York Chamber of Commerce, *Seventeenth Annual Report* (New York, 1875), 1:101–125; Henry V. Poor, "Sketch of the Rise and Progress of the Internal Commerce, of the United States," in his *Manual of the Railroads of the United States for 1881* (New York, 1881), i–xvii. The statistics of tonnage upon the New York canals show that not until 1847 did the products of the West surpass those of the home state (*ibid.,* xv).

10. George R. Taylor, *The Transportation Revolution* (New York, 1951), 160–167, 173–175; Emory R. Johnson and others, *History of Domestic and Foreign Commerce of the United States* (Washington, 1915), 1:224–253, 327–356.

11. See the eulogy to the canal system in New York Chamber of Commerce, *Annual Report, 1858* (New York, 1858), 50–51.

12. For the financial benefits to New York, see Margaret G. Myers, *The New York Money Market* (New York, 1931), 3–9, 222–230.

13. Contemporary recognition of the changed order of things was widespread. See *Report by Thomas S. Fernon Submitted to J. Edgar Thomson, December 9th, 1852* (Philadelphia?, 1852?). Another pamphlet in much the same vein is, *Letters of Prof. Edward D. Mansfield, of Cincinati, to Job R. Tyson, Esq., LL.D. of Philadelphia* (Philadelphia, 1853). For a Boston variation on the same theme see Boston Board of Trade, *Fourteenth Annual Report* (Boston, 1868), 27–40. In addition to numerous reports by New York legislative committees cited in the previous chapter, see the comprehensive analysis of the railroad danger to the metropolis contained in an anonymous pamphlet signed "New York." *Legislative Restrictions on the Carrying Trade of the Railways of the State of New York: Viewed in Connection with Outside Competition. Addressed to the Citizens of the City and State of New York* (New York, 1860).

14. "Remonstrance of the Chamber of Commerce, Against the Passage of 'An Act in Relation to the Transportation of Freight on the Several Railroads of This State,' etc.," New York State *Assembly Document,* No. 59 (1860). See also the memorials adopted by the Chamber in 1868 and 1870 which stress the significance of the railroads' breaking the monopoly once enjoyed by New York. "Up to 1852, the Erie Canal was the only avenue to the Lakes and to the West, and controlled the whole Western trade to New York . . ." *Tenth Annual Report* (New York, 1868), 1:73–80 [Reports of Special Committees]; *Twelfth Annual Report* (New York, 1870), 1:39–40.

15. *Report of the New York Commerce Commission* (Albany, 1900), 1:395.

16. The grain merchants at New York were particularly worried about water competition, regarding it in the early seventies as more to be feared than railroads to the other cities. New York Produce Exchange, *Annual Report, 1872–1873* (New York, 1873), 231–295.

17. Joseph Nimmo, Jr., *Report on the Internal Commerce of the United States . . . for the Fiscal Year 1881–'82* (Washington, 1884), 67–79. The export business on through bills of lading began with the opening of the Grand Trunk Railroad before the Civil War and grew thereafter. Hepburn Committee, *Proceedings*, 3:3139–3168.

18. New York continued to supply Boston with substantial quantities of grain until 1872. Windom Committee, *Report*, 1:31.

19. Joseph Nimmo, Jr., *Report on the Internal Commerce of the United States . . . Submitted December 21, 1884* (Washington, 1885), 8–9; *The Commercial Interests of New York as Related to Our System of Transportation, No. 2* (New York?, 1873?), 10–17. This anonymous pamphlet was almost certainly written during the summer of 1873 by Francis B. Thurber, a leading New York wholesale grocer. It is a significant manifestation of the metropolitan reaction to the changes in transportation.

20. *Commercial and Financial Chronicle*, 39:451–452 (October 25, 1884).

21. Nimmo, *Internal Commerce of the United States, 1881–82*, 67–79.

22. *Report of New York Commerce Commission*, 1:395–396. A comprehensive study of New York's foreign trade over a long period is presented in David M. Ellis, "New York and the Western Trade," *New York History*, 33: 379–396 (October 1952).

23. Albert Fink, *Report Upon the Adjustment of Railroad Transportation Rates to the Seaboard* (New York, 1882), 50, Statement D.

24. *Report of New York Commerce Commission*, 1:1068–1069.

25. New York Chamber of Commerce, *Twentieth Annual Report* (New York, 1878), 1:116–117.

26. By early 1874 the merchants of the New York Cheap Transportation Association were listening to a grim paper reminding them of the rise and fall of great European cities like Venice, Hamburg, Trieste, and others, and exhorting them to constant vigilance. See its *Minutes,* March 10, 1874.

27. For an excellent contemporary analysis summing up New York's reactions to the changed conditions see Simon Sterne's closing address in Hepburn Committee *Proceedings*, 4:3934–3941, and *passim.* The secondary source which best depicts the changes in ocean shipping is John G. B. Hutchins, *The American Maritime Industries and Public Policy, 1789–1914* (Cambridge, Mass., 1941), 371–516.

28. In the late 1850's New Yorkers could not foresee the time when trunk-line officials would deliberately decide to divert trade from the metropolis, no matter what advantages she possessed. See "Railroads," in New York Chamber of Commerce, *Annual Report, 1858,* 1:62, 64.

29. Penetrating analyses of the impact of transportation changes upon urban rivalries are scattered throughout Joseph Nimmo, Jr.'s six reports on internal commerce from 1876 to 1885. See his "First Annual Report on the Internal Commerce of the United States . . . for the Fiscal Year Ending June 30, 1876," *House Executive Document 46,* 44 Congress, 2 Session, Part 2, serial 1761 (Washington, 1877), 47–59, 62–67, 74–85; "Report on the Internal Commerce of the United States . . . Submitted December 1, 1879," *House Executive Document 32,* 45 Congress, 3 Session, Part 3, serial 1857 (Washington, 1879), 141–157; "Report on the Internal Commerce of the United States . . . Submitted July 1, 1881," *House Executive Document 7,* 46 Congress, 3 Session, Part 2, serial 1966 (Washington, 1881), 70–71, 72–151; "Report on the Internal Commerce of the United States, 1881–82," 8–11, 61–67; "Report on the Internal Commerce of the United States . . . Submitted December 31, 1884," 8–10, 23–29; "Report on the Internal Commerce of the United States . . . Submitted May 6, 1885" (Washington, 1885), 330–401. Also the *Commercial and Financial Chronicle*, 19:179–180 (August 22, 1874); *Railroad Gazette,* 8:482–483 (November 3, 1876), 10:244 (May 17, 1878), 11:355 (June 27, 1879).

30. John Moody, *The Railroad Builders* (New Haven, 1919), 15. For various aspects of railroad development and innovation after 1850 see Bureau of the Census, *Historical Statistics of the United States, 1789–1945* (Washington, 1949), Series K 1,

200; William Z. Ripley, *Railroads, Rates and Regulation* (New York, 1912), 13–16; Caroline E. MacGill, ed. *History of Transportation Before 1860*, 565–570; Rolland H. Maybee, *Railroad Competition and the Oil Trade, 1855–1873* (Mount Pleasant, Mich., 1940), 80–99, 140–193; Hepburn Committee, *Proceedings*, 3:2960–2970; Emerson D. Fite, *Social and Industrial Conditions in the North During the Civil War* (New York, 1910), 54–67.

31. New York *Times*, March 31, 1877.

32. These developments were not limited to railroads. In fact the pooling device has been traced at least as far back as a clearing house of the proprietors of stagecoaches in England. When railroads began to run into traffic exchange problems they adopted an analogous system, and in 1842 the Railway Clearing House was established. Edward McDermott, *The Railway Clearing House: Its Place in Relation to the Working and Management of English Railways* (New York, 1846?), 1–6. This 64-page pamphlet described the English system and was published in America by H. V. and H. W. Poor. Steamship and canal boat pools appeared in the 1840's in the United States, and railroad pools were in operation in New England during the fifties. William Z. Ripley, *Railroads, Finance and Organization* (New York, 1915), 582–583; Edward C. Kirkland, *Men, Cities, and Transportation* (Cambridge, Mass., 1948), 1:184–185. Albert Fink stressed the successful workings of the English Clearing House in appealing for federal legislation to aid the American railroads to achieve like results. Fink's statements suggest that it may well have been the inspiration for the Southern Railway and Steamship Association of 1875 which he headed. *The Railroad Problem and Its Solution. Argument of Albert Fink, Before the Committee on Commerce of the U.S. House of Representatives, in Opposition to the Bill to Regulate Interstate Traffic, January 14, 15 & 16, 1880* (New York, 1882), 17, 51–53; *United States Senate Committee on Labor and Education. Testimony of Albert Fink, New York. Sept. 17, 1883* (New York?, 1883?), 6–7.

33. Maybee, *Railroad Competition*, 80–100; George M. Burgess and Miles C. Kennedy, *Centennial History of the Pennsylvania Railroad Company* (Philadelphia, 1949), 233–235; Edward Hungerford, *Men and Iron* (New York, 1938), 107–116.

34. *Railroad Gazette*, 8:174 (April 21, 1876).

35. Nimmo, *Report on the Internal Commerce of the United States for 1876*, 70–71, 73–74.

36. Hepburn Committee, *Proceedings*, 3:3112–3113, 4:3934–37; *The Power of New York's Capital to Retain New York's Commerce. A Letter From a New York Merchant* (New York?, 1878?), 1–3; *Report of the Committee on Railway Transportation of the American Board of Transportation and Commerce at the Third Annual Convention of That Body, Held in Chicago, December 18th, 1875* (New York?, 1876?), 5–8.

37. *Railroad Gazette*, 9:88–89 (February 23, 1877).

38. See Fink, *Adjustment of Seaboard Rates*, 50, Statement D. I have rounded out the statistics to the nearest million.

39. *Railroad Gazette*, 8:332, 361 (July 27, August 18, 1876); *Commercial and Financial Chronicle*, 28:28–29, 81–82 (July 12, 26, 1879).

40. Nimmo, *Report on the Internal Commerce of the United States, 1876*, 67.

41. The tables are taken from the *Report of the New York Commerce Commission*, 1:1068–1071. Montreal is not included but there is no reason to believe that the statistics would show any significant change had she been. The coast-wise traffic brought to New York was relatively insignificant.

42. As evidence that merchants were ahead of railroaders in appreciating the problems involved in developing railroads as high-volume, low-cost carriers, see *Report of the Committee on Railway Transportation of the New York Cheap Transportation Association* (New York?, 1873?), 11–14.

43. *Railroad Gazette*, 6:306, 442, 7:75 (August 7, November 14, 1874, February 20, 1875); New York *Times*, September 12, 1874, March 17, June 9, 1875.

44. A series of letters and cables between President John W. Garrett of the Baltimore and Ohio and his subordinates make clear his aggressive confidence, and

the importance of the passenger traffic in the 1873–1874 rate war. See in particular Garrett to John King, January 8, 1874. Inside accounts of the relations between the Pennsylvania and the Baltimore and Ohio are given in King to Garrett, January 5, July 3, 11, September 1, 5, 9, October 24, November 18, December 30, 1873, January 1, July 3, 1874. Among other communications of considerable interest, John King to John Thomson, December 20, 22, 1873, Thomson to King, December 20, 1873, H. J. Jewett to King, December 21, 1873, King to Jewett, December 22, 1873, George Roberts to King, March 13, 1874, King to Roberts, March 14, 1874, Thomas Scott to King, March 16, 1874, King to Scott, March 16, 1874. Robert Garrett Collection, Library of Congress. Garrett correspondence cited below is from the same collection.

45. Hepburn Committee, *Proceedings*, 3:3171–3172, 4:3508–3509.

46. *Ibid.*, 3:3172; New York *Times*, November 15, 1874, March 18, 1875.

47. *Commercial and Financial Chronicle*, 19:504, 595 (November 14, December 12, 1874); *Railroad Gazette*, 6:306, 442 (August 8, November 14, 1874); New York *Times*, September 12, November 18, 1874. See Charles F. Adams, Jr., *Railroads: Their Origin and Problems* (rev. ed., New York, 1887), 150–156, for an interesting interpretation of the Saratoga Compact's significance in railroad history.

48. *Railroad Gazette*, 7:75, 286, 532–533 (February 20, July 10, December 25, 1875); New York *Times*, March 6, 1875.

49. *Ibid.*, March 17, 18, 1875.

50. *Ibid.*, June 17, July 6, 1875; *Railroad Gazette*, 7:278, 346–347 (July 3, August 21, 1875).

51. Hepburn Committee, *Proceedings*, 4:3934–3937.

52. *Railroad Gazette*, 7:346–347, 8:46–47, 185 (August 21, 1875, January 28, April 28, 1876); New York *Times*, December 28, 1875, March 11, 1876; Massachusetts Board of Railroad Commissioners, *Eighth Annual Report, January 1877* (Boston, 1878), 46–47.

53. *Hepburn Committee, Proceedings*, 3:3040–3041.

54. *Railroad Gazette*, 7:286, 8:279 (July 10, 1875, June 23, 1876). Writing in 1881, Albert Fink flatly stated, "The past history of competition between the Trunk Lines fully establishes this fact, that arbitrary differentials have been maintained only so long as it suited the interests of the competing roads." *Adjustment of Rates to the Seaboard*, 15.

55. New York Cheap Transportation Association, *Minutes*, May 12, 1874; *The Relations of Railroads to the Public. A Statement Prepared by F. B. Thurber, Esq., of New York City, in Reply to Inquiries Submitted to Him by the Chief of the Bureau of Statistics, Washington, D.C.* (New York?, 1879?), 2; Massachusetts Board of Railroad Commissioners, *Seventh Annual Report* (Boston, 1876), 65–66; Kirkland, *Men, Cities and Transportation*, 1:505–506.

56. *Railroad Gazette*, 7:536 (December 25, 1875).

57. New York Cheap Transportation Association, *Minutes*, November 9, December 7, 30, 1875. The association's Committee on Claims and Grievances offered documents to support its charges of discrimination, including a circular issued by a New England manufacturer boasting, "Wholesale merchants take notice — Freight from Boston to Southern and Western points is usually less than from New York." See also Massachusetts Railroad Commissioners, *Tenth Annual Report* (Boston, 1879), 50–53.

58. New York *Times*, December 24, 1875.

59. New York *Times*, December 9, 19, 22, 24, 28, 31, 1875; New York *Tribune*, December 7, 9, 22, 1875; Massachusetts Railroad Commissioners, *Seventh Annual Report*, 66–68.

60. It was evident that New York's supremacy had caused her merchants and railroads to neglect keeping pace with rivals, and had brought about higher costs in some auxiliary services. New York Produce Exchange, *Annual Report, 1873–1874*, 33–34.

61. Massachusetts Railroad Commissioners, *Eighth Annual Report*, 46–53; *Rail-*

road Gazette, 8:174, 185 (April 21, 28, 1876); New York *Times,* May 2, 1876; Hepburn Committee, *Proceedings,* 3:3172–3173. The Hepburn Committee hearings constitute probably the best single source of information concerning the rate wars of the mid-seventies. The testimony of George R. Blanchard, second vice-president of the Erie Railroad, is particularly valuable. A leading figure in those wars, Blanchard was able to give a revealing inside picture of their development. And his testimony appears reliable because he was interested in showing how they led to the pooling agreement of 1877 which he strongly favored.

A public letter by William H. Vanderbilt claimed that the other roads failed to carry out the agreement of March 2. New York *Tribune,* May 4, 1876.

62. *Railroad Gazette,* 8:195, 267, 279, 361, 568 (May 5, June 16, 23, August 18, December 29, 1876); *Commercial and Financial Chronicle,* 22:448, 582–583, 23:5–6 (May 6, June 17, 1876, January 6, 1877); Adams, *Railroads,* 162–168; Hepburn Committee, *Proceedings,* 3:3173–3179.

63. Wheaton J. Lane, *Commodore Vanderbilt* (New York, 1942), 297–298. The *Railroad Gazette* had another explanation than love of justice for the Commodore's belligerency. Grain had been diverted to Philadelphia and Baltimore, and the Grand Trunk was becoming more irritating. Since conferences had failed to achieve binding results, perhaps a show of force might. The war, thus, had the purpose of extending the combination and making it stick. *Ibid.,* 8:195 (May 5, 1876). This interpretation is consonant with subsequent events which saw the Central abandon its stand against differentials and proclaim their inherent justice.

64. New York *Times,* May 2, October 17, November 13, December 17, 27, 1876, January 31, 1877; New York Cheap Transportation Association, *Minutes,* May 9, 1876; New York Produce Exchange, *Annual Report, 1875–1876* (New York, 1877), 28–29, 221–223.

65. *Railroad Gazette,* 8:279 (June 23, 1876).

66. *Commercial and Financial Chronicle,* 23:620 (December 23, 1876). For the actual rates during the war, see Hepburn Committee, *Proceedings,* 3:3177–3178. By August most of the through traffic was being carried at "extremely low rates, such as never were known before." *Railroad Gazette,* 8:361 (August 18, 1876).

67. Drexel to Garrett, December 8, 16, 1876. Also Drexel to Garrett, November 21, December 13, 23, 1876, George W. Childs to Garrett, December 19, 1876, January 3, 1877. Childs was the proprietor of the Philadelphia *Public Ledger* and a close intimate and partner of Drexel. An undated letter from him to Garrett, probably written early in 1877, refers to the fact that Drexel and Moses Taylor owned considerable stock in the Baltimore and Ohio. Drexel's role was extremely significant in the rate wars, particularly because of his relationship with the House of Morgan. Apparently he made the first attempts at financier-induced harmony among major railroads, the policy which really came to fruition with the "Morganization" of the railroad system in the 1890's. The first letter seen from Drexel to Garrett urging peaceful relations is dated November 20, 1871. The letters cited previously reveal that Drexel was not only a stockholder in the Baltimore and Ohio, but that his firm was helping to finance the road's short term obligations.

68. Drexel to Garrett, January 3, 1877.

69. *Railroad Gazette,* 8:556–557, 571, 572, 573, 9:18, 100, 167 (December 22, 29, 1876, January 12, March 2, April 13, 1877).

70. There is a keen analysis of the December 16, 1876 agreement in the Massachusetts Railroad Commission, *Eighth Annual Report,* 54–60.

71. *Railroad Gazette,* 9:167, 280 (April 13, June 22, 1877); New York *Times,* April 8, July 4, 1877; Hepburn Committee, *Proceedings,* 3:3015–3025, 3040–3051, 3173–3175; Fink, *Adjustment of Seaboard Rates,* 5–11. The measure of New York City's anger can perhaps best be seen in the editorials of the *Commercial and Financial Chronicle,* 24:308–309, 380–381, 430–433, 529–530 (April 7, 28, May 12, June 9, 1877).

72. See the copy of the agreement in John B. Daish, *The Atlantic Port Differen-*

tials (Washington, 1918), 2–3. This volume contains the major documents pertinent to the differential system from 1877 through 1912 and is a valuable source.

73. The most comprehensive analysis I have found of the trunk-line pool and its predecessors is a series of articles, "Railroad Apportionment Schemes," in the *Railroad Gazette*, 9:542–543, 552–553, 564–565, 574–575 (December 7, 14, 21, 28, 1877), also 10:4 (January 4, 1878). Another interesting survey is in Massachusetts Railroad Commissioners, *Ninth Annual Report* (Boston, 1878), 65–94.

74. Fink, *Railroad Problem and Its Solution . . . 1880*, 60–67.

75. Hepburn Committee, *Proceedings*, 1:481–490, 512–519, 3:3015–3051. The information elicited here, and in other places from George Blanchard and Albert Fink concerning the trunk-line pools is particularly valuable because it was in response to the sharp questioning of Simon Sterne. Sterne represented the New York merchants and the exchanges between these three men provide much of the material upon which the conclusion stated below is based.

76. *Ibid.*, 1:501, 512–541, 3:3034–3035; Nimmo, *Report on the Internal Commerce of the United States, 1876*, Appendix, 12–24, 45–47; *Argument Before the Committee of Commerce of the Senate of the United States on the Reagan Bill, for the Regulation of Inter-State Commerce. By Albert Fink. Washington, February 11, 1879* (New York, 1879), 9–12. Adams' views, towards which he had been tending since 1875, are most clearly expressed in his *Railroads, Their Origins and Problems*, first published in 1878. The entire book constituted an argument for the pooling system, and for government aid in helping to strengthen it. Although Adams' reputation had been made as a railroad commissioner, he had more personal reasons for concern with the proper workings of the transportation system. His diaries indicate that he had been speculating in railroad stocks, and serving on various boards of directors in important capacities from 1869 on. See, for example, entries dated January 12, February 18, April 2, 1869, August 14–19, 1872, October 1, 30, November 12–16, 1873, March 24, 1874, June 18, 1875, October 22, 1876, January 4, 11, 13, 1878. At the very time he was writing the book, railroad affairs were of vital financial interest to him. The diaries are in the Adams' Family Collection at the Massachusetts Historical Society.

77. Massachusetts Railroad Commissioners, *Ninth Annual Report*, 66. See also *Railroad Gazette*, 10:624 (December 27, 1878).

78. Albert Fink, *Cost of Railroad Transportation, Railroad Accounts, and Governmental Regulations of Railroad Tariffs . . . Extract from Annual Report of the Louisville & Nashville Railroad Company, for the Year Ending June 30, 1874* (New York, 1882), 23.

79. *Senate Committee on Labor and Education. Testimony of Albert Fink, 1883*, 6–7. Fink continued to pay lip service to the popular belief in the efficacy of competition by pointing to the Erie Canal as a "regulator" but his basic argument was the impossibility of competition's achieving desirable results among railroads. The *Railroad Gazette*, 19:96 (February 11, 1887) caustically observed — in another connection — that the canal as "regulator" was the reverse of reality (after the rate wars of the seventies and eighties). "So far from the Canal regulating the rates of the railroads, it is the railroads and their attitude toward one another which decides the amount of traffic that may go by Canal."

80. See the exchange between Simon Sterne and Edwin D. Worcester, secretary of the Central and president of the Lake Shore, in Hepburn Committee, *Proceedings*, 3:1073–1074.

81. Garrett to J. S. Morgan, January 28, 1874. A number of other letters of the same year indicate the intimate relationship developing, and the great respect which Morgan held for the president of the Baltimore & Ohio. J. S. Morgan to Garrett, February 4, 6, 14, 1874; Garrett to J. S. Morgan, July 31, 1874; George Childs to Garrett, January 6, 1875.

82. J. S. Morgan to Garrett, June 29, 1876.

83. J. S. Morgan to Garrett, September 23, 1876.

84. J. S. Morgan to Garrett, December 9, 1876.

85. J. S. Morgan to Garrett, January 24, 27, 1877. The cablegram from Garrett was copied in the January 27 letter.

86. J. S. Morgan to Garrett, February 7, 1877. Other letters revealing increasing European concern with "all" American railroad securities are J. S. Morgan to Garrett, February 10, 17, 24, 1877.

87. Garrett to J. S. Morgan, March 9, 1877.

88. E. P. Fabri (of Drexel, Morgan & Company) to Garrett, March 16, 1877. Garrett had apparently written to the American branch of the banking firm as well, and his son had paid a personal call upon its officers.

89. Garrett to J. S. Morgan, May 2, 1877. A. J. Drexel was also taking a hand in settling the rate war because its pressure had again strained relations between the Baltimore & Ohio and the Pennsylvania. But the managers of the New York roads apparently were not as peaceably inclined as Garrett had intimated, and there is reason to doubt his own desire for peace. See A. J. Drexel to Garrett, May 23, 1877, and telegram of same date; New York *Times*, March 31, 1877.

90. J. S. Morgan to Garrett, June 30, 1877.

91. J. Pierpont Morgan to Garrett, July 13, 1877.

92. E. P. Fabri to Garrett, July 25, 1877.

93. This was the position taken by Simon Sterne all throughout the Hepburn inquiry and is conveniently summed up in his closing argument. See its *Proceedings*, 4:3930–3942.

94. Kirkland, *Men, Cities, and Transportation*, 1:526–528.

95. The trunk-line plan was to control the traffic out of New York at first and then gradually extend the pool to other ports. Events soon tended to reinforce New Yorkers' doubts that the pool would find universal application, particularly since the Grand Trunk was not a member.

96. Perhaps the clearest demonstration of this point is found in the statement by Simon Sterne on "The Pooling Arrangements" in Hepburn Committee, *Proceedings*, 4:3973–3996.

97. It must be stressed here that men like Albert Fink and George R. Blanchard conceded the existence of railroad abuses prior to the pools. Their contention, however, was that unrestricted competition had been responsible and that a better day was dawning. *Ibid.*, 1:481–541, 556–636, 3:3006–3037.

Chapter III. New York Fights Back

1. The pamphlet bears no date or place of publication, but Jones supplied this information a year later in his testimony before the Windom Committee. *Transportation Routes to the Seaboard*, 2:107. Jones' appearance at the committee hearings had been arranged by the New York Cheap Transportation Association.

2. Jones, *Merchants and Property Owners of New York City*, 1–9.

3. *Ibid.*, 5–6; Windom Committee, *Transportation Routes to the Seaboard*, 2:104–108, 309–328. That Commodore Vanderbilt had not originated the practice of stock watering on the Central is demonstrated in Irene Neu, "A Business Biography of Erastus Corning" (Ph.D. dissertation, Cornell University, 1950), 253–296. By May 1854 the *American Railroad Journal* was charging "that the company was beginning to show the effects of the excessive watering its stock had undergone in the process of consolidation." According to Dr. Neu, had the true story been known, the journal's condemnation would have been more severe. *Ibid.*, 254.

4. Jones, *Merchants and Property Owners of New York City*, 9–12.

5. *Ibid.*, 14–15.

6. *Ibid.*, 11.

7. *Ibid.*, 16.

8. *Ibid.*, 15.

9. Chamber of Commerce, *Fifteenth Annual Report* (New York, 1873), 1:69–70, 73.

10. New York *Times,* May 6, 1873. This information was given to the *Times* reporter by S. M. Smith, the secretary of the association, who also said that the plan was to convert the state association to a national one.

11. *Times,* November 26, 1874; *Proceedings of the First Annual Meeting of the American Cheap Transportation Association, Held in New York, May 6th and 7th, 1873* (Troy, New York, 1873), 5–7, 22–23. The *Times'* account of the association's convention in 1874 gives the details of the organization's history.

12. The meetings were held at New York, May 6–7, 1873, Washington, January 14–17, 1874, Richmond, December 1–4, 1874, Chicago, December 15–17, 1875. Both the New York *Times* and New York *Tribune* gave full accounts of these meetings, and their columns, plus the published reports of proceedings at the several meetings, are the major sources for the material presented in this section. The organization's name was changed to the American Board of Transportation and Commerce at the Richmond meeting. In addition to the *Proceedings* of its preliminary meeting cited in n. 11 above, see *National Convention of the American Cheap Transportation Association Held at Washington, D. C., January 14–16, 1874* (Troy, N. Y., 1874); *Report of the Committee on Railway Transportation of the American Cheap Transportation Association . . . Presented at the Annual Convention, Held at Richmond, Va., December 1st to 4th, 1874* (New York, 1874); *Third Annual Convention of the American Board of Transportation and Commerce Held at the Grand Pacific Hotel, December, 15th, 16th, 17th, 1875* (Chicago, 1876); *Report of the Committee on Railway Transportation of the American Board of Transportation and Commerce, at the Third Annual Convention of That Body, Held in Chicago, December 18th, 1875* (New York, 1876?).

13. New York *Times,* September 1, 1873, in a front page article headed "The Western Grangers — The War Against the Railroads, — Origins, Purposes, and Progress of the Farmers' Movement in Illinois and the North-West." The article is interesting in many respects and its sympathy for the antirailroad position makes its assessment even more reliable. The article's main contention was that politicians had attempted to take over the agitation for partisan purposes.

14. *Times,* December 16, 1875.

15. Josiah Quincy, Jr., *Public Interest and Private Monopoly. An Address Delivered Before the Boston Board of Trade, October 16, 1867. By Josiah Quincy* (Boston, 1867). Quincy had been a leading figure in the League. The first *printed* use I recall having seen of the term "robber barons" is Quincy's presidential address in May 1873. *Proceedings of the American Cheap Transportation Association, May, 1873,* 15. It appears significant that many of the contemporary polemics by merchants and farmers were directed against feudalism, new or old style. The conditions under which nineteenth-century liberalism had developed were no longer present and the increasing limitations upon economic mobility were likened to medieval restrictions. "Robber barons" as the favorite epithet of the period serves as an excellent illustration. The first use I recall having seen of the "robber barons" *concept,* as distinct from the specific term, was in an address by Josiah Quincy, Jr., on January 14, 1869. There he used "feudal barons" but a letter written by C. F. Adams, Jr., bearing the exact date suggests that the latter was in the audience; Adams wrote it "robber barons" but his letter merely paraphrased Quincy unless a remarkable coincidence took place. Quincy's statement is in *Cheap Food Dependent on Cheap Transportation, an Address Delivered Before the Boston Social Science Association, Jan. 14, 1869, By Josiah Quincy, Its President* (Boston, 1869), 12; Adams' letter is quoted in Joseph Dorfman, *The Economic Mind in American Civilization* (New York, 1949), 3:23, and n. 48 on p. x of "Appendix and Bibliographic Notes."

16. *Proceedings of the American Cheap Transportation Association, May, 1873,* 14. The several reports of the railroad committee appear to have been written by Thurber; certainly the phrasing and ideas are almost identical with those contained in his reports to the New York Cheap Transportation Association, an auxiliary. The reports on railroads of the national association also conform closely to Thurber's speeches from the floor at the various conventions.

17. Information concerning the monetary affairs of the association is contained

in R. H. Ferguson to Thurber, May 14, June 1, 1873, Josiah Quincy, Jr., to Thurber, May 27, 1873.

18. Quincy to Thurber, May 27, 1873.

19. S. M. Smith to Thurber, May 23, 1873; S. M. Thorp to Thurber, June 11, 1873.

20. *Railroad Gazette,* 6:485 (December 12, 1874).

21. See in this connection, *Annual Meeting of the New York Cheap Transportation Association, January 18, 1876. Copy of Minutes* . . . (New York, 1876), 7–8.

22. New York Chamber of Commerce, *Eighteenth Annual Report* (New York, 1876), 1:71. The delegates of the Chamber were also the leaders of the New York Cheap Transportation Association, an example of the successful "boring from within" strategy they adopted soon after organization.

23. *Third Annual Convention of the American Board of Transportation and Commerce,* 8. Windom Committee, *Transportation Routes to the Seaboard,* 1:140–141, contains a flattering reference to the association's members, although not by name. Correspondence between Senator Windom, the secretary of his committee, Joseph Nimmo, Jr., and Benjamin Sherman and Thurber on behalf of the New York merchants, indicates that the association's claim to influence was no idle boast. Windom to Benjamin Sherman, August 6, 1873, Sherman to Windom, September 8, 12, 1873, Nimmo to Thurber, November 16, 1874 (all in the Thurber papers).

24. See, for example, New York *Tribune,* May 17, 1873; New York *Times,* May 17, 27, 1873; *Nation* 16:349 (May 22, 1873).

25. "Report of the Select Committee Appointed . . . to Investigate Alleged Mismanagement on the Part of the Erie Railway Company, Together with the Testimony Taken Before Said Committee," New York State *Assembly Document,* No. 98 (1873), 551–552.

26. New York Chamber of Commerce, *Sixteenth Annual Report* (New York, 1874), 1:21.

27. New York State *Assembly Document,* No. 98 (1873), xx. See also the bitter editorial in the New York *Times,* April 13, on "The Dictator of Four States."

28. The articles were reprinted in a pamphlet called *Facts for the People* (New York?, 1873?). F. B. Thurber and his brother, Horace K., owned an interest in the paper, and later were to buy it out completely. Horace K. Thurber to F. B. Thurber, December 25, 1876. This long letter, together with several others written while the latter was on a trip around the world, gives a good deal of information concerning their business.

29. Thurber's hand is revealed by many characteristic phrases and ideas. The articles in the *American Grocer* were also obviously written by the same man. Compare them, for example, with New York Cheap Transportation Association, *Report of the Railway Committee* (New York?, 1873?), and Thurber's article, "Steam and Electricity, Their Commercial, Political and Economical Bearing Upon Life in the Nineteenth Century." The copy I have seen of the article is reprinted from the *International Review* of September and October 1875. These are significant pamphlets for they reveal an excellent contemporary grasp of the implications of the Communication Revolution. These pamphlets, and numerous others printed around that time, foreshadow David A. Wells, *Recent Economic Changes* (New York, 1889). In turn, however, Thurber was clearly anticipated, if indeed he had not borrowed the ideas directly, by men such as Hiram Walbridge and James S. Stranahan. See in this connection the *Proceedings* of the National Board of Trade cited previously.

The crux of the matter is that at a time when knowledge had not yet become the exclusive property of specialists, merchants in the seaboard towns were in a strategic position to analyze the nature of the rapid changes in society. As will be suggested throughout this study, much of the basic thinking in the decades after the Civil War can be attributed to cosmopolitan merchants in close touch commercially and intellectually with Europe.

30. *Commercial Interests of New York* (No. 1), 6–8; *Commercial Interests of New York* (No. 2), 11–17.

31. *Ibid.*, 15.

32. Minutes of the New York Cheap Transportation Association, p. 1. The citation refers to the manuscript copy of the minutes now in the possession of the New York Board of Trade. Apparently printed minutes were issued even before the formal organization of the association in September 1873, but only one has been found.

33. *Ibid.*, 1–3. Thurber was the leading spirit in the Importers' and Grocers' Board of Trade and it sparked the drive for the association. New York *Times*, July 30, 1873.

34. *Commercial Interests of New York* (No. 2), 12–13.

35. The call containing these sentiments is found in the manuscript Minutes, p. 3.

36. New York *Herald*, August 1, 1873. A clipping of this article was found in the Thurber papers, as is the case of a number of other citations below to newspapers which I have not used systematically. The tremendous amount of clippings from a wide variety of sources which came into the possession of Thurber — he employed a clipping service and associates apparently forwarded pertinent articles to him — have enabled me to get a much more comprehensive coverage of newspaper sources than should otherwise have been possible.

37. New York *Tribune*, September 10, 1873.

38. New York *Times*, September 10, 1873. The meeting was advertised as representing the views of men having $500,000,000 capital investment and doing $5,000,000,000 business annually. Windom Committee, *Transportation Routes to the Seaboard*, 2:175.

39. Letter of that date addressed to B. F. [*sic*] Sherman, Esq., Chairman of Special Committee, Importers and Grocers Board of Trade.

40. Nimmo to Thurber, August 22, 1873.

41. A number of lengthy letters from Nimmo to Thurber, from 1873 to 1883, afford revealing insights into the thinking of both men. They also help to explain why Nimmo framed questionnaires for public response by Thurber, Sterne, and others, which enabled the New York position to be well advertised in his annual reports on internal commerce. In addition, the letters contain a good deal of valuable information concerning the progress of railroad regulation in the United States.

42. New York *Tribune*, September 11, 1873.

43. *Ibid.*; New York *Times*, September 11, 1873.

44. *The Relations of Railroads to the Public. A Statement Prepared by F. Thurber, Esq., of New York City, in Reply to Inquiries Submitted to Him by the Chief of the Bureau of Statistics, Washington, D.C.* (New York?, 1879?), 7–8.

45. As quoted in New York Cheap Transportation Association, *Facts for New Yorkers* (New York?, 1874?), 13. "One house in this city — the largest in the wholesale dry goods [H. B. Claflin & Company] — which has been doing a business of $50,000,000 per annum, is now doing, and is only calculating on doing a business of $20,000,000." *Ibid.*, 12.

46. Chicago *Tribune*, August 31, 1874; Cincinnati *Gazette*, March 31, 1876, reprinted in the New York *Times*, April 2, 1876. The *Herald* was not the only New York paper to comment upon the loss of the jobbing trade; the Chicago *Tribune* quoted from the *Bulletin* and *Graphic* to the same effect.

47. Cincinnati *Gazette*, March 31, 1876, reprinted in New York *Times*, April 2, 1876. The firm was E. S. Jaffray & Company.

48. *Arguments of the New York Cheap Transportation Association . . . Made Before the Joint Committees on Railways of the Senate and Assembly. March 12th, 1874* (New York?, 1874?), 17.

49. New York Cheap Transportation Association, *Report of the Committee on Railway Transportation* (New York?, 1873?), 1, 9. The report had been delivered on December 9, 1873. A copy of it is found in New York *Times*, December 10, 1873.

50. The dim view taken by the association of the canal and waterways in gen-

eral is best illustrated by its sharp *Review of the Report of U.S. Senate Committee on Transportation Routes by the Committee on Railway Transportation of the New York Cheap Transportation Association. May 12, 1874* (New York?, 1874?).

51. The main basis for the statements above are the *Annual Reports* of the Produce Exchange from 1872 to 1878. The address of President William A. Cole to the annual meeting of the Exchange on May 28, 1878 is in marked contrast to those which preceded it. New York Produce Exchange, *Annual Report, 1878* (New York, 1879), 34.

52. The reversal of opinion in the East is cited in Chapter I, n. 123.

53. An example of this line of attack is found in New York Chamber of Commerce, *Seventeenth Annual Report* (New York, 1875), 1:11–12.

54. The first pamphlet has been previously cited in the chapter but its title is given here in full to make the point clearer. *Arguments of the New York Cheap Transportation Association in Favor of Senate Bill No. 98, Providing a Board of Railway Commissioners for This State; And Senate Bill No. —, to Provide for Minority Representation in Boards of Direction of Railroad Companies; Made Before the Joint Committee on Railways, of the Senate and Assembly, March 12th, 1874*, 3–12, 20; *Arguments of the New York Cheap Transportation Association in Favor of Senate Bill No. — Providing a Board of Railway Commissioners for This State; Made Before the Committee on Railways, of the Senate, March 28, 1876* (New York?, 1876?), 3, 8–9; *Argument of Simon Sterne, Esq., Delivered at Albany, March 7th, 1878, Before the Committee on Railroads, on "Bill to Create a Board of Railroad Commissioners, and to Regulate Their Powers"* (New York?, 1878?), 3–5.

55. By 1878 the revulsion against Grangerism had gone so far that Sterne, in pressing for a railroad commission, assured the legislature: "Those who are foremost in the advocacy of this bill (the Chamber of Commerce and the Board of Trade and Transportation, which I here represent) are as far removed from having any strong predilections for Granger legislation as the gentlemen who represent the railway interests of the State can be." *Argument of Simon Sterne Before Committee on Railroads, 1878*, 6.

56. Pratt's role in the Oil War, and the subsequent absorption of his firm by Rockefeller, is treated in Ida M. Tarbell, *The History of the Standard Oil Company* (New York, 1904), 88–148; Rolland H. Maybee, *Railroad Competition and the Oil Trade* (Mount Pleasant, Michigan, 1940), 341–384. His part in founding the Cheap Transportation Association has been noted previously in the present study.

57. New York Board of Trade and Transportation, *Minutes*, February 14, 1883.

58. Letters from James Penfield to Thurber, August 12, October 14, 1872.

59. This judgment is based upon acquaintance with Henry's actions and speeches in the 1870's and 1880's.

60. *Dictionary of American Biography*. See also the obituary in the New York *Times*, September 23, 1901. An interesting letter in the Simon Sterne collection at the New York Public Library indicates that he had access to the inner sanctums of the Democratic party. "My friend Mr. Simon Sterne desires to talk over the situation with you and you may safely do so, as he is in earnest in what he undertakes, and to be trusted for advice and conclusions faithfully yours," Abram S. Hewitt to John Kelly, February 19, 1873.

61. New York Cheap Transportation Association, *Minutes*, November 11, 1873. Published statements of its membership apparently cannot be relied upon for they are not consistent with each other, nor with other indications of the association's strength. They do provide some basis, however, for impressionistic judgments, and I have so used them.

62. *Commercial Interests of New York* (No. 2), 16.

63. Circular of the association, dated New York, October 1873; New York Cheap Transportation Association, *Minutes*, November 11, 1873. The circular lists Carlos Cobb as a director.

64. This report has been cited previously, and will be referred to as *Report of the Railway Committee, 1873*. For editorial comment upon its importance see New York *Tribune*, December 11, 1873.

65. *Report of the Railway Committee*, 3–14, 14–16.

66. *Ibid.*, 10.

67. *Ibid.*, 11.

68. *Ibid.*, 16.

69. *Facts for New Yorkers* (1874?) 4–5.

70. See the Address of President B. P. Baker in the association's *Minutes*, Annual Meeting, January 9, 1877.

71. Hepburn Committee, *Proceedings*, 2:1263. His testimony before the Hepburn Committee is especially revealing on the subject of special rates. See *ibid.*, 2:1263–1309. Also the testimony of James H. Rutter and Samuel Goodman, General Freight Agent and Assistant General Freight Agent, respectively, of the New York Central.

72. For a summary of the New York City position on special rates, see Hepburn Committee, *Proceedings*, 4:3908–3930. Suggestive evidence concerning the personal profits of railroad managers rigging rates is contained in the testimony of Harlan A. Pierce, editor of the *American Railroad Journal* in *Proceedings*, 3:2506–2519. Typical editorials on the subject over the time span covered by this study are in the *Commercial and Financial Chronicle*, 18:4–5 (January 3, 1874); *Railroad Gazette*, 10:612 (December 20, 1878): *Nation*, 44:525 (June 23, 1887).

As Chester Destler has observed, the personal interest in Standard Oil by various railroad magnates needs to be considered in understanding the otherwise peculiarly favorable treatment given that particular company. "The Standard Oil Company, Child of the Erie Ring, 1868–1872," *Mississippi Valley Historical Review*, 33:89–114 (June 1946).

73. See the discussion of the "Car-Load Cases," initiated by the New York Board of Trade and Transportation, in William Z. Ripley, *Railroads, Rates and Regulation* (New York, 1912), 325–329.

74. Simon Sterne argued that national legislation was not enough to stamp out the evil — even apart from the fact, he noted, that the "suggestion for national legislation does not come in perfect good faith from the railway corporations . . . A large branch . . . of the subject must necessarily always remain within the scope of State Legislatures only." Hepburn Committee, *Proceedings*, 4:4031–4032.

75. *Arguments of the New York Cheap Transportation Association, 1874*, 5, 20–22. See also, *Review of Report of U.S. Senate Committee on Transportation Routes by the Committee on Railway Transportation of the New York Cheap Transportation Association, 1874*, 7.

76. New York Cheap Transportation Association, *Facts for New Yorkers*, 7–8; *Arguments of the New York Cheap Transportation Association in Favor of Senate Bill No. — Providing a Board of Railway Commissioners for this State; Made before the Committee on Railways, of the Senate, March 28, 1876*, 8.

77. New York Cheap Transportation Association, *Minutes*, Annual Meeting, January 25, 1875. That the association was operating on a considerable scale for those days can be seen from the fact that its balance sheet showed expenditures of nearly $14,000 in little more than a year; its income had been a little more than $15,000. Retrospective analyses of the early troubles of the association are found in the *Minutes* of the New York Board of Trade and Transportation, September 12, 1877, and Annual Meeting, January 9, 1878. The name was formally changed at the September 12, 1877 meeting. See also a letter to the editor of the New York *Times*, May 26, 1874, signed "Merchant" (possibly Thurber — he was prone to the sobriquet).

78. New York Chamber of Commerce, *Seventeenth Annual Report*, 1:39–40. John F. Henry nominated Thurber, Baker, Edson, etc. for membership at the meeting. Thereafter, both he and Thurber made wholesale nominations and a comparison between these names and the membership of the Cheap Transportation Association

reveals the infiltration. The association printed its list of members in the *Minutes* of its annual meetings. While reliable enough for this purpose, the membership lists can not be used to calculate the strength of the association at specific times.

79. *Ibid.*, 1:46–47, 56–57.

80. New York *Times,* December 9, 19, 24, 28, 31, 1875; New York *Tribune,* December 7, 9, 22, 1875; *Railroad Gazette,* 7:546 (December 25, 1875); New York Cheap Transportation Association, *Minutes,* November 11, December 7, 30, 1875.

81. *Ibid.*, May 9, 1876.

82. *Arguments of New York Cheap Transportation Association, 1876,* 1, and *passim;* New York Cheap Transportation Association, *Minutes,* Annual Meeting, January 9, 1877.

83. *Arguments of New York Cheap Transportation Association, 1876,* 11.

84. *Ibid.*, 14.

85. New York Chamber of Commerce, *Eighteenth Annual Report,* 1:107–108.

86. That the New Yorkers were factually accurate can be seen in a letter from the president of the Boston & Albany, C. W. Chapin to Edward Atkinson, December 12, 1874. On the tie-up between the Boston & Albany and the New York Central, see Edward C. Kirkland, *Men, Cities and Transportation* (Cambridge, Mass., 1948), 1:372–376.

87. New York *Times,* November 13, December 27, 1876; *Commercial and Financial Chronicle,* 23:620 (December 23, 1876). The *Chronicle* was the leading national investment journal but it always identified itself with the interests of New York City. It was an uncompromising opponent of differentials against the city and fought any "scheme" to divert commerce from it. As a result, despite its extreme laissez-faire approach, it frequently joined the merchants in attacking railroad policy. See its editorial, "Artificial vs. Natural courses of Trade," 24:529–530 (June 9, 1877). The *Chronicle* was a very influential journal, no less an expert than John Moody adjudged it to be the best authority in the country on railroad matters after 1870. *The Railroad Builders* (New Haven, 1919), 245.

88. For Vanderbilt and Jewett's defense of their concessions, see Hepburn Committee, *Proceedings,* 1:72, also 1:645, 4:3768–3770, and *Railroad Gazette,* 8:434 (October 10, 1876).

89. See the *Railroad Gazette*'s analysis of Vanderbilt's later admission that the differentials had been largely offset by secret rebates, 13:716 (December 16, 1881). Moreover, secret rebates meant that place discrimination was lessened but it increased the prevalence of personal discrimination — a practice far more in the interests of individual railroad officials.

90. *Railroad Gazette,* 10:197 (April 19, 1878). The importance of the export trade in the over-all commerce of the city was such that the entire New York mercantile community, not just grain merchants, was acutely interested in the problem.

91. New York *Times,* April 8, 1877.

92. "Is the Railroad War a Stock-Jobbing Trick?" *Commercial and Financial Chronicle,* 24:308–309 (April 7, 1877); also 24:430–434, 577–578 (May 12, June 23, 1877).

93. *Ibid.*, 24:430–434 (May 12, 1877); New York *Times,* May 12, 1877. That railroad managers used their strategic position to acquire fortunes on the stock exchange is a theme that runs through the contemporary literature. For typical examples of journalistic denunciation of the practice, both before and after 1877, see the *Times,* November 2, 1883, April 5, 1884; *Commercial and Financial Chronicle,* 18:4–5 (January 3, 1874), 29:289 (September 20, 1879), 34:301–302 (March 18, 1882), 37:87–89 (July 28, 1883); *Railroad Gazette,* 5:361 (September 6, 1873), 7:210 (May 22, 1875), 15:486 (July 31, 1885).

94. As early as 1875 the Cheap Transportation Association looked to the railroad war then in progress to bring about a liquidation of watered stock. See its *Minutes,* June 8, 1875. It may be speculated that the stock-holding interests of

merchants who entertained such hopes were either secondary to their commercial interests, or were in different roads than those in which they looked forward to liquidation. See Chapter VI for a more detailed analysis of the controversy over stock watering, and the basis for settling the Central's dividends at approximately 32 per cent.

95. *Commercial and Financial Chronicle,* 25:27 (July 14, 1877). The extent of mercantile hard times during the seventies is treated in 28:57 (January 18, 1879).

96. New York *Times,* August 4, 9, September 11, 25, 1877, October 11, 1877, January 10, 1878.

97. *Times,* January 20, 21, 23, 25, 1878; *Railroad Gazette,* 10:44, 54, 70, 84, 98 (January 25, February 1, 8, 15, 22, 1878); Massachusetts Railroad Commissioners, *Tenth Annual Report* (Boston, 1879), 50–68. The Massachusetts Commissioners' *Report* is particularly informative and perceptive; it covered both the westbound and eastbound traffic problems, and it pointed out that Chicago as well as New York was discriminated against.

98. New York Chamber of Commerce, *Twentieth Annual Report* (New York, 1878), 1:100–109.

99. *Argument by Hon. Chauncey M. Depew . . . Before the Assembly Railroad Committee . . . , March 9th, 1882* (Albany, 1882), 5–6, 13.

100. New York Chamber of Commerce, *Twentieth Annual Report,* 1:115–130.

Chapter IV. The Patrons of Husbandry in New York

1. *Husbandman* (Elmira, New York), November 28, 1877, p. 4. A careful study of this paper, the unofficial organ of the New York Grange, has been the major source for the material in this and the next chapter. It gave almost complete coverage to the activities of every farm group in New York, including town bodies, and almost invariably reprinted addresses, resolutions, proceedings, etc. Its semi-official status forced it to give space to all factions within the Grange and other organizations, and to an extent unusual in farm journals it was critical of the "sturdy yeomanry" when its editors believed the criticism warranted.

2. *Thirteenth Census of the United States . . . 1910* (Washington, 1913), 5:73, 90, Tables 25, 33. The 1910 *Census* was used because it contains percentage tables from 1850 to 1910 which clearly express the relative standings of each state.

3. Bruce L. Melvin, "Rural Population of New York, 1855 to 1925," Cornell University Agricultural Experiment Station, *Memoir 116,* June 1928, 26, Table 6.

4. David M. Ellis, *Landlords and Farmers in the Hudson-Mohawk Region* (Ithaca, N. Y., 1946), 184–224; R. A. Mordhoff, "The Climate of New York State," *Cornell Extension Bulletin, 764,* December 1949, *passim;* Frank B. Howe, "Classification and Agricultural Value of New York Soils," Cornell University Agricultural Experiment Station, *Bulletin 619,* January 1935, *passim.*

5. The Cornell University Agricultural Experiment Station has published roughly two dozen of these surveys, usually under the title "An Economic Study of Land Utilization in ——— County, New York." Their findings, particularly the land classification maps, form the basis for the conclusion stated above. It is almost impossible to exaggerate the importance of New York's varied agricultural patterns in discussing its farmers' socio-political history during the late nineteenth century. At this time the variations were not nearly as great as those shown in the agricultural surveys of the twentieth century, but the same fundamental factors of soil, climate topography, location obtained. In this connection, see R. S. Beck, "Types of Farming in New York," Cornell University Agricultural Experiment Station, *Bulletin 704,* August 1938, *passim.*

6. Mordhoff, *Climate of New York,* 3.

7. For example, the cheese market was affected by international prices and conditions, butter-makers were more concerned with domestic production and home

markets, the milk farmers were worried about competitors in the next county and the milk dealers in the large cities (particularly New York). Orange County farmers wanted *intrastate* pro rata freights to preserve their location advantages, but Cattaraugus and St. Lawrence counties could hardly be expected to agree.

8. The varied agriculture of the state makes it difficult to assemble accurate statistics of land values. In contrast with the prairie and plains states, an extraordinarily wide range of values exists in the majority of townships in New York. It thus becomes difficult to assemble a statistically reliable pattern. But enough data can be pieced together to justify the generalizations above. For township studies, see Herrell DeGraff, "Farming in Newfane, New York" (Ph.D. dissertation, Cornell University, 1941); F. F. Hill and others, *Erin — The Economic Characteristics of a Rural Town in Southern New York* (Ithaca, New York, 1943). Interesting, albeit sketchy, surveys of the late nineteenth-century agricultural depression in New York, by agricultural economists who could draw upon first-hand experience, are found in G. F. Warren, "Land Values and Land Prices in the East and in the West," New York Department of Agriculture, *Circular No. 18* (Albany, 1911); M. C. Burritt, "An Account of the History and Development of Agriculture in Western New York" (M.S. thesis, Cornell University, 1910).

9. Hill, *Erin*, passim; Lawrence M. Vaughan, "Abandoned Farm Areas in Southern New York" (Ph.D. dissertation, Cornell University, 1928). Vaughan summarized his findings in "Abandoned Farm Land in New York," *Journal of Farm Economics*, 11:436–444 (July 1929).

10. An example of the antagonism expressed by farmers noncontiguous to the Erie Canal is found in the contest over the constitutional amendment of 1882 freeing it of tolls. Virtually every issue of the *Orange County Farmer* (Port Jervis, New York) during that year attacked the canal in unmeasured language and printed extracts from rural papers throughout the state taking a similar position.

11. Some aspects of these intrastate rivalries are treated in Frederick Jackson Turner, *The United States, 1830–1850* (reprinted ed., New York, 1950), 133–135. Other material is scattered in his chapter on "The Middle Atlantic States" in the same volume.

12. New York Agricultural Society, *Transactions*, 1865, 25:4 (Albany, 1866). Henceforth cited as *Transactions*.

13. Samuel E. Ronk, "Prices Received by Producers in New York State, 1841–1933" (Ph.D. dissertation, Cornell University, 1934), 1:47–48 (Table 10), 53–54 (Table 12). In 1867 wheat reached an average price of $2.67.

14. *Transactions*, 31:681 (Albany, 1872). An illustration of the fact that the figure given above is not far out of line for good farm land is provided by the discussions of Seneca County Grangers in 1875 — several years past the peak of the boom. After numerous sessions devoted to the cost of producing wheat, and based upon careful study, they came to the conclusion that the average cost of a bushel was $1.15 — on land worth $100 an acre. The use of such a figure under these circumstances suggests its reliability. *Husbandman*, April 7, 1875, p. 4.

15. *Transactions*, 25: 675–676.

16. *Ibid.*, 31:443–446.

17. *Transactions*, 30:68–73 (Albany, 1871).

18. *Ibid.*, 31:46. Resentment against town bonding definitely existed in various New York rural localities but doesn't seem to have played as important a role in hostility to railroads as in the West. The major resentment of New York farmers against railroads stemmed from relatively low rates to western through freight: the cry for pro rata antedated the demand for wiping out the town-bonding act. Resentment against town bonding probably was stimulated by western agitation on the subject; at least the New York *Times* maintained that it had been. See its editorial, February 6, 1878, entitled "Railroad Debts of New York."

19. New York State Grange, Patrons of Husbandry, *Journal of Proceedings*, 1:34–37 (Elmira, N. Y., 1874); *Husbandman*, December 2, 1874, p. 4.

20. *Transactions*, 33:287 (Albany, 1874).

21. *Transactions*, 34:293–294 (Albany, 1875).

22. Ronk, *Prices Paid to New York Producers,* 1:47–48 (Table 10). The same source supplies the statistics for 1875 and 1876, given below.

23. *Transactions,* 36:302 (Albany, 1877).

24. For an interesting interpretation of the relation between agrarian economic interests and agrarian politics, see Arthur N. Holcombe, *The Political Parties of To-Day* (2nd ed., New York, 1924), particularly pp. 39–129, 185–213.

25. The emphasis in New York rural areas upon individual prowess and prestige, based upon income variations, is extensively treated in a pioneering work of historical social psychology: James M. Williams, *Our Rural Heritage — the Social Psychology of Rural Development* (New York, 1925).

26. Unfortunately the Census did not get around to classifying farmers by sources of income until 1900; hence it is difficult, prior to that date, to depict accurately the contrasts between New York and western agriculture. For a discussion of the basic factors determining New York diversification, with some historical material, see R. S. Beck, *Types of Farming in New York.*

27. Thus, serious western competition in the butter market only developed years after western wheat hit the Genesee Valley. Furthermore, wheat growers throughout New York tended to shift their type of farming and became dairymen to the detriment of Orange County (and other) producers. Such an indirect result of western development is hardly to be compared with the competition offered by prairie wheat. As noted below, the Genesee Valley became the center of the New York Farmers' Alliance because of this direct competition. Typical discussions of the problems inherent in organizing farmers engaged in various types of farming are found in *Husbandman,* July 14, 1875, p. 4, September 8, 1875, p. 2, December 1, 1875, p. 4, October 25, 1876, p. 4, February 21, 1877, p. 3.

28. The subtle effects of regional qualities pervading the life of all groups in a given region are difficult to document precisely. The statement above is based upon extensive reading in New York contemporary sources, particularly a large number of rural journals and local newspapers, the bulk of which are not cited in the present study. The leaders of New York farm organizations in particular were susceptible to non-agrarian, non-rural interests.

29. Solon J. Buck, *The Granger Movement* (Cambridge, Mass., 1913), 45.

30. *Husbandman,* March 22, 1876, p. 2.

31. New York Grange, *Proceedings,* 1:5–6.

32. *Ibid.,* 1:10.

33. *Ibid.,* 1:11, 13.

34. For example, see the editorial sympathizing with western farmers in *Husbandman,* November 11, 1874, p. 4, and an indignant letter signed "Patron," attacking the editorial, *ibid.,* December 2, 1874, p. 4. The letter referred to the prewar pro rata agitation and to the long-haul, short-haul bill introduced in the legislature in 1872. Its heavy stress upon the damage to interior "business interests" points up an important feature of New York agrarian movements. The leaders were men whose major source of income tended to derive from agricultural service industries rather than from tilling the soil.

35. New York Grange, *Proceedings,* 1:34–36.

36. *Ibid.,* 1:36–37.

37. *Husbandman,* April 21, 1875, p. 4, March 22, 1876, p. 2, December 20, 1876, p. 4, March 21, 1877, p. 3, May 30, 1877, p. 4.

38. New York Grange, *Proceedings,* 2:13, 22–24, 30; Buck, *Granger Movement,* 257–258.

39. *Husbandman,* September 9, 16, 1874, p. 4, May 19, 1875, p. 2, June 2, 1875, p. 5, September 8, 1875, p. 2, March 7, 1877.

40. New York Grange, *Proceedings,* 3:39. This figure is based on the secretary's report and is not thoroughly reliable. Not until the Grange became strong in the 1890's were detailed statistics of its membership published.

41. *Ibid.,* 5:18. Calculated from the roundabout statements given by the secretary in 1878, and in the annual *Proceedings* thereafter.

42. Leonard L. Allen, *History of the New York State Grange* (Waterford, New

York, 1934), 94. The numerical increase became pronounced in the mid-eighties, soared in the nineties, and really zoomed thereafter.

43. *Husbandman,* January 5, 19, 1876, p. 4; New York Grange, *Proceedings,* 8:20.

44. This statement is based upon reading literally hundreds of accounts of Grange meetings, addresses to Granges, speeches at county fairs, agricultural society meetings, etc.

45. Almost without exception, when I have been able to secure information concerning the sources of income or wealth of Grange leaders, farming either turns out to be subordinate, or, in a minority of cases, carried out on a large scale. Thus, of the leading Grangers during 1873–1896, William A. Armstrong was primarily a newspaper owner and journalist; William C. Wayne had made his money in non-agricultural enterprises and in 1876 purchased one of the "finest lake side farms in the State"; William C. Gifford owned a factory making farm equipment and a very large farm in Chautauqua County; H. H. Goff was a produce dealer; J. S. Van Duzer owned a cheese factory; and General E. F. Jones was a nationally famous producer of weight scales. The testimony of Goff before the Hepburn Committee demonstrates that he was hostile to the railroads because business rivals had special rates and he was not so favored. All the "farmers" testifying before the Hepburn Committee either belonged to the Grange or to the Farmers' Alliance or both, and by far the greatest proportion indicated that business interests were their over-riding consideration; the others were large landowners. Hepburn Committee, *Proceedings,* 2:1837–1995. In addition, see the biographical sketches of Grange and Alliance leaders in the *Husbandman,* March 17, 1875, p. 2, April 28, 1875, p. 4, June 23, 1875, p. 2, July 21, 1875, p. 5, March 8, 1876, p. 4, April 12, 1876, p. 5, July 26, 1876, p. 4, April 25, 1877, p. 2, June 13, 1877, p. 5, March 19, 1879, p. 2, September 10, 1879, p. 2, August 10, 1881, p. 4, July 4, 1883, p. 4. My conclusions as to the social origins of New York farm leaders are based not only on published material but on extensive correspondence with their descendants, and weeks spent in traveling through the New York countryside visiting these descendants, and speaking to octogenarians and nonogenerians who knew them. Their memories were surprisingly good, at least in those cases which could be checked with other sources.

46. William M. White of Livingstone County, George W. Hoffman and James McCann of Chemung. See "The New York State Agricultural Society," Department of Farms and Markets of the State of New York, *Agricultural Bulletin 161* (January 1924, Albany, N. Y.), 27. For accounts of their estates see the *Husbandman,* March 8, 1876, p. 4, July 26, 1876, p. 4, September 10, 1879, p. 2. Dean I. P. Roberts of Cornell University, another president of the State Agricultural Society, was also a Granger. A. S. Diven, although not a member of the Order, belonged to the Elmira Farmers' Club, and worked closely with the Grange.

47. New York Grange, *Proceedings,* 2:35.

48. See the reports of the delegates from the several counties in the New York Grange, *ibid.,* 6:35–50 (Elmira, N. Y., 1878).

49. As the depression got worse money outlays for dues and initiation fees became increasingly burdensome. See, for example, the comments in New York Grange, *Proceedings,* 5:26–27 (Elmira, N. Y., 1878).

50. *Ibid.,* 3:10–12, 21, 28; 4:9; 5:23; 6:31, 35–50. *Husbandman,* December 8, 1875, p. 4, December 6, 1876, p. 2, December 27, 1876, p. 4, March 21, 1877, p. 4, July 10, 1878, p. 4, November 19, 1879, p. 4.

51. *Ibid.,* May 15, 1878, p. 4, October 6, 1880, p. 4.

52. *Ibid.,* September 2, 1874, p. 2, August 18, 1875, p. 4, 5, September 22, 1875, p. 4, August 30, 1876, p. 4, October 4, 1876, p. 4.

53. *Ibid.,* August 26, 1874, p. 4, June 14, 1876, p. 5, August 9, 1876, p. 4, March 28, 1877, p. 3, April 11, 1877, p. 2, December 19, 1877, p. 4, December 22, 1880, p. 2, December 31, 1884, p. 4. The quotation from the *Times* is found in the August 9, 1876 issue. The Elmira Farmers' Club appears to have been an im-

portant organization; its national reputation caused many farm leaders to subscribe to the *Husbandman*. As a result, the concepts, program, and activities of New York Grangers received wide publicity and the paper served as a "carrier" of the New York emphasis on independent political action. The quotation concerning the national status of the *Husbandman* is from a letter signed "W. Maxwell, President S.W.A.," Owachita, La., in the March 28, 1877 issue.

54. The estimate of its circulation is based upon several roundabout editorials on the subject, August 10, 1881, p. 4, January 17, 1883, p. 4.

55. See the editorial attacking the *Country Gentleman* for calling the *Husbandman* an organ of the Grange, May 5, 1875, p. 4.

Chapter V. Railroad Rate Wars and the Farmers' Alliance

1. For a summary history of the Alliance's origins, see *American Rural Home,* December 24, 1881, p. 414. See also its editorial, January 11, 1879, p. 19, claiming credit for having founded the organization. Perspective concerning the origin of the Alliance early in 1877 is best gained by noting that 1876 marked the year in which rate wars on eastbound freight broke out in full force.

2. Angry editorials calling for public discussion of the inequities of the trunk lines' rate policy began to sound late in 1876. See the *Husbandman,* October 25, November 8, 15, 1876, p. 4.

3. Place discrimination affected New York farmers indirectly as well by hurting interior market towns which they supplied with perishables. *Ibid.,* October 3, 1877, p. 4. Historical continuity of agrarian concern with railroad discrimination was an important factor in New York. For prewar complaints against railroads, see *The Farming Interest of Western New York, as Affected by the Various Means of Transportation to the East and West. Address of Dr. Sanford B. Hunt, Delivered Before the Genesee County Agricultural Society, September 15th, 1859* (Batavia, New York, 1859?) Instead of the notion that the more "radical" farmers went off to the West, a more likely explanation would be that favorable freight rates available there after trunk lines developed, in relative terms, made the move seem logical to some of the more business-minded farmers.

4. Hepburn Committee, *Proceedings,* 2:1975–1994. Root's land was probably worth more than $100 an acre before the middle seventies as it constituted some of the best farming property in the state.

5. *Husbandman,* April 19, 1876, p. 4.

6. *American Rural Home,* March 3, 1877, p. 69.

7. The annual meeting of the State Grange early in 1877 was characterized by a number of speeches in this vein. "The influence of the farmers of the State of New York is less felt in its Legislature at present than at any other time for the past thirty years." New York Grange, *Proceedings,* 4:22–24 (Elmira, N. Y., 1877).

8. *Rural Home,* March 3, 1877, p. 69.

9. *Ibid.*

10. *Ibid.,* March 17, 1877, p. 85. See also the editorial on p. 91.

11. *Yates County Chronicle,* March 15, 1877.

12. *Rural Home,* March 31, 1877, p. 101.

13. *Ibid.,* pp. 101–102; *Husbandman,* March 28, April 4, 1877, p. 4. See also the account in the Rochester *Union and Advertiser* March 21, 22, 1877. Some time later, Victor E. Piollet, master of the Pennsylvania State Grange, and very active in the Alliance work, stated that the Alliance "was got up for those farmers that don't want to go into the Grange." *Husbandman,* October 16, 1878, p. 3.

14. For perceptive analyses of the nativist movements which enable us to place the postwar reformist agitation in historical perspective, see Louis D. Scisco, *Political Nativism in New York State* (New York, 1901), 242–254; Oscar Handlin, *Boston's Immigrants, 1790–1865* (Cambridge, Mass., 1941), 184–215.

15. *Husbandman,* April 11, p. 3, April 18, p. 4, April 25, p. 4, May 16, p. 203, 4, June 13, p. 2 (all 1877).

16. *Rural Home,* September 15, 1877, p. 294; *Husbandman,* September 12, 1877, p. 4; Rochester *Union and Advertiser,* September 6, 1877.

17. The presidents of the State Agricultural Society elected as officers of the Alliance were Harris Lewis (president), Alexander S. Diven, George W. Hoffman, and James Geddes. Also present were Patrick Barry, I. P. Roberts, Milo Ingalsbee, George Geddes, and General N. M. Curtis. Based upon comparison of the list of delegates at the meeting as reported in the *Husbandman,* and the list of past presidents of the society, in New York State Department of Farms and Markets, *Agricultural Bulletin 161,* 27. The four others noted as delegates at later meetings of the Alliance, were William M. White, James McCann, R. J. Swan, and Horatio Seymour.

18. Although not a delegate at Alliance meetings, John Johnston of Geneva, the "father" of tile drainage in the United States, supported its position. His complaint against the railroads was typical: "Stock feeding proved profitable with me, and at the same time enriched my lands. But now the railroad management is such that stock is taken to New York and other Eastern markets from the far West at less rates than are charged for shipping the same class of freight from near-by points. This robs us of an advantage legitimately belonging to our location." *Husbandman,* July 31, 1878, p. 4.

19. *Ibid.,* September 12, 1877, p. 4; *Rural Home,* September 15, 1877, pp. 293–295.

20. *Ibid.,* September 15, 1877, pp. 294–295.

21. *Rural Home,* January 5, 1878, p. 5; *Husbandman,* December 26, 1877, p. 4, January 2, 1878, p. 2; Rochester *Union and Advertiser,* December 22, 1878.

22. This estimate is based upon the Alliance's call somewhat later for financial support from 600 Granges, Farmers' Clubs, and Agricultural Societies in the state. *Husbandman,* October 2, 1878, p. 4.

23. *Rural Home,* January 5, 1878, p. 5. The quotation below is also found there.

24. For a study of taxation in New York after 1887 but applicable to the seventies see M. Slade Kendrick, "An Index Number of Farm Taxes in New York, and Its Relation to Various Other Economic Factors," Cornell University Agricultural Experiment Station, *Bulletin 457,* December, 1926. The split in the Alliance over taxation is summed up by this editorial comment in the *Husbandman,* April 23, 1879, p. 4: "That some plan should be devised to equalize taxation by making every class of property bear its share, is a proposition not disputed, but how to do it is the puzzling question."

25. Late in 1877, and all through 1878, it was a rare issue of the *Husbandman* that did not carry a letter, article or editorial on the "money question." Armstrong, its editor, belonged to the orthodox school of hard money and was obviously determined to root out financial "heresies" among his readers. But both sides of the question received more than adequate space — most issues carried several eight-column pages devoted to the subject — and the paper constitutes a valuable source of information for agrarian views.

26. Ronk, *Prices Paid to New York Producers,* 1:47–48, Table 10. The month-by-month course of wheat prices showing the sharp rise beginning in October 1879 is traced on p. 121, Table 36. But prior to that time prices were extremely low.

27. The respectable origins of inflationary proposals are treated in Joseph Dorfman, *The Economic Mind in American Civilization* (New York, 1949), 3:3–20.

28. For revealing editorials, see *Husbandman,* March 27, June 5, August 21, 1878, p. 4.

29. *The Tribune Almanac and Political Register for 1879* (New York, n.d.), 87, 103. Note the strong vote in Allegany, Cattaraugus, Chenango, Chemung, Delaware, Greene, Steuben, etc. Most of the Greenback strength was in the Southern Tier, and in part probably reflects the labor vote resulting from the railroad strikes of 1877.

30. *The Tribune Almanac and Political Register for 1881* (New York, n.d.), 77. Harris Lewis, the maverick president of the Farmers' Alliance, was the Greenback candidate for governor in 1879.

31. *Rural Home,* August 30, 1879, p. 290.

32. *Ibid.,* August 30, 1879, 290, 295; *Husbandman,* August 27, 1879, p. 4. No eastbound pool was in effect at this time and the European demand for grain had not yet materialized. As a result, eastbound rates were "demoralized." Agrarian militancy in New York was closely tied to the level of freight rates from the West.

33. This conclusion is based upon a comparison of the personnel in the two organizations.

34. *Rural Home,* August 30, 1879, p. 290.

35. *Husbandman,* September 6, 1879, p. 4.

36. *Ibid.,* May 10, 1876, p. 4, and March 22, August 16, 1876, p. 4, January 10, 1877, p. 4, April 25, 1877, p. 2.

37. *Ibid.,* September 20, 1876, p. 4, October 25, 1876, p. 6, January 3, March 28, August 29, September 5, 12, October 10, 1877, p. 4, May 1, 8, September 4, 1878, p. 4.

38. *Ibid.,* March 6, 1878, p. 4.

39. Compare the statements by Thurber and others at the meetings of the Chamber, January 30 and June 6, 1878, in its *Twentieth Annual Report* (New York, 1878), 1:101–108; *Twenty-First Annual Report* (New York, 1879), 1:37–42. The resolution quoted above is on p. 40 of the latter *Report.* In connection with the reversal by the merchants see the editorials in the *Husbandman,* June 12, 19, 1878, p. 4, and the letter signed John Livingstone, June 12, 1878, p. 5.

40. *Ibid.,* October 16, 1878, p. 3; *Rural Home,* September 14, 1878, p. 294.

41. *Tribune Almanac for 1880,* pp. 19–21.

42. *Husbandman,* November 5, 1879, p. 4.

43. "The Railroads and Middle States Farming," New York *Commercial Bulletin,* May 23, 1879, reprinted in the *Husbandman,* June 4, 1879, p. 6. This article, and others written in similar vein as a result of the Hepburn investigation, attracted a good deal of attention. The *Railroad Gazette,* 9:313 (June 6, 1879) noted that it was a remarkable article for a journal "especially devoted to the interest of the commerce of the city of New York, and the foremost exponent of low through rates to the metropolis."

44. New York Grange, *Proceedings,* 7:75–76, 8:23–24, 93.

45. New York *Times,* February 6, 1879. The bill in question had been introduced by A. Brundage, a Steuben County Granger and Alliance leader.

46. *Husbandman,* June 16, 23, p. 4, July 7, p. 1, 4, July 28, p. 5, August 4, 11, 18, 25, p. 4 (all 1880); *Rural Home,* August 21, 1880, p. 271; New York Grange, *Proceedings,* 8:72, 93.

47. *Rural Home,* September 25, 1880, p. 311.

48. *Argument of Albert Fink Before the Committee on Commerce of the United States House of Representatives — Washington, March 17 and 18, 1882* (Washington, 1882), 3.

49. For a clear statement on this point by charter members, see *Husbandman,* January 2, 1878, p. 4.

50. In addition to the journals cited in the text, accounts of Alliance activities were found in the Rochester *Union and Advertiser* and the *Yates County Chronicle* (Penn Yan, New York).

51. *Husbandman,* November 3, 1875, p. 4.

52. *Ibid.,* May 3, 1876, p. 2.

53. *Ibid.,* October 17, 1877, p. 3.

54. *Ibid.,* June 6, 1877, p. 2, September 5, 1877, p. 8, September 12, 1877, p. 2. These letters also demonstrate that "Practicus" was an ardent Greenbacker, and a close reader of the *Husbandman.*

55. *Ibid.,* January 30, 1878, p. 6. Other letters from R. T. Kennedy and W. W. Lang, secretary and master, respectively, of the Texas State Grange are in the issues for June 25, 1879, p. 2, and May 19, 1880, p. 1. Importance is attached here to Texas' knowledge of the New York Alliance because the impression exists that the Farmers' Alliance originated in the Lone Star State. That erroneous impression largely stems from the volume edited by N. A. Dunning, *The Farmers' Alliance*

History and Agricultural Digest (Washington, 1891). Dunning was then an associate editor of the *National Economist,* the organ of the Southern Farmers' Alliance, and played up Texas' role in the movement. Ironically, most of the basic facts concerning the Alliance's real origins were set forth by its first president, F. P. Root, in the *Farmers' Alliance History,* 230–232. But Dunning's hosannas were sounded for, and the attention of his readers directed towards, "the Alliance in Texas."

56. *Husbandman,* September 8, 1875, p. 4, September 15, 1875, p. 4, November 11, 1875, p. 5, April 11, 1877, p. 4, January 1, March 26, June 11, 1879, p. 4. There are numerous letters from the men named above and from other Grange leaders on various subjects in the *Husbandman.* The tone of these letters, and other evidence, suggests that Armstrong was on close personal terms with most of them. To illustrate the paper's far-flung influence, it printed an essay read before the Mannsville Grange, Iowa, and by vote of the Grange, its publication was requested in the *Husbandman* for May 9, 1877, p. 2.

57. *Ibid.,* February 6, 1878, p. 2.

58. Piollet's intense feelings are evident in addresses printed in the *Husbandman,* October 16, 1878, p. 3, September 29, 1880, p. 2.

59. *Rural Home,* June 11, 1879, p. 199.

60. *Prairie Farmer,* June 28, 1879, p. 201. For its account of the "New York 'Alliance'" activities, see March 22, 1879, p. 92, October 4, 1879, p. 313.

61. *Husbandman,* November 19, 1879, pp. 2–3. But the editor of the *Husbandman* was well aware of the difficulties in achieving national unity. See the issue for November 11, 1879, p. 4.

62. National Grange, *Journal of Proceedings of the Thirteenth Session . . . 1879* (Philadelphia, 1879), 122. This bold step towards independent political action had been foreshadowed the year before with the accession of Wayne and Piollet to the Committee on Transportation. The interest of the National Grange in transportation languished with the coming of the rate wars of the mid-seventies and 1878 marked a revival. Piollet called for farmers "to sever their relation with the political party organizations that have heretofore dominated them," and also urged them to collect petitions to end discriminations in freight. *Journal of Proceedings of the Twelfth Session . . . 1878* (Philadelphia, 1878), 96.

63. Solon Buck has observed that Grange influence was pronounced from the start of the Farmers' Alliance in Texas. *Granger Movement,* 303. Even N. A. Dunning did not claim that the name "Farmers' Alliance" was applied to local vigilante groups in Texas before 1879. *Farmers' Alliance History,* 18–19.

64. *Husbandman,* August 11, 1880, p. 5.

65. Rochester *Union and Advertiser,* September 16, 1880; *Rural Home,* September 25, 1880, p. 311.

66. *Husbandman,* September 29, 1880, p. 2.

67. *Prairie Farmer,* October 23, 1880, p. 340, November 13, 1880, p. 364, November 27, 1880, p. 380.

68. Chicago *Tribune,* October 15, 1880.

69. Thurber was then in the process of laying down foundations for what later became the National Anti-Monopoly League; a League designed to give organizational expression to joint efforts of merchants and farmers on behalf of railroad regulation. A letter from William J. Fowler to Thurber, August 10, 1880, indicated that the plan was well advanced in New York. The National Anti-Monopoly League will be treated below.

70. Chicago *Tribune,* October 15, 1880.

71. *Ibid.,* October 15, 1880. At the annual meeting of the Monroe County Alliance some months later, Fowler reported on the formation of the National Alliance. The fact that he found it necessary to attempt to reconcile the interests of eastern and western farmers indicates the ambivalent nature of New York agrarian movements. Agricultural fundamentalism resulted in a definite feeling of class solidarity but the real conflict in interests put a severe strain upon it. Rochester *Union and Advertiser,* December 9, 1880.

72. This reference is to the discussion of economic location in agriculture by J. H. Von Thünen in his classic work, *The Isolated State.*

Chapter VI. The Hepburn Committee Investigation

1. *Railroad Gazette,* 12:65 (January 30, 1880).

2. John Foord, *The Life & Public Services of Simon Sterne* (London, 1903), 22–23. Unfortunately, the Sterne papers now in the possession of the New York Public Library contain only a handful of letters, most of them of little significance. I have attempted to learn what happened to the extensive correspondence described by Foord — with no success to date.

3. The pamphlet was signed with the pseudonym "Average Citizen" — a favorite nom-de-plume employed by Francis B. Thurber. It was an elaboration of an earlier article printed in the *American Grocer.* As was true of virtually all of Thurber's pamphlets it was made up in large measure of extracts from various newspapers.

4. New York *Times,* May 9, 11, 1879; New York *Evening Post,* May 19, 1879. The quotations are from the *Times,* but the *Post's* editorial on "The Calamity in California" is in a similar vein. Compare these editorials with the attitudes of Progressive leaders in George E. Mowry, "The California Progressive and His Rationale: A Study in Middle Class Politics," *Mississippi Valley Historical Review,* 36:239–250 (September 1949).

5. New York *Evening Post,* May 9, 16, 23, 1879. Letters signed "Anti-Communist," "Merchant," "Anti-Communist."

6. The grievances of the merchants can be found summarized briefly in the "indictment" drawn up by them before the inquiry was underway, and in considerable detail in Simon Sterne's closing argument. Hepburn Committee, *Proceedings,* 1:3–32; 4:3881–4036. Resentment against the roads for not having taken over the function of the Erie Canal as an instrument of New York's commercial warfare is perhaps best brought out in Sterne's sharp questioning of William H. Vanderbilt. See *ibid.,* 2:1252–1254.

7. New York *Commercial Bulletin,* June 17, 1879.

8. Hepburn Committee, *Proceedings,* 1:481, 4:3910, 5:120–148 (section of volume 5, entitled "exhibits").

9. *Ibid.,* 1:50.

10. National Anti-Monopoly League, *Document No. 7 . . . Speech of Hon. John H. Reagan . . . and Speech of Hon. W. J. Fowler . . . At the Mass Meeting of the National Anti-Monopoly League, Held at Cooper Institute, New York, February 21, 1881* (New York?, 1881?), 12.

11. The printed minutes for the January 30, 1878, meeting merely note "a full attendance of members" but the original manuscript in the Chamber's possession is more explicit. Thirty-five leading figures are mentioned by name, "and other members of the Chamber representing all the principal branches of trade of the city." Minutes, 7:262–266 (manuscript). The request for the special meeting charged gross discrimination against New York, and was signed by 174 of the leading firms in the city. New York Chamber of Commerce, *Twentieth Annual Report,* 1:100. This seems to bear out Sterne's claim, made some time later, that "The request for the call of the meeting was signed by the largest number of representative houses in every department of trade and commerce that had signed any request for any meeting of the Chamber of Commerce since the beginning of the war of 1861. The signatures appended to the request for the call represented a capital three times over the combined capital of the New York Central and Erie railways, water, fraud and all." Hepburn Committee, *Proceedings,* 4:3884.

12. *Ibid.,* 1:101–102.

13. New York *Times,* January 31, 1878. See also the *Times* editorial on the meeting in the same issue.

14. *Twentieth Annual Report*, 1:108–109. The three leaders of the Board of Trade and Transportation named to the committee were Benjamin G. Arnold, Francis B. Thurber, and Benjamin B. Sherman.

15. *Ibid.*, 1:108.

16. *Ibid.*, 1:119.

17. *Ibid.*, 1:121.

18. New York Board of Trade and Transportation, *Minutes*, February 13, 1878. Henceforth referred to as N.Y.B.T.T., *Minutes*.

19. Chamber of Commerce, *Twentieth Annual Report*, 1:121.

20. *Facts for the People. A Short Report Showing How Railroad Influence Controls in Our Legislature; Referring Particularly to How the Senate of 1878–9 Refused to Allow Citizens the Common Right of Investigation of Grievances* (New York?, 1879?), 4–5; New York Produce Exchange, *Annual Report 1878* (New York, 1879), 61. The memorial emphasized that rapid changes in transportation had not been accompanied by corresponding changes in the relation between the railroads and the state.

21. *Argument of Simon Sterne, Esq., Delivered at Albany March 7th, 1878 Before the Committee on Railroads* . . . (New York?, 1878?).

22. *Ibid.*, 9.

23. Chamber of Commerce, *Twentieth Annual Report*, 1:161–162.

24. Chamber of Commerce, *Twenty-First Annual Report*, 1:7.

25. N.Y.B.T.T., *Minutes*, January 9, 1878; New York *Times*, January 10, 1878.

26. *Address of Simon Sterne Before the Merchants and Business Men of New York, at Steinway Hall, April 19, 1878* (New York, 1878), 3.

27. *Ibid.*, 3–5. The original petition is in the Sterne Collection and next to each signature is the firm or institution with which the individual is connected.

28. New York *Times*, April 20, 1878.

29. *Address of Simon Sterne . . . April 19, 1878*, 25–26.

30. *Ibid.*, 29.

31. *Ibid.*, 35–37.

32. *Nation*, 26:303 (May 9, 1878).

33. Chamber of Commerce, *Twenty-First Annual Report*, 1:38.

34. The letter, dated May 28, 1878, is in the Thurber papers.

35. Chamber of Commerce, *Twenty-First Annual Report*, 1:38, 42–43.

36. *Ibid.*, 1:40.

37. H. K. Thurber to F. B. Thurber, August 6, December 25, 1876, March 1, 20, 1877.

38. Smith to Thurber, July 9, 1878.

39. New York *Times*, June 27, 1878.

40. *Ibid.*, July 16, 1878.

41. *Co-Operation for Self Preservation — Non-Partisan Political Movement, for the Protection of Our Material Interests, Which May Lead to Important Results* (New York?, 1878?), 3, 9–10.

42. *Ibid.*, 5.

43. *New York Times*, June 15, 1878.

44. New York *Journal of Commerce*, June 29, 1878.

45. Chamber of Commerce, *Twenty-First Annual Report*, 1:112–113.

46. New York *Daily Graphic*, June 4, 1879.

47. Chamber of Commerce, *Twenty-Second Annual Report* (New York, 1880), 1:98–99.

48. Hepburn Committee, *Proceedings*, 1:1–2.

49. *Ibid.*, 1:2–14.

50. *Ibid.*, 1:16–36.

51. Hepburn Committee, *Report*, 50–51.

52. Hepburn Committee, *Proceedings*, 1:37–84.

53. An excellent and typical example of Depew's invention is his confident statement before the Assembly Committee on Railroads that the Massachusetts Board

of Railroad Commissioners would now concede their own uselessness. Sterne promptly wrote to Charles Francis Adams, Jr., asking if that were true. The Bostonian replied, "When Depew, or anyone else . . . ventures to assert that, if questioned, I will admit that it [Mass. Bd.] has been of no . . . practical use, I can only say that he is guilty of a piece of excessively gratuitous impertinence. Most emphatically I admit nothing of the sort; and further, accustomed as I am to what is known as 'cheek' in railroad attorneys, this display of it by Mr. Depew fairly robs me of my breath." Adams to Sterne, April 1, 1878.

54. Chamber of Commerce, *Twenty-Second Annual Report,* 1:18–19.

55. The headline and article on p. 34 of the New York *Herald Tribune,* April 18, 1951, might well have been written in the nineteenth century. "Port Committee Asks End to Rail Rate Handicaps — Report Proposes 7-Point Program to Regain Trade." The article noted that "The Port Committee was established last summer by former Mayor William O'Dwyer in an effort to ascertain why New York was losing trade to other American ports." Among other sentences that sounded reminiscent was this one: "The rail industry was urged to abolish entirely all port differentials." With inconsequential alterations the article might have been printed in the New York *Herald* or *Tribune* of April 18, 1881.

56. Hepburn Committee, *Proceedings,* 1:40.

57. New York *Evening Post,* June 19, 1879.

58. Hepburn Committee, *Proceedings,* 1:42, 81–84.

59. *Ibid.,* 1:53.

60. *Ibid.,* 1:53.

61. *Ibid.,* 1:8–9, 104.

62. Edwin C. Worcester, secretary of the New York Central, conceded that the limitation in the charters of the roads was not based upon the amount of capital stock but upon the actual cost of the road. Windom Committee, *Transportation Routes to the Seaboard,* 2:143.

63. Hepburn Committee, *Proceedings,* 1:53.

64. *Ibid.,* 1:56–59.

65. *Ibid.,* 1:58, 70.

66. *Ibid.,* 1:11.

67. *Ibid.,* 1:72–73.

68. *Ibid.,* 1:74–75.

69. *Ibid.,* 1:63.

70. *Ibid.,* 4:3929.

71. New York *Evening Post,* June 19, 1879.

72. For representative samples of their testimony, consult the index of the Hepburn Committee *Proceedings* under the names Conway W. Ball, Henry E. Boardman, Alexander S. Diven, C. P. Eastman, James A. Hinds, Harris Lewis, William M. Hunt, Arthur G. Newton, Frederick P. Root, Thomas Thornton.

73. New York *Commercial Advertiser,* August 21, 1879. As noted in the previous chapter, newspapers closely allied with the merchants suddenly discovered in 1879 that railroads were ruining New York agriculture. The *Advertiser* was referring to the wide circulation given an editorial reprinted in pamphlet form as "The Railroads and Middle States Farming."

Chapter VII. Investigation Adds Light and Heat

1. Hepburn Committee, *Proceedings,* 1:86–95; 2:1355–1356.

2. New York Chamber of Commerce, *Twenty-Second Annual Report* (New York, 1880), 1:100.

3. This statement is based upon the large quantities of newspaper clippings dealing with the hearings found in the F. B. Thurber papers.

4. New York *Journal of Commerce,* August 25, 1879.

5. New York *Evening Post,* August 29, 1879.

6. Hepburn Committee, *Proceedings*, 2:1264–1265, 1235–1240, 1241–1245, 1309–1311, 1293–1297, 1567–1577, 1285–1291. Editorials are found in the New York *Commercial Bulletin*, August 22, 1879; *Daily Graphic*, August 22, 1879; *Evening Post*, August 29, 1879. Consult the index of the *Proceedings* for the testimony of James Rutter and Samuel Goodman. Their admissions concerning special rates constituted some of the most damaging evidence against the roads.

7. *Ibid.*, 4:3902.

8. The Hepburn Committee placed the minimum "water" in the Erie and Central at approximately $50,000,000 in each case. *Report*, 18–22. But as noted above, George O. Jones demonstrated that the figure would be closer to $100,000,-000, for the Central; the evidence presented at the hearing would seem to indicate that the Erie was in the same class. The $180,000,000 estimate was made by the *American Exchange*, August 26, 1879.

9. Hepburn Committee, *Proceedings*, 1:1116.

10. Hepburn Committee, *Report*, 18.

11. For a typical Vanderbilt statement complaining that he wasn't earning enough on his railroad see Hepburn Committee, *Proceedings*, 2:1674.

12. For the most accurate public statement available concerning the New York Central's earnings and dividends, 1872–1885, see the "Investors Supplement," *Commercial and Financial Chronicle*, December 19, 1885, p. 10.

13. Jones had actually been charitable in accepting the Hudson River Railroad's capitalization as roughly accurate. Wheaton Lane's account shows that before its merger with the New York Central only $12,500,000 of its stock represented paid in capital. See his *Commodore Vanderbilt* (New York, 1942), 227–228.

14. Hepburn Committee, *Proceedings*, 4:3768–3771.

15. *Ibid.*, 4:3895–3897. The valuable local traffic of the New York Central enabled it to bear the vicissitudes of rate wars, stock watering, cut-rates to favorites, and vagaries of management with ease until the eighties.

16. Sterne had been the first secretary of the American Free Trade League and an avowed disciple of the classical economists. Perhaps the chief significance of the part played by railroad discrimination in the emergence of the Standard Oil near-monopoly is that it seemed to give substance to the popular charge that such discrimination was the primary, if not the only, reason for its emergence.

17. Hepburn Committee, *Proceedings*, 4:3970–3971.

18. *The Tribune Almanac . . . for 1877* (New York, 1878), 35–39; *The Tribune Almanac . . . for 1879* (New York, 1880?), 23–26; *The Evening Journal Almanac, 1879* (Albany, n.d.), 148.

19. *The Tribune Almanac . . . for 1880* (New York, n.d.), 19–21.

20. Miller to Thurber, September 3, 1879.

21. Miller to Thurber, September 13, 1879.

22. Smith to Thurber, September 18, 1879.

23. John Moody, *The Railroad Builders* (New Haven, 1919), 36–37. Burton J. Hendrick estimated that in 1879 Vanderbilt owned "not far from 550,000 shares" of the 894,280 total. "The Vanderbilt Fortune," *McClure's Magazine*, November 1908, p. 60. Contemporary guesses ranged from 500,000 to 600,000 shares. New York *Tribune*, November 29, 1879.

24. Herbert L. Satterlee, *J. Pierpont Morgan* (New York, 1939), 192.

25. New York *Sun*, November 29, 1879; New York *Times*, November 29, 1879.

26. *Railroad Gazette*, 12:158 (March 19, 1880). Thurber's role in the reform movement will be elaborated upon below.

27. The quotation is from pp. 5–8; the one below is from p. 26.

28. Hendrick in *McClure's Magazine*, 1908, p. 60.

29. Hepburn Committee, *Proceedings*, 4:3712–3716, 3720–3721, 3726, 3775.

30. *Ibid.*, 4:3873–3880.

31. New York State, *Assembly Document*, No. 2 (1880), 14–15.

32. New York *Times*, December 4, 1879.

33. Hepburn Committee, *Report,* 8–17. The remainder of the *Report* upholds the indictment against the roads.

34. *Ibid.,* 77–78.

35. The bills formed the Appendix to the committee's *Report.*

36. New York Chamber of Commerce, *Twenty-Second Annual Report,* 1:105.

37. *Ibid.,* 1:105.

38. N.Y.B.T.T., *Minutes,* February 11, 1880.

39. *Proceedings Before the Assembly Committee on Railroads on the Bill Entitled An Act to Regulate the Transportation of Freight by Railroad Corporation — Remarks of Hon. Barton A. Hepburn in Support of the Bill. Albany, March, 1880* (Albany, 1880), *passim.*

40. For the mercantile reaction to the Senate's action, see *Report of the Committee on Railway Transportation of the New York Board of Trade and Transportation — Adopted June 9th, 1880* (New York?, 1880?), 9–12.

41. New York *Times,* May 7, 1880.

42. New York Chamber of Commerce, *Twenty-Third Annual Report,* 1:53–55. The Board of Trade's position is found in the pamphlet cited above in n. 40.

43. N.Y.B.T.T., *Minutes,* February 18, 1880.

44. New York *Times,* March 7, 1880.

45. *Commercial and Financial Chronicle,* 30:368–369 (April 10, 1880).

46. New York *Commercial Advertiser,* April 29, 1880.

47. *Husbandman,* April 28, 1880, p. 4.

48. For the state of public opinion concerning the antidiscrimination bill, and the other Hepburn legislation see the editorials in the New York *Times,* February 6, April 15, 27, 29, May 7, 15, 19, 27, 1880.

49. *Husbandman,* July 28, 1880, p. 4.

50. *Ibid.,* August 11, 1880, p. 4.

51. Fowler to Thurber, August 10, 1880.

52. Hepburn Committee, *Proceedings,* 3:2710–2750. The information about the Commission is found on pp. 2723–2725.

53. *Husbandman,* July 7, 1880, pp. 1, 4, July 28, 1880, p. 5. August 4, 11, 18, 25, p. 4.

54. Rochester *Union and Advertiser,* August 25, 1880.

55. Hepburn Committee, *Proceedings,* 4:3728.

56. Rochester *Union and Advertiser,* December 9, 1880.

57. N.Y.B.T.T., *Minutes,* June 9, 1880.

58. *National Grange, Journal of Proceedings . . . 1880* (Philadelphia, 1880), 30.

59. New York Chamber of Commerce, *Twenty-Third Annual Report,* 1:80–83, 115. A large number of the replies to these questionnaires were found in the Thurber papers.

60. Black's letter was republished by the New York Board of Trade as a tract under the title, *A Half-Hour with One of the Great Questions of the Day* (New York? 1880?). In addition to the tens of thousands of copies broadcast by the board, the Farmers' Alliance printed 15,000 copies of Black's letter for distribution. *Husbandman,* December 22, 1880, p. 8.

61. *A Half Hour with One of the Great Questions of the Day,* 9.

62. *Ibid.,* 15.

63. *Railroad Gazette,* 12:656 (December 10, 1880); New York *Times,* December 3, 1880; New York *Commercial Advertiser,* December 9, 1880; New York *Tribune,* December 7, 1880.

64. *Letter to the Hon. H. J. Jewett, on the Relations of Railroads to the State and the United States, in the Matter of Freight Charges. In Answer to Judge Black. By George Ticknor Curtis* (New York, 1880).

65. New York *Times,* December 17, 1880.

66. See the brief but interesting interpretation of Gould's activities by Alexan-

der D. Noyes, *Forty Years of American Finance* (New York, 1909), 62–65. For a penetrating contemporary analysis of railroad consolidation see the editorial in the New York *Times,* December 6, 1880.

Chapter VIII. The National Anti-Monopoly League

1. New York *Evening Mail,* January 7, 1881; New York *Sunday Mercury,* February 20, 1881.
2. The League's "Address to the People," issued almost immediately after its organization, emphasized the Supreme Court's affirmation of the right of governments to regulate enterprises "affected with a public interest."
3. *Argument by Hon. Chauncey M. Depew before the Assembly Railroad Committee Against the Railroad Commission Bills and the Anti-Freight Discrimination Bills, in the Assembly Chamber* (Albany, 1882), 5–6.
4. *Ibid.,* 5.
5. *Nation,* 32:254–255 (April 14, 1881).
6. Nimmo to Thurber, July 10, 1882.
7. Letter signed "John Livingstone," in *Husbandman,* June 12, 1878.
8. New York *Daily Graphic,* February 1, 1881.
9. The Address consisted for the most part of Thurber's favorite quotations on the evils of monopoly but it is an excellent summation of the League's philosophy, objects, and methods of organization. A close reading demonstrates its derivatory nature; Thurber was not so much an original thinker as an excellent, hard working promoter, well attuned to popular currents and generally sympathetic to them.
10. Thurber later admitted that the League had been essentially a New York organization for some period of time. See his pamphlet, *Democracy and Anti-Monopoly. An Address . . . before the Thomas Jefferson Club of Brooklyn, April 16, 1883* (Brooklyn, 1883?), 7.
11. The information is contained in a printed letter of that date to the membership.
12. Printed letter to editor dated February 12, 1881.
13. New York *Times,* February 22, 1881. Even the *Tribune,* vigorously opposed to the League, conceded that it was "large" and most of those in attendance were "sincere and honest." Editorial, "Anti-Monopoly," February 23, 1881. The *Railroad Gazette,* 13:112 (February 25, 1881), hopefully expressed the opinion that the League wouldn't "get anywhere" because railroad rates were far lower than in Granger times. It did admit, however, that "there is doubtless a good deal of opposition on the part of many because of the great consolidations, and the union of a great number of companies, still independent, under the control of a comparatively small body of capitalists." For an interesting editorial emphasizing the strength of this opposition to "consolidation," and to "monopolies," see "The Impending Shadow," New York *Evening Post,* February 4, 1881.
14. New York *Times,* February 22, 1881.
15. New York *World,* February 25, 1881.
16. *Railroad Gazette,* 13:146 (March 11, 1881).
17. *Nation,* 32:199–200 (March 24, 1881).
18. *Ibid.,* 32:203 (March 24, 1881).
19. Charles Francis Adams, Jr., manuscript Diary, entries dated April 19, 20, 21, 23, 1881, in the Adams Collection, Massachusetts Historical Society.
20. *Nation,* 32:199–200, 242, 254–255, 258, 273–274, 295–296 (March 24, April 7, 14, 21, 28, 1881).
21. *Railroad Gazette,* 13:186 (April 1, 1881).
22. N.Y.B.T.T., *Minutes,* February 9, 1881.
23. Another factor influencing the decision to press for the railroad commission was that the Senators who had defeated the anti-discrimination bill of 1880 were still at Albany. New York *Times,* April 7, 1881.

24. *Argument of Chauncey M. Depew Before the Assembly Committee on Opposition to the Bills Providing for the Creation of a Board of Railroad Commissioners. March 16, 1881* (Chicago, 1882), 31. The *Times* (March 18, 1881) was of the opinion that Depew would not be successful in ridiculing the demand for a railroad commission. It was true, the paper maintained, that the roads had been more discreet since the Hepburn inquiry but that only proved the need for publicity in transportation. A good deal of weight is given to the *Times'* editorials in this chapter, because, on balance, it was found to be the best New York paper for the purposes of the present study. Its news coverage of the various movements for railroad reform was thorough and its editorial policy was sympathetic yet critical.

25. *Ibid.*, April 21, 1881. The vote was 74 to 33. The paper's comment upon the message is revealing: "It now remains to be seen what treatment the bill will receive in the Senate; in other words, what the disposition of the corporations toward it may be."

26. On the differences between the Stalwarts and Half-Breeds see Matthew Josephson, *The Politicos* (New York, 1938), 276–315; Thomas C. Cochran and William Miller, *The Age of Enterprise* (New York, 1942), 154–168.

27. Windom Committee, *Transportation Routes to the Seaboard*, 2:142–156, 312–322. I do not mean to suggest that Conkling was antirailroad by conviction but merely that he, as a professional politician whose main asset was popular support, was not adverse to posing as the sword-bearer of the people on properly dramatic or important occasions.

28. Josephson, *Politicos*, 304–305.

29. An incisive analysis of railroad methods of control, in both major parties, naming names and citing chapter and verse, was made at a conference held in Utica in the summer of 1881. What makes the analysis of particular interest is that the delegates approving the "Address to the People" were from the leading commercial and agricultural organizations in the state. Among numerous others, the New York Chamber of Commerce, Board of Trade and Transportation, Buffalo Board of Trade, Utica Board of Trade, New York State Miller's Association, New York State Grange, New York State Dairymen's Association. *Shall Railroads Be Servants or Masters? Abstract from Proceedings of Conference at Utica, August 18, 1881* (New York?, 1881?), 20–23. Depew's lieutenants are listed in De Alva S. Alexander, *A Political History of the State of New York* (New York, 1909), 3:466–469.

30. *Truth*, April 7, 1881.

31. A copy of the letter, dated March 25, 1881, is in the Thurber papers. The announcement of Robertson's appointment was made public March 23, 1881. It would be reasonable to conclude that Thurber's letter and the impressive mercantile petition two weeks later against the appointment was a factor in Conkling's decision to fight. It was guessed at the time that Conkling was shrewd enough to see that an Anti-Monopoly wind was blowing and set his sails accordingly. Brooklyn *Eagle*, May 20, 21, 22, 1881.

32. Alexander, *Political History of New York*, 3:408–475; Donald B. Chidsey, *The Gentleman from New York: A Life of Roscoe Conkling* (New Haven, 1935), 296–356. These accounts are adequate for the personal and intraparty aspects of the fight; they have nothing upon the underlying differences between Half-Breeds and Stalwarts. Robertson's employment by Vanderbilt, Chauncey Depew's affiliations, etc., also do not figure in these treatments. Robertson's nomination to the collectorship was flagrantly political. The incumbent, Edwin Merritt, had been appointed in 1878 after scandals forced President Hayes to remove Chester Arthur from the position. Merritt was not a Conkling man but Robertson was an open foe of the senator, and had split the New York delegation at the National Republican Convention in 1880 and helped to defeat Grant. The ex-president had been Conkling's candidate and Robertson's subsequent appointment to the juiciest political plum in New York was obviously intended, and taken, as a deliberate declaration of war.

33. Alexander, *Political History of New York*, 3:476–480.

34. As quoted in Chidsey, *Roscoe Conkling*, 257. Again no implication is in-

tended that Conkling actively opposed dominant groups on crucial issues; the point is he was not committed to support their stand at any cost. In this sense he was an independent politician, careful not to go out on unpopular limbs which might be sawed off and lose him control of votes. Depew, for example, was simply a railroad agent in politics — no question as to which way he would go on important issues. Conkling was primarily a politician who might or might not see eye to eye with railroad officers or other entrepreneurs. He called his own shots and when the pressures were strong enough could not be counted upon to do his duty to quell the populace.

35. Alexander, *Political History of New York*, 3:479. Alexander has nothing on the Central's role in the fight; that information comes from other sources. The Brooklyn *Eagle*, for example, some months later (October 1, 1881) summed up the matter in this fashion: "The main strength of the opposition to his [Conkling] return to the Senate was the political strength of the Central Railroad."

36. *Ibid.*, May 20, 1881. See also its editorial the next day warning against the Stalwart pretensions to antimonopoly, and New York *Times*, May 20, 1881.

37. New York *Commercial Advertiser*, June 9, 13, August 23, 1881; New York *Daily Graphic*, June 10, 1881.

38. New York *Herald*, June 22, 1881.

39. New York *Times*, May 6, 1881.

40. New York Chamber of Commerce, *Twenty-Third Annual Report*, 1:115–121.

41. Some of the comments upon Stanford's letter were printed in the pamphlet put out by the Chamber. *Report of the Special Committee on Railroad Transportation of the Chamber of Commerce . . . on the Reply Made by Hon. Leland Stanford . . . April 7th, 1881* (New York, 1881), 31–34.

42. *Ibid.*, 34.

43. Henry V. Poor, *Manual of the Railroads of the United States* (New York, 1881), li.

44. *Ibid.*, li–lxvi.

45. *Ibid.*, lxvi.

46. *Ibid.*, lxvii–lxxiii. The quotation is from p. lxxiii.

47. New York Chamber of Commerce, *Twenty-Fourth Annual Report* (New York, 1882), 1:45–47; New York *Times*, August 13, 1881.

48. N.Y.B.T.T., *Minutes*, May 11, June 8, 1881.

49. *Ibid.*, July 13, 1881. Handwritten lists of the officers of the branch leagues found in the Thurber papers are the basis for statements made below concerning the League's strength in New York City.

50. N.Y.B.T.T., *Minutes*, July 26, 1881.

51. New York *Times*, August 18, 19, 1881; New York *Daily Graphic*, August 19, 1881.

52. *Shall Railroads Be Servants or Master? — Abstract from Conference at Utica, August 18, 1881* (New York?, 1881?), 3–5, 10–11, 16–27.

53. *Ibid.*, 22–23, 27–28.

54. *Ibid.*, 10–11, 29.

55. New York *Times*, August 19, 1881.

56. Printed circular bearing the letterhead "The State Committee of the Utica Conference," found in the Thurber papers.

57. Alexander, *New York Political History*, 3:485.

58. New York *Daily Graphic*, October 13, 1881.

59. *The Tribune Almanac for 1882* (New York, n.d.), 19–20.

60. Alexander, *New York Political History*, 3:483–485.

61. New York *Times*, August 31, 1881.

62. *Ibid.*, October 4, 1881.

63. *Christian Union*, October 12, 1881.

64. New York *Times*, October 27, 1881.

65. New York *Evening Telegram*, November 18, 1881.

66. New York *Daily Graphic,* November 9, 10, 1881.

67. New York *Evening Telegram,* November 18, 1881; *Husbandman,* November 23, 1881, p. 4. For an interesting editorial on the significance of the election results, see New York *Daily Graphic,* November 10, 1881. For other views, see New York *Times,* November 12, December 12, 1881.

68. N.Y.B.T.T., *Proceedings, Annual Meeting,* January 11, 1882 (New York, 1882), 10–11.

69. National Grange, *Journal of Proceedings . . . 1880* (Philadelphia, 1880), 23, 28–31.

70. Woodman to Thurber, May 14, 1881.

71. National Grange, *Journal of Proceedings . . . 1881* (Philadelphia, 1881), 19–22. The quotation is from p. 21.

72. *Ibid.,* 97–101.

73. This observation is based largely on a close reading of the National Grange *Proceedings,* but it is supported by impressionistic material from a wide variety of other sources.

74. *Journal of Proceedings . . . 1880,* 74–78.

75. New York *Star,* January 19, 1882.

76. The situation is discussed in detail in the New York *Times,* February 2, 5, 9, 19, 1882. There are numerous newspaper clippings in the Thurber papers which indicate the wide publicity given to the League.

77. Albany *Argus,* February 3, 1882. A detailed description of the meeting was given in the paper's news columns the day before.

78. *Argument by Hon. Chauncey M. Depew before the Assembly Railroad Committee . . . March 9th, 1882,* 4, 13–14. Depew maintained that both the Board of Trade and Transportation and the Chamber of Commerce had so much confidence in Thurber that they endorsed the Boyd bill (patterned after the Georgia Commission) without knowing what it was.

79. Albany *Argus,* February 2, 1882.

80. Telegram signed Thomas Carroll, dated February 2, 1882.

81. Nichols to Thurber, February 4, 1882.

82. Nichols to Thurber, February 15, 1882.

83. New York *Times,* February 5, 1882.

84. Francis B. Thurber, *Democracy and Anti-Monopoly. An Address . . . before the Thomas Jefferson Club of Brooklyn, April 16th, 1883* (New York?, 1883?), 6.

85. The clipping containing this statement in the Thurber papers appears to have been printed in the March 1, 1881, issue.

86. New York *Times,* March 1, 2, 1882.

87. Nichols to Thurber, March 1, 1882. For Anti-Monopoly statements repudiating the *Times'* interpretation see the *Husbandman,* March 8, 1882, p. 4.

88. Printed letter dated March 25, 1882, bearing the National Anti-Monopoly League heading.

89. These statements are based upon handwritten receipts for expenses paid found in the Thurber papers and a letter from Gardner to Thurber, December 28, 1881.

90. Memorandum dated February 2, 1882, signed, "Sabin Hough."

91. Full accounts of the preliminaries and the meeting itself are found in the *Husbandman,* April 12, 19, 1882, p. 4, May 3, 1882, p. 2, May 10, p. 2, 4, 8, May 17, 1882, p. 2. The letters and speeches of Peter Cooper, Thomas Kinsella, John Kelly, and L. E. Chittenden rang all the changes on the corporation threat to Jeffersonian ideals.

92. The Produce Exchange, Chamber of Commerce, Board of Trade and Transportation, and numerous other commercial organizations strongly supported the amendment, but the League and its membership actually carried out most of the work.

93. As an undated note from George Proctor to Thurber put it, "The papers of the interior counties Delaware for instance oppose free canals hotly."

94. *Husbandman,* November 15, 1882, p. 4. For the views of a farm journal opposed to the free canal amendment, see, *Orange County Farmer,* October 6, 1881, p. 4, December 8, 1881, p. 4, March 2, 1882, p. 4, January 9, 1882, p. 4, March 2, 1882, p. 4, May 11, 1882, p. 4, June 6, 1882, p. 4, September 14, 1882, p. 4, December 27, 1883, p. 4, February 21, 1884, p. 4. The *Farmer* quoted extensively from numerous rural papers throughout the state in opposition to the canal amendment and accurately reflected agrarian views as the *Husbandman,* self-confessedly, did not.

95. *Orange County Farmer,* April 19, 1883, p. 4.

96. New York *Times,* May 26, 1882.

97. New York *Evening Post,* May 26, 1882.

Chapter IX. Justice for All

1. Armstrong to Thurber, June 20, 1882.

2. Nimmo to Thurber, July 13, 1882.

3. For extensive press comment on the legislature's record see the New York *Times,* June 5, 1882.

4. As quoted in *Justice,* August 26, 1881, p. 1. "We have received a unique pamphlet from the Anti-Monopoly League . . . This pamphlet is the first of the kind ever published, and as a work of ready reference will be invaluable to every politician and voter."

5. New York *Times,* June 16, 17, 1882.

6. *Ibid.,* June 16, 1882.

7. *The Anti-Monopoly League Presents with Sorrow the Following Concerning the Record of the Legislature of 1882* (New York?, 1882?), 21. Without developing the point here, the phrase "millionaires and tramps," usually associated with the Populists of the 1890's, suggests the role of the Anti-Monopoly League in paving the way for later reform movements. Numerous other slogans, symbols, and concepts can be pointed to in this connection.

8. The paper's masthead only identified it as published "under the auspices, and with the advice, of leading members of the Anti-Monopoly League." But a form letter written by Thurber stated that "Mr. Peter Cooper, Mr. F. B. Thurber, and two or three other gentlemen are backing the paper." That Thurber wrote the letter is clear from the fact that in the original copy the word "myself" was struck out and "Mr. F. B. Thurber" substituted. An extensive, although not complete, file of the paper was found in the Thurber papers.

The letter referred to above states that 30,000 copies were published weekly during the first four months. Its paid circulation, however, judging from a few weekly reports made up for Thurber's information, ranged from 4,000 to 5,000 during the first year of publication, and appeared to be tapering off after the summer of 1883. A memorandum from Frank S. Gardner to Thurber gave the breakdown of the copies distributed gratis: politicians, clergymen, college presidents, "Men who Make Public Opinion," "Labor Men," Grange officers, judges, newspapers in New York State, etc.

9. Smith to Thurber, August 20, 1882.

10. Copy of a letter from Thurber to Weaver, November 21, 1881.

11. Thurber's remarks weren't printed in *Justice* but he wrote a summary of them which indicates what he said. The summary was found in his papers.

12. *Justice,* August 26, 1882, p. 1.

13. *Ibid.* The editorial on p. 2 obviously was intended to pave the way for a declaration of political independence: "We must have *Justice for all! —* and perhaps the only way we can obtain it is to cut loose from the old parties."

14. See the letter by L. E. Chittenden to the leader of the freight-handlers' union in the same issue on p. 1.

15. The quotation and the platform are found in "The Impending Crisis," *Document No. 14 Issued by the National Anti-Monopoly League* (New York?, 1882?), 15–17.

16. See, for example, his paper read before the XIX Century Club, *Our Country* (New York?, 1885?), a title which may have been inspired by Josiah Strong's famous tract of the same year.

17. *Justice,* August 5, 1882, p. 4. This "Socialistic Manifesto" was a reprint of an editorial from *Truth,* a New York daily paper supporting Henry George.

18. See an editorial taking this line in *Justice,* August 5, 1882, p. 2.

19. Anti-Monopoly League, *Document No. 14,* 4, 6, 12, 13, 14.

20. *Justice,* August 12, 1882, p. 1.

21. New York *Sun,* September 7, 1882.

22. New York *Times,* September 12, 15, 1882.

23. See the editorial "Jay Gould's New Man," in the New York *Times,* August 17, 1882; *Justice,* September 2, 1882, p. 2.

24. New York *Sun,* August 26, 1882; *Justice,* September 2, 1882, p. 2.

25. *Ibid.,* September 23, 1882, p. 1.

26. *Ibid.,* September 23, 1882, p. 1.

27. New York *Times,* September 14, 1882.

28. *Ibid.,* September 14, 1882.

29. *Justice,* September 23, 1882, p. 1.

30. *Ibid.,* September 30, 1882, p. 1.

31. *Ibid.,* p. 1. The issue contained a roundup of editorials from leading Republican papers.

32. *Ibid.,* p. 1.

33. *Ibid.,* September 23, 1882, p. 2.

34. *Ibid.,* September 9, 1882, p. 2.

35. *Ibid.,* October 14, 1882, pp. 1, 2.

36. *Ibid.,* p. 2.

37. Allan Nevins, *Grover Cleveland* (New York, 1947 printing), 76–77.

38. The League's policy of swallowing the Democratic ticket whole apparently caused a good deal of uneasiness even among those Republicans who agreed to accept it. See the editorial in the *Husbandman,* October 11, 1882, p. 4. Alexander S. Diven, however, felt so strongly about the endorsement of the Democrats that he resigned from the League.

39. *Justice,* October 14, 1882, p. 2.

40. *Ibid.,* October 28, 1882, p. 4.

41. *Ibid.,* October 14, 1882, p. 1.

42. The quotation is from the New York *Herald* as printed in *Justice,* September 30, 1882, p. 2. In its next issue (October 7) the paper printed a roundup press criticism of Gould's threat. The three papers owned or controlled by Gould and his partner, Cyrus Field, were the New York *Tribune, World,* and *Mail and Express.*

43. *Justice,* October 14, 1882, p. 1.

44. For a copy of the interview see the New York *Times,* October 9, 1882. That the expression was not new to Mr. Vanderbilt is evident from the testimony of one of the *Graphic's* editorial writers. In an interview with him Vanderbilt had "used the same exclamation regarding various matters at least a dozen times." *Justice,* October 28, 1882, p. 2.

45. See, for example, Hepburn Committee, *Report,* 76.

46. New York *Times,* October 9, 1882. See also the editorial the next day entitled, "The Contentment of Croesus."

47. See the use to which Vanderbilt's phrase was put in *Justice,* October 28, 1882, p. 1.

48. New York *Evening Post,* November 8, 1882.

49. New York *Times,* November 8, 1882.

50. Compiled from the statistics in the *Tribune Almanac for 1881,* 42, 48, 54, 62–64, 77, and the *Tribune Almanac for 1883,* 47, 52, 58, 67–70, 79. Though the percentage shift was slightly greater in Massachusetts, Ben Butler's personal following in the Bay State largely accounts for the Democratic sharp gains in that state, in my opinion.

51. *Justice,* October 21, 1882, p. 1.

52. New York *Times,* November 14, 1882.

53. *Husbandman,* November 29, 1882, p. 2. The quotations below are from the same page.

54. *Ibid.,* May 9, 1883, p. 4. The attack on Cleveland was in the form of an open letter from J. G. Shepard, a Democrat and one of the men responsible for Cleveland's endorsement by Anti-Monopoly.

55. Letter signed "Kings County," *Justice,* March 17, 1883, p. 3. The League appears to have been fairly strong in Brooklyn for the letter pointed out that every Kings County Assemblyman — Republican as well as Democratic — voted to override Cleveland's veto of the five-cent fare bill. As indicated below this was the occasion for Cleveland's repudiation of the Democratic platform on transportation.

56. *Husbandman,* May 9, 1883, p. 4.

57. For a contrary view, see Nevins, *Cleveland,* 107–124.

58. New York *Times,* February 26, 1883. The *Times'* Albany correspondent apparently had excellent sources of information; at least his predictions of the course Cleveland would take on various issues were fulfilled.

59. New York *Herald,* January 11, 1883.

60. New York *Times,* September 12, 1882. McCarthy, Sr., was a leading Half-Breed politician, and worked hand in hand with Chauncey Depew. The information that John D. Kernan was the legal counsellor of the "Merchants, Manufacturers, and Farmers' Union," is found in *Justice,* August 9, 1884, p. 10. The Albany correspondent of the New York *Times,* discussing the appointments on January 11, 1883, had this to say of Kernan: "In a movement of merchants and manufacturers last Spring against the Railroad Commission Act Kernan acted with them."

61. Letter signed "A Friend of the Canals," *Justice,* August 2, 1884, p. 9.

62. *Ibid.,* p. 9. See also New York *Herald,* January 11, 1883; New York *Times,* January 11, 1883.

63. *Ibid.*

64. *Ibid.,* January 15, 1883.

65. This letter is cited in n. 55 above. It was reprinted in *Justice,* June 28, 1884, pp. 9–10, and was used extensively against Cleveland during the 1884 campaign. In this connection, see the letter signed "A Friend of the Canals," the letter on the same page by L. E. Chittenden, and New York *Times,* January 15, 1883.

66. *Ibid.,* March 3, 1883.

67. New York *Tribune,* March 2, 1883. On March 8, after Cleveland acceded to the petition and was upheld by the legislature, the Rochester *Union and Advertiser* termed it "The Triumph of a Billion Dollars and the Corporation."

68. New York *World,* March 3, 1883.

69. New York *Tribune,* March 3, 1883.

70. The usual accounts of Cleveland's veto only mention the $13,000,000 of water added to the elevated roads by Jay Gould, but this is a gross understatement. Even Cleveland's two nominees to the railroad commission found that of the $47,318,000 capital claimed by the elevated roads, only $22,683,253.14 represented actual cost of production. New York State Board of Railroad Commissioners, *Annual Report . . . for the Fiscal Year Ending September 30, 1883* (Albany, 1884), 1:111–112.

71. *Ibid.,* 1:119–131. The quotation is from p. 130. The information is found in Commissioner O'Donnell's minority report on the elevated roads. For a more favorable assessment of Cleveland's veto, see Nevins, *Grover Cleveland,* 115–118.

72. New York *Herald,* March 3, 1883. See also the strongly critical editorials in the *Times,* March 3, 4, 7, 8, 1883.

73. *Ibid.,* March 6, 1883.

74. New York *Times,* January 15, 1883.

75. *Ibid.,* February 26, 1883. Further information about Cary's relation to Cleveland is found in the issue for March 8, 1883.

76. *Ibid.,* March 3, 1883.

77. W. A. Poucher to Cleveland, February 14, 1883. Cleveland papers, Library of Congress.

78. S. S. Cox to John Reagan, April 29, 1883. A microfilm copy of the Reagan papers held by the University of Texas is in the Columbia University Library, and all Reagan letters cited below are from the microfilm copy.

79. Letter signed Charles Wyllys Elliot, *Justice,* May 5, 1883, p. 3. There is a gap of several months in the file of *Justice* I used, and this is the first indication I noticed of its disapproval. Elliot was a leading figure in New York and there is even a possibility that he was editing the paper at the time.

80. Burrows to Thurber, May 19, 1882. The continuity of the relationship, and the respect in which Thurber was held by the Nebraskan, is indicated in another letter to Thurber, December 17, 1883.

81. The circular bears the date line, May, 1882, and is signed by J. Burrows, secretary of the State Alliance. Burrows was an important figure in the movement and later became president of the National Farmers' Alliance, that is, the Northern Alliance.

82. *Justice,* May 5, 1883, p. 3.

83. *Ibid.,* June 30, 1883, p. 4.

84. *Ibid.,* July 14, 1883, pp. 1, 3.

85. *Ibid.,* p. 3.

86. *Ibid.* The New York *Times* commented on July 5, 1883, that the Anti-Monopoly "party" was already split over the tariff question.

87. *Justice,* July 14, 1883, p. 3.

88. *Ibid.,* p. 1.

89. *Ibid.,* August 11, 1883, p. 4. The resolution to dissolve stated that the original League had consisted "largely of citizens of New York."

90. *Ibid.,* October 6, 1883, pp. 4–5.

91. In addition to these issues which split the farmers away from the Anti-Monopolists, New York City opposition to an equalization of the tax burden between real estate and personal property aroused rural hostility.

92. *Justice,* November 10, 1883, pp. 4, 5.

93. New York *Times,* November 7, 1883.

94. *Justice,* December 15, 1883, p. 9.

95. *John Swinton's Paper,* October 14, 1883.

96. *Justice,* May 24, 1884, pp. 3–4, 8.

97. Butler explained his course of action in this fashion: "The nomination of Mr. Cleveland I looked upon as a victory of the free traders of New York City . . . Looking at the men who were gathered around Mr. Cleveland and at the doctrines they entertained, I thought I foresaw great danger to the country in his election. If the Republican party won, the preservation of the tariff was assured. I thought I would see, by a fusion of the Greenback party and the Democrats in the Western States and in New Jersey and New York, if enough votes could not be procured to prevent the election of Mr. Cleveland by getting enough electoral votes for the fusion ticket.

"I labored assiduously throughout the campaign to this end." Benjamin F. Butler, *Butler's Book* (Boston, 1892), 982–983. Butler ran on the Greenback as well as on the Anti-Monopoly ticket which hampered the independent movement considerably. He seems to have done everything possible both to prevent Cleveland's election and the emergence of a strong third party.

98. *Justice,* June 28, 1884, pp. 1, 8, 9–10, July 5, 1884, p. 8, August 2, 1884, pp. 8, 9–10, August 9, 1884, pp. 9–10, August 16, 1884, pp. 8–9; *Husbandman,* August 20, 1884, p. 1. In considering the reasons for the precipitous drop in Cleveland's plurality from approximately 192,000 in 1882 to approximately 1,000 in 1884, historians might do well to weigh the violent antipathy to his record as governor and the all-out attack upon him by Anti-Monopoly and labor groups.

99. As reprinted in *Justice,* October 11, 1884, pp. 9–10.

100. *Nation,* 37:368 (October 30, 1884); New York *Times,* October 7, 1884.

101. *Husbandman,* August 27, 1884, p. 1.

102. National Grange, *Journal of Proceedings . . . 1885* (Philadelphia, 1885), 103; *Journal of Proceedings . . . 1886* (Philadelphia, 1886), 127–128.

103. James F. Hudson, *The Railways and the Republic* (New York, 1886), 345–348.

Chapter X. New York and the Interstate Commerce Act

1. Josiah Quincy, *Public Interest and Private Monopoly. An Address Delivered Before the Boston Board of Trade, October 16, 1867* (Boston, 1867); *Cheap Food Dependent on Cheap Transportation. An Address Delivered Before the Boston Social Science Association, Jan. 14, 1869 by Josiah Quincy, Its President* (Boston, 1869).

2. Charles Francis Adams, *Railroad Legislation* (Boston, 1868), 3, 22, 29. This is a reprint of an article which had previously appeared in both the *American Law Review* and *Hunt's Merchants' Magazine.*

3. The substance of several articles from 1868 to 1871 is conveniently found in Charles F. Adams, Jr., and Henry Adams, *Chapters of Erie* (Boston, 1871), 333–429. See also, *Speech of Charles Francis Adams, Jr., on Behalf of the Mass. Board of Railroad-Commissioners, Made Before the Joint Standing Legislative Committee on Railways, February 14, 1873* (Boston, 1873); *The Railroad Problem; A Lecture by Charles Francis Adams, Jr. Delivered at the Lowell Institute, in Boston, February 26, 1875* (New York, 1875); *Railroads; Their Origins and Problems* (rev. ed., New York, 1887). Adams' reference to William Galt's influence probably refers to the latter's *Railway Reform: Its Importance and Practicability Considered as Affecting the Nation, the Shareholders, and the Government* (London, 1865).

4. *Report from the Joint Select Committee of the House of Lords and the House of Commons on Railway Companies Amalgamation. . . . 2 August 1872.* That the western agrarian leaders were cognizant of, and impressed by, the Parliamentary *Report* can be seen from W. C. Flagg's references to it in his address at the Northwestern Farmer's Convention, October 1873, reprinted in Windom Committee, *Transportation Routes to the Seaboard,* 2:662. Flagg obviously was also impressed with the comments of C. F. Adams, Jr. on the reports, and his entire address is indicative of the European and eastern influences upon American thinking about railroads. For other references to the *Report* see *ibid.,* 1:112–115; S. Shellabarger, "The Domestic Commerce of the United States," *International Review,* 1:839–840 (November–December 1874); *Nation,* 18:295 (May 7, 1874); Adams, *Speech Before Legislative Committee, 1873,* 28–30. I am indebted to James C. Malin of the University of Kansas for suggesting to me the basic importance of the Parliamentary *Report's* impact upon American economic thought relative to railroads.

5. Parliamentary Select Committee, *Report, 1872,* 1:xviii. For the investigation and the subsequent legislation see Edward Cleveland-Stevens, *English Railways; Their Development and Their Relation to the State* (London, 1915), 251–279. That American railroad agitation after the Civil War needs to be viewed against the background of developments in England and Europe is seen from this contemporary observation by Arthur T. Hadley: "The years 1870–3 are marked by a change in the aims of railroad legislation, more obvious perhaps than in principles of railroad management twenty years earlier. A noticeable thing about the changes of legislative

aim was the suddenness with which they made themselves felt all over the world . . . In the years immediately following 1872, the Granger movement did its work in the United States; the Railway Commission was established in England; Belgium and Prussia determined to change from a mixed system to a system of state ownership pure and simple; France and Italy began a policy — eventually unsuccessful — of state purchase and management. The general object was the same in every case. Hitherto legislation had been conceived from the standpoint of the investor — whether that investor was a private company or the state itself, mattered little. Hence-forward things were looked at from the standpoint of the shipper, and especially of those shippers who under the old system were being driven to the wall." *Railroad Transportation: Its History and Its Laws* (impression 15, New York, 1903), 22–23. Hadley's book was first published in 1885.

6. Adams, *Speech Before Legislative Committee, 1873,* 28–30, 33–39. Apparently Adams read the Parliamentary *Report* soon after publication. See entry in his manuscript Diary, October 21, 1872. While in Europe in 1873 he conscientiously sought out information concerning railroad legislation everywhere he went. See manuscript Diary, June 11, 14, 17, July 29, August 1, 20, 21, 23, September 2, 3, 1873.

7. Originally printed in 1883, the article is conveniently found in his *Railways in the United States* (New York, 1912). The report to Cleveland is published as a separate: "Report to the Honorable Thomas F. Bayard, Secretary of State of the United States, On the Relations of the Governments of the Nations of Western Europe to the Railways, By Simon Sterne, January 18, 1887," *Senate Miscellaneous Document,* No. 66, 49 Congress, 2 Session (Washington, 1887).

8. Hepburn Committee, *Proceedings,* 4:4010–4012.

9. Sterne, *Report on Relation of Government to Railways,* 7–8; Charles L. Raper, *Railway Transportation: A History of Its Economics and of Its Relation to the State* (New York, 1912), 254–255.

10. Sterne, *Report on the Relations of Governments to Railways,* 20.

11. The difference in emphasis is seen in *Review of the Report of U.S. Senate Committee on Transportation Routes by the Committee on Railway Transportation of the New York Cheap Transportation Association, May 12, 1874* (New York?, 1874?).

12. *Proceedings of the National Commercial Convention, Held in Boston, February, 1868* (Boston, 1868), 121–124; *Proceedings of the Second Annual Meeting of the National Board of Trade, Held in Richmond, December, 1869* (Boston, 1870), 74–123.

13. *Proceedings of the Adjourned Meeting of the National Board of Trade, Held in Baltimore, January, 1874* (Chicago, 1874), 144–157.

14. Even a generous list would number less than a dozen names: Charles Francis Adams, Jr., Henry C. Adams, Edward Atkinson, George R. Blanchard, Thomas M. Cooley, Albert Fink, Arthur T. Hadley, Joseph Nimmo, Jr., Henry V. Poor, Simon Sterne, Francis B. Thurber. Possibly others might be included but the main point here is the relative scarcity of personnel equipped to deal with the complexities of the American railroad system.

15. Massachusetts Railroad Commissioners, *Ninth Annual Report* (Boston, 1878), 79. The *Report* is dated "Boston, Dec. 14, 1877."

16. Solon J. Buck, *The Granger Movement* (Cambridge, Mass., 1913), 226.

17. *Proceedings of the Seventh Annual Meeting of the National Board of Trade, Held in Philadelphia, June 1875* (Chicago, 1875), 30–31, 37–38.

18. *Ibid.,* 92–105.

19. *Ibid.,* 192–211.

20. New York Cheap Transportation Association, *Minutes,* July 13, 1875.

21. *Proceedings of the Eighth Annual Meeting of the National Board of Trade, Held in New York, June 1876* (Chicago, 1876), 173–174. The Philadelphia Board of Trade also introduced a resolution concerning railroads but it did not involve

government legislation, and the debate reveals that it was overshadowed by the New York proposal.

22. *Ibid.,* 174–184. The report of the Executive Council, while critical of various aspects of the railroad system, demonstrates that rate wars ended complaints against railroad extortion. "The era of high charges has in many instances, especially on the great lines of inter-state traffic, been succeeded by rates formerly deemed wholly inadequate for the service, and the popular sympathy would now perhaps be more properly extended to the carriers than to their patrons." *Ibid.,* 21.

23. A printed report was distributed to delegates on the topic of Bills of Lading which had sharp things to say about the railroad system and called for Congressional investigation of the railroad system. But the committee having the matter in charge "had no resolutions in regard to it [the report]." *Proceedings of the Ninth Annual Meeting of the National Board of Trade, Held in Milwaukee, August, 1877* (Chicago, 1877), 179–188. Attendance at the 1877 session was limited, action was inconclusive, and the board's failure to meet in 1878 suggests that the pressures of deepening economic crisis found its constituent bodies at a loss to grapple with the problems of the first modern depression.

24. This statement is based upon the compilation in Samuel W. Briggs, *Regulation of Interstate Commerce. History of Bills and Resolutions Introduced in Congress Respecting Federal Regulation of Interstate Commerce by Railways, etc., from the Thirty-Seventh Congress to the Sixty-Second Congress, Inclusive, 1862–1913* (Washington, 1913), 5–9. The peak of agitation in the decade, using the number of bills introduced as the index, was in the 1872–1874 period. No comparable interest was shown until the early eighties. *Ibid.,* 9–13.

25. New York Board of Trade and Transportation, *Minutes,* September 12, 1877.

26. For summary statements of various local movements for railroad regulation in the South and Far West during the middle and late seventies see Solon J. Buck, *The Granger Movement* (Cambridge, Mass., 1913), 194–205; Maxwell Ferguson, *State Regulation of Railroads in the South* (New York, 1916), 41–45; James F. Doster, *Alabama's First Railroad Commission: 1881–1885* (University, Alabama, 1949), 10–24. The last work cited contains material which suggests that intensive study of railroad regulatory movements in the South would demonstrate that, as in the West and East, merchants rather than Patrons of Husbandry were the dominant figures.

27. *Railroad Combinations and Discriminations — Speech of Honorable James H. Hopkins, of Pennsylvania, in the House of Representatives, May 29, 1876* (Washington, 1876), 3–5, 6–7.

28. *Congressional Record,* 13:146 (Appendix, 47 Congress, 1 Session); *ibid.,* 16:63, 97 (48 Congress, 2 Session).

29. See the exchange between Reagan and one of the promoters of those local roads, Rep. Phelps, in *Congressional Record,* 16:523.

30. *Ibid.,* 7:3404 (45 Congress, 2 Session); 13:134 (Appendix, 47 Congress, 1 Session).

31. Reagan's report to Samuel S. Randall is found in the National Archives as "Original Report No. 245" of the 45 Congress, 2 Session. It contains George B. Hibbard's pamphlet, carefully edited so as to form part of the report. The pamphlet is *Memoranda as to Authorities, etc. Establishing the Power of Congress to Pass a Law Providing for Equality in Rates of Freight, etc. upon Property Carried Wholly or Partly by Railroad, in Commerce between the States or with Foreign Nations* (Buffalo, N. Y., February 6, 1878). For Hibbard's role in the Reagan Bill, see Ida M. Tarbell, *The History of the Standard Oil Company* (New York, 1904), 213–215.

32. *Congressional Record,* 16:63. See also the comment by Rep. Rice, *ibid.,* 16:97.

33. *Ibid.,* 7:3326.

34. *Ibid.,* 7:3275–3280, 8:94–96, 10:4020–4026, 11:362–364, 1156, 13: 4542, and 130–142 (Appendix), 16:25–31, 287–294.

35. *Ibid.*, 7:3276–3277.

36. *Ibid.*, 7:3397–3398.

37. *Ibid.*, 7:3392–3408, 8:99–101, 16:47–48, 60–62, 119, 199, 397, 400, 524. The quotation is from 8:100 (Rep. Phillips of Kansas). Sectional unanimity didn't exist. Local considerations somewhat complicated the pattern but the generalization made above is not thereby invalidated.

38. *Ibid.*, 8:96.

39. *Ibid.*, 7:3392–3394.

40. A clear expression of the process whereby States' Rights views were used to rationalize western opposition to essential features of the bill is provided by Rep. Bragg of Wisconsin. *Ibid.*, 7:3392–3393. Rep. Henderson's attack on Thurber, quoted below, is found in 10:4030–4031.

41. N.Y.B.T.T., *Minutes*, February 13, 1878, Annual Meeting, January 8, 1879.

42. *Minutes*, March 13, April 10, 1878, Annual Meeting, January 8, 1879.

43. *Husbandman*, January 15, 1879, p. 4. See also the issue for July 30, 1879, p. 2, for a reprinted article from the New Orleans *Picayune* describing the pigeon-holing of Reagan's bill.

44. N.Y.B.T.T., *Minutes*, March 12, June 11, 1879.

45. *American Grocer*, 22:125–126 (July 17, 1879). See also Simon Sterne's statement on "National and State Legislation" in Hepburn Committee, *Proceedings*, 4:4031–4034.

46. *Argument of Albert Fink before the Committee on Commerce of the United States House of Representatives: Washington, March 17 and 18, 1882* (Washington, 1882), 37. See also Edwin R. A. Seligman, "Railway Tariffs and the Interstate Commerce Law," *Political Science Quarterly*, 2: 240 (June 1887).

47. *Proceedings of the Tenth Annual Meeting of the National Board of Trade . . . December, 1879* (Boston, 1880), 46–83, 113–114. The quotation is from p. 46. Citations to the *Proceedings* henceforth will take the same form: the first note will give all the pages pertinent to railroad regulation and only direct quotations will be cited by page. Unless the entire discussion at each meeting is read the arguments appear out of context.

48. *Ibid.*, 70.

49. *Ibid.*, 47.

50. *Ibid.*, 64.

51. *Husbandman*, December 17, 1878, p. 8.

52. Letter dated February 24, 1880, New York Board of Trade and Transportation, found in the Reagan collection. It was sent to him along with the letter cited in n. 53 below.

53. N.Y.B.T.T. per A. B. Miller, to Reagan, March 2, 1880

54. Miller to Reagan, March 18, 1880.

55. N.Y.B.T.T., *Minutes*, June 9, 1880.

56. The petitions are found in the National Archives filed under the symbol, Senate 46A–H8.

57. New York Chamber of Commerce, *Twenty-Third Annual Report*, 1:53–55.

58. Milwaukee *Sentinel*, November 27, 1880. The *Sentinel* answered the questionnaire in the proper spirit.

59. *Proceedings of the Eleventh Annual Meeting of the National Board of Trade . . . December, 1880* (Boston, 1881), 96–98. All meetings of the board were held in Washington after 1879 to facilitate the process of bringing its views to the attention of Congress. Almost invariably, they were held just before or at the same time as the Congressional hearings on interstate commerce.

60. New York Chamber of Commerce, *Twenty-Third Annual Report*, 1:80–87.

61. See Reagan's comments in *Congressional Record*, 13:141 (Appendix), 16:31.

62. Reagan to Thurber, September 16, 1879. The Texan's position grew more inflexible in the course of time. In 1882 he was still willing to agree to a commission as an "experiment"; by December 1884 he was warning that no matter how

patriotic and honest the president who would make such appointments "we must remember that the railroad corporations, few in numbers as to the heads that control them, can easily combine their influence and bring to bear by indirection, if they dare not do it directly, influences which will be likely to control in the appointment of commissioners . . . In my judgment, when we look at what has occurred in the majority of the States that have appointed commissioners, when we remember that State Legislatures have been suborned, that courts of justice have been corrupted, that even governors of States have been improperly influenced in their action by the power of these corporations, we should rather trust the rights of the people in the hands of the courts of the country than to commit them to three particular individuals, whose jurisdiction at most can be partial." He acknowledged that other genuine advocates of control favored a commission; he also noted, however, that all the railroad companies and their attorneys did. *Congressional Record*, 13:141 (Appendix), 16:31.

63. The effect of the division in the ranks was emphasized since other Congressmen could oppose Reagan's bill, plump for a mild commission along the lines of Massachusetts or New York, and point to support for a commission by L. E. Chittenden, Simon Sterne, J. J. White, J. G. Shepard — leaders of New York City merchants and upstate farmers. Candor did not compel the admission, however, that these men nonetheless favored Reagan's bill, as well as a stronger commission than that proposed by Representative Davis of Illinois. *Ibid.*, 16:117–119.

64. *Proceedings of the Fourteenth Annual Meeting of the National Board of Trade . . . January 1884* (Boston, 1884), 111–116. Sterne conceded, however, that America was not yet ready to go as far as England had.

65. National Anti-Monopoly League, *Address to the People* (New York?, 1881?), 14. For Stanford's position see *Report of the Special Committee on Railroad Transportation of the Chamber of Commerce of the State of New York, on the Reply Made by Hon. Leland Stanford. . . . to the Questions on the Railroad Problem, Propounded by the Committee. April 7th, 1881* (New York, 1881), 11–24.

66. *Address to the People*, 19. In the midst of the Conkling-Depew fight, and after President Garfield's appointments gave rise to the conviction that railroads controlled the Presidency, the League issued a document entitled, *Is There Any Danger?* I have not found any copies, but *Justice*, Thurber's paper, published an extract which expresses well the sense of foreboding developing in the early eighties concerning corporate designs on the national government. "Recent political events have induced the National Anti-Monopoly League to call attention to some significant facts, indicating a settled purpose on the part of the great railway and telegraph monopolies of the United States.

"The decision of the Supreme Court of the United States in the Granger cases which affirmed the right of the people through their legislatures, to control corporations, was one of the most important declarations of public rights since the Declaration of Independence, and indications have since been frequent that the monopolists have decided upon a settled programme to: 1st. Elect a President in their interest. 2nd. Reconstitute the Supreme Court, and reverse the Granger decisions. 3rd. Pack the Senate of the United States." As quoted in *American Grocer*, 25:1224–1225 (May 26, 1881).

67. Reagan's speech was printed as part of a *Document* of the National Anti-Monopoly League. *Speech of Hon. John H. Reagan . . . and Speech of Hon. W. J. Fowler . . . at the Mass Meeting of the National Anti-Monopoly League, Held at Cooper Institute, New York, February 21, 1881* (New York? 1881?), 3–11. Secretary Windom did not actually attend the meeting but sent a strong letter, frequently quoted thereafter. He soon resigned from the cabinet and was reëlected to the Senate; however, he does not appear to have played a significant role in railroad agitation subsequently.

68. Henry Nichols to Reagan, January 16, 1884; Thomas Cator to Reagan, January 30, 1884; Frank S. Gardner to Reagan, February 15, 1884.

69. Atkinson to J. H. Reall, January 11, 1881. All Atkinson correspondence is

in the collection bearing his name at the Massachusetts Historical Society. His letter-books have been preserved and contain contemporary indexes. Unfortunately, some of the most intriguing entries listed have been ripped out. For a sympathetic but critical evaluation of his work and its influence see Harold Williamson, *Edward Atkinson: The Biography of an American Liberal, 1827–1905* (Boston, 1934).

70. Atkinson to Reall, March 7, 1881.

71. Reall to Atkinson, March 14, 1881.

72. Atkinson to Luigi Cossa, May 4, 1881.

73. Correspondence flew thick and fast and will only be cited here in part to indicate the roads' deep interest in the article. Atkinson to Albert Fink, March 21, 1881, Fink to Atkinson, March 25, 1881, Atkinson to Fink, March 28, 1881; Atkinson to J. M. Forbes, April 4, 1881; C. P. Huntington to Atkinson, June 13, 1881; Charles E. Perkins to Atkinson, June 7, 15, 1881; Atkinson to Reall, April 5, 12, 13, 14, June 16, July 19, 1881; Reall to Atkinson, April 13, June 10, July 21, August 1, September 17, 1881; Atkinson to G. H. Putnam, September 22, 1884; Atkinson to Chauncey Depew, September 9, 1884; Atkinson to treasurer of the New York Central Railroad, September 30, 1884; Atkinson to Theodore E. Lees, October 7, December 4, 1884, January 7, 1885; Lees to Atkinson, October 22, 1884. The article caused a great hullabaloo — the Anti-Monopoly League replied, Atkinson rejoindered, and so it went.

74. Perkins to Atkinson, June 15, 1881. An earlier letter from Perkins had asked him to demonstrate that the agitators were all wrong in citing Standard Oil as an example of railroad discrimination; it was simply a product of the "natural laws of trade." Perkins to Atkinson, June 7, 1881. Atkinson's replies have been ripped out of the letterbook but the June 15th letter indicates that he had told Perkins that Standard Oil *was* the result of railroad abuse, not the product of natural law.

75. *Proceedings of the Twelfth Annual Meeting of the National Board of Trade . . . January 1882* (Boston, 1882), 112–119, 123–135.

76. *Ibid.*, 112. Reagan was still willing to go along with a commission as an experiment in 1882 so Henry probably was speaking with authorization.

77. *Ibid.*, 127.

78. *Ibid.*, 135.

79. The petitions are in the National Archives, filed under Senate 47A–H8. These boxes contain other petitions but they are from organizations, state legislatures, etc. The files are obviously incomplete since they don't contain a single petition from New York City or from New York organizations, petitions cited by Reagan on the floor of Congress. The Grange had been selected to circulate the petition in the rural districts. National Grange, *Journal of Proceedings . . . 1881* (Philadelphia, 1881), 21. Petitions drawn up by the Grange itself were found dated in 1879 and early in 1880, especially the latter year. Senate Archives, 45A–H21, 46A–H8. The November 1879 meeting of the Grange had made a strong pitch for petitions. *Journal of Proceedings . . . 1879* (Philadelphia, 1879), 86, 121–122, 135–136. Woodman and Piollet were instrumental in getting this drive authorized.

The 1881–1882 Congressional session was the last one for which I found any substantial number of petitions from individuals, as distinct from organizations, in the Senate Archives. The House of Representatives had not yet thrown its archives open to public inspection in 1952.

80. *Argument of the Hon. John H. Reagan of Texas, Before the Committee on Commerce of the House of Representatives, on the Railroad Problem, Made on the 28th, 29th, and 30th of March, 1882* (Washington, 1882), 29. Reagan was not precisely a paragon of accuracy in his statements. For example, he tended to give the unwarranted impression that all petitions favoring regulation supported his bill. But the material in the Archives seems to bear him out here.

81. *Argument of Albert Fink, 1882*, 3.

82. *Argument by Hon. Chauncey M. Depew . . . Before the Assembly Railroad Committee, Against the Railroad Commission Bills, and the Anti-Freight Discrimination Bills . . . March 9th, 1882* (Albany, 1882), 5–6. "I never yet have seen

a petition in favor of a freight or a commission bill, or a tract on railroads that was not traced to Thurber's printing press and written or dictated by himself . . ." Depew's motive is transparent but close inspection of the language and typefaces of the numerous pamphlets found in the Thurber papers, and other documents, bear out his assertion. Thurber was in an excellent position to agitate because of his wide business acquaintance with interior retailers; moreover, the *American Grocer* provided him with an excellent vehicle to bring his views to the attention of merchants all over the nation. In effect, he had a far-flung network of agents both feeding information to New York and disseminating its views.

83. *Argument of Albert Fink, 1882,* 4–5.

84. *Ibid.,* 5.

85. *Ibid.,* 5.

86. *Ibid.,* 7, 9, 10, 21, 37, 38.

87. *United States Senate Committee on Labor and Education. Testimony of Albert Fink. New York, September 17, 1883* (New York?, 1883?), 33, 38–39, 60–62; *Argument Before the Committee on Commerce of the United States House of Representatives by Albert Fink. Washington, January 26, 1884* (Washington, 1884), 5–6.

88. N.Y.B.T.T., *Minutes,* March 15, 1882.

89. National Grange, *Journal of Proceedings . . . 1882* (Philadelphia, 1882), 58–60

90. *Argument of John Reagan, 1882,* 29–30.

91. *Railroad Gazette,* 14:105–106 (February 17, 1882).

92. *Testimony of Albert Fink, 1883,* 59–60.

93. The first pamphlet in the organized campaign to get these slogans popularized appears to have been the *Report of the Committee on Railway Transportation of the New York Board of Trade and Transportation. Adopted June 9th, 1880* (New York?, 1880?). The National Anti-Monopoly League's *Address to the People* emphasized them, and thereafter they are found in virtually every publication of the League.

94. National Grange, *Journal of Proceedings . . . 1882,* 58–60.

95. *Ibid.,* 13–14.

96. Nimmo to Thurber, July 13, 1882.

97. New York Board of Trade, *Minutes,* Annual Meeting, January 10, February 14, May 9, 1883.

98. The Chamber's return to normalcy quickened in pace after 1883. By June 1884, the Executive Committee was refusing to reappoint the Special Committee on Transportation, Francis Thurber's pleas to the contrary notwithstanding. *Twenty-Seventh Annual Report* (New York, 1885), 1:16.

99. *Proceedings of the Thirteenth Annual Meeting of the National Board of Trade . . . January 1883* (Boston, 1883), 23–35. Thurber's renunciation of "radicalism" is on p. 27.

100. Secretary Jay Burrows to Thurber, December 17, 1883.

101. *Proceedings of the Fourteenth Annual Meeting of the National Board of Trade . . . January 1884* (Boston, 1884), 102–136.

102. *Ibid.,* 136.

103. *Proceedings of the Fifteenth Annual Meeting of the National Board of Trade . . . January 1885* (Boston, 1885), 68–71. The resolution is on p. 68. Debate at this session was brief. Apparently the inevitability of regulation was now recognized. A committee of five was appointed to consider the matter further but I find no record of it subsequently.

104. *Ibid.,* 68–69.

105. *Proceedings of the Sixteenth Annual Meeting of the National Board of Trade . . . January 1886* (Boston, 1886), 13–14, 127–160. The committee reporting favorably on this resolution contained only one member from New York, A. Foster Higgins of the Chamber of Commerce. The Chamber, however, no longer followed

the lead of the Board of Trade and Transportation and Higgins took a leading role in defending the committee report.

106. *Proceedings of the Seventeenth Annual Meeting of the National Board of Trade . . . January 1887* (Boston, 1887), 11–12, 24–43, 50–51. The National Archives contain a number of petitions from leading organizations remonstrating against the long-haul short-haul clause but favoring some kind of legislation. The petitions from western organizations, in particular, opposed the clause. Senate Archives, 49A–H22.

107. See also Buck, *Granger Movement*, 230. But some weight must be given to agrarian activities, especially those of the New York and Pennsylvania Granges and the New York Farmers' Alliance, in the over-all campaigns for regulation in the late seventies and early eighties. And after 1880 various Farmers' Alliances in the West had some impact on the regulation front.

108. Hepburn Committee, *Proceedings,* 1:482–483; 3:3119–3130.

109. *Railroad Gazette,* 13:669 (November 25, 1881); *Report upon the Adjustment of Railroad Transportation Rates to the Seaboard by Albert Fink* (New York, 1882), 10–12.

110. *Railroad Gazette,* 10:294 (June 14, 1878).

111. *Ibid.,* 8:288–289 (June 30, 1876).

112. Adams, *Railroad Origins and Problems,* 189–216.

113. Adams, manuscript Diary, entries dated June 24, November 11, 1878, April 30, 1879. Numerous other entries, before and after, indicate that Adams was working away with characteristic vigor to make the pool a success.

114. Fink. *Argument Before the Senate Committee on Commerce, 1879,* 7–10; *Railroad Problem and Its Solution, 1880,* 38–71; George Blanchard, "Politico-Railway Problems and Theorists," reprinted from *National Quarterly Review,* April 1880. Adams' respect for Fink is evident from his *Railroad Origins and Problems,* 172–175, 191.

115. Fink, *Railroad Problem and Its Solution, 1880,* 69.

116. *Ibid.,* 51–53.

117. Adams to John D. Long, January 3, 1884, in the Long collection at the Massachusetts Historical Society.

118. Reprinted in the *Husbandman,* April 27, 1881, p. 5. Four years later the *Bulletin* pointed to the dismal state of American railroads, and said, in effect, "We told you so." Reprinted in the *Husbandman,* June 17, 1885, p. 2. Also reprints of articles from *Bradstreet's* on the same subject in the issues for July 13, 1881, p. 1, and August 5, 1885, p. 1.

119. *Reply of John W. Garrett to William H. Vanderbilt, September 30, 1881* (New York?, 1881?), 5–7.

120. New York *Times,* April 5, 1884; James F. Hudson, *The Railways and the Republic* (New York, 1886), 230–233, 268–271; Lewis Corey, *The House of Morgan* (New York, 1930), 148–149.

121. *Commercial and Financial Chronicle,* 33:542–543 (November 19, 1881).

122. *Railroad Gazette,* 13:347, 414, 554, 716 (June 24, July 29, October 7, December 16, 1881.

123. *Ibid.,* 13:440 (August 12, 1881).

124. *Reply of John W. Garrett to William H. Vanderbilt,* 13–15.

125. *Commercial and Financial Chronicle,* 33:369–370 (October 8, 1881).

126. *Ibid.,* 33:426 (October 22, 1881).

127. *Ibid.,* 33:672–673 (December 17, 1881).

128. *Railroad Gazette,* 13:716, 14:24 (December 16, 1881, January 13, 1882).

129. Adams, manuscript Diary, entries dated December 8, 31, 1881. There are a number of other entries from the beginning of serious trouble in 1880 through the spring of 1882 which suggest the course of events. In particular, September 6, 1880, June 13, July 1, December 9, 28, 1881, January 4, 7, 14, February 3, 4, 1882.

130. *Commercial and Financial Chronicle,* 34:72–73, 301–302 (January 21, March 18, 1882).

131. *Ibid.,* 34:99 (January 28, 1882).

132. New York *Times,* February 14, 1882.

133. New York Chamber of Commerce, *Twenty-Fourth Annual Report,* 1:147–152; New York Board of Trade and Transportation, *Minutes,* April 15, 1882; New York Produce Exchange, *Annual Report, 1882* (New York, 1883), 72–81.

134. Alden G. Thurman, E. B. Washburne, and Thomas M. Cooley, *Report of Messrs. Thurman, Washburne & Cooley, Constituting an Advisory Commission on Differential Rates by Railroads between the West and the Seaboard* (New York, 1882).

135. *Argument of Albert Fink, 1882,* 33–34.

136. *Argument of Albert Fink, 1882,* 37–38; New York *Times,* February 27, 1882. Fink credited Adams with having formulated the plan.

137. *Commercial and Financial Chronicle,* 34:304–305 (March 18, 1882).

138. *Nation,* 34:182 (March 2, 1882). For its earlier prophecy, see the *Nation,* 16:250 (April 10, 1873).

139. *Commercial and Financial Chronicle.* 36:341, 37:448–449, 532, 666, 38:163, 197, 256–257, 520, 613 (October 25, November 15, December 13, 1884, February 7, 14, 28, May 2, 23, 1885).

140. *Ibid.,* 37:534 (November 15, 1884).

141. *Ibid.,* "Investors Supplement," October 25, 1884, p. 1. See also New York Chamber of Commerce, *Twenty-Sixth Annual Report,* 1:68.

142. *Report of the Senate Select Committee on Interstate Commerce (Testimony)* (Washington, 1886), 182.

143. A comprehensive summary of the grievances throughout the country is found in the *Report,* 180–198. The committee particularly stressed resentment against stock watering which was believed to result in high rates.

144. *Congressional Record,* 16:290.

145. Even Democratic supporters of Reagan's bill referred to Arthur's stand to emphasize the wide national interest in railroad regulation. *Ibid.,* 16:112.

146. *The Tribune Almanac . . . for 1885* (New York, 1885?), 18.

147. *Our Country. A Paper by F. B. Thurber, Read before the XIX Century Club, New York, November 17, 1885* (New York?, 1885?), 28.

148. Cullom Committee, *Testimony,* 274.

149. *Railroad Gazette,* 17:486 (July 31, 1885).

150. Hudson, *Railways and the Republic,* 201–206; Corey, *House of Morgan,* 147–153.

151. *Ibid.,* 150.

152. Although it needs to be treated skeptically, some fragmentary evidence in this direction is the interpretation placed on Morgan's settlement of the West Shore troubles by his son-in-law many years later. "The idea of government regulation was still nebulous. The present practice of strict supervision of new construction was then a matter of debate only, and it was not until a year later that the Interstate Commerce was passed by the Congress of the United States in the effort to control what had become a menace to investors, as well as to curb the evil of railroad monopoly and disregard of the public's rights.

"Railroads for which there was no necessity had been built, and when they failed were operated by the courts, through receivers, at rates which brought their solvent competitors dangerously near the bankruptcy line. The practice had become a scandal and was injuring the market for American securities abroad. This had challenged Pierpont's attention because he was profoundly interested in the possibility of the development of United States railroads and industries with foreign capital. It was probably his passion for order that made him concentrate on the conditions which prevailed in 1885 . . ." Herbert L. Satterlee, *J. Pierpont Morgan: An Intimate Portrait* (New York, 1939), 224–225. These reminiscences are at least consonant with the material presented in previous chapters concerning the role of the House of Morgan in the trunk-line wars.

153. New York Chamber of Commerce, *Twenty-Sixth Annual Report,* 1:42.

154. Cullom Committee, *Testimony,* 41–42.

155. Hudson, *Railways and the Republic,* 347. The views of the commissioners are found in New York Railroad Commissioners, *Annual Report, 1883* (Albany, 1884), 1:63–65; *Annual Report, 1884* (Albany, 1885), 1:vii–ix; *Annual Report, 1885* (Albany, 1886, 1:xxix.

156. N.Y.B.T.T., *Minutes,* March 19, 1885.

157. *Commercial and Financial Chronicle,* 41:734–735 (December 26, 1885).

158. *Commercial and Financial Chronicle,* 45:660–661 (November 19, 1887).

159. Corey, *House of Morgan,* 166–177.

160. William Z. Ripley, *Railroads: Rates and Regulations* (New York, 1912), 456–486.

161. Cullom to Sterne, September 8, 1885.

162. Cullom to Sterne, June 16, 1886.

163. Sterne, *Report to the Secretary of State, 1887,* 1.

164. Until the very day on which the Senate approved the bill, the New York Board of Trade and Transportation worked tirelessly in behalf of railroad regulation. See *Congressional Record,* 18:718–719.

Index

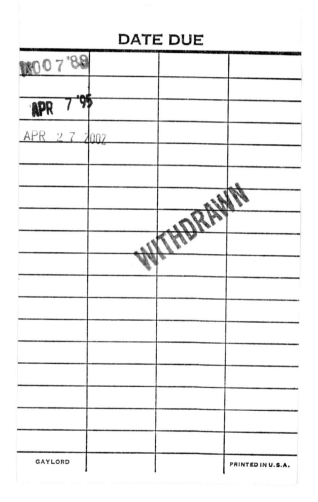